# BAKUMAN

# 2

CHOCOLATE
and
AKAMARU

STORY BY
TSUGUMI OHBA

ART BY
TAKESHI OBATA

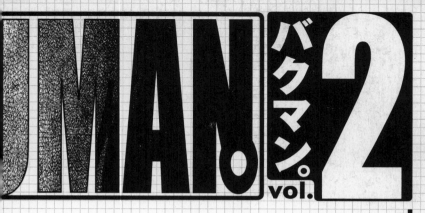

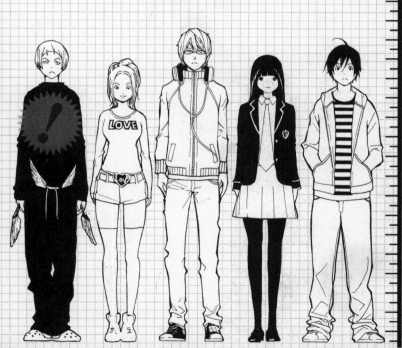

**EIJI**
**Nizuma**

A prodigy who received the Tezuka Award at just age 15. He's in the same age group as Moritaka and Akito.

Age: 15

**KAYA**
**Miyoshi**

Miho's best friend who thinks Akito has a crush on her.

Age: 15

**AKITO**
**Takagi**

Aspiring manga writer. An extremely smart guy who gets the best grades in his class. A cool guy who becomes very passionate when it comes to manga.

Age: 14

**MIHO**
**Azuki**

A girl who dreams of becoming a voice actress. She promised to marry Moritaka under the condition that they not see each other until their dreams come true.

Age: 14

**MORITAKA**
**Mashiro**

Aspiring manga artist. An extreme romantic who believes that he will marry Miho Azuki once their dreams come true.

Age: 14

*These ages are from August 2008.

**STORY** In order to attain the glory that only a handful of people can, two young men decide to walk the rough "path of manga" and become professional manga creators. This is the story of a great artist, Moritaka Mashiro, a talented writer, Akito Takagi, and their quest to become manga legends!

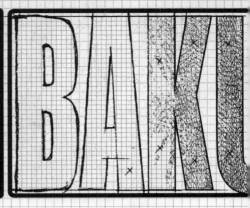

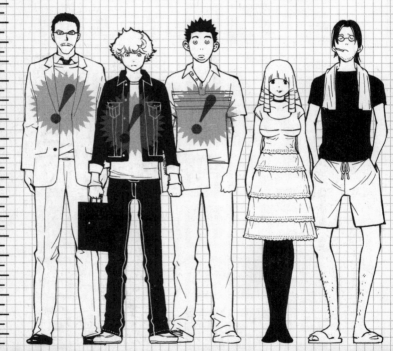

| EDITOR IN CHIEF Sasaki | YUJIRO Hattori | AKIRA Hattori | MIYUKI Azuki | NOBUHIRO Mashiro |
|---|---|---|---|---|
| Editor in Chief at *Jump* | Editor at *Jump* | Editor at *Jump* | Miho's mother. She used to exchange letters with Nobuhiro in the past to cheer him up. | Moritaka's uncle was a manga artist under the pseudonym Taro Kawaguchi. He has already passed away. |
| Age: 46 | Age: 26 | Age: 28 | Age: 42 | Age at death: 39 |

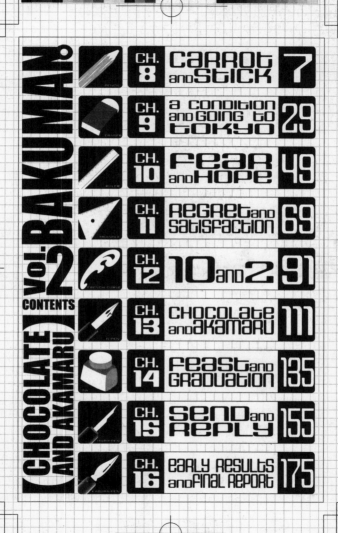

# BAKUMAN。

## VOL.2 (CHOCOLATE AND AKAMARU)

### CONTENTS

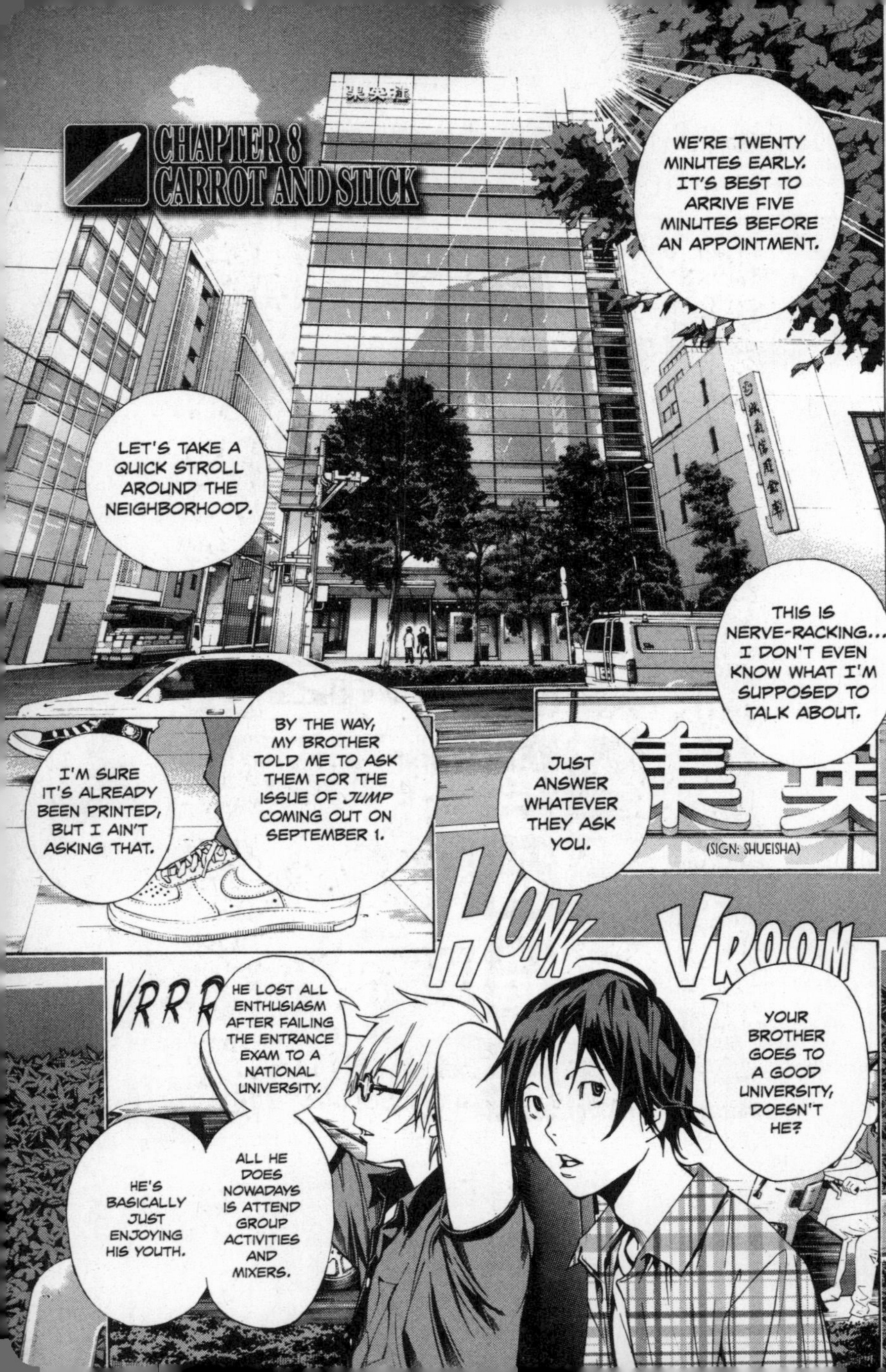
CHAPTER 8 CARROT AND STICK
WE'RE TWENTY MINUTES EARLY. IT'S BEST TO ARRIVE FIVE MINUTES BEFORE AN APPOINTMENT.
LET'S TAKE A QUICK STROLL AROUND THE NEIGHBORHOOD.
THIS IS NERVE-RACKING... I DON'T EVEN KNOW WHAT I'M SUPPOSED TO TALK ABOUT.
JUST ANSWER WHATEVER THEY ASK YOU.
(SIGN: SHUEISHA)
BY THE WAY, MY BROTHER TOLD ME TO ASK THEM FOR THE ISSUE OF *JUMP* COMING OUT ON SEPTEMBER 1.
I'M SURE IT'S ALREADY BEEN PRINTED, BUT I AIN'T ASKING THAT.
VROOM
HONK
YOUR BROTHER GOES TO A GOOD UNIVERSITY, DOESN'T HE?
HE LOST ALL ENTHUSIASM AFTER FAILING THE ENTRANCE EXAM TO A NATIONAL UNIVERSITY.
VRRR
ALL HE DOES NOWADAYS IS ATTEND GROUP ACTIVITIES AND MIXERS.
HE'S BASICALLY JUST ENJOYING HIS YOUTH.

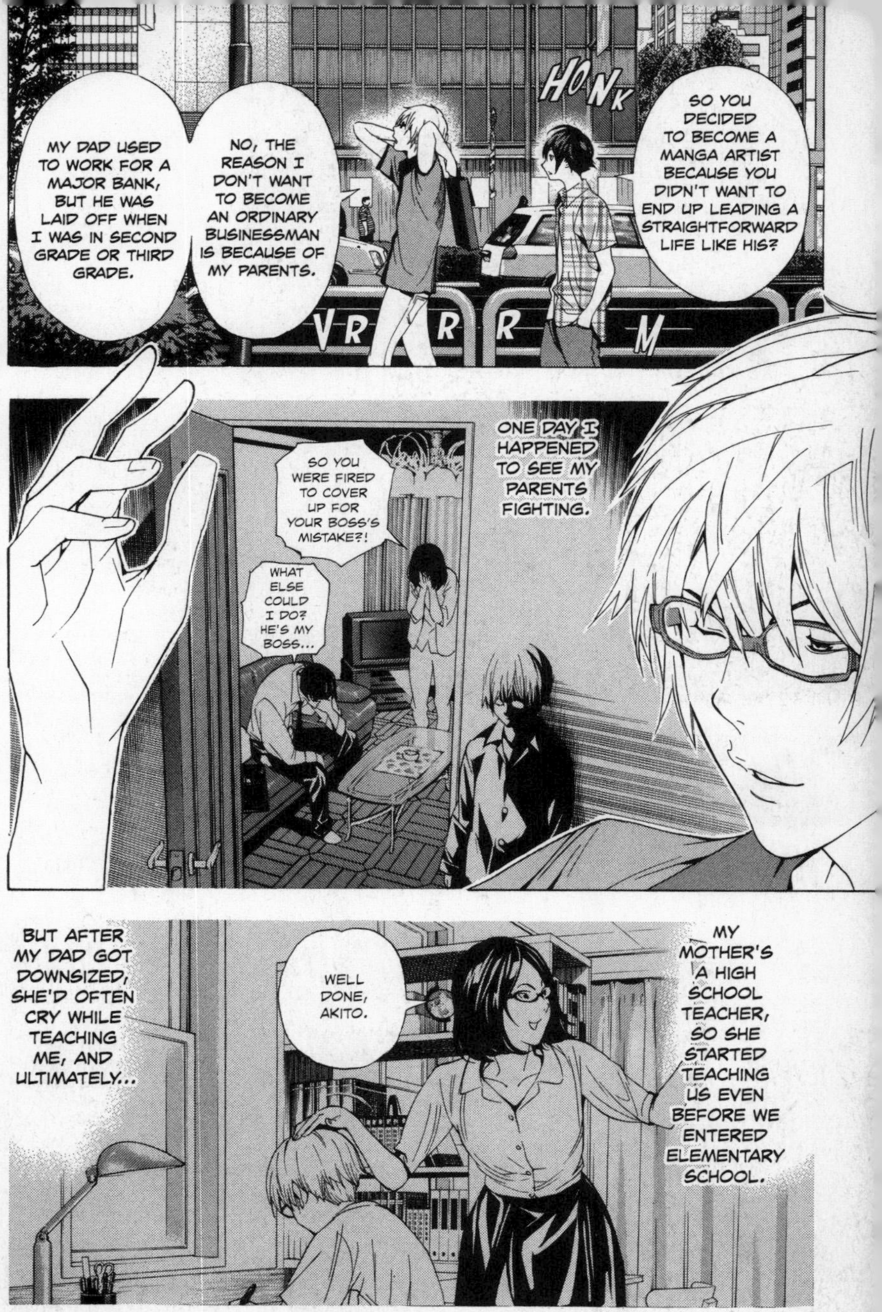
HONK
SO YOU DECIDED TO BECOME A MANGA ARTIST BECAUSE YOU DIDN'T WANT TO END UP LEADING A STRAIGHTFORWARD LIFE LIKE HIS?
NO, THE REASON I DON'T WANT TO BECOME AN ORDINARY BUSINESSMAN IS BECAUSE OF MY PARENTS.
MY DAD USED TO WORK FOR A MAJOR BANK, BUT HE WAS LAID OFF WHEN I WAS IN SECOND GRADE OR THIRD GRADE.
VRRRM
ONE DAY I HAPPENED TO SEE MY PARENTS FIGHTING.
SO YOU WERE FIRED TO COVER UP FOR YOUR BOSS'S MISTAKE?!
WHAT ELSE COULD I DO? HE'S MY BOSS...
MY MOTHER'S A HIGH SCHOOL TEACHER, SO SHE STARTED TEACHING US EVEN BEFORE WE ENTERED ELEMENTARY SCHOOL.
WELL DONE, AKITO.
BUT AFTER MY DAD GOT DOWNSIZED, SHE'D OFTEN CRY WHILE TEACHING ME, AND ULTIMATELY...

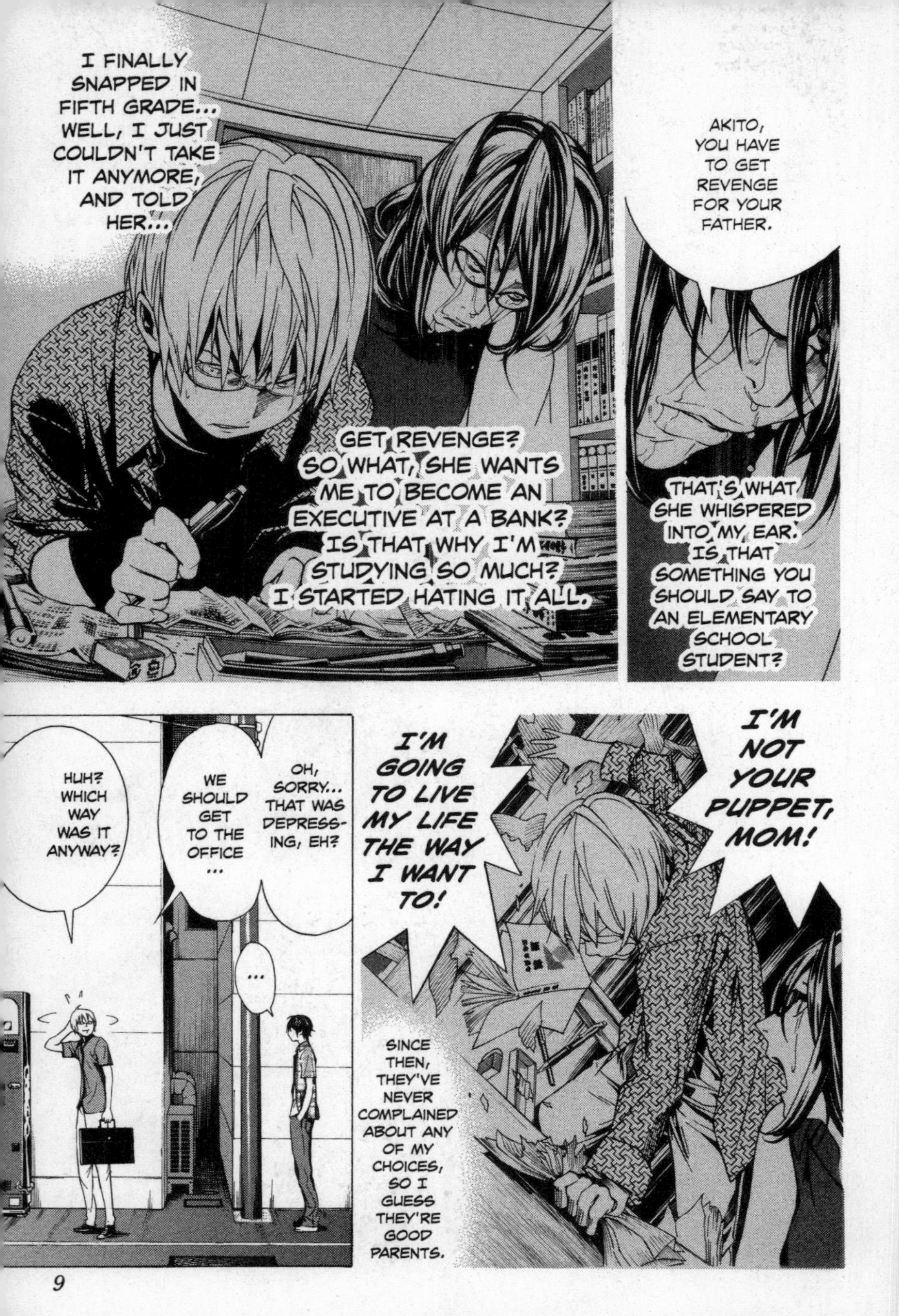
AKITO, YOU HAVE TO GET REVENGE FOR YOUR FATHER.
THAT'S WHAT SHE WHISPERED INTO MY EAR. IS THAT SOMETHING YOU SHOULD SAY TO AN ELEMENTARY SCHOOL STUDENT?
I FINALLY SNAPPED IN FIFTH GRADE... WELL, I JUST COULDN'T TAKE IT ANYMORE, AND TOLD HER...
GET REVENGE? SO WHAT, SHE WANTS ME TO BECOME AN EXECUTIVE AT A BANK? IS THAT WHY I'M STUDYING SO MUCH? I STARTED HATING IT ALL.
I'M NOT YOUR PUPPET, MOM!
I'M GOING TO LIVE MY LIFE THE WAY I WANT TO!
SINCE THEN, THEY'VE NEVER COMPLAINED ABOUT ANY OF MY CHOICES, SO I GUESS THEY'RE GOOD PARENTS.
OH, SORRY... THAT WAS DEPRESSING, EH?
WE SHOULD GET TO THE OFFICE ...
...
HUH? WHICH WAY WAS IT ANYWAY?

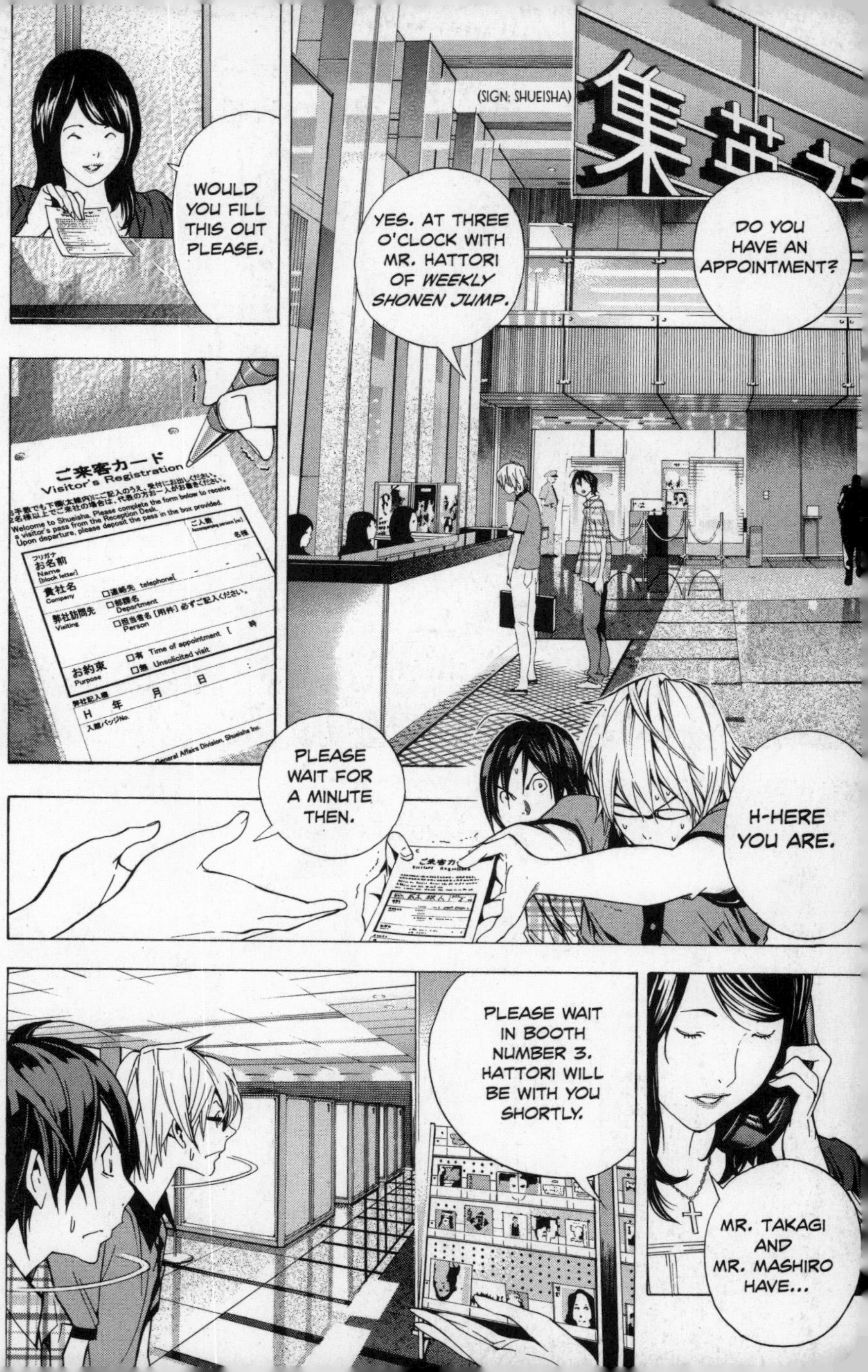
(SIGN: SHUEISHA)
DO YOU HAVE AN APPOINTMENT?
YES. AT THREE O'CLOCK WITH MR. HATTORI OF *WEEKLY SHONEN JUMP*.
WOULD YOU FILL THIS OUT PLEASE.
ご来客カード
Visitor's Registration
H-HERE YOU ARE.
PLEASE WAIT FOR A MINUTE THEN.
MR. TAKAGI AND MR. MASHIRO HAVE...
PLEASE WAIT IN BOOTH NUMBER 3. HATTORI WILL BE WITH YOU SHORTLY.

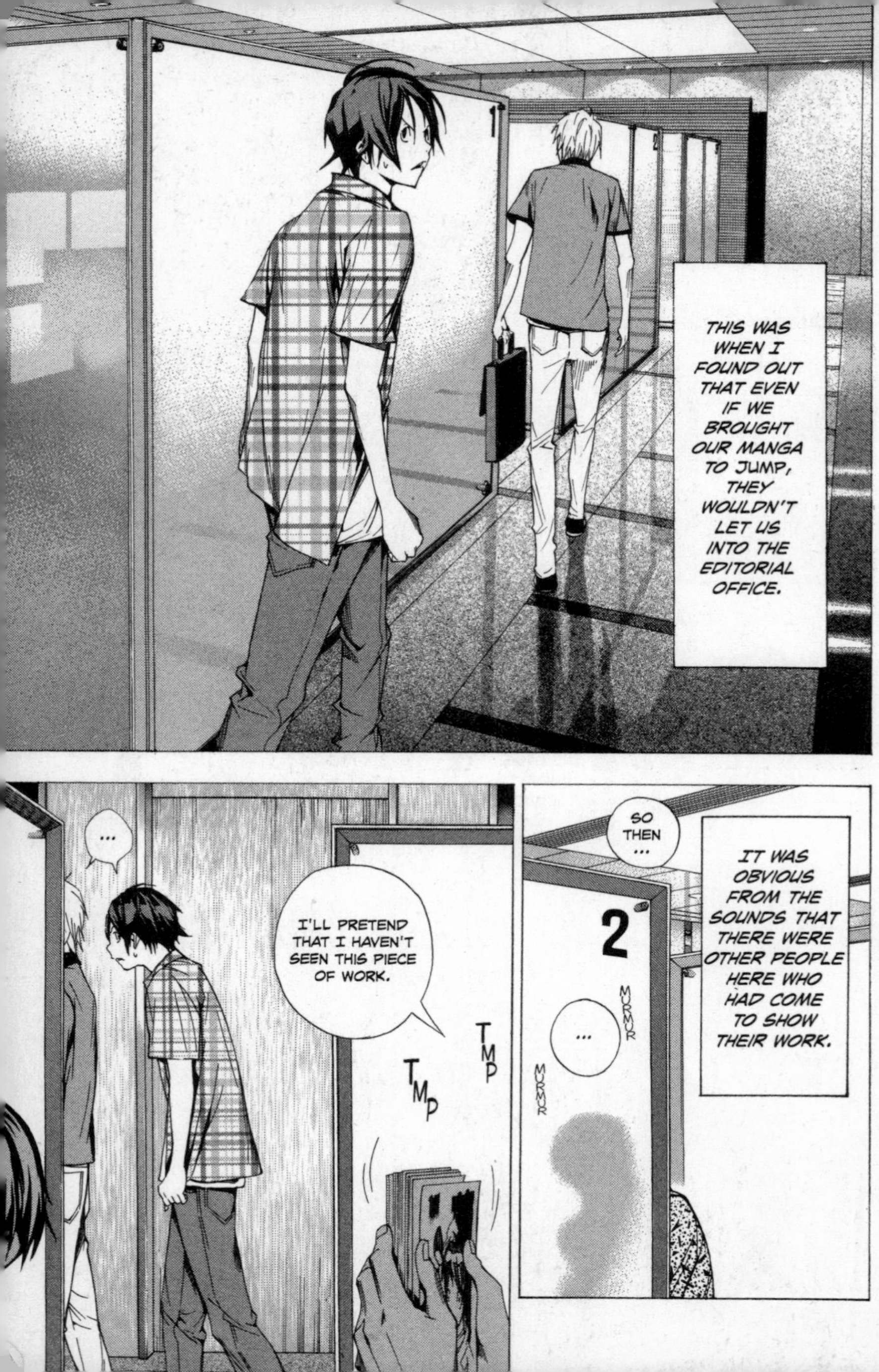
THIS WAS WHEN I FOUND OUT THAT EVEN IF WE BROUGHT OUR MANGA TO JUMP, THEY WOULDN'T LET US INTO THE EDITORIAL OFFICE.
IT WAS OBVIOUS FROM THE SOUNDS THAT THERE WERE OTHER PEOPLE HERE WHO HAD COME TO SHOW THEIR WORK.
SO THEN ...
2
MURMUR
...
MURMUR
I'LL PRETEND THAT I HAVEN'T SEEN THIS PIECE OF WORK.
TMP
TMP
...

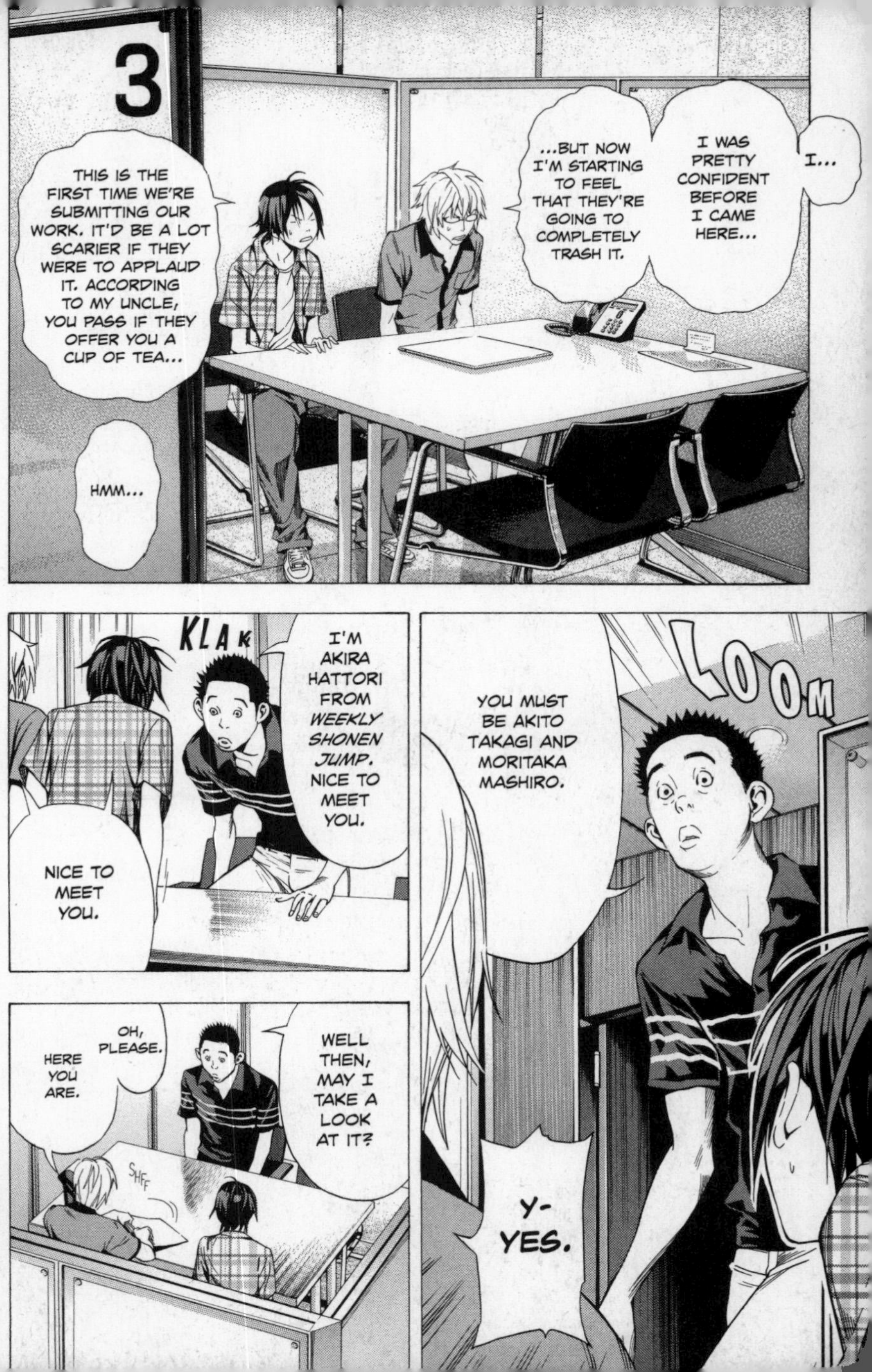

3
I...
I WAS PRETTY CONFIDENT BEFORE I CAME HERE...
...BUT NOW I'M STARTING TO FEEL THAT THEY'RE GOING TO COMPLETELY TRASH IT.
THIS IS THE FIRST TIME WE'RE SUBMITTING OUR WORK. IT'D BE A LOT SCARIER IF THEY WERE TO APPLAUD IT. ACCORDING TO MY UNCLE, YOU PASS IF THEY OFFER YOU A CUP OF TEA...
HMM...
LOOM
YOU MUST BE AKITO TAKAGI AND MORITAKA MASHIRO.
Y- YES.
KLAK
I'M AKIRA HATTORI FROM *WEEKLY SHONEN JUMP*. NICE TO MEET YOU.
NICE TO MEET YOU.
WELL THEN, MAY I TAKE A LOOK AT IT?
OH, PLEASE.
HERE YOU ARE.
SHFF

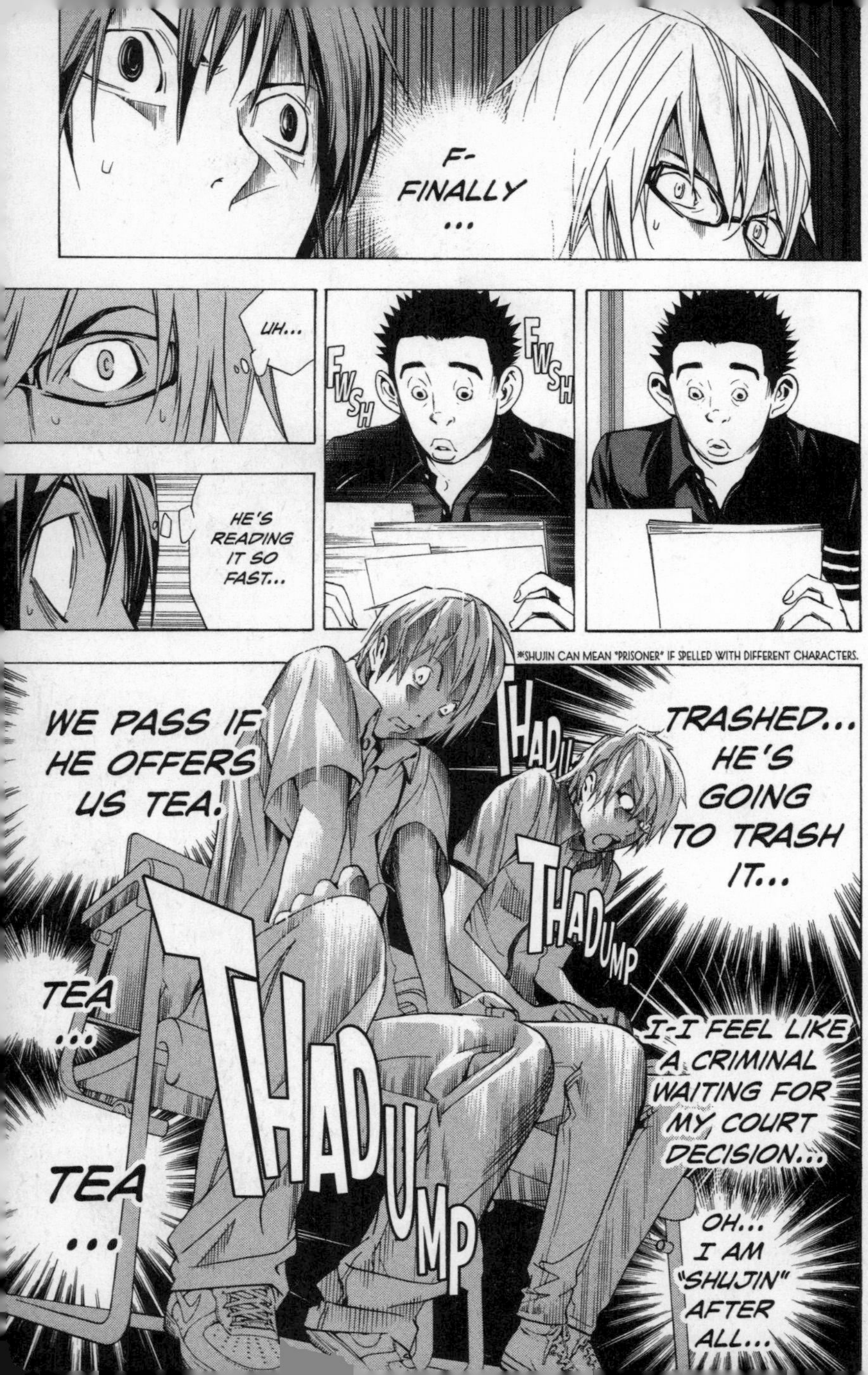
F- FINALLY ...
FWSH
FWSH
UH...
HE'S READING IT SO FAST...
TRASHED... HE'S GOING TO TRASH IT...
THADUMP
THADUMP
WE PASS IF HE OFFERS US TEA.
I-I FEEL LIKE A CRIMINAL WAITING FOR MY COURT DECISION...
OH... I AM "SHUJIN" AFTER ALL...
THADUMP
TEA ...
TEA ...

*SHUJIN CAN MEAN "PRISONER" IF SPELLED WITH DIFFERENT CHARACTERS.

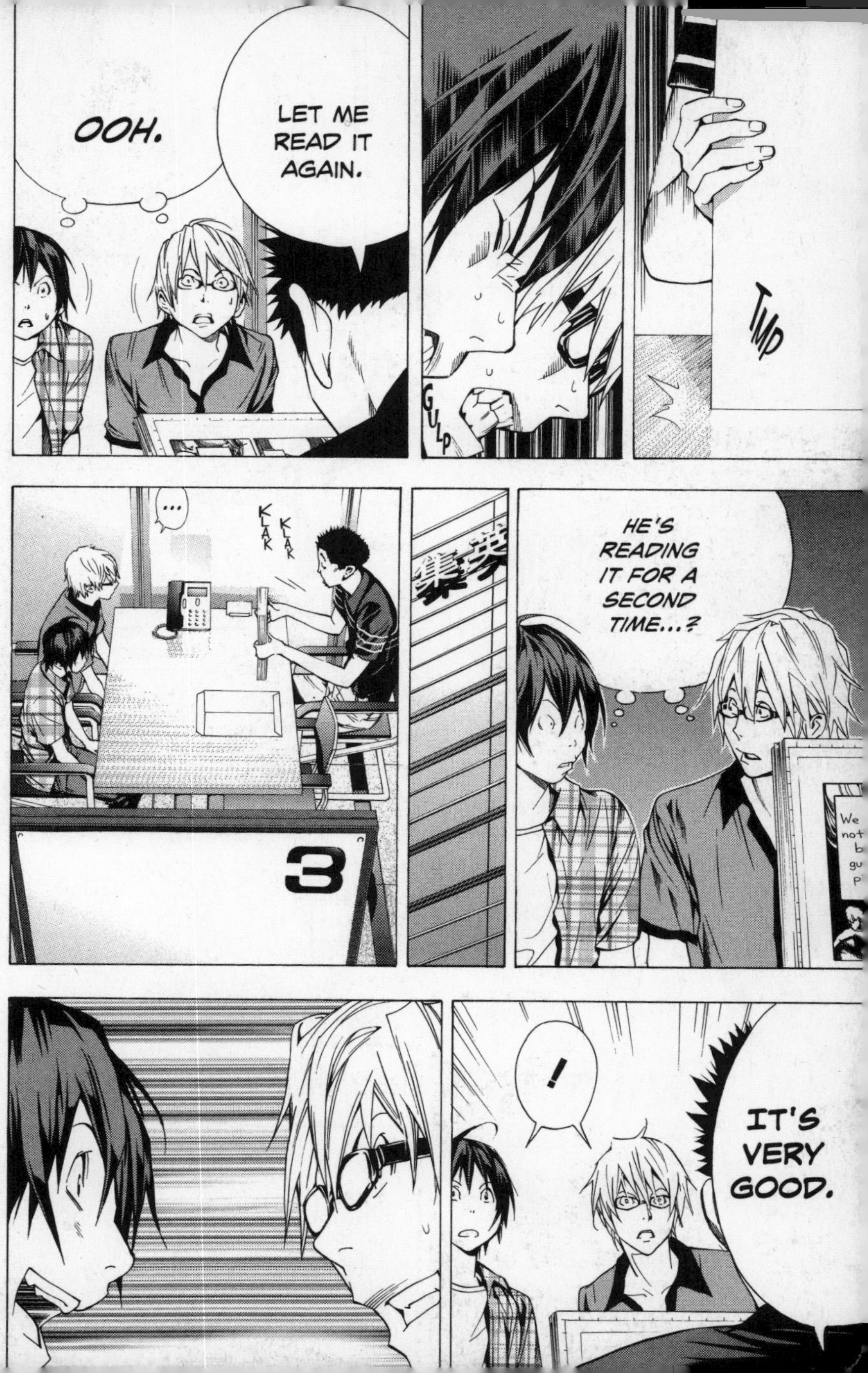
TMP
GULP
LET ME READ IT AGAIN.
OOH.
HE'S READING IT FOR A SECOND TIME...?
集英
...
KLAK KLAK
IT'S VERY GOOD.
!

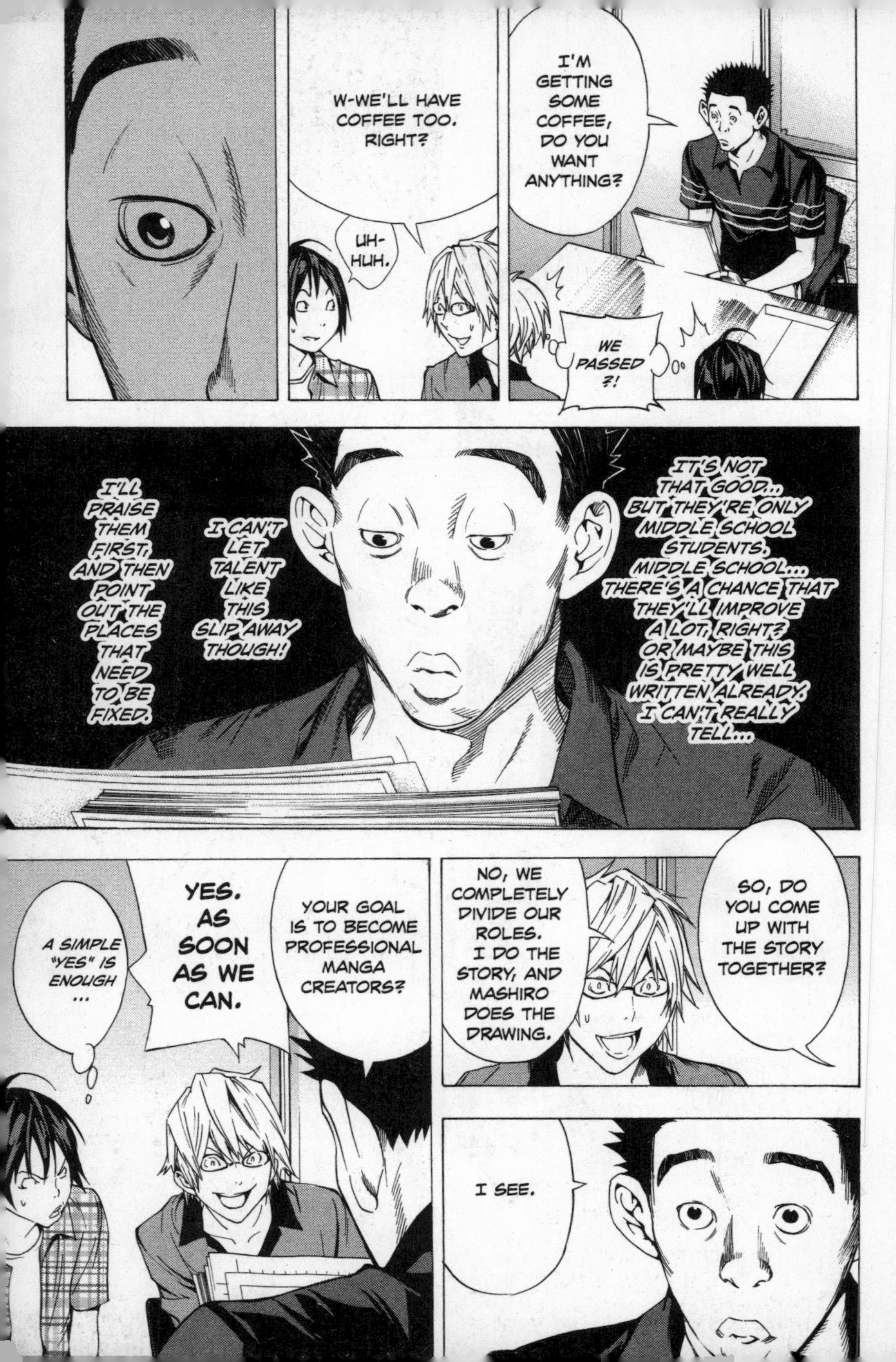
I'M GETTING SOME COFFEE, DO YOU WANT ANYTHING?
WE PASSED?!
W-WE'LL HAVE COFFEE TOO. RIGHT?
UH-HUH.
IT'S NOT THAT GOOD... BUT THEY'RE ONLY MIDDLE SCHOOL STUDENTS. MIDDLE SCHOOL... THERE'S A CHANCE THAT THEY'LL IMPROVE A LOT, RIGHT? OR MAYBE THIS IS PRETTY WELL WRITTEN ALREADY. I CAN'T REALLY TELL...
I CAN'T LET TALENT LIKE THIS SLIP AWAY THOUGH!
I'LL PRAISE THEM FIRST, AND THEN POINT OUT THE PLACES THAT NEED TO BE FIXED.
SO, DO YOU COME UP WITH THE STORY TOGETHER?
NO, WE COMPLETELY DIVIDE OUR ROLES. I DO THE STORY, AND MASHIRO DOES THE DRAWING.
I SEE.
YOUR GOAL IS TO BECOME PROFESSIONAL MANGA CREATORS?
YES. AS SOON AS WE CAN.
A SIMPLE "YES" IS ENOUGH...

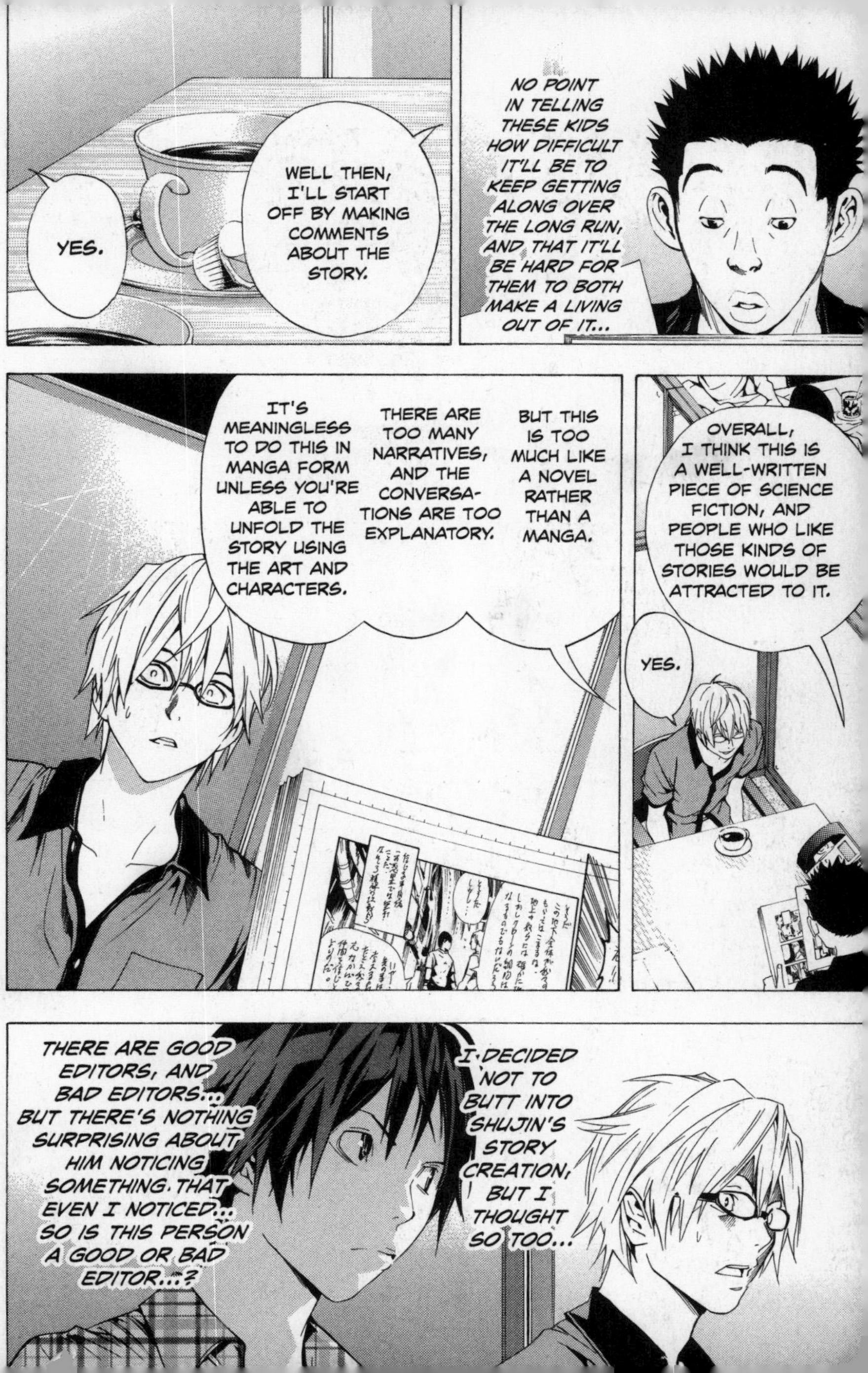
NO POINT IN TELLING THESE KIDS HOW DIFFICULT IT'LL BE TO KEEP GETTING ALONG OVER THE LONG RUN, AND THAT IT'LL BE HARD FOR THEM TO BOTH MAKE A LIVING OUT OF IT...
WELL THEN, I'LL START OFF BY MAKING COMMENTS ABOUT THE STORY.
YES.
OVERALL, I THINK THIS IS A WELL-WRITTEN PIECE OF SCIENCE FICTION, AND PEOPLE WHO LIKE THOSE KINDS OF STORIES WOULD BE ATTRACTED TO IT.
YES.
BUT THIS IS TOO MUCH LIKE A NOVEL RATHER THAN A MANGA.
THERE ARE TOO MANY NARRATIVES, AND THE CONVERSATIONS ARE TOO EXPLANATORY.
IT'S MEANINGLESS TO DO THIS IN MANGA FORM UNLESS YOU'RE ABLE TO UNFOLD THE STORY USING THE ART AND CHARACTERS.
I DECIDED NOT TO BUTT INTO SHUJIN'S STORY CREATION, BUT I THOUGHT SO TOO...
THERE ARE GOOD EDITORS, AND BAD EDITORS... BUT THERE'S NOTHING SURPRISING ABOUT HIM NOTICING SOMETHING THAT EVEN I NOTICED... SO IS THIS PERSON A GOOD OR BAD EDITOR...?

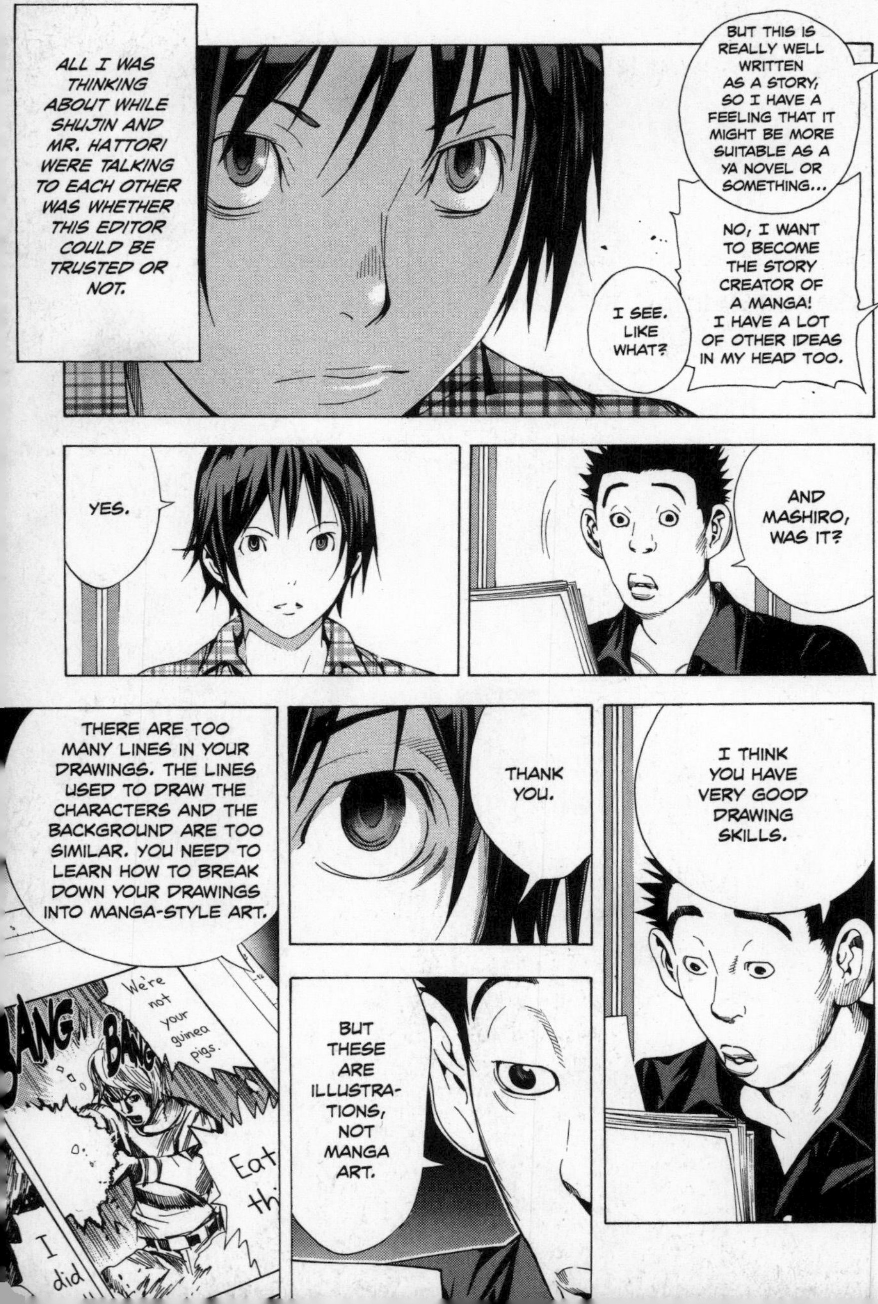
BUT THIS IS REALLY WELL WRITTEN AS A STORY, SO I HAVE A FEELING THAT IT MIGHT BE MORE SUITABLE AS A YA NOVEL OR SOMETHING...
...
NO, I WANT TO BECOME THE STORY CREATOR OF A MANGA! I HAVE A LOT OF OTHER IDEAS IN MY HEAD TOO.
I SEE. LIKE WHAT?
ALL I WAS THINKING ABOUT WHILE SHUJIN AND MR. HATTORI WERE TALKING TO EACH OTHER WAS WHETHER THIS EDITOR COULD BE TRUSTED OR NOT.
AND MASHIRO, WAS IT?
YES.
I THINK YOU HAVE VERY GOOD DRAWING SKILLS.
THANK YOU.
BUT THESE ARE ILLUSTRATIONS, NOT MANGA ART.
THERE ARE TOO MANY LINES IN YOUR DRAWINGS. THE LINES USED TO DRAW THE CHARACTERS AND THE BACKGROUND ARE TOO SIMILAR. YOU NEED TO LEARN HOW TO BREAK DOWN YOUR DRAWINGS INTO MANGA-STYLE ART.
We're not your guinea pigs.
BANG

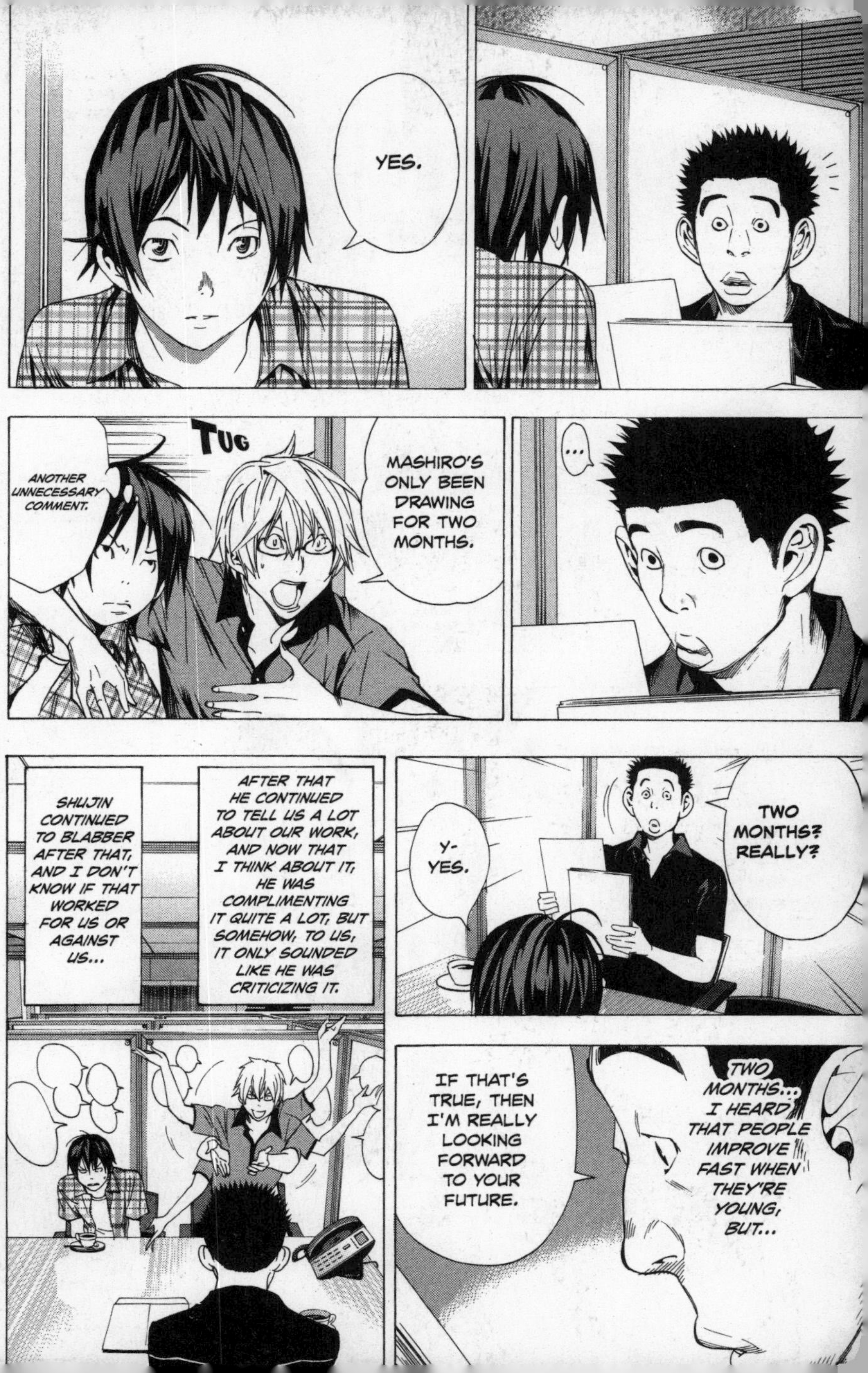
YES.
...
MASHIRO'S ONLY BEEN DRAWING FOR TWO MONTHS.
TUG
ANOTHER UNNECESSARY COMMENT.
TWO MONTHS? REALLY?
Y- YES.
AFTER THAT HE CONTINUED TO TELL US A LOT ABOUT OUR WORK, AND NOW THAT I THINK ABOUT IT, HE WAS COMPLIMENTING IT QUITE A LOT, BUT SOMEHOW, TO US, IT ONLY SOUNDED LIKE HE WAS CRITICIZING IT.
SHUJIN CONTINUED TO BLABBER AFTER THAT, AND I DON'T KNOW IF THAT WORKED FOR US OR AGAINST US...
TWO MONTHS... I HEARD THAT PEOPLE IMPROVE FAST WHEN THEY'RE YOUNG, BUT...
IF THAT'S TRUE, THEN I'M REALLY LOOKING FORWARD TO YOUR FUTURE.

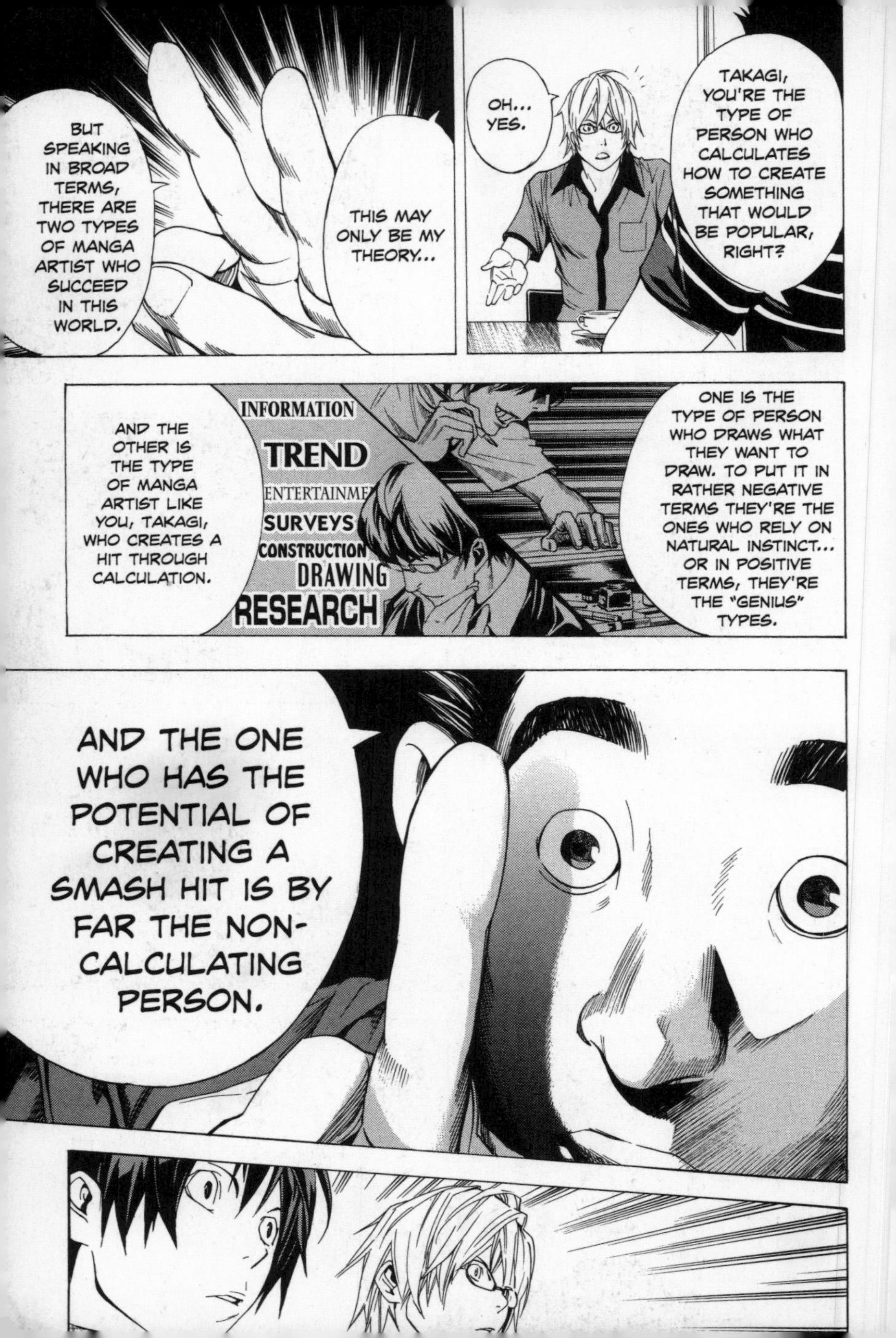
TAKAGI, YOU'RE THE TYPE OF PERSON WHO CALCULATES HOW TO CREATE SOMETHING THAT WOULD BE POPULAR, RIGHT?
OH... YES.
THIS MAY ONLY BE MY THEORY...
BUT SPEAKING IN BROAD TERMS, THERE ARE TWO TYPES OF MANGA ARTIST WHO SUCCEED IN THIS WORLD.
ONE IS THE TYPE OF PERSON WHO DRAWS WHAT THEY WANT TO DRAW. TO PUT IT IN RATHER NEGATIVE TERMS THEY'RE THE ONES WHO RELY ON NATURAL INSTINCT... OR IN POSITIVE TERMS, THEY'RE THE "GENIUS" TYPES.
INFORMATION
TREND
ENTERTAINME
SURVEYS
CONSTRUCTION
DRAWING
RESEARCH
AND THE OTHER IS THE TYPE OF MANGA ARTIST LIKE YOU, TAKAGI, WHO CREATES A HIT THROUGH CALCULATION.
AND THE ONE WHO HAS THE POTENTIAL OF CREATING A SMASH HIT IS BY FAR THE NON-CALCULATING PERSON.

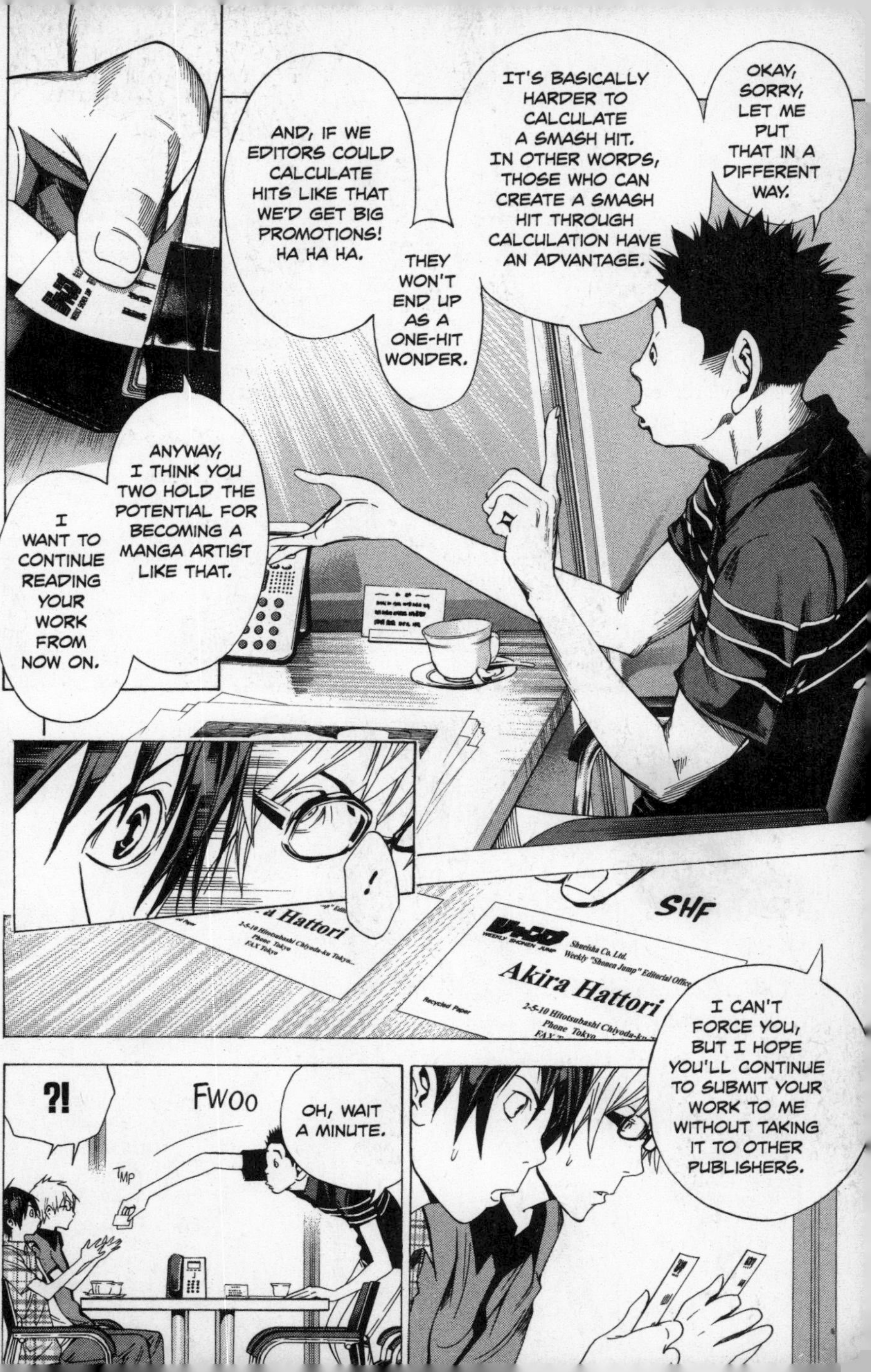
OKAY, SORRY, LET ME PUT THAT IN A DIFFERENT WAY.
IT'S BASICALLY HARDER TO CALCULATE A SMASH HIT. IN OTHER WORDS, THOSE WHO CAN CREATE A SMASH HIT THROUGH CALCULATION HAVE AN ADVANTAGE.
THEY WON'T END UP AS A ONE-HIT WONDER.
AND, IF WE EDITORS COULD CALCULATE HITS LIKE THAT WE'D GET BIG PROMOTIONS! HA HA HA.
ANYWAY, I THINK YOU TWO HOLD THE POTENTIAL FOR BECOMING A MANGA ARTIST LIKE THAT.
I WANT TO CONTINUE READING YOUR WORK FROM NOW ON.
!
SHF
WEEKLY SHONEN JUMP
Shueisha Co. Ltd.
Weekly "Shonen Jump" Editorial Office
Akira Hattori
2-5-10 Hitotsubashi Chiyoda-ku
Phone Tokyo
Recycled Paper
I CAN'T FORCE YOU, BUT I HOPE YOU'LL CONTINUE TO SUBMIT YOUR WORK TO ME WITHOUT TAKING IT TO OTHER PUBLISHERS.
OH, WAIT A MINUTE.
FWOO
?!
TMP

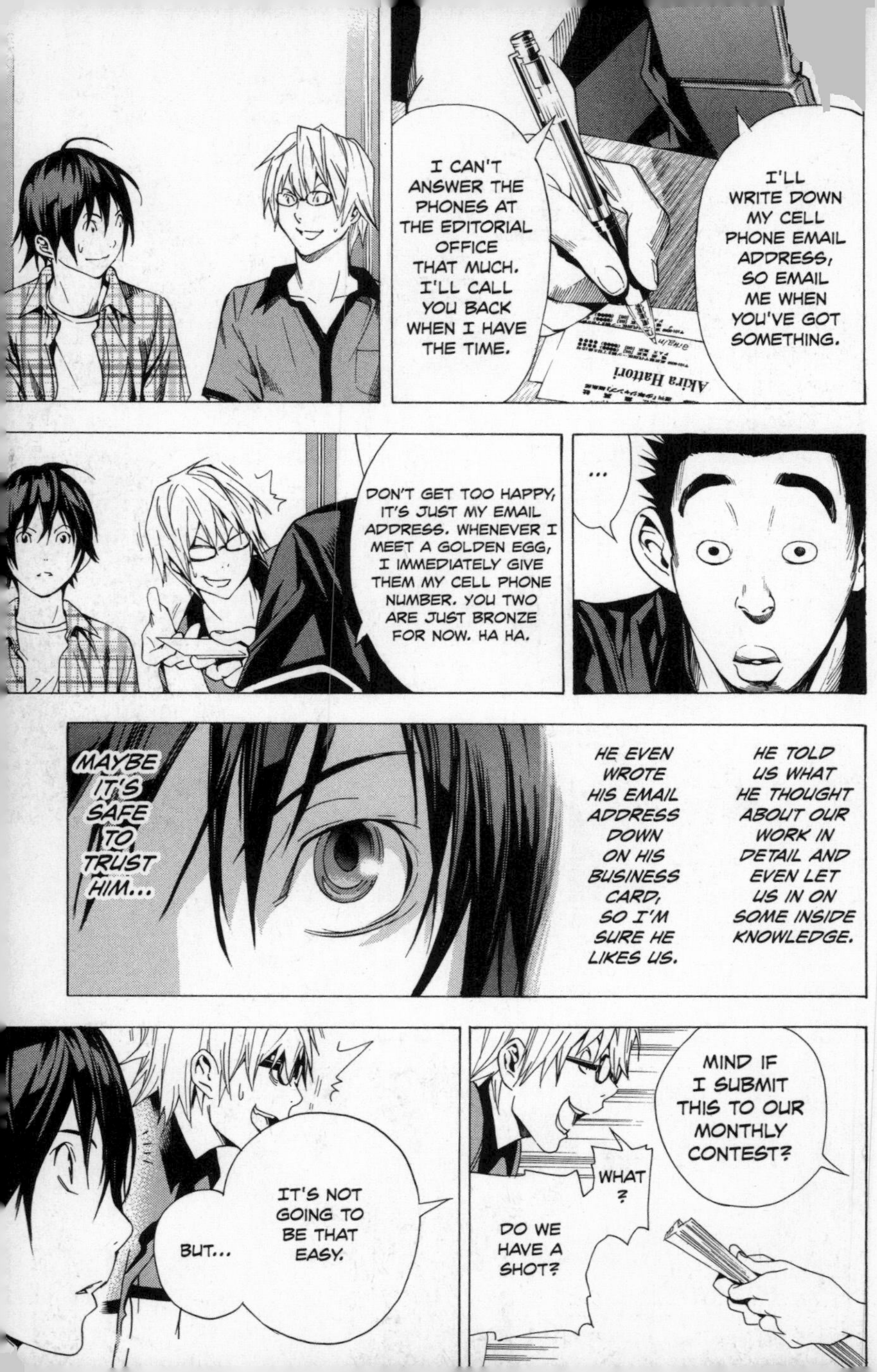
I CAN'T ANSWER THE PHONES AT THE EDITORIAL OFFICE THAT MUCH. I'LL CALL YOU BACK WHEN I HAVE THE TIME.
I'LL WRITE DOWN MY CELL PHONE EMAIL ADDRESS, SO EMAIL ME WHEN YOU'VE GOT SOMETHING.
Akira Hattori
...
DON'T GET TOO HAPPY, IT'S JUST MY EMAIL ADDRESS. WHENEVER I MEET A GOLDEN EGG, I IMMEDIATELY GIVE THEM MY CELL PHONE NUMBER. YOU TWO ARE JUST BRONZE FOR NOW. HA HA.
HE TOLD US WHAT HE THOUGHT ABOUT OUR WORK IN DETAIL AND EVEN LET US IN ON SOME INSIDE KNOWLEDGE.
HE EVEN WROTE HIS EMAIL ADDRESS DOWN ON HIS BUSINESS CARD, SO I'M SURE HE LIKES US.
MAYBE IT'S SAFE TO TRUST HIM...
MIND IF I SUBMIT THIS TO OUR MONTHLY CONTEST?
WHAT?
DO WE HAVE A SHOT?
BUT...
IT'S NOT GOING TO BE THAT EASY.

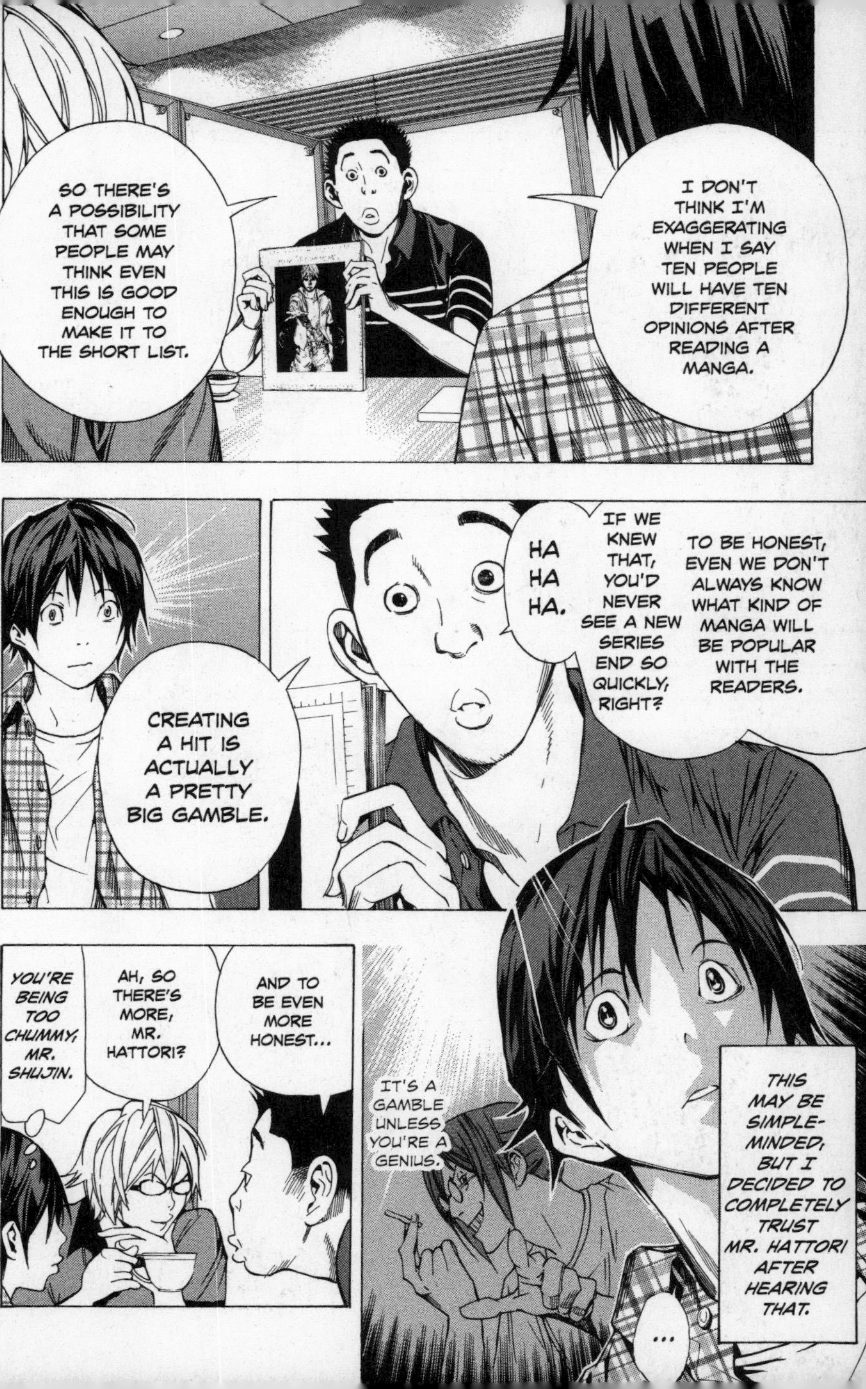
I DON'T THINK I'M EXAGGERATING WHEN I SAY TEN PEOPLE WILL HAVE TEN DIFFERENT OPINIONS AFTER READING A MANGA.
SO THERE'S A POSSIBILITY THAT SOME PEOPLE MAY THINK EVEN THIS IS GOOD ENOUGH TO MAKE IT TO THE SHORT LIST.
TO BE HONEST, EVEN WE DON'T ALWAYS KNOW WHAT KIND OF MANGA WILL BE POPULAR WITH THE READERS.
IF WE KNEW THAT, YOU'D NEVER SEE A NEW SERIES END SO QUICKLY, RIGHT?
HA HA HA.
CREATING A HIT IS ACTUALLY A PRETTY BIG GAMBLE.
THIS MAY BE SIMPLE-MINDED, BUT I DECIDED TO COMPLETELY TRUST MR. HATTORI AFTER HEARING THAT.
IT'S A GAMBLE UNLESS YOU'RE A GENIUS.
...
AND TO BE EVEN MORE HONEST...
AH, SO THERE'S MORE, MR. HATTORI?
YOU'RE BEING TOO CHUMMY, MR. SHUJIN.

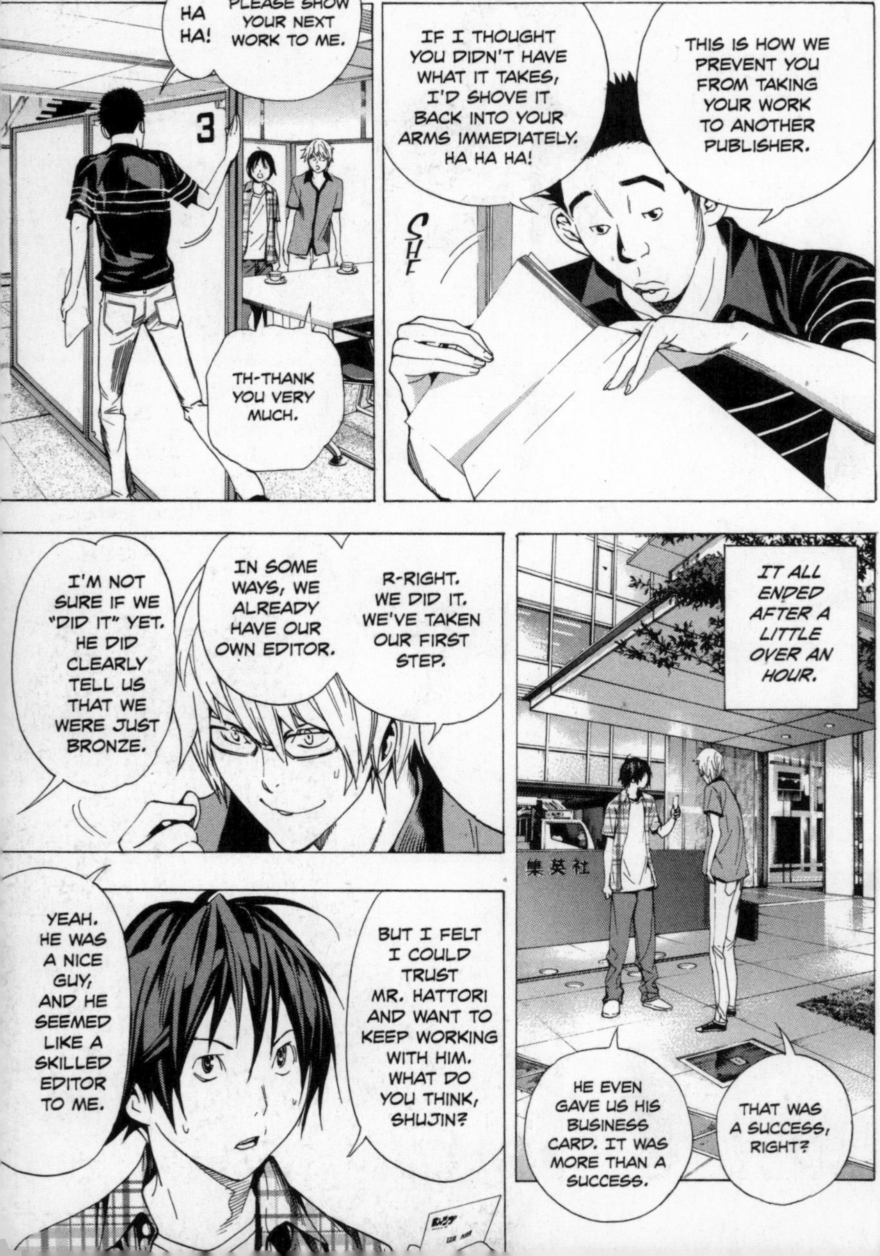
THIS IS HOW WE PREVENT YOU FROM TAKING YOUR WORK TO ANOTHER PUBLISHER.
IF I THOUGHT YOU DIDN'T HAVE WHAT IT TAKES, I'D SHOVE IT BACK INTO YOUR ARMS IMMEDIATELY. HA HA HA!
SHF
PLEASE SHOW YOUR NEXT WORK TO ME.
HA HA!
3
TH-THANK YOU VERY MUCH.
IT ALL ENDED AFTER A LITTLE OVER AN HOUR.
集英社
THAT WAS A SUCCESS, RIGHT?
HE EVEN GAVE US HIS BUSINESS CARD. IT WAS MORE THAN A SUCCESS.
R-RIGHT. WE DID IT. WE'VE TAKEN OUR FIRST STEP.
IN SOME WAYS, WE ALREADY HAVE OUR OWN EDITOR.
I'M NOT SURE IF WE "DID IT" YET. HE DID CLEARLY TELL US THAT WE WERE JUST BRONZE.
BUT I FELT I COULD TRUST MR. HATTORI AND WANT TO KEEP WORKING WITH HIM. WHAT DO YOU THINK, SHUJIN?
YEAH. HE WAS A NICE GUY, AND HE SEEMED LIKE A SKILLED EDITOR TO ME.

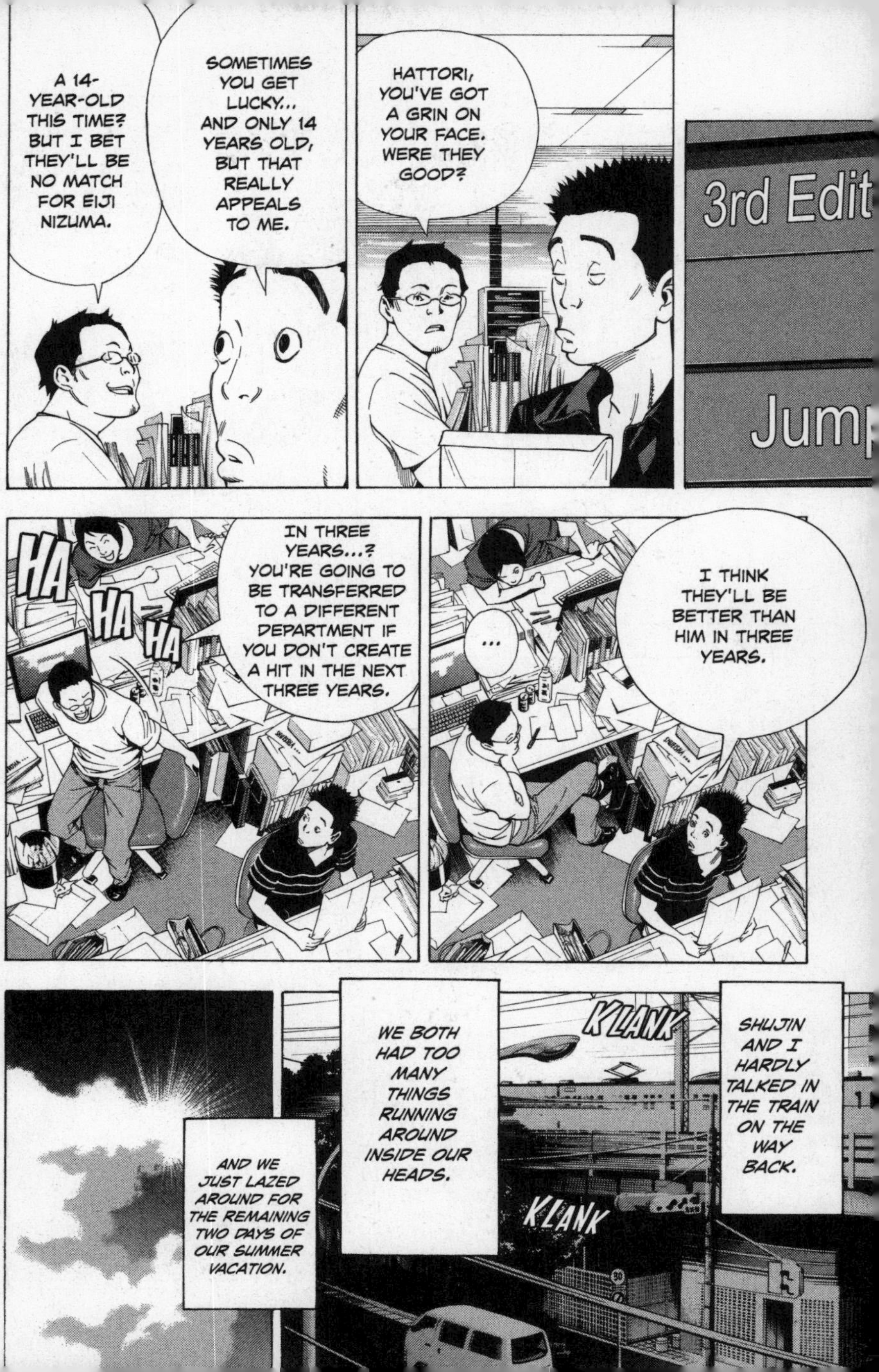
3rd Edit
Jump
HATTORI, YOU'VE GOT A GRIN ON YOUR FACE. WERE THEY GOOD?
SOMETIMES YOU GET LUCKY... AND ONLY 14 YEARS OLD, BUT THAT REALLY APPEALS TO ME.
A 14-YEAR-OLD THIS TIME? BUT I BET THEY'LL BE NO MATCH FOR EIJI NIZUMA.
I THINK THEY'LL BE BETTER THAN HIM IN THREE YEARS.
...
IN THREE YEARS...? YOU'RE GOING TO BE TRANSFERRED TO A DIFFERENT DEPARTMENT IF YOU DON'T CREATE A HIT IN THE NEXT THREE YEARS.
HA
HA
HA
SHUJIN AND I HARDLY TALKED IN THE TRAIN ON THE WAY BACK.
KLANK
WE BOTH HAD TOO MANY THINGS RUNNING AROUND INSIDE OUR HEADS.
KLANK
AND WE JUST LAZED AROUND FOR THE REMAINING TWO DAYS OF OUR SUMMER VACATION.

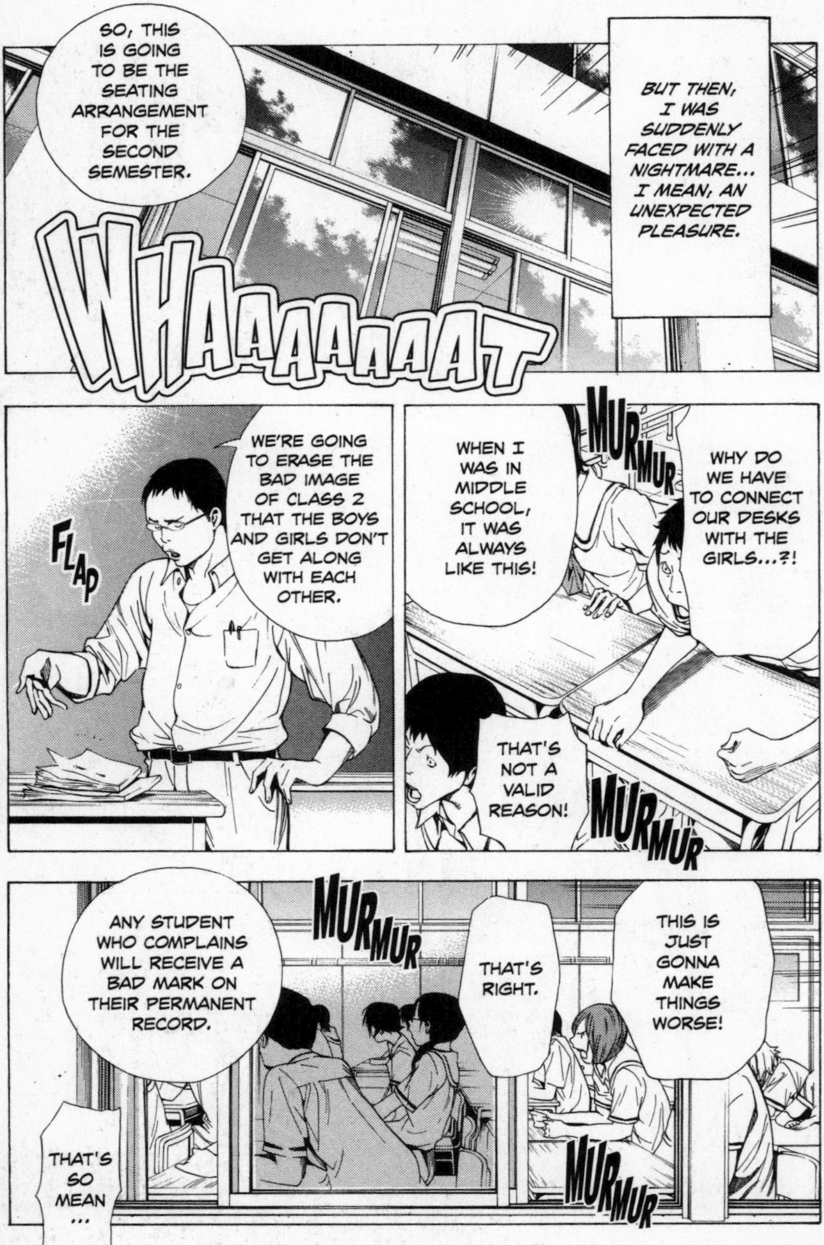
BUT THEN, I WAS SUDDENLY FACED WITH A NIGHTMARE... I MEAN, AN UNEXPECTED PLEASURE.
SO, THIS IS GOING TO BE THE SEATING ARRANGEMENT FOR THE SECOND SEMESTER.
WHAAAAAAAT
WHY DO WE HAVE TO CONNECT OUR DESKS WITH THE GIRLS...?!
MURMUR
WHEN I WAS IN MIDDLE SCHOOL, IT WAS ALWAYS LIKE THIS!
THAT'S NOT A VALID REASON!
MURMUR
WE'RE GOING TO ERASE THE BAD IMAGE OF CLASS 2 THAT THE BOYS AND GIRLS DON'T GET ALONG WITH EACH OTHER.
FLAP
THIS IS JUST GONNA MAKE THINGS WORSE!
THAT'S RIGHT.
MURMUR
ANY STUDENT WHO COMPLAINS WILL RECEIVE A BAD MARK ON THEIR PERMANENT RECORD.
MURMUR
THAT'S SO MEAN...

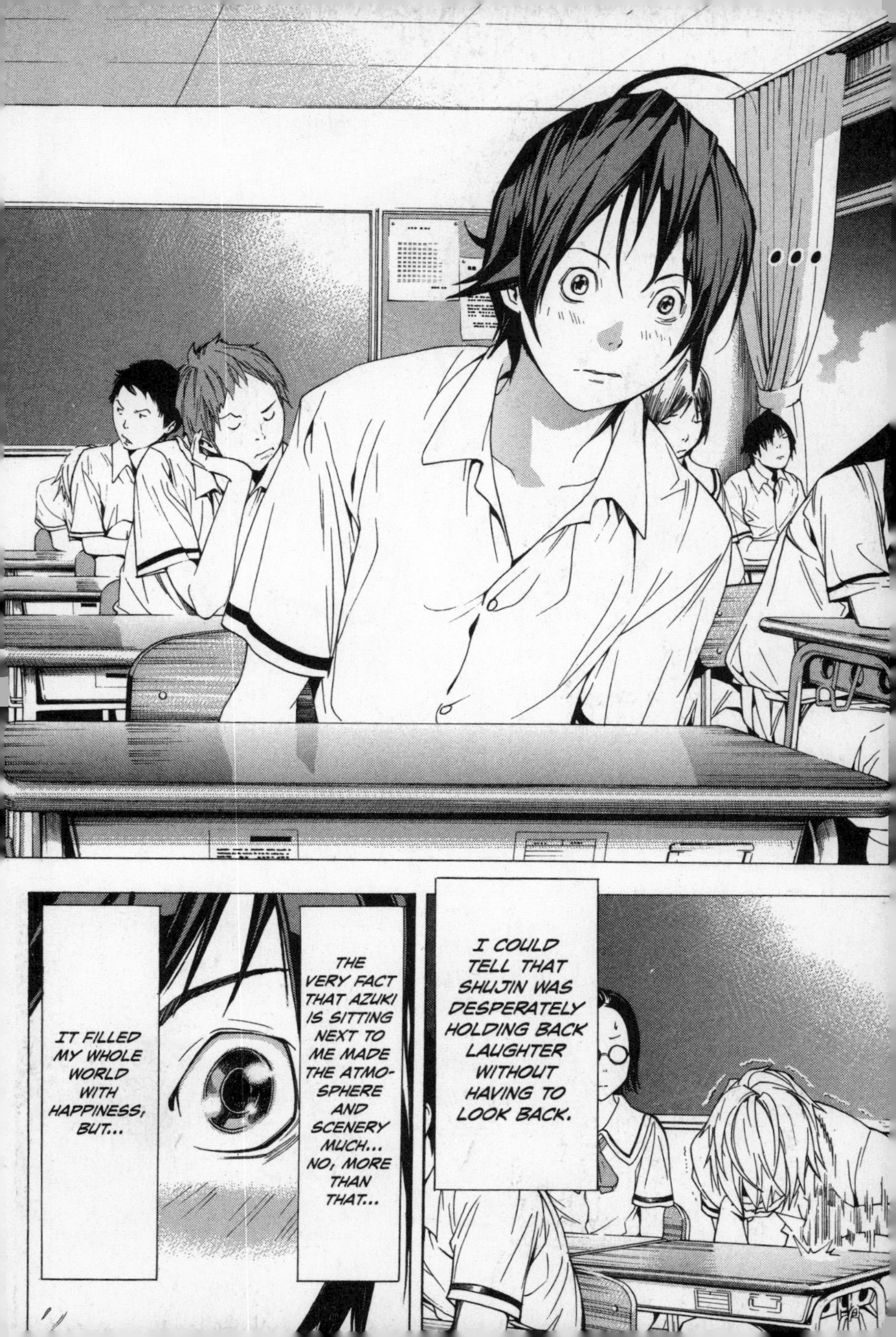
...
I COULD TELL THAT SHUJIN WAS DESPERATELY HOLDING BACK LAUGHTER WITHOUT HAVING TO LOOK BACK.
THE VERY FACT THAT AZUKI IS SITTING NEXT TO ME MADE THE ATMO-SPHERE AND SCENERY MUCH... NO, MORE THAN THAT...
IT FILLED MY WHOLE WORLD WITH HAPPINESS, BUT...

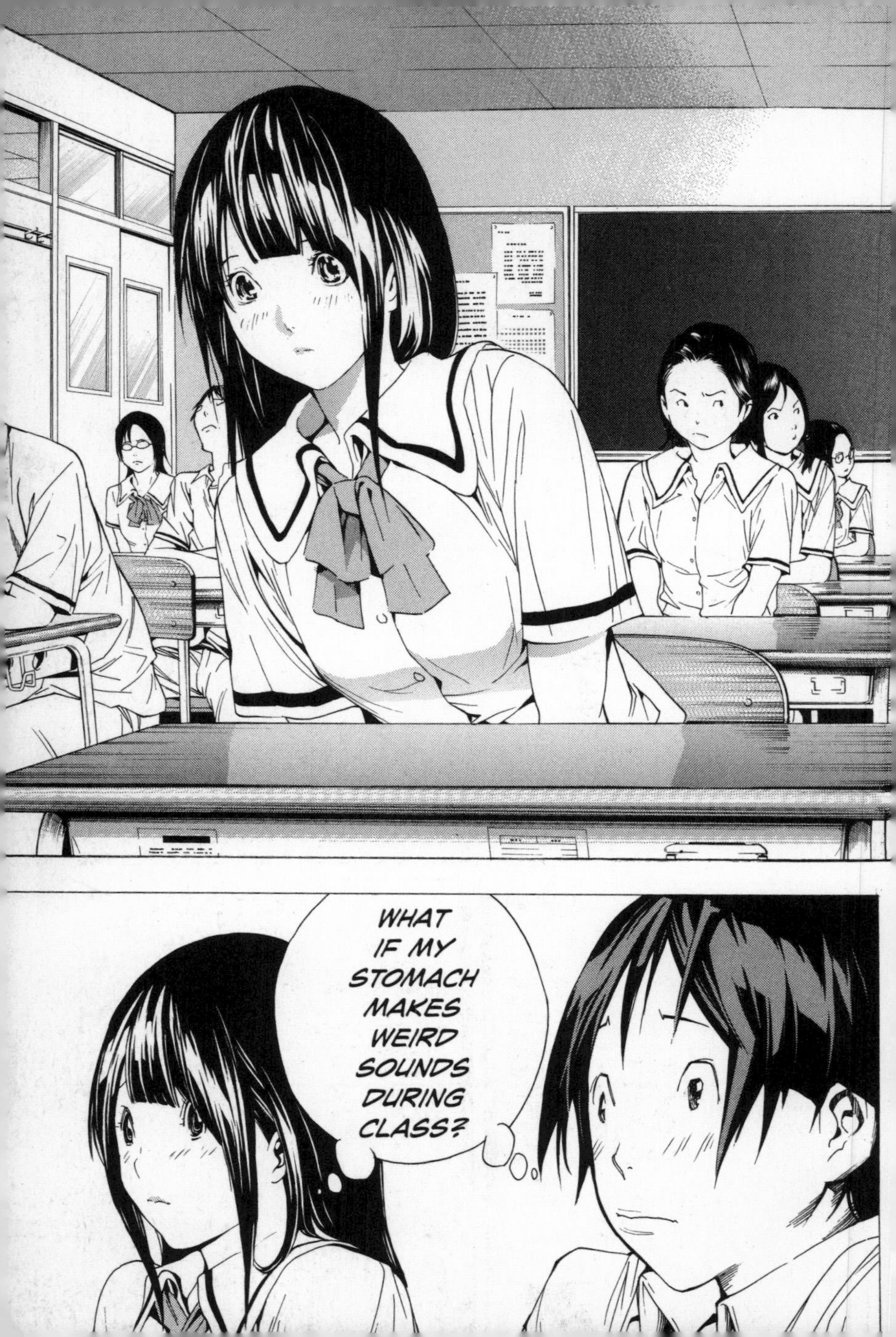
WHAT IF MY STOMACH MAKES WEIRD SOUNDS DURING CLASS?

OHBA'S STORYBOARD

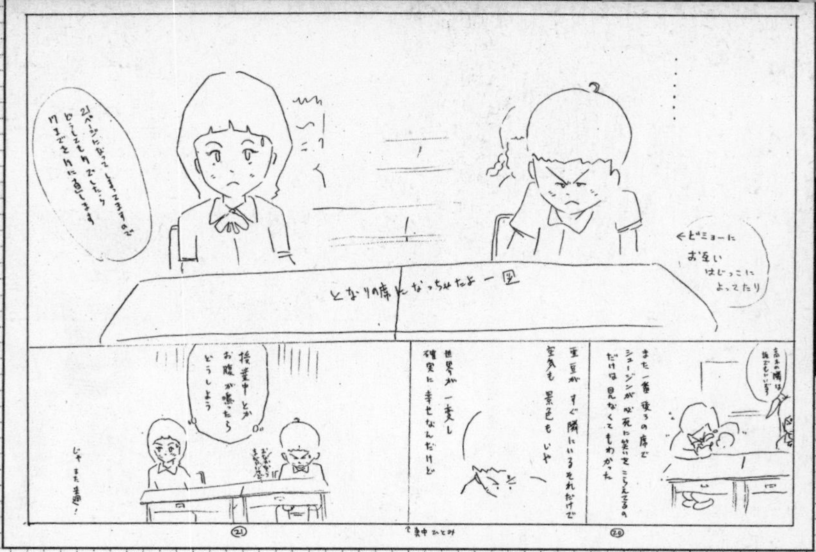
……
←ビミョーに お互い はじっこに よってたり
となりの席になっちゃったよー
また一番後ろの席で シュージンが必死に笑いをこらえてるのだけは 見なくてもわかった
亜豆がすぐ隣にいるそれだけで 空気も 景色も いや
世界が一変し 確実に幸せなんだけど
授業中とか お腹が鳴ったら どうしよう
じゃまた来週!
20
21

OBATA'S STORYBOARD

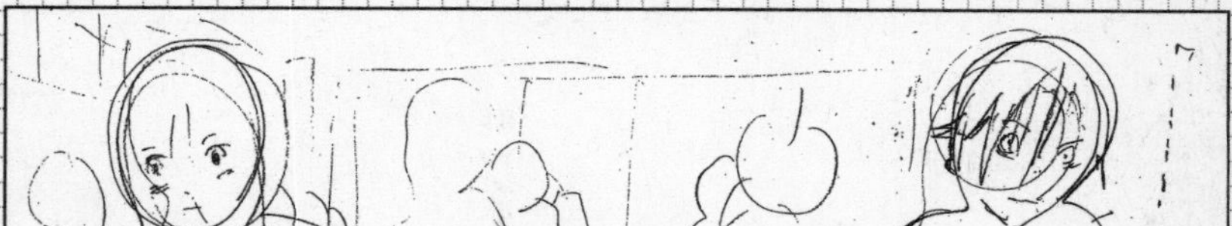
また一番後ろの席でシュージンが必死に笑いをこらえてるのだけは見なくてもわかった
亜豆がすぐとなりにいるってだけで 空気も景色も いや
世界が一変し 確実に幸せなんだけど
授業中とか お腹が鳴ったらどうしよう
20
21

COMPLETE!

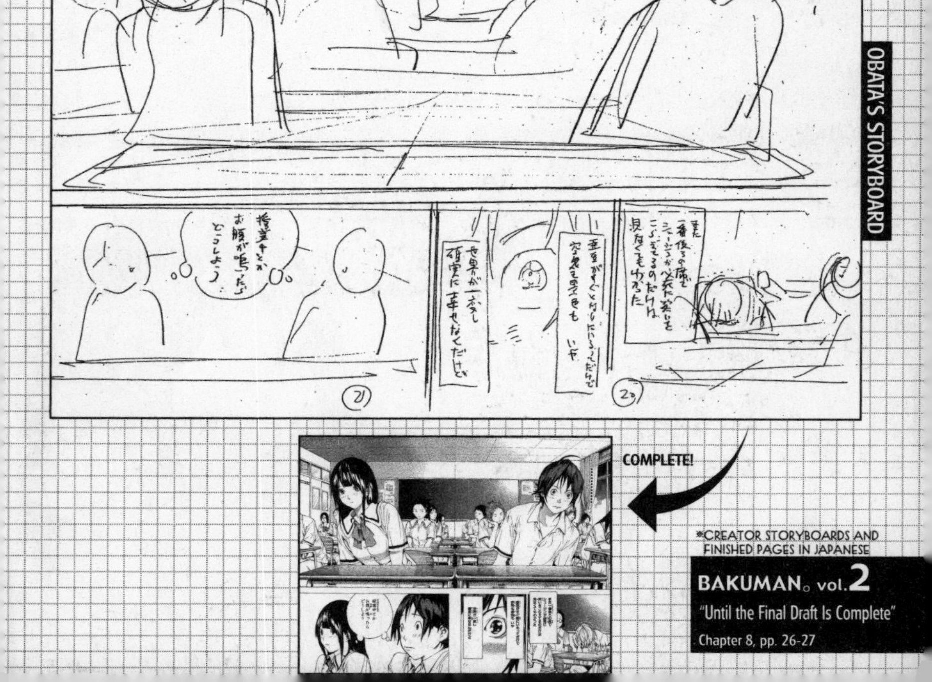

*CREATOR STORYBOARDS AND FINISHED PAGES IN JAPANESE

**BAKUMAN。 vol. 2**

"Until the Final Draft Is Complete"

Chapter 8, pp. 26-27

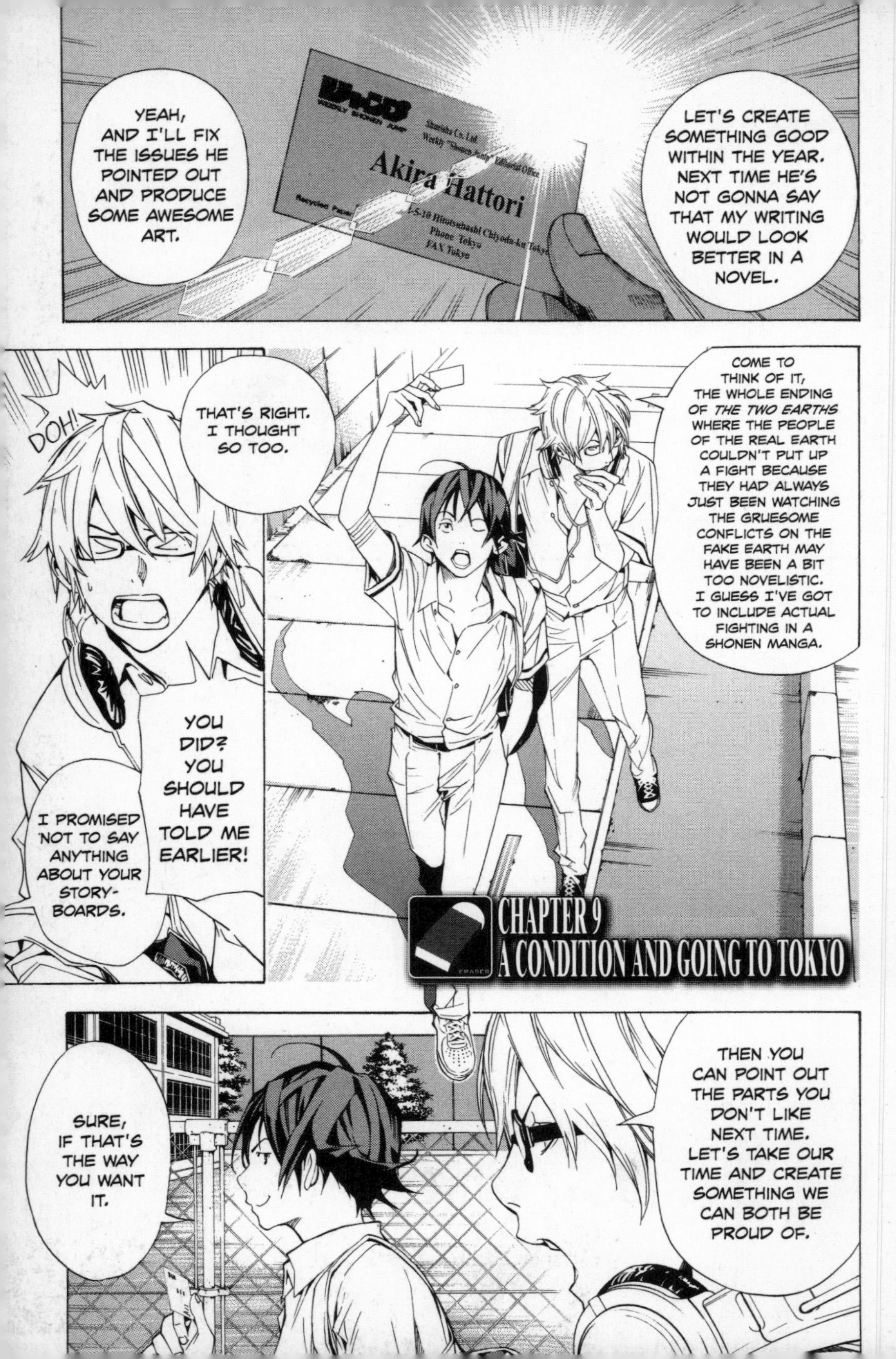
LET'S CREATE SOMETHING GOOD WITHIN THE YEAR. NEXT TIME HE'S NOT GONNA SAY THAT MY WRITING WOULD LOOK BETTER IN A NOVEL.
Akira Hattori
YEAH, AND I'LL FIX THE ISSUES HE POINTED OUT AND PRODUCE SOME AWESOME ART.
COME TO THINK OF IT, THE WHOLE ENDING OF *THE TWO EARTHS* WHERE THE PEOPLE OF THE REAL EARTH COULDN'T PUT UP A FIGHT BECAUSE THEY HAD ALWAYS JUST BEEN WATCHING THE GRUESOME CONFLICTS ON THE FAKE EARTH MAY HAVE BEEN A BIT TOO NOVELISTIC. I GUESS I'VE GOT TO INCLUDE ACTUAL FIGHTING IN A SHONEN MANGA.
THAT'S RIGHT. I THOUGHT SO TOO.
DOH!
YOU DID? YOU SHOULD HAVE TOLD ME EARLIER!
I PROMISED NOT TO SAY ANYTHING ABOUT YOUR STORY-BOARDS.
CHAPTER 9
A CONDITION AND GOING TO TOKYO
THEN YOU CAN POINT OUT THE PARTS YOU DON'T LIKE NEXT TIME. LET'S TAKE OUR TIME AND CREATE SOMETHING WE CAN BOTH BE PROUD OF.
SURE, IF THAT'S THE WAY YOU WANT IT.

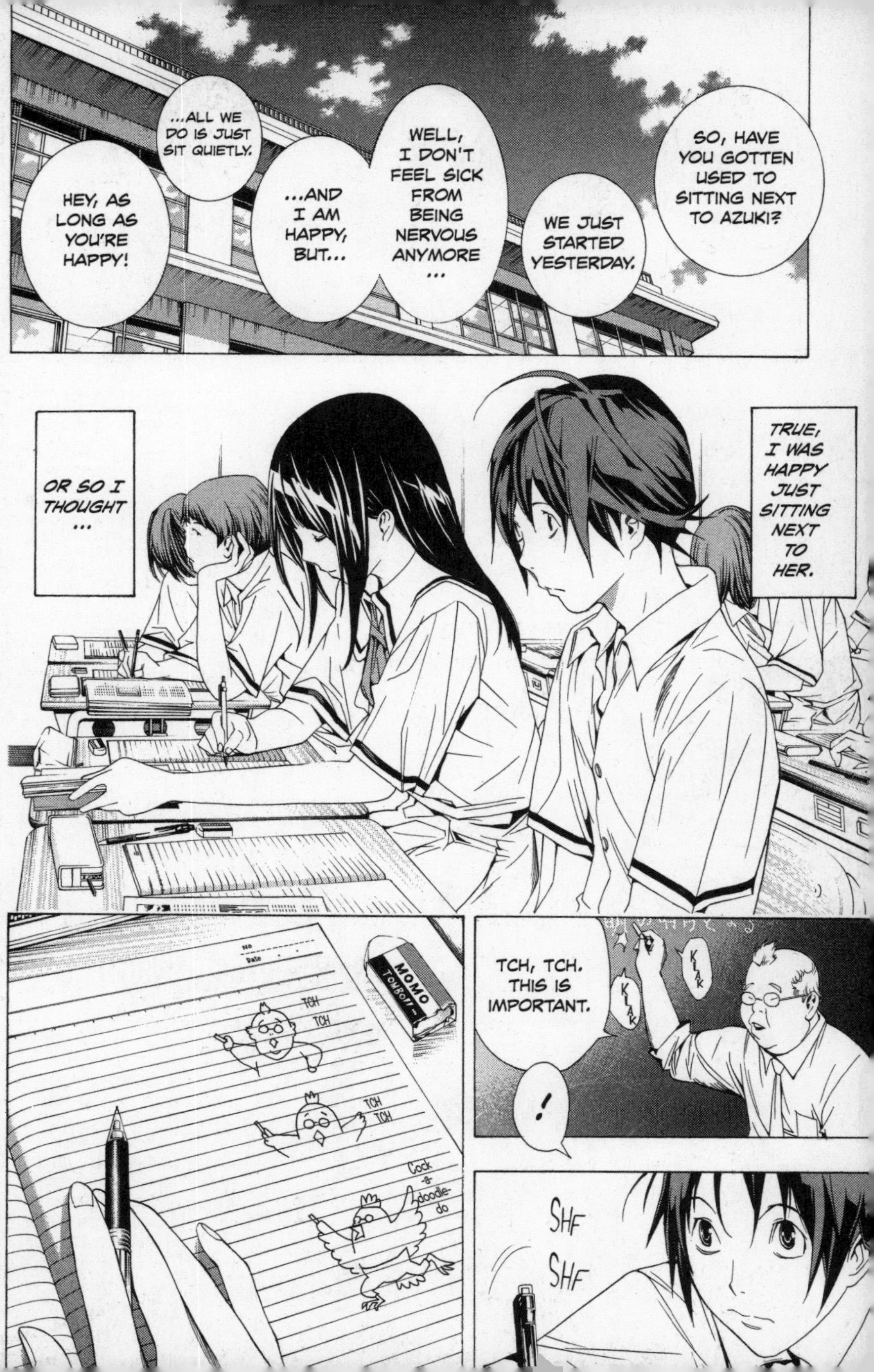
SO, HAVE YOU GOTTEN USED TO SITTING NEXT TO AZUKI?
WE JUST STARTED YESTERDAY.
WELL, I DON'T FEEL SICK FROM BEING NERVOUS ANYMORE ...
...AND I AM HAPPY, BUT...
...ALL WE DO IS JUST SIT QUIETLY.
HEY, AS LONG AS YOU'RE HAPPY!
TRUE, I WAS HAPPY JUST SITTING NEXT TO HER.
OR SO I THOUGHT ...
KLAK
KLAK
TCH, TCH. THIS IS IMPORTANT.
!
SHF
SHF
No
Date
MOMO
TOMBOW
TCH
TCH
TCH
TCH
Cock-a-doodle-do

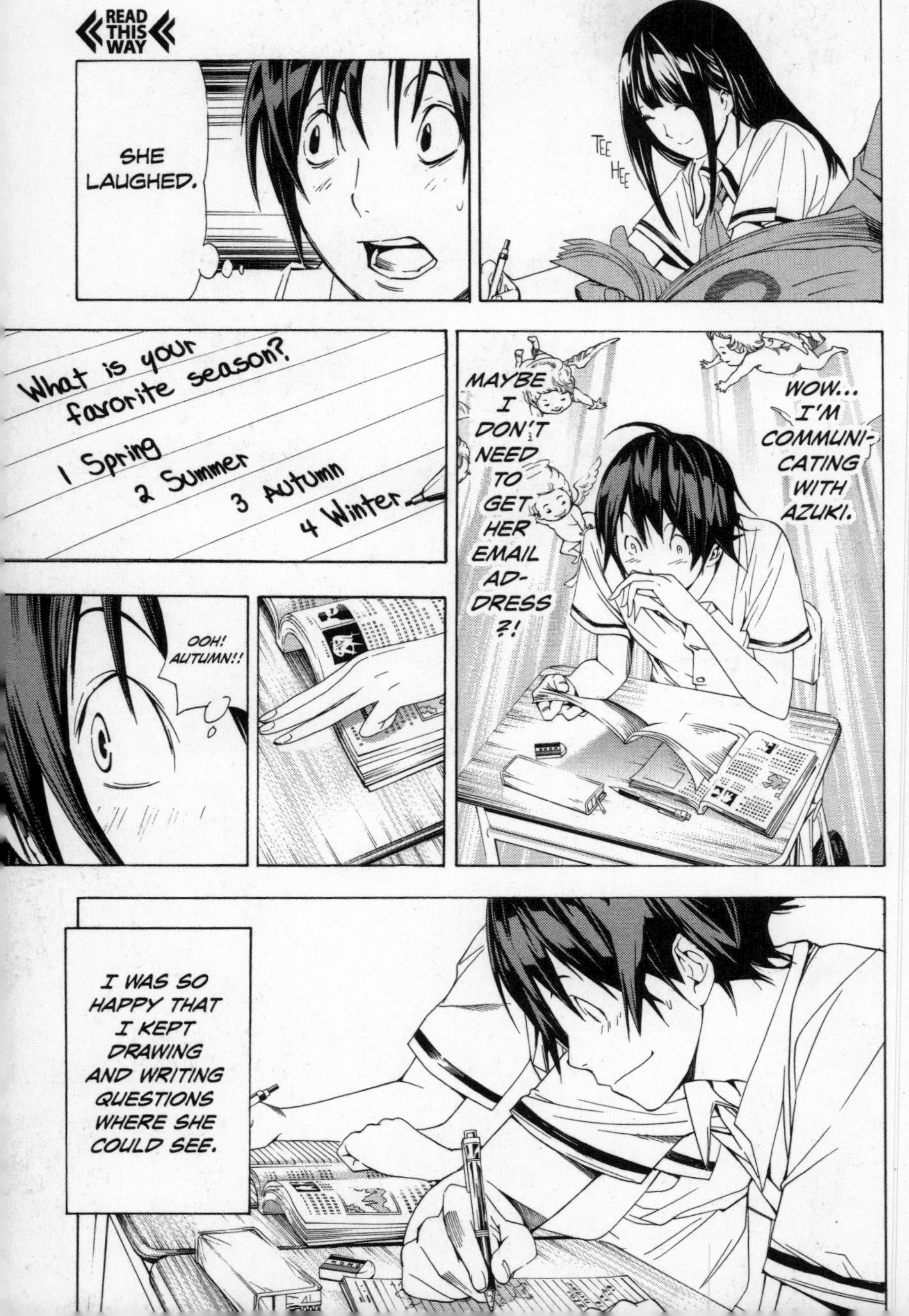
READ THIS WAY
TEE HEE
SHE LAUGHED.
WOW... I'M COMMUNI-CATING WITH AZUKI.
MAYBE I DON'T NEED TO GET HER EMAIL AD-DRESS?!
What is your favorite season?
1 Spring
2 Summer
3 Autumn
4 Winter
OOH! AUTUMN!!
I WAS SO HAPPY THAT I KEPT DRAWING AND WRITING QUESTIONS WHERE SHE COULD SEE.

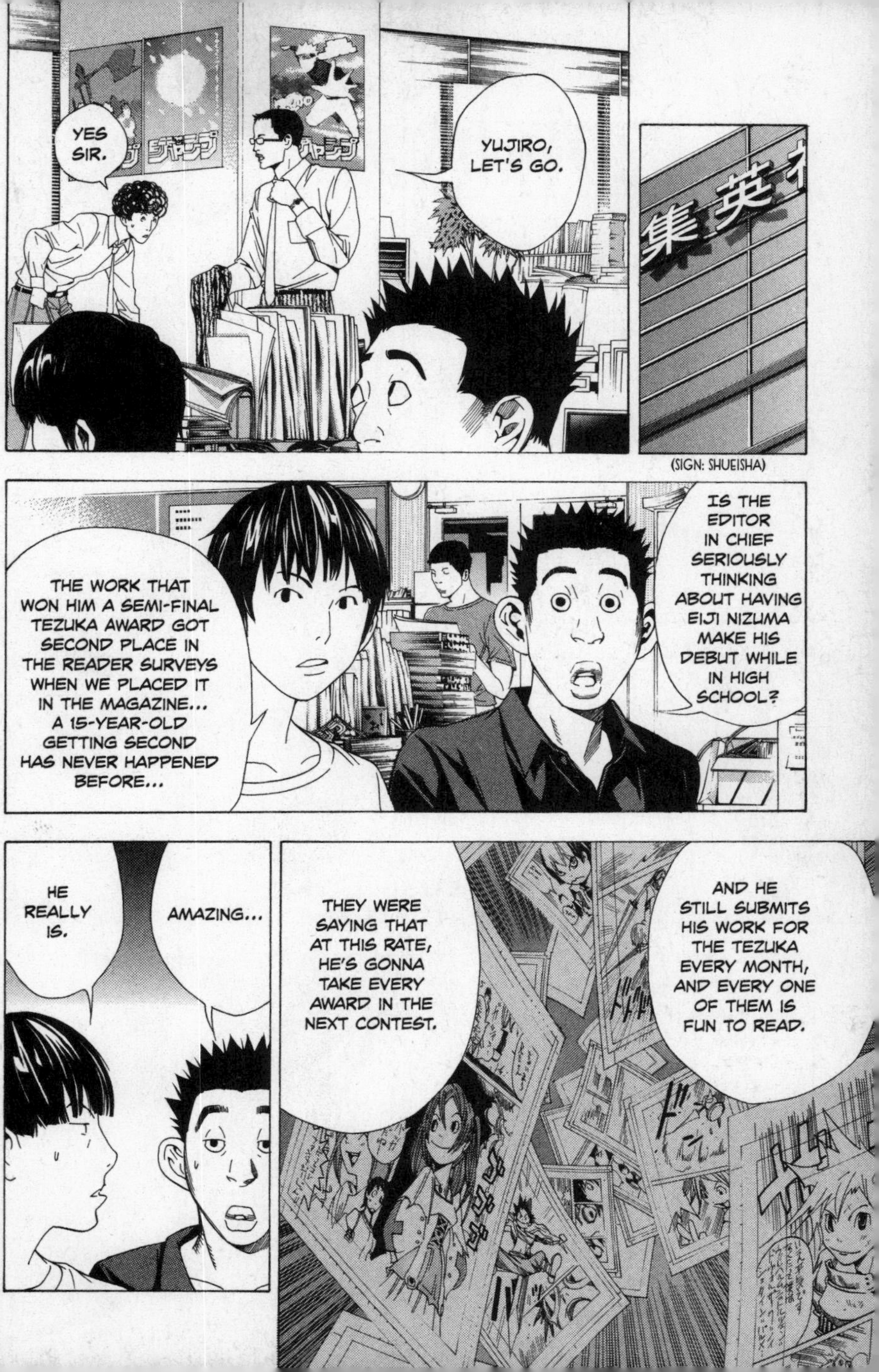
集英
(SIGN: SHUEISHA)
YUJIRO, LET'S GO.
YES SIR.
IS THE EDITOR IN CHIEF SERIOUSLY THINKING ABOUT HAVING EIJI NIZUMA MAKE HIS DEBUT WHILE IN HIGH SCHOOL?
THE WORK THAT WON HIM A SEMI-FINAL TEZUKA AWARD GOT SECOND PLACE IN THE READER SURVEYS WHEN WE PLACED IT IN THE MAGAZINE... A 15-YEAR-OLD GETTING SECOND HAS NEVER HAPPENED BEFORE...
AND HE STILL SUBMITS HIS WORK FOR THE TEZUKA EVERY MONTH, AND EVERY ONE OF THEM IS FUN TO READ.
THEY WERE SAYING THAT AT THIS RATE, HE'S GONNA TAKE EVERY AWARD IN THE NEXT CONTEST.
AMAZING...
HE REALLY IS.

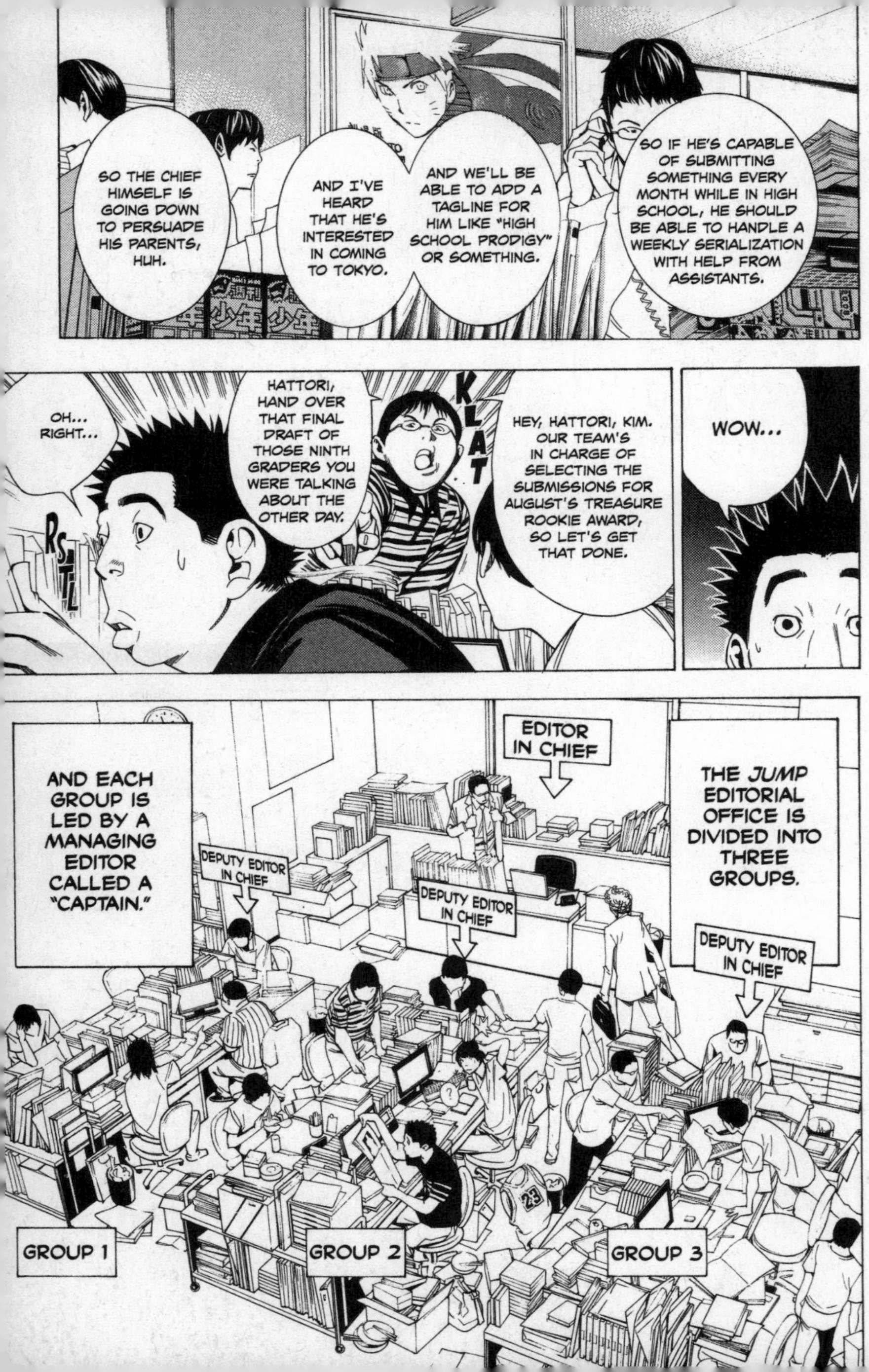
SO IF HE'S CAPABLE OF SUBMITTING SOMETHING EVERY MONTH WHILE IN HIGH SCHOOL, HE SHOULD BE ABLE TO HANDLE A WEEKLY SERIALIZATION WITH HELP FROM ASSISTANTS.
AND WE'LL BE ABLE TO ADD A TAGLINE FOR HIM LIKE "HIGH SCHOOL PRODIGY" OR SOMETHING.
AND I'VE HEARD THAT HE'S INTERESTED IN COMING TO TOKYO.
SO THE CHIEF HIMSELF IS GOING DOWN TO PERSUADE HIS PARENTS, HUH.
WOW...
HEY, HATTORI, KIM. OUR TEAM'S IN CHARGE OF SELECTING THE SUBMISSIONS FOR AUGUST'S TREASURE ROOKIE AWARD, SO LET'S GET THAT DONE.
KLAT
HATTORI, HAND OVER THAT FINAL DRAFT OF THOSE NINTH GRADERS YOU WERE TALKING ABOUT THE OTHER DAY.
OH... RIGHT...
RSTL
THE JUMP EDITORIAL OFFICE IS DIVIDED INTO THREE GROUPS.
EDITOR IN CHIEF
DEPUTY EDITOR IN CHIEF
DEPUTY EDITOR IN CHIEF
DEPUTY EDITOR IN CHIEF
AND EACH GROUP IS LED BY A MANAGING EDITOR CALLED A "CAPTAIN."
GROUP 3
GROUP 2
GROUP 1

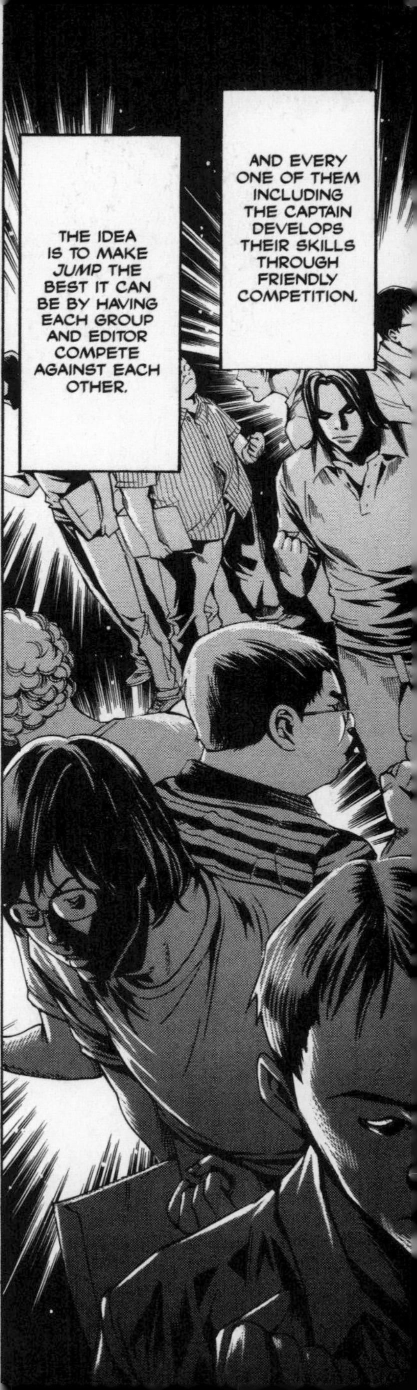
AND EVERY ONE OF THEM INCLUDING THE CAPTAIN DEVELOPS THEIR SKILLS THROUGH FRIENDLY COMPETITION.
THE IDEA IS TO MAKE *JUMP* THE BEST IT CAN BE BY HAVING EACH GROUP AND EDITOR COMPETE AGAINST EACH OTHER.

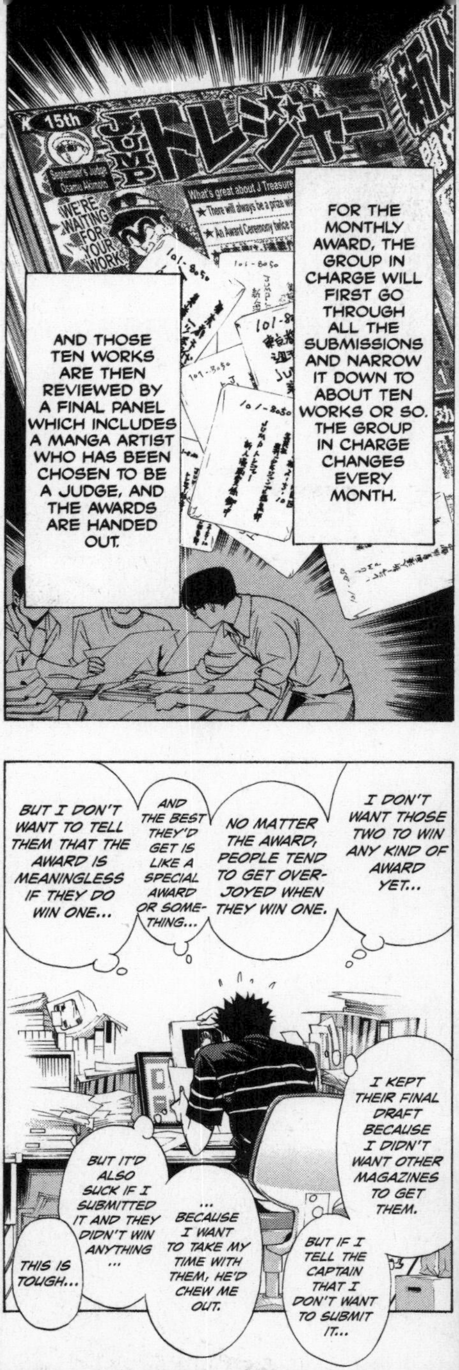
15th
JUMP
WE'RE WAITING FOR YOUR WORK
What's great about J Treasure
FOR THE MONTHLY AWARD, THE GROUP IN CHARGE WILL FIRST GO THROUGH ALL THE SUBMISSIONS AND NARROW IT DOWN TO ABOUT TEN WORKS OR SO. THE GROUP IN CHARGE CHANGES EVERY MONTH.
AND THOSE TEN WORKS ARE THEN REVIEWED BY A FINAL PANEL WHICH INCLUDES A MANGA ARTIST WHO HAS BEEN CHOSEN TO BE A JUDGE, AND THE AWARDS ARE HANDED OUT.
I DON'T WANT THOSE TWO TO WIN ANY KIND OF AWARD YET...
NO MATTER THE AWARD, PEOPLE TEND TO GET OVER-JOYED WHEN THEY WIN ONE.
AND THE BEST THEY'D GET IS LIKE A SPECIAL AWARD OR SOME-THING...
BUT I DON'T WANT TO TELL THEM THAT THE AWARD IS MEANINGLESS IF THEY DO WIN ONE...
I KEPT THEIR FINAL DRAFT BECAUSE I DIDN'T WANT OTHER MAGAZINES TO GET THEM.
BUT IF I TELL THE CAPTAIN THAT I DON'T WANT TO SUBMIT IT...
...BECAUSE I WANT TO TAKE MY TIME WITH THEM, HE'D CHEW ME OUT.
BUT IT'D ALSO SUCK IF I SUBMITTED IT AND THEY DIDN'T WIN ANYTHING...
THIS IS TOUGH...

READ THIS WAY

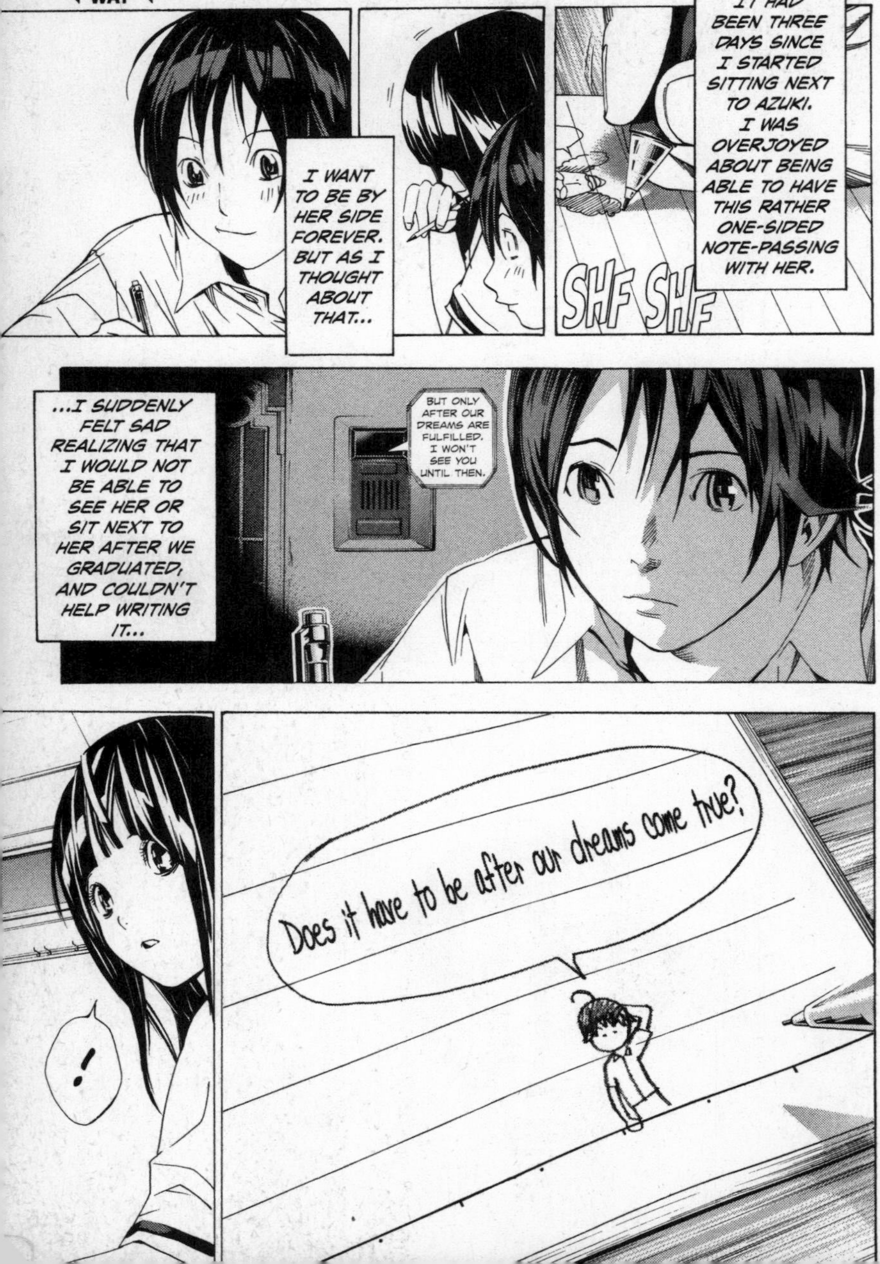
IT HAD BEEN THREE DAYS SINCE I STARTED SITTING NEXT TO AZUKI. I WAS OVERJOYED ABOUT BEING ABLE TO HAVE THIS RATHER ONE-SIDED NOTE-PASSING WITH HER.
SHF SHF
I WANT TO BE BY HER SIDE FOREVER. BUT AS I THOUGHT ABOUT THAT...
BUT ONLY AFTER OUR DREAMS ARE FULFILLED. I WON'T SEE YOU UNTIL THEN.
...I SUDDENLY FELT SAD REALIZING THAT I WOULD NOT BE ABLE TO SEE HER OR SIT NEXT TO HER AFTER WE GRADUATED, AND COULDN'T HELP WRITING IT...
Does it have to be after our dreams come true?
!

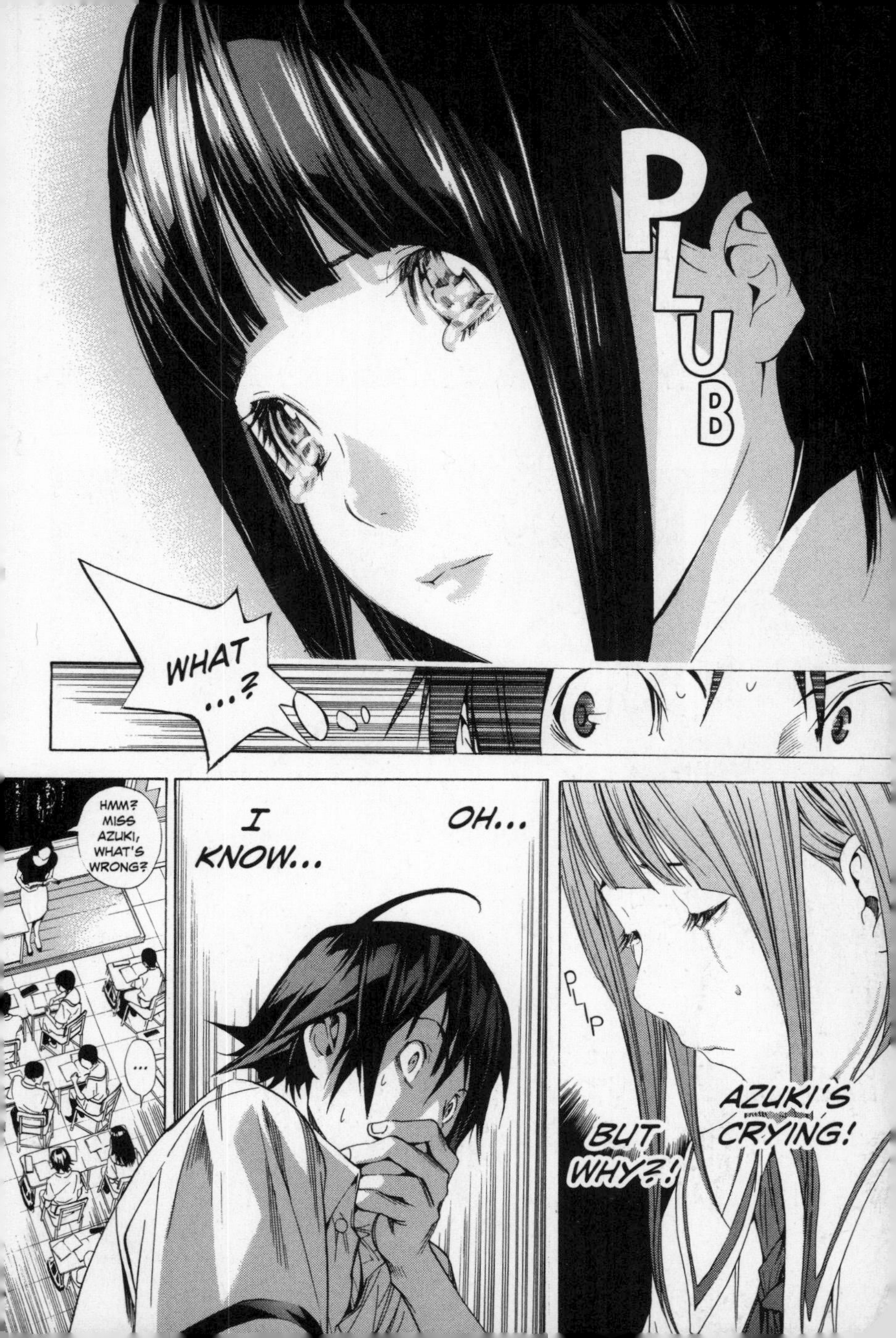
PLUB
WHAT ...?
PLIP
AZUKI'S CRYING!
BUT WHY?!
OH...
I KNOW...
HMM? MISS AZUKI, WHAT'S WRONG?
...

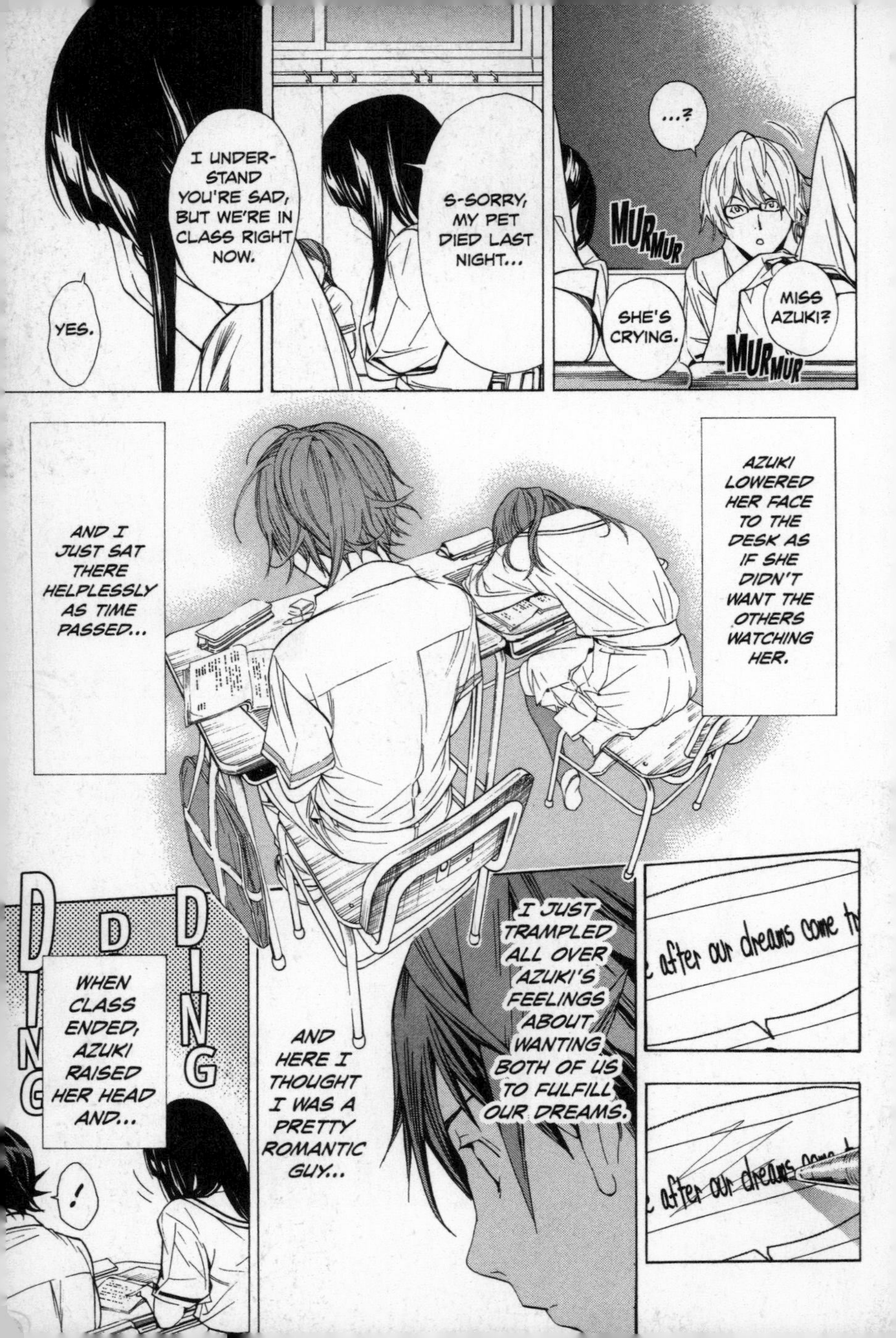

...?
MURMUR
MISS AZUKI?
SHE'S CRYING.
MURMUR
S-SORRY, MY PET DIED LAST NIGHT...
I UNDERSTAND YOU'RE SAD, BUT WE'RE IN CLASS RIGHT NOW.
YES.
AZUKI LOWERED HER FACE TO THE DESK AS IF SHE DIDN'T WANT THE OTHERS WATCHING HER.
AND I JUST SAT THERE HELPLESSLY AS TIME PASSED...
after our dreams come
after our dreams
I JUST TRAMPLED ALL OVER AZUKI'S FEELINGS ABOUT WANTING BOTH OF US TO FULFILL OUR DREAMS.
AND HERE I THOUGHT I WAS A PRETTY ROMANTIC GUY...
DING
DING
DING
WHEN CLASS ENDED, AZUKI RAISED HER HEAD AND...
!

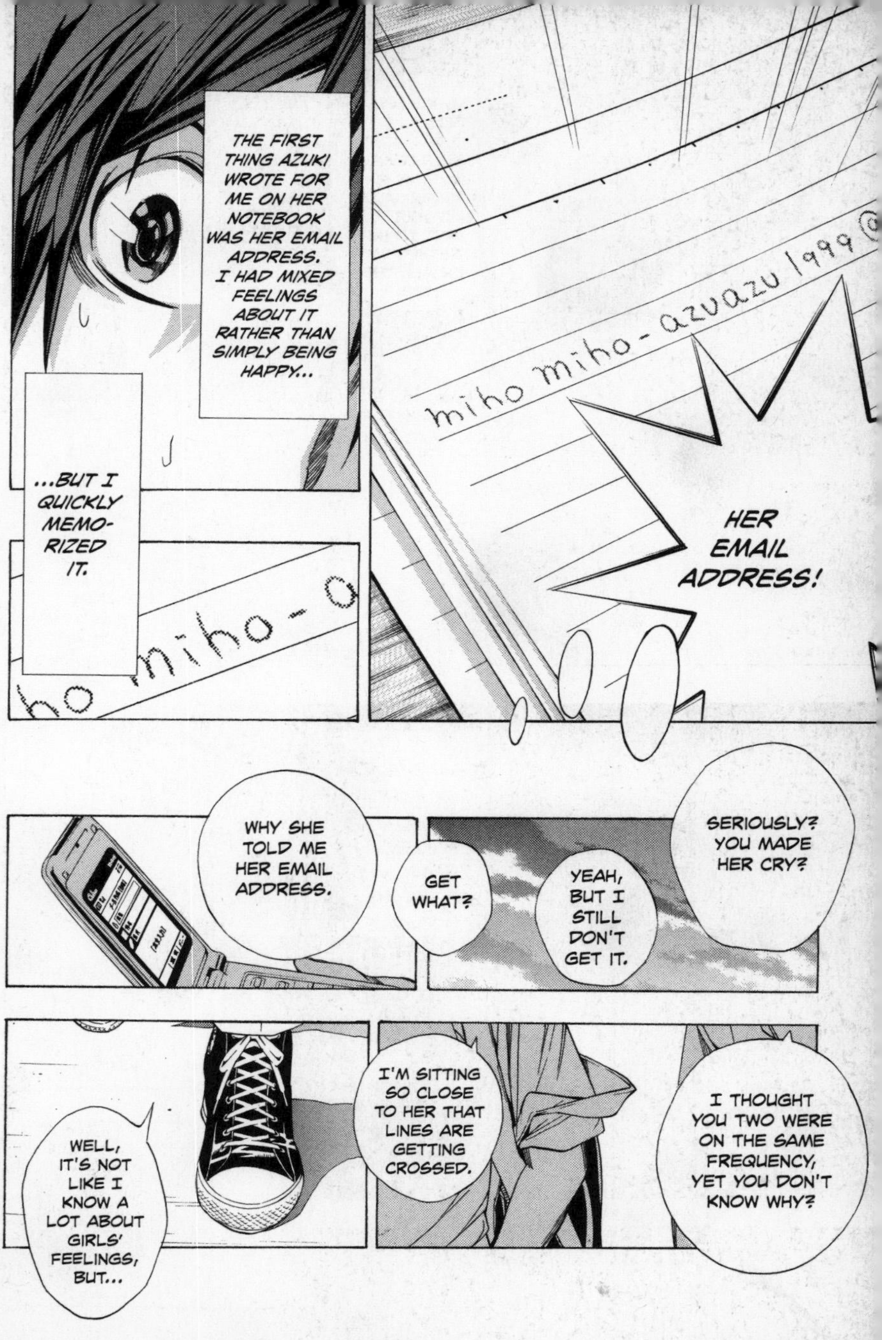
miho miho-azuazu1999@
HER EMAIL ADDRESS!
THE FIRST THING AZUKI WROTE FOR ME ON HER NOTEBOOK WAS HER EMAIL ADDRESS. I HAD MIXED FEELINGS ABOUT IT RATHER THAN SIMPLY BEING HAPPY...
...BUT I QUICKLY MEMORIZED IT.
ho miho-a
SERIOUSLY? YOU MADE HER CRY?
YEAH, BUT I STILL DON'T GET IT.
GET WHAT?
WHY SHE TOLD ME HER EMAIL ADDRESS.
I THOUGHT YOU TWO WERE ON THE SAME FREQUENCY, YET YOU DON'T KNOW WHY?
I'M SITTING SO CLOSE TO HER THAT LINES ARE GETTING CROSSED.
WELL, IT'S NOT LIKE I KNOW A LOT ABOUT GIRLS' FEELINGS, BUT...

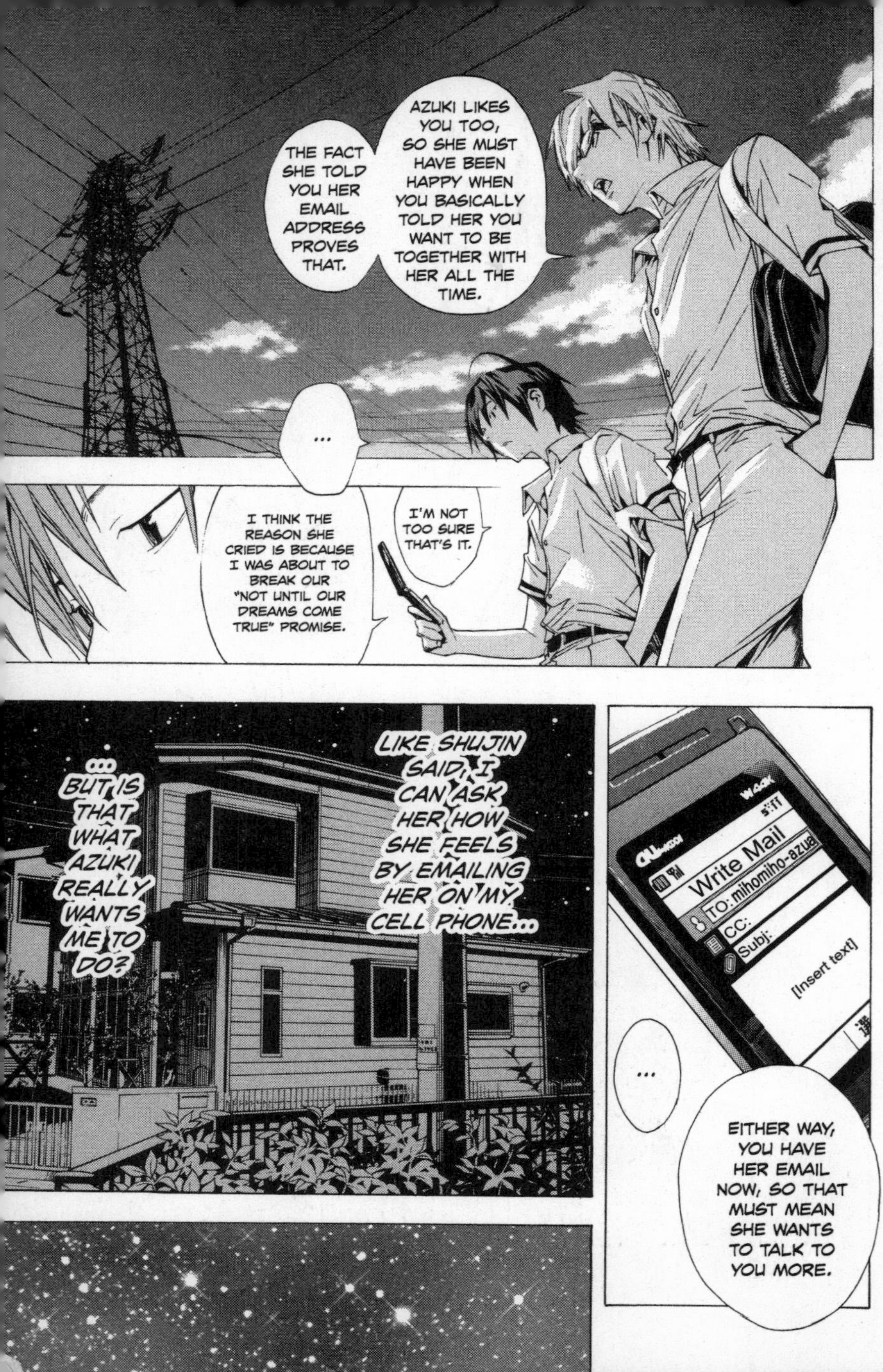
AZUKI LIKES YOU TOO, SO SHE MUST HAVE BEEN HAPPY WHEN YOU BASICALLY TOLD HER YOU WANT TO BE TOGETHER WITH HER ALL THE TIME.
THE FACT SHE TOLD YOU HER EMAIL ADDRESS PROVES THAT.
...
I'M NOT TOO SURE THAT'S IT.
I THINK THE REASON SHE CRIED IS BECAUSE I WAS ABOUT TO BREAK OUR "NOT UNTIL OUR DREAMS COME TRUE" PROMISE.
Write Mail
TO: mihomiho-azue
CC:
Subj:
[Insert text]
...
EITHER WAY, YOU HAVE HER EMAIL NOW, SO THAT MUST MEAN SHE WANTS TO TALK TO YOU MORE.
LIKE SHUJIN SAID, I CAN ASK HER HOW SHE FEELS BY EMAILING HER ON MY CELL PHONE...
...BUT IS THAT WHAT AZUKI REALLY WANTS ME TO DO?

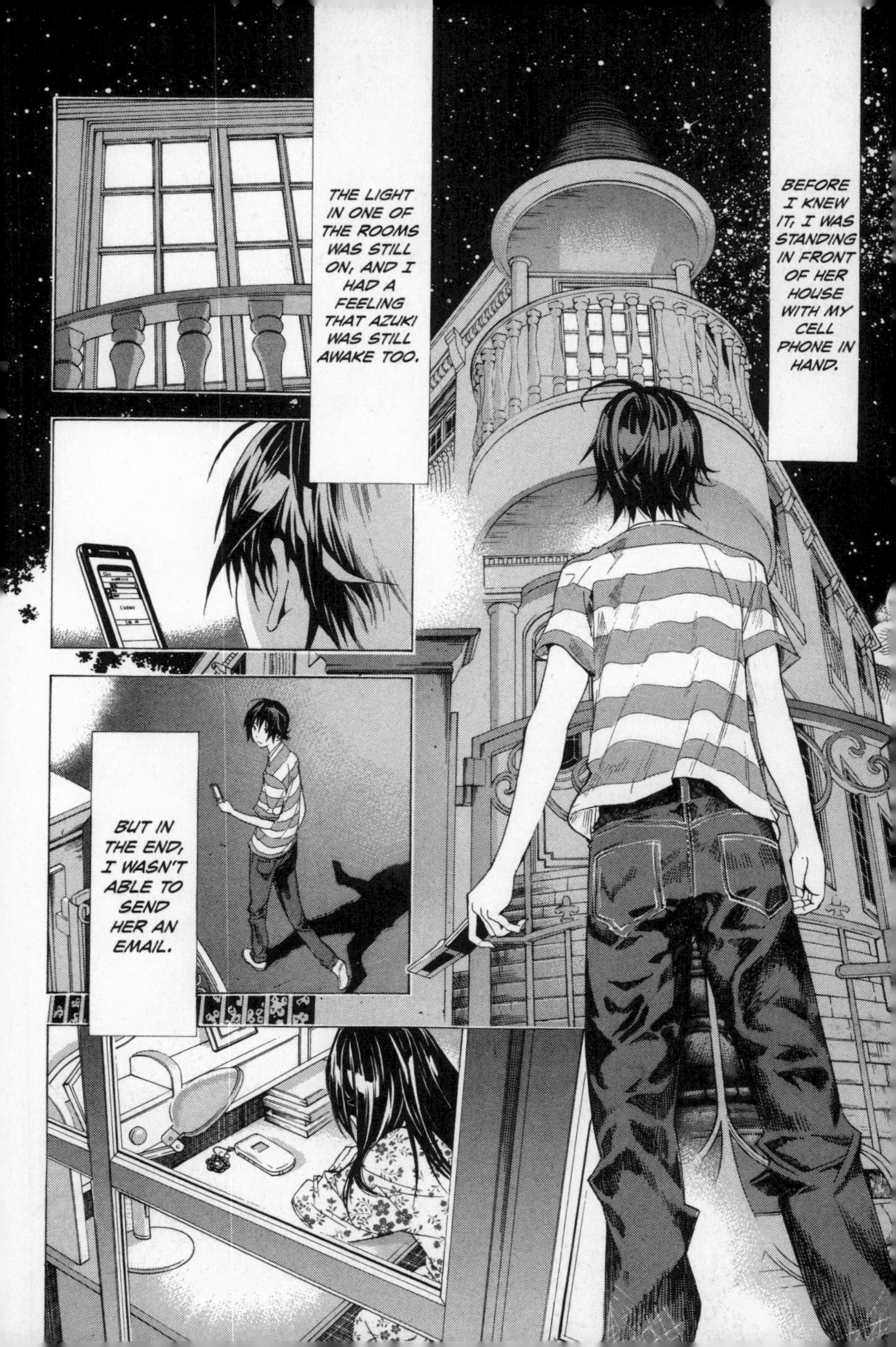
BEFORE I KNEW IT, I WAS STANDING IN FRONT OF HER HOUSE WITH MY CELL PHONE IN HAND.
THE LIGHT IN ONE OF THE ROOMS WAS STILL ON, AND I HAD A FEELING THAT AZUKI WAS STILL AWAKE TOO.
BUT IN THE END, I WASN'T ABLE TO SEND HER AN EMAIL.

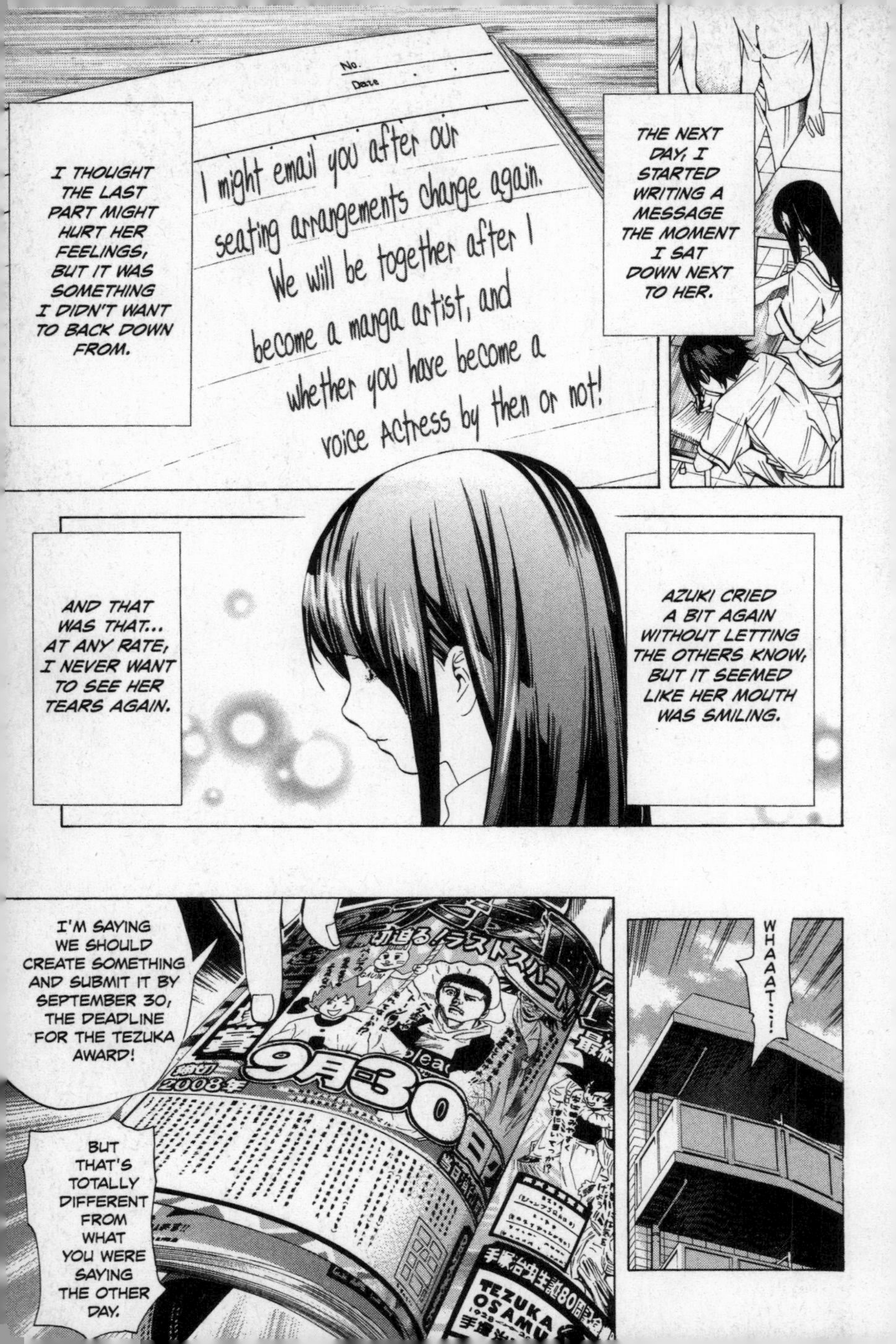
THE NEXT DAY, I STARTED WRITING A MESSAGE THE MOMENT I SAT DOWN NEXT TO HER.
No.
Date
I might email you after our seating arrangements change again. We will be together after I become a manga artist, and whether you have become a voice Actress by then or not!
I THOUGHT THE LAST PART MIGHT HURT HER FEELINGS, BUT IT WAS SOMETHING I DIDN'T WANT TO BACK DOWN FROM.
AZUKI CRIED A BIT AGAIN WITHOUT LETTING THE OTHERS KNOW, BUT IT SEEMED LIKE HER MOUTH WAS SMILING.
AND THAT WAS THAT... AT ANY RATE, I NEVER WANT TO SEE HER TEARS AGAIN.
WHAAAT...!
I'M SAYING WE SHOULD CREATE SOMETHING AND SUBMIT IT BY SEPTEMBER 30, THE DEADLINE FOR THE TEZUKA AWARD!
TEZUKA OSAMU
BUT THAT'S TOTALLY DIFFERENT FROM WHAT YOU WERE SAYING THE OTHER DAY.

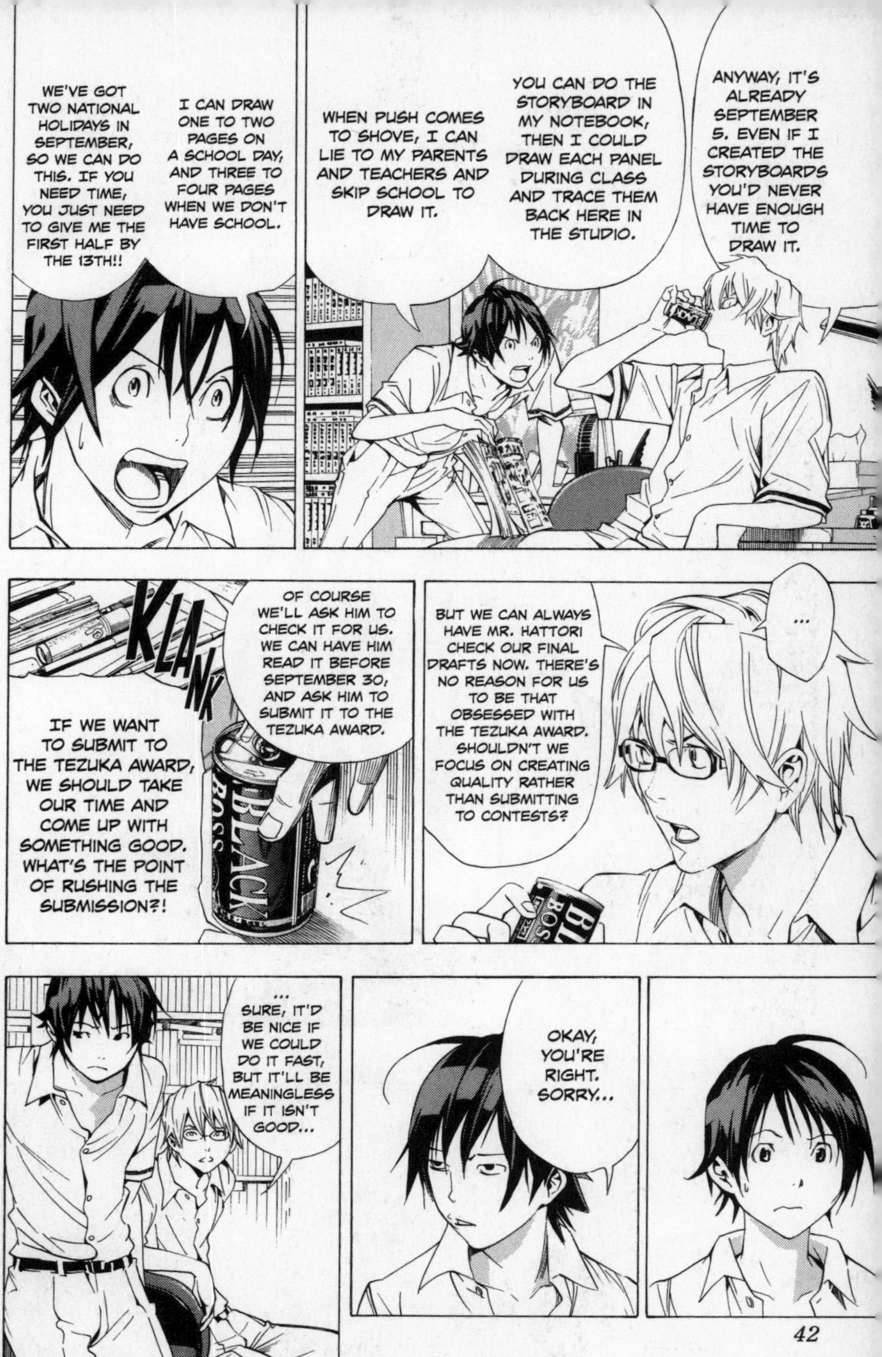
ANYWAY, IT'S ALREADY SEPTEMBER 5. EVEN IF I CREATED THE STORYBOARDS YOU'D NEVER HAVE ENOUGH TIME TO DRAW IT.
YOU CAN DO THE STORYBOARD IN MY NOTEBOOK, THEN I COULD DRAW EACH PANEL DURING CLASS AND TRACE THEM BACK HERE IN THE STUDIO.
WHEN PUSH COMES TO SHOVE, I CAN LIE TO MY PARENTS AND TEACHERS AND SKIP SCHOOL TO DRAW IT.
I CAN DRAW ONE TO TWO PAGES ON A SCHOOL DAY, AND THREE TO FOUR PAGES WHEN WE DON'T HAVE SCHOOL.
WE'VE GOT TWO NATIONAL HOLIDAYS IN SEPTEMBER, SO WE CAN DO THIS. IF YOU NEED TIME, YOU JUST NEED TO GIVE ME THE FIRST HALF BY THE 13TH!!
...
BUT WE CAN ALWAYS HAVE MR. HATTORI CHECK OUR FINAL DRAFTS NOW. THERE'S NO REASON FOR US TO BE THAT OBSESSED WITH THE TEZUKA AWARD. SHOULDN'T WE FOCUS ON CREATING QUALITY RATHER THAN SUBMITTING TO CONTESTS?
KLANK
OF COURSE WE'LL ASK HIM TO CHECK IT FOR US. WE CAN HAVE HIM READ IT BEFORE SEPTEMBER 30, AND ASK HIM TO SUBMIT IT TO THE TEZUKA AWARD.
IF WE WANT TO SUBMIT TO THE TEZUKA AWARD, WE SHOULD TAKE OUR TIME AND COME UP WITH SOMETHING GOOD. WHAT'S THE POINT OF RUSHING THE SUBMISSION?!
OKAY, YOU'RE RIGHT. SORRY...
... SURE, IT'D BE NICE IF WE COULD DO IT FAST, BUT IT'LL BE MEANINGLESS IF IT ISN'T GOOD...

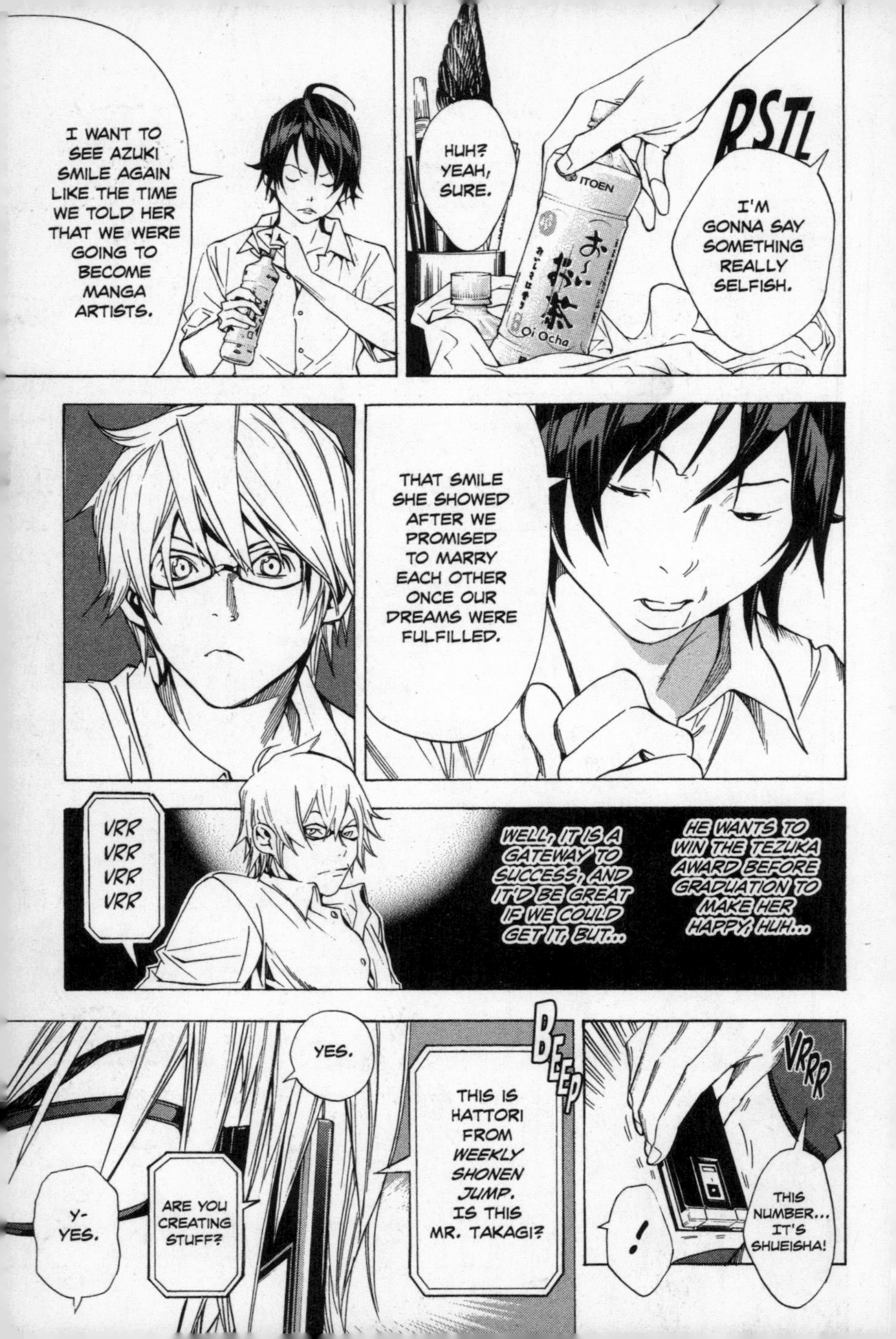
RSTL
I'M GONNA SAY SOMETHING REALLY SELFISH.
HUH? YEAH, SURE.
I WANT TO SEE AZUKI SMILE AGAIN LIKE THE TIME WE TOLD HER THAT WE WERE GOING TO BECOME MANGA ARTISTS.
THAT SMILE SHE SHOWED AFTER WE PROMISED TO MARRY EACH OTHER ONCE OUR DREAMS WERE FULFILLED.
HE WANTS TO WIN THE TEZUKA AWARD BEFORE GRADUATION TO MAKE HER HAPPY, HUH...
WELL, IT IS A GATEWAY TO SUCCESS, AND IT'D BE GREAT IF WE COULD GET IT, BUT...
VRR VRR VRR VRR
VRRR
THIS NUMBER... IT'S SHUEISHA!
!
BEEP
THIS IS HATTORI FROM WEEKLY SHONEN JUMP. IS THIS MR. TAKAGI?
YES.
ARE YOU CREATING STUFF?
Y- YES.

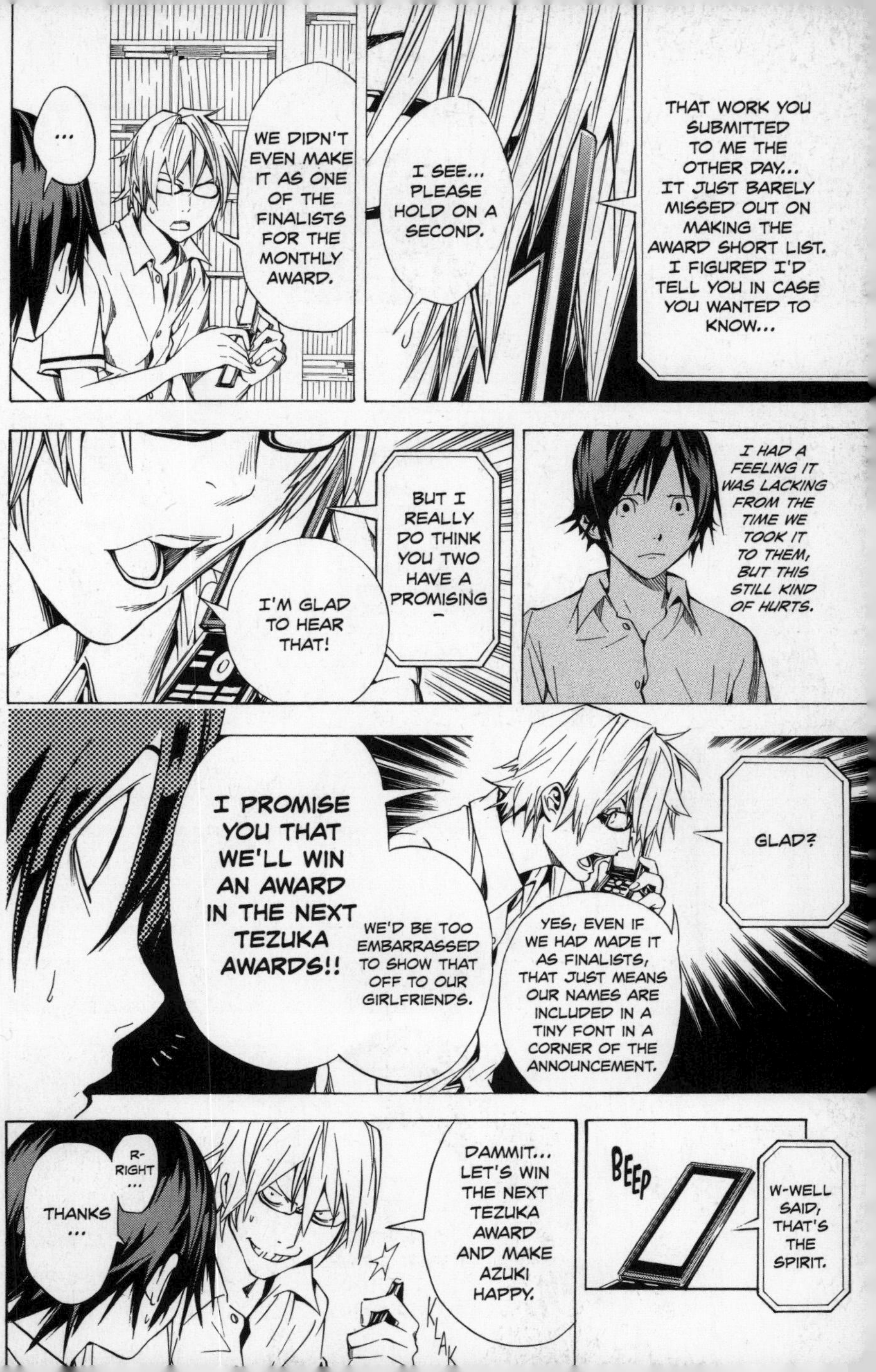
THAT WORK YOU SUBMITTED TO ME THE OTHER DAY... IT JUST BARELY MISSED OUT ON MAKING THE AWARD SHORT LIST. I FIGURED I'D TELL YOU IN CASE YOU WANTED TO KNOW...
I SEE... PLEASE HOLD ON A SECOND.
WE DIDN'T EVEN MAKE IT AS ONE OF THE FINALISTS FOR THE MONTHLY AWARD.
...
I HAD A FEELING IT WAS LACKING FROM THE TIME WE TOOK IT TO THEM, BUT THIS STILL KIND OF HURTS.
BUT I REALLY DO THINK YOU TWO HAVE A PROMISING –
I'M GLAD TO HEAR THAT!
GLAD?
YES, EVEN IF WE HAD MADE IT AS FINALISTS, THAT JUST MEANS OUR NAMES ARE INCLUDED IN A TINY FONT IN A CORNER OF THE ANNOUNCEMENT.
WE'D BE TOO EMBARRASSED TO SHOW THAT OFF TO OUR GIRLFRIENDS.
I PROMISE YOU THAT WE'LL WIN AN AWARD IN THE NEXT TEZUKA AWARDS!!
BEEP
W-WELL SAID, THAT'S THE SPIRIT.
DAMMIT... LET'S WIN THE NEXT TEZUKA AWARD AND MAKE AZUKI HAPPY.
KLAK
R-RIGHT...
THANKS...

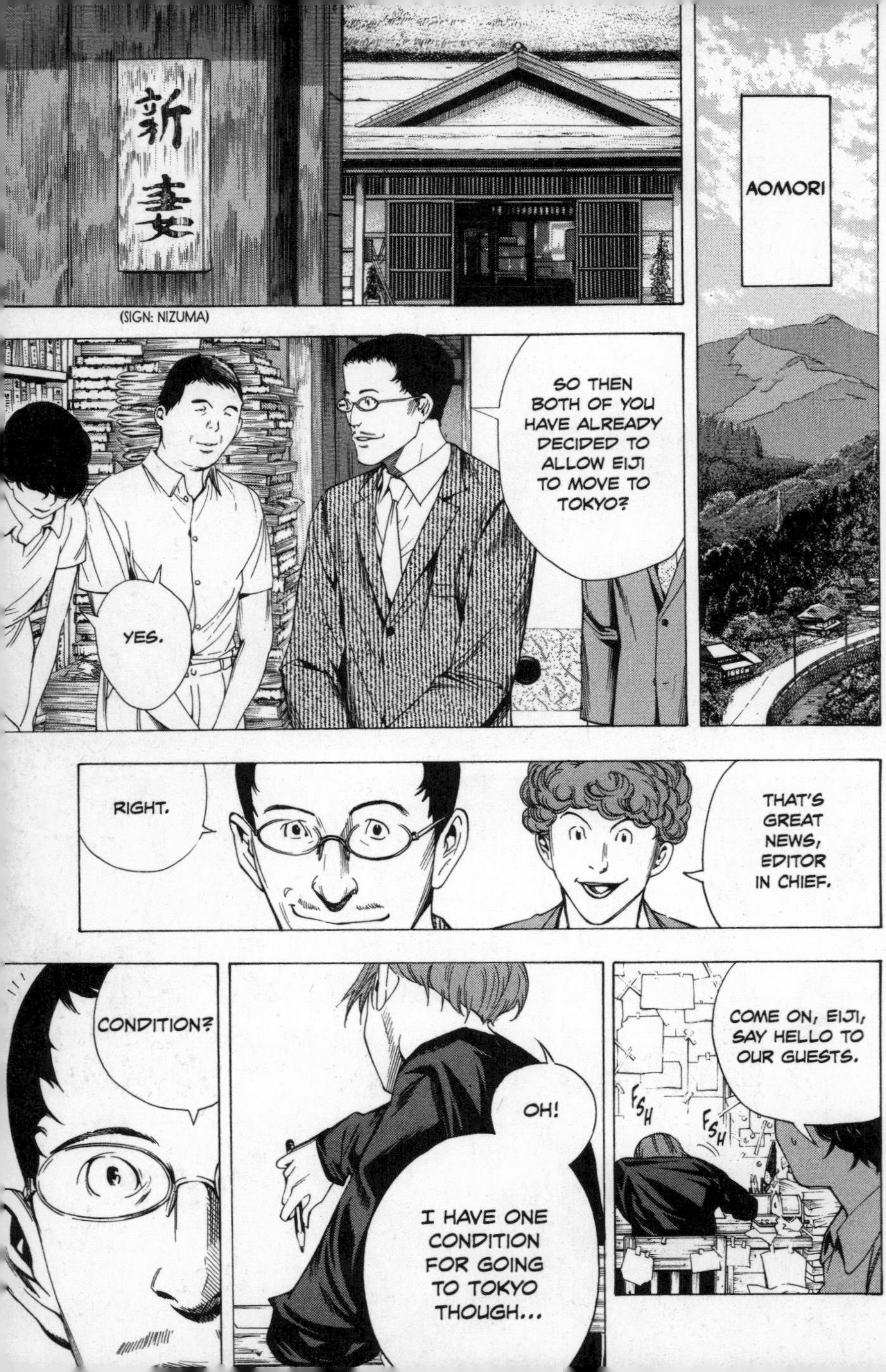
AOMORI
新妻
(SIGN: NIZUMA)
SO THEN BOTH OF YOU HAVE ALREADY DECIDED TO ALLOW EIJI TO MOVE TO TOKYO?
YES.
THAT'S GREAT NEWS, EDITOR IN CHIEF.
RIGHT.
COME ON, EIJI, SAY HELLO TO OUR GUESTS.
FSH
FSH
OH!
I HAVE ONE CONDITION FOR GOING TO TOKYO THOUGH...
CONDITION?

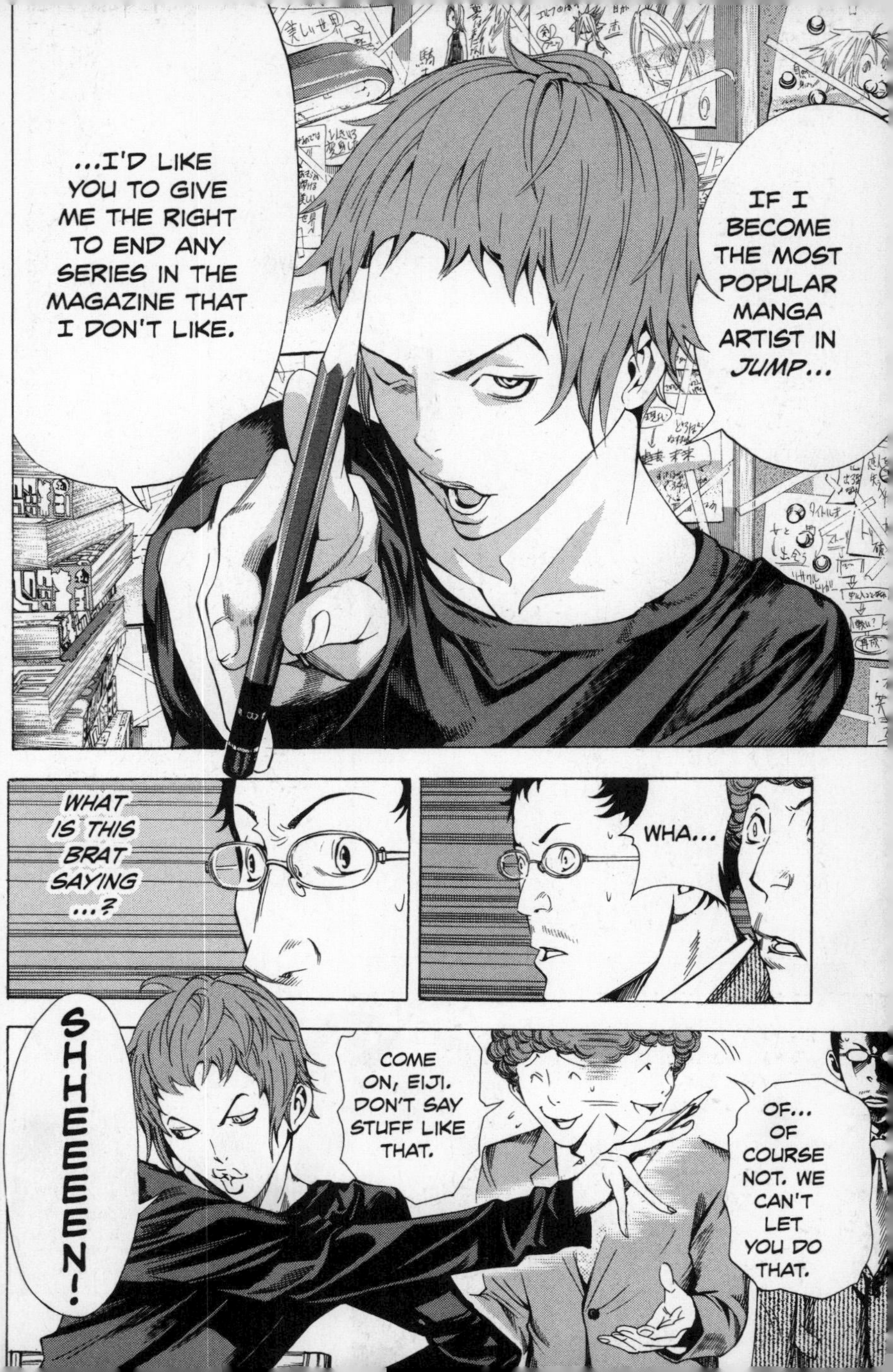
IF I BECOME THE MOST POPULAR MANGA ARTIST IN *JUMP*...
...I'D LIKE YOU TO GIVE ME THE RIGHT TO END ANY SERIES IN THE MAGAZINE THAT I DON'T LIKE.
WHA...
WHAT IS THIS BRAT SAYING ...?
OF... OF COURSE NOT. WE CAN'T LET YOU DO THAT.
COME ON, EIJI. DON'T SAY STUFF LIKE THAT.
SHHEEEEEN!

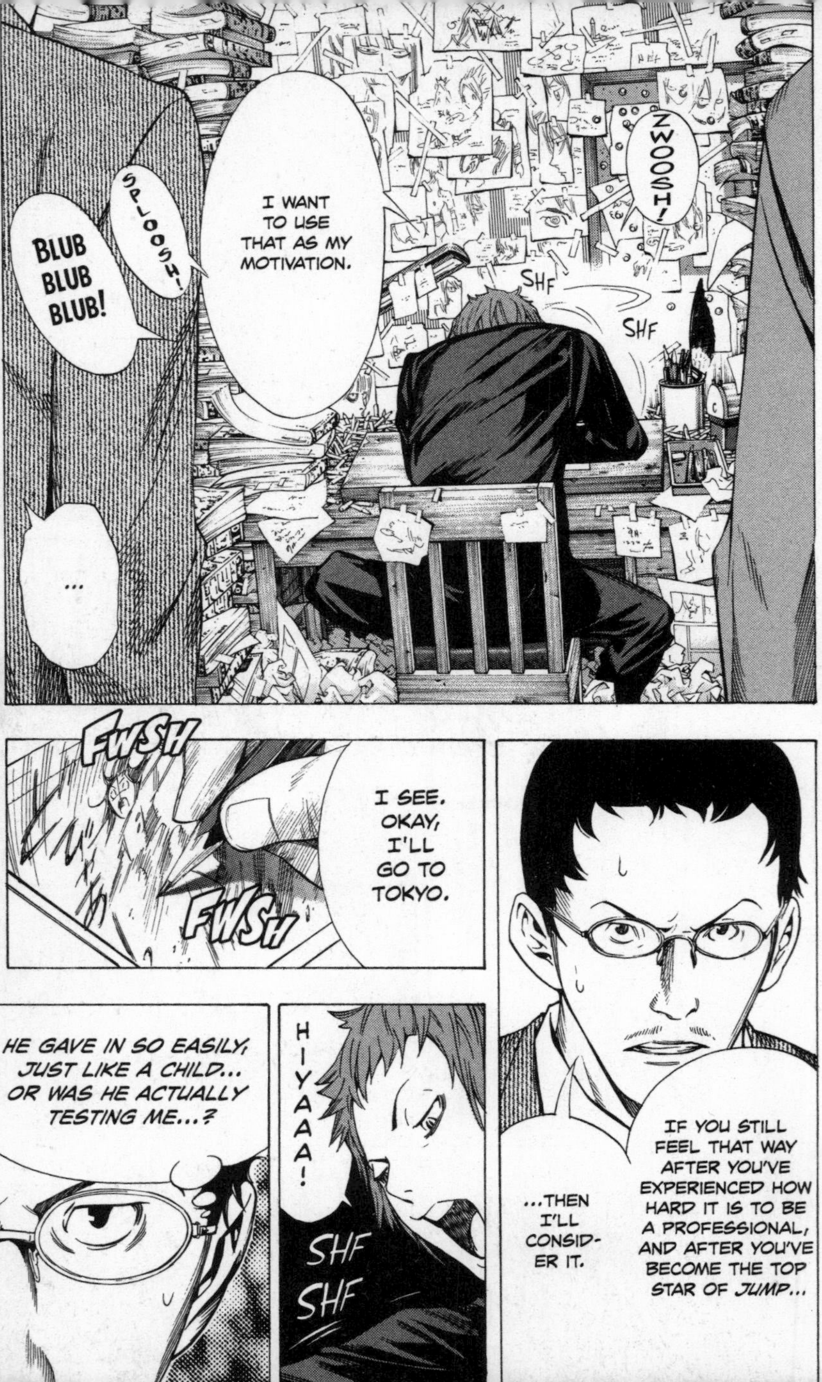
ZWOOSH!
SHF
SHF
I WANT TO USE THAT AS MY MOTIVATION.
SPLOOSH!
BLUB BLUB BLUB!
...
IF YOU STILL FEEL THAT WAY AFTER YOU'VE EXPERIENCED HOW HARD IT IS TO BE A PROFESSIONAL, AND AFTER YOU'VE BECOME THE TOP STAR OF *JUMP*...
...THEN I'LL CONSID-ER IT.
FWSH
I SEE. OKAY, I'LL GO TO TOKYO.
FWSH
HIYAAA!
SHF
SHF
HE GAVE IN SO EASILY, JUST LIKE A CHILD... OR WAS HE ACTUALLY TESTING ME...?

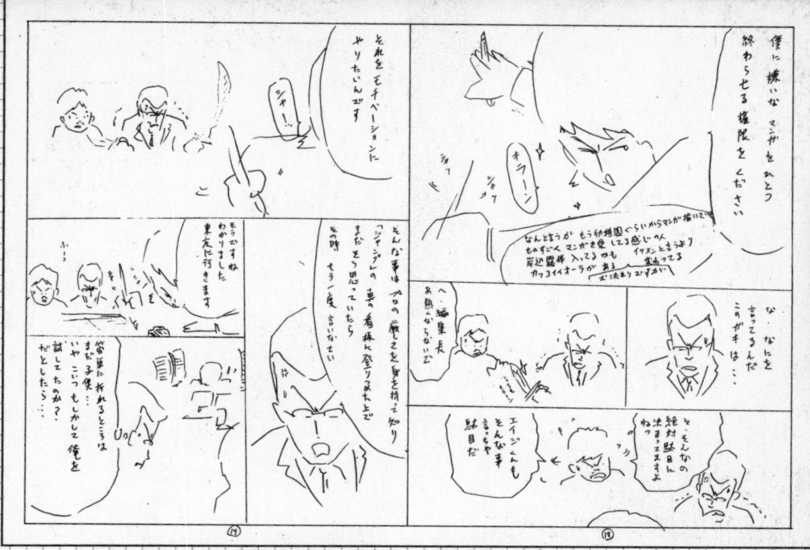
僕に嫌いなマンガをひとつ終わらせる権限をください
キラーン
なんと言うか もう幼稚園ぐらいからマンガが描いてる
ものすごくマンガを愛してる感じの人
岸辺露伴入ってるかも イケメンと言うより 変わってる
カッコイイオーラがある
お決まりですが
な、なにを言ってるんだこのガキは…
へ、編集長お熱くならないで
そ、そんなの絶対駄目に決まってますよねっ
エイジくんもそんな事言っちゃ駄目だ
それをモチベーションにヤりたいんです
シャー…
そんな事はプロの厳しさを身を持って知り「ジャンプ」の真の看板に登りつめた上でまだそう思っていたら
その時もう一度言いなさい
そうですね わかりました 東京に行きます
ふー…
簡単に折れるところはまだ子供… いや こいつもしかして俺を試してたのか？ だとしたら…

OHBA'S STORYBOARD

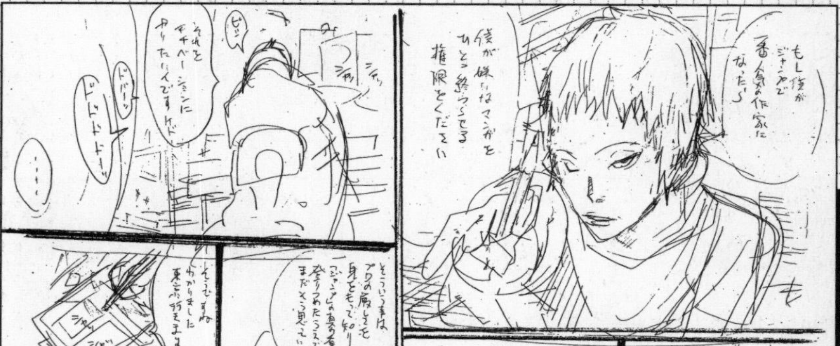
もし僕がジャンプで一番人気の作家になったら
僕が嫌いなマンガをひとつ終わらせる権限をください
何を言ってるんだ
このガキは
しゅぴーん
そ、そんなの絶対駄目に決まってますよねっ
エイジくんもそんな事言っちゃ駄目だ
それをモチベーションにヤりたいんですけど
ピン
ドバーン
ドドドドドーッ
…
そうですね わかりました 東京に行きます
そういう事はプロの厳しさを身をもって知り「ジャンプ」の真の看板に登りつめたうえでまだそう思っていたら
その時 その話をもう一度
簡単に折れるところはまだ子供！
いや こいつもしかして俺を試したのか
ぐぎゃーん

OBATA'S STORYBOARD

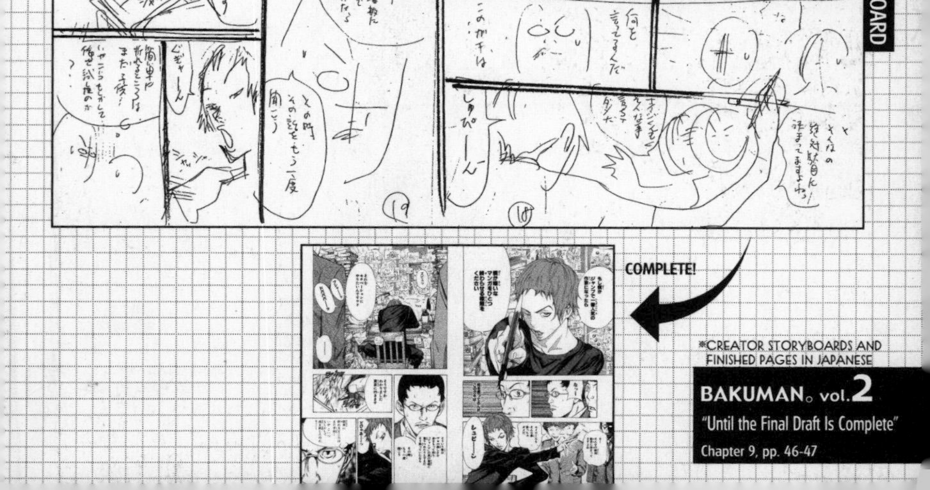

COMPLETE!

※CREATOR STORYBOARDS AND FINISHED PAGES IN JAPANESE

**BAKUMAN。 vol.2**

"Until the Final Draft Is Complete"

Chapter 9, pp. 46-47

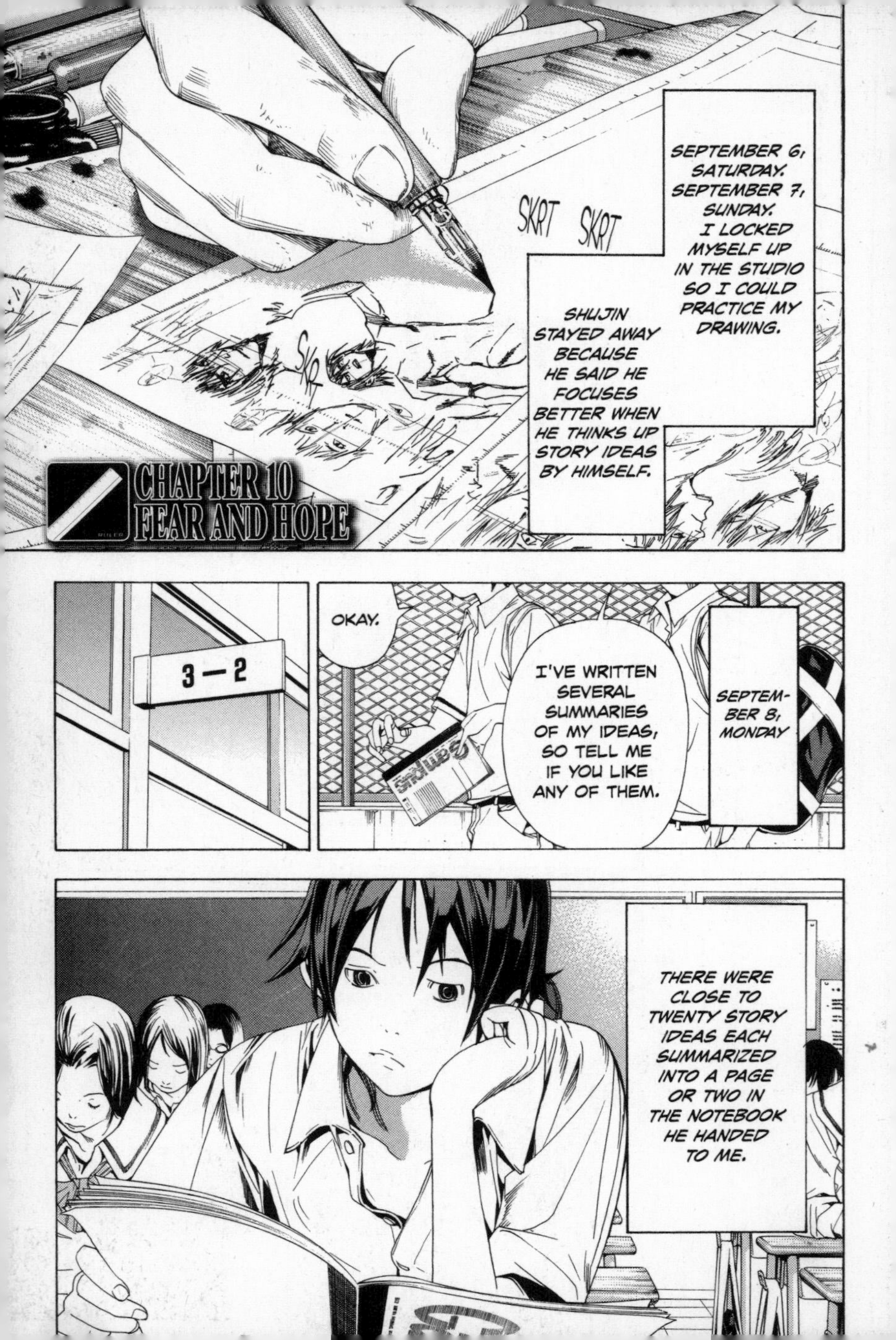
SEPTEMBER 6, SATURDAY. SEPTEMBER 7, SUNDAY. I LOCKED MYSELF UP IN THE STUDIO SO I COULD PRACTICE MY DRAWING.
SHUJIN STAYED AWAY BECAUSE HE SAID HE FOCUSES BETTER WHEN HE THINKS UP STORY IDEAS BY HIMSELF.
SKRT SKRT
SKR
CHAPTER 10 FEAR AND HOPE
SEPTEMBER 8, MONDAY
I'VE WRITTEN SEVERAL SUMMARIES OF MY IDEAS, SO TELL ME IF YOU LIKE ANY OF THEM.
OKAY.
3—2
THERE WERE CLOSE TO TWENTY STORY IDEAS EACH SUMMARIZED INTO A PAGE OR TWO IN THE NOTEBOOK HE HANDED TO ME.

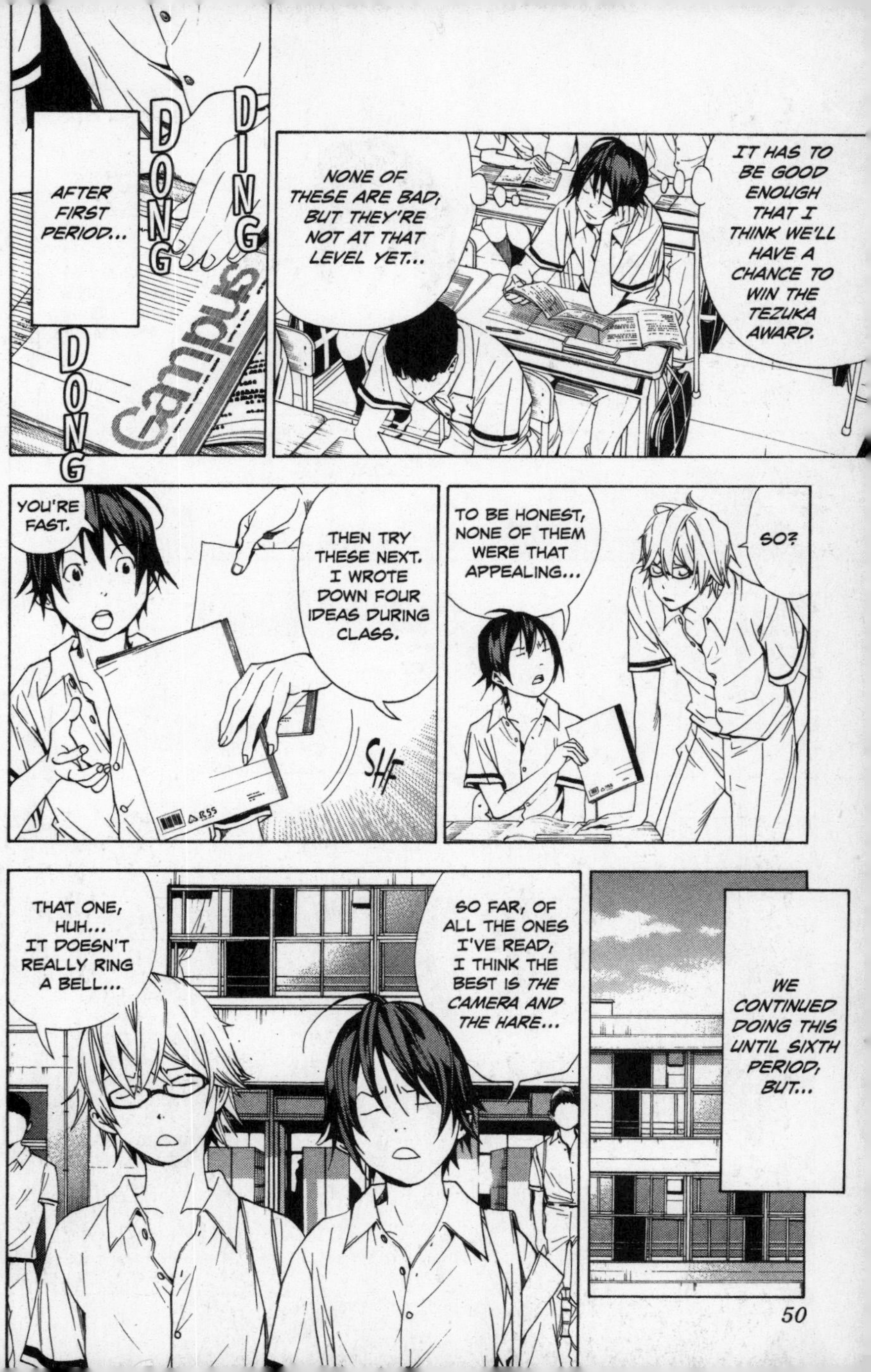
IT HAS TO BE GOOD ENOUGH THAT I THINK WE'LL HAVE A CHANCE TO WIN THE TEZUKA AWARD.
NONE OF THESE ARE BAD, BUT THEY'RE NOT AT THAT LEVEL YET...
DING
DONG
AFTER FIRST PERIOD...
DING
DONG
Campus
SO?
TO BE HONEST, NONE OF THEM WERE THAT APPEALING...
THEN TRY THESE NEXT. I WROTE DOWN FOUR IDEAS DURING CLASS.
YOU'RE FAST.
SHF
WE CONTINUED DOING THIS UNTIL SIXTH PERIOD, BUT...
SO FAR, OF ALL THE ONES I'VE READ, I THINK THE BEST IS THE CAMERA AND THE HARE...
THAT ONE, HUH... IT DOESN'T REALLY RING A BELL...

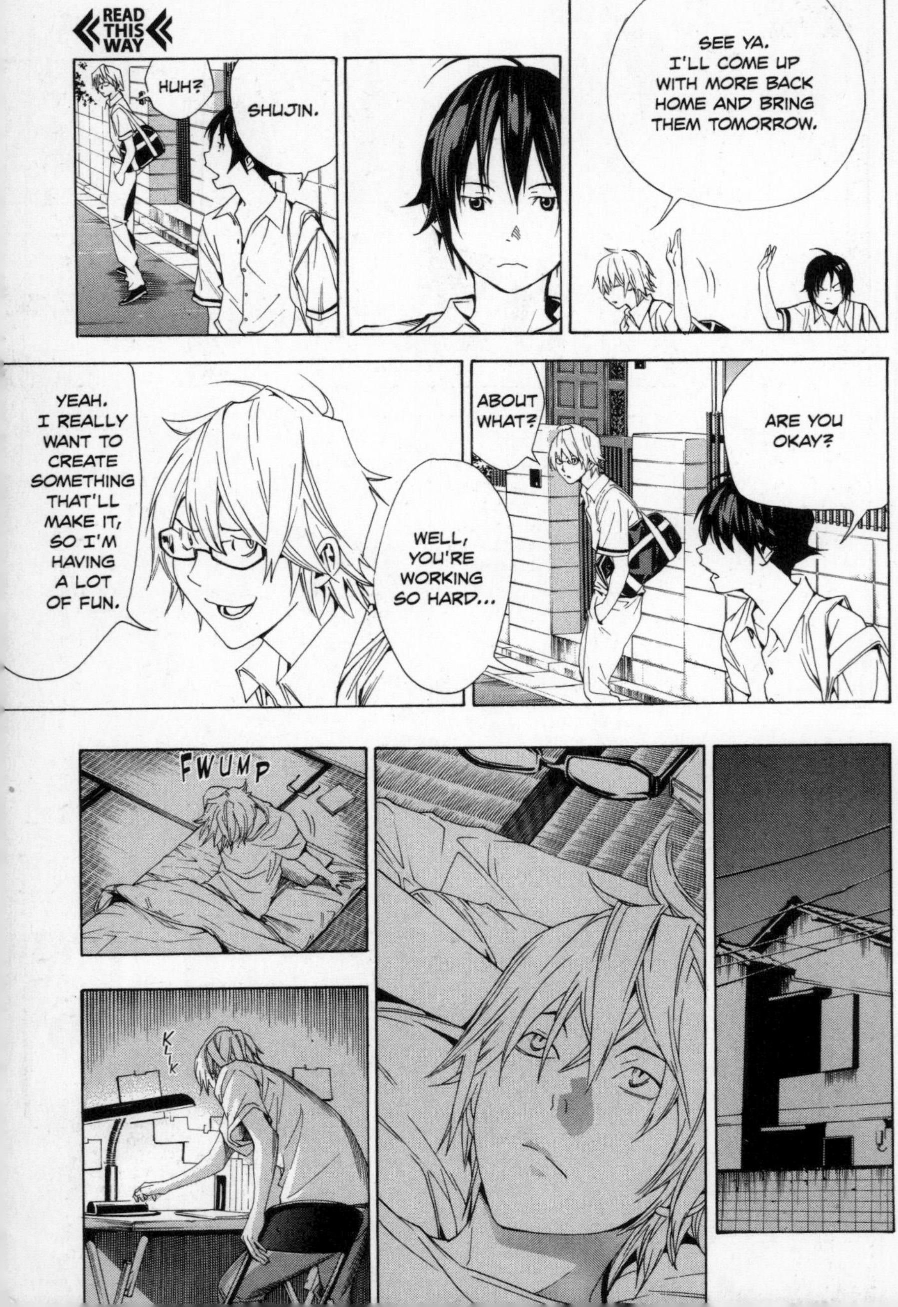
READ THIS WAY
SEE YA. I'LL COME UP WITH MORE BACK HOME AND BRING THEM TOMORROW.
SHUJIN.
HUH?
ARE YOU OKAY?
ABOUT WHAT?
WELL, YOU'RE WORKING SO HARD...
YEAH. I REALLY WANT TO CREATE SOMETHING THAT'LL MAKE IT, SO I'M HAVING A LOT OF FUN.
FWUMP
KLIK

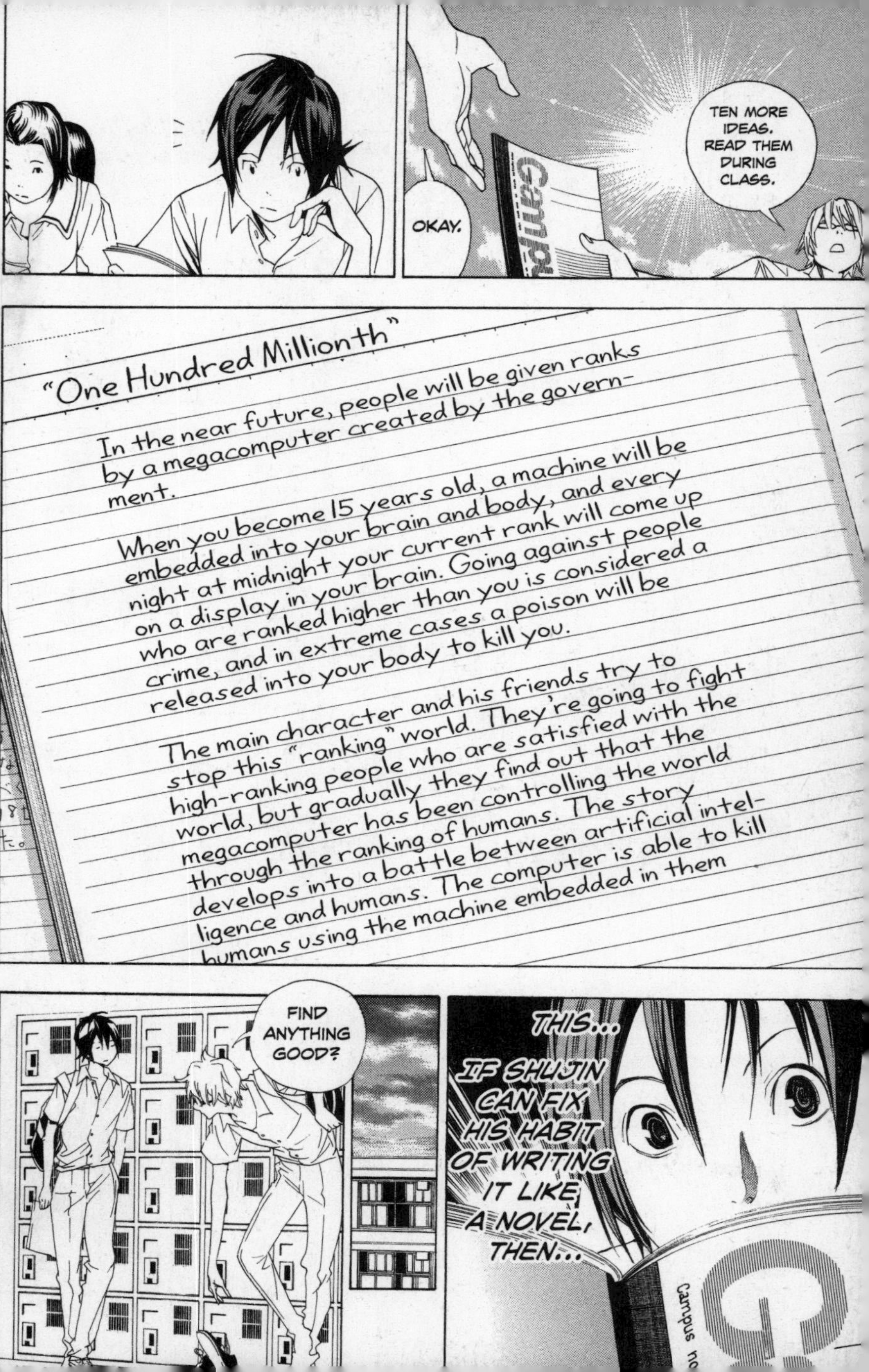
TEN MORE IDEAS. READ THEM DURING CLASS.
OKAY.
"One Hundred Millionth"
In the near future, people will be given ranks by a megacomputer created by the government.
When you become 15 years old, a machine will be embedded into your brain and body, and every night at midnight your current rank will come up on a display in your brain. Going against people who are ranked higher than you is considered a crime, and in extreme cases a poison will be released into your body to kill you.
The main character and his friends try to stop this "ranking" world. They're going to fight high-ranking people who are satisfied with the world, but gradually they find out that the megacomputer has been controlling the world through the ranking of humans. The story develops into a battle between artificial intelligence and humans. The computer is able to kill humans using the machine embedded in them
THIS...
IF SHUJIN CAN FIX HIS HABIT OF WRITING IT LIKE A NOVEL, THEN...
Campus
FIND ANYTHING GOOD?

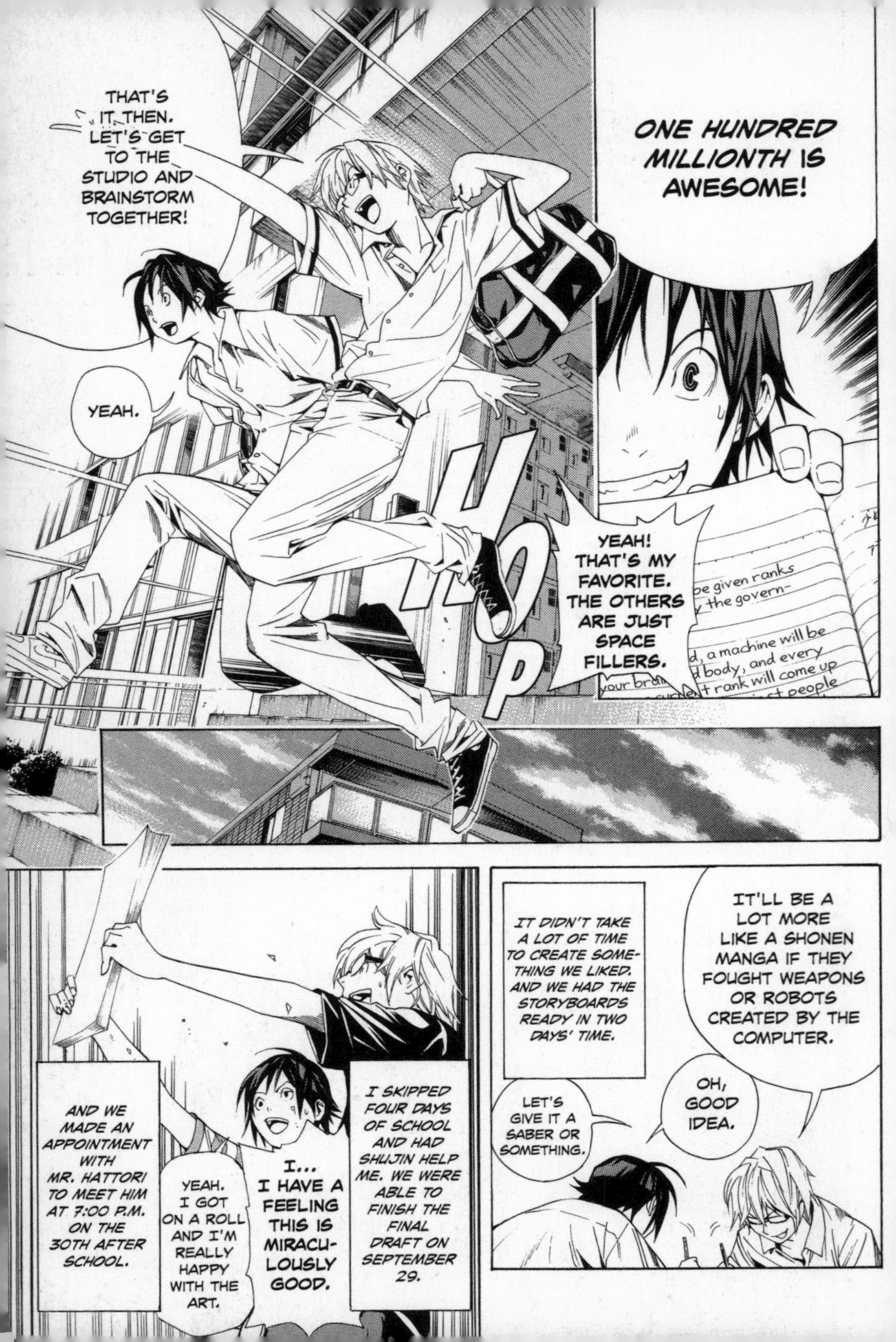
ONE HUNDRED MILLIONTH IS AWESOME!
YEAH! THAT'S MY FAVORITE. THE OTHERS ARE JUST SPACE FILLERS.
THAT'S IT THEN. LET'S GET TO THE STUDIO AND BRAINSTORM TOGETHER!
YEAH.
HOP
IT'LL BE A LOT MORE LIKE A SHONEN MANGA IF THEY FOUGHT WEAPONS OR ROBOTS CREATED BY THE COMPUTER.
IT DIDN'T TAKE A LOT OF TIME TO CREATE SOMETHING WE LIKED. AND WE HAD THE STORYBOARDS READY IN TWO DAYS' TIME.
OH, GOOD IDEA.
LET'S GIVE IT A SABER OR SOMETHING.
I SKIPPED FOUR DAYS OF SCHOOL AND HAD SHUJIN HELP ME. WE WERE ABLE TO FINISH THE FINAL DRAFT ON SEPTEMBER 29.
I... I HAVE A FEELING THIS IS MIRACULOUSLY GOOD.
YEAH. I GOT ON A ROLL AND I'M REALLY HAPPY WITH THE ART.
AND WE MADE AN APPOINTMENT WITH MR. HATTORI TO MEET HIM AT 7:00 P.M. ON THE 30TH AFTER SCHOOL.

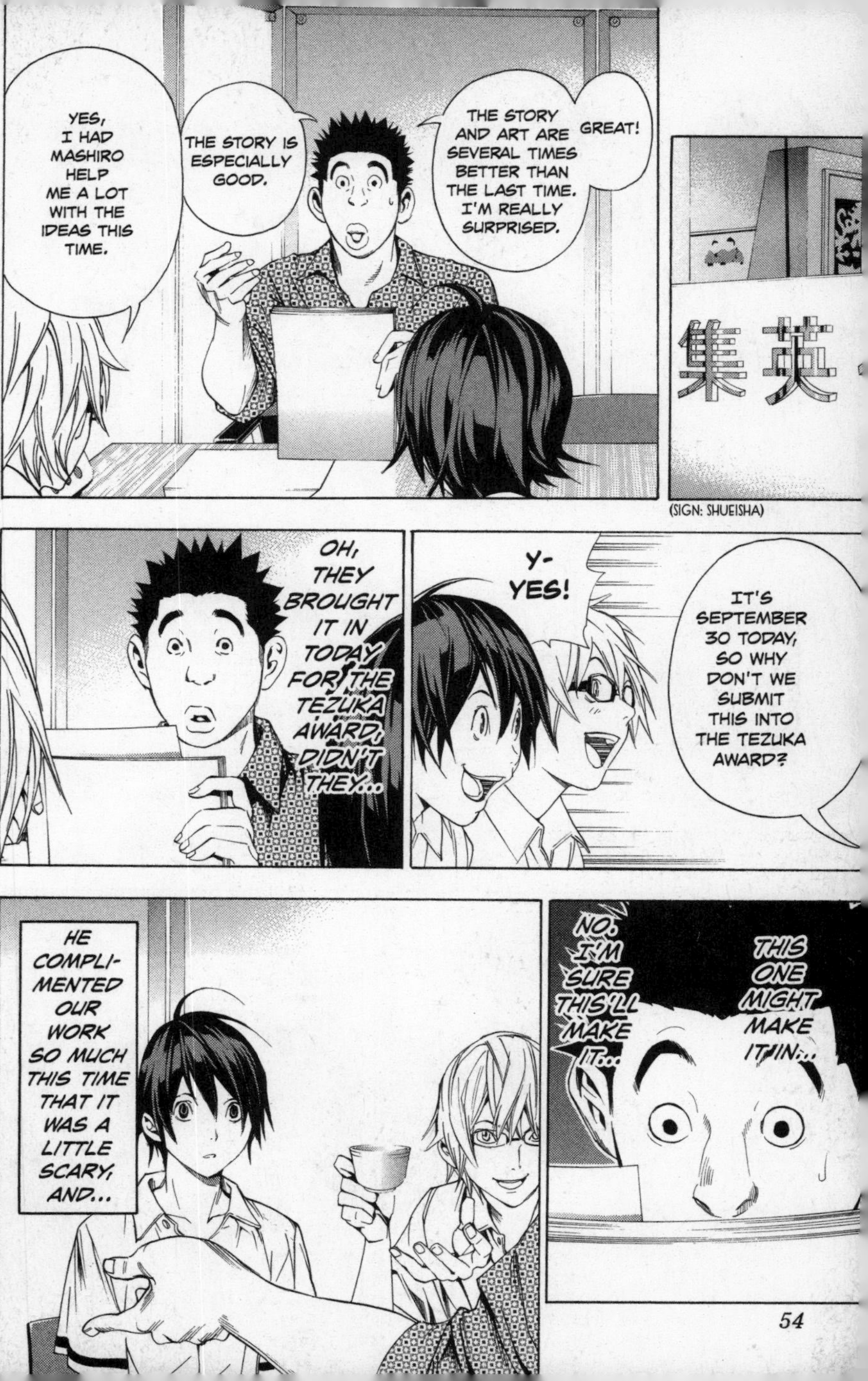
集英
(SIGN: SHUEISHA)
GREAT!
THE STORY AND ART ARE SEVERAL TIMES BETTER THAN THE LAST TIME. I'M REALLY SURPRISED.
THE STORY IS ESPECIALLY GOOD.
YES, I HAD MASHIRO HELP ME A LOT WITH THE IDEAS THIS TIME.
IT'S SEPTEMBER 30 TODAY, SO WHY DON'T WE SUBMIT THIS INTO THE TEZUKA AWARD?
Y- YES!
OH, THEY BROUGHT IT IN TODAY FOR THE TEZUKA AWARD, DIDN'T THEY...
THIS ONE MIGHT MAKE IT IN...
NO. I'M SURE THIS'LL MAKE IT...
HE COMPLIMENTED OUR WORK SO MUCH THIS TIME THAT IT WAS A LITTLE SCARY, AND...

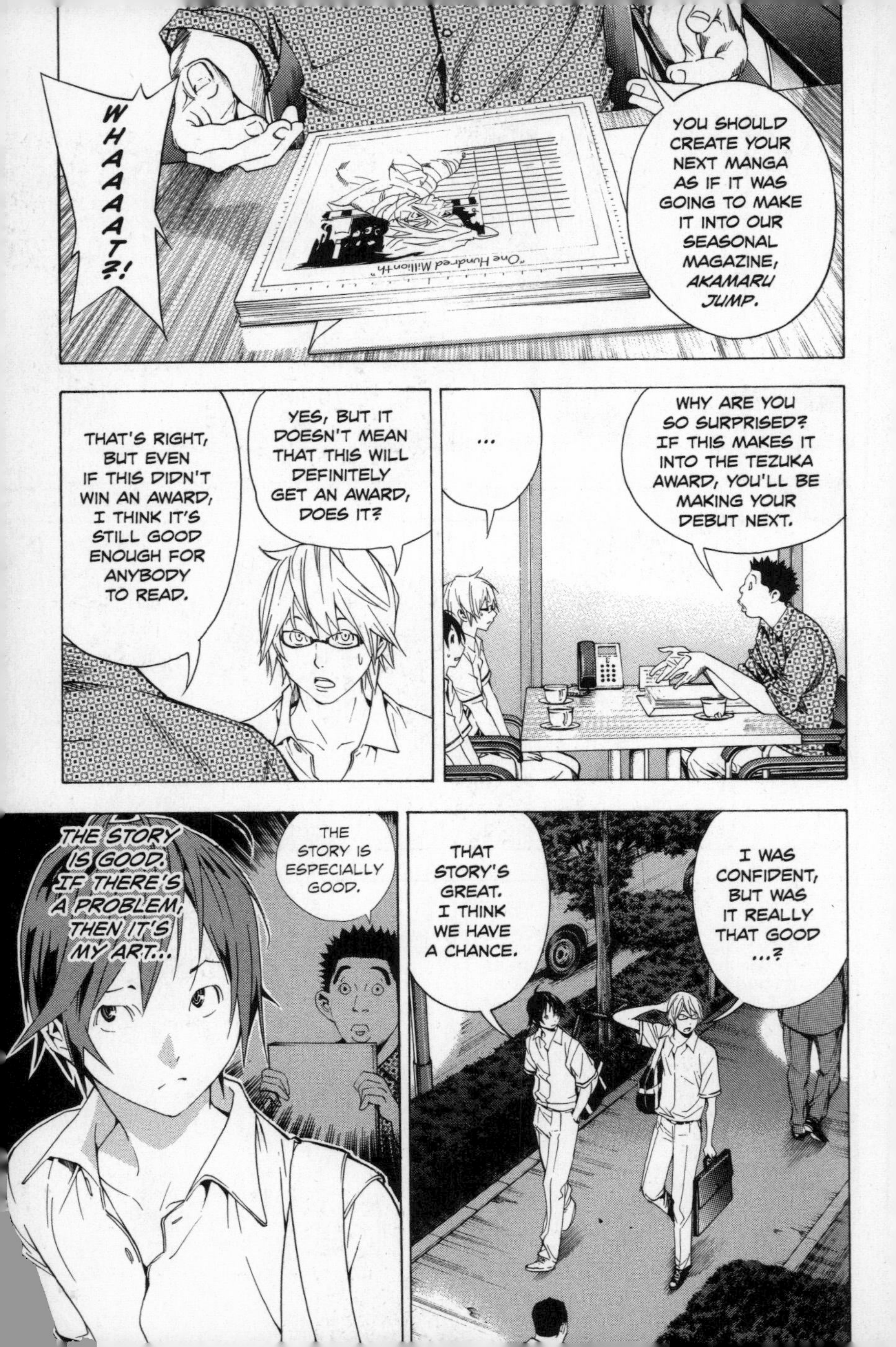
YOU SHOULD CREATE YOUR NEXT MANGA AS IF IT WAS GOING TO MAKE IT INTO OUR SEASONAL MAGAZINE, *AKAMARU JUMP*.
"One Hundred Millionth"
WHAAAAT?!
WHY ARE YOU SO SURPRISED? IF THIS MAKES IT INTO THE TEZUKA AWARD, YOU'LL BE MAKING YOUR DEBUT NEXT.
...
YES, BUT IT DOESN'T MEAN THAT THIS WILL DEFINITELY GET AN AWARD, DOES IT?
THAT'S RIGHT, BUT EVEN IF THIS DIDN'T WIN AN AWARD, I THINK IT'S STILL GOOD ENOUGH FOR ANYBODY TO READ.
I WAS CONFIDENT, BUT WAS IT REALLY THAT GOOD ...?
THAT STORY'S GREAT. I THINK WE HAVE A CHANCE.
THE STORY IS ESPECIALLY GOOD.
THE STORY IS GOOD. IF THERE'S A PROBLEM, THEN IT'S MY ART...

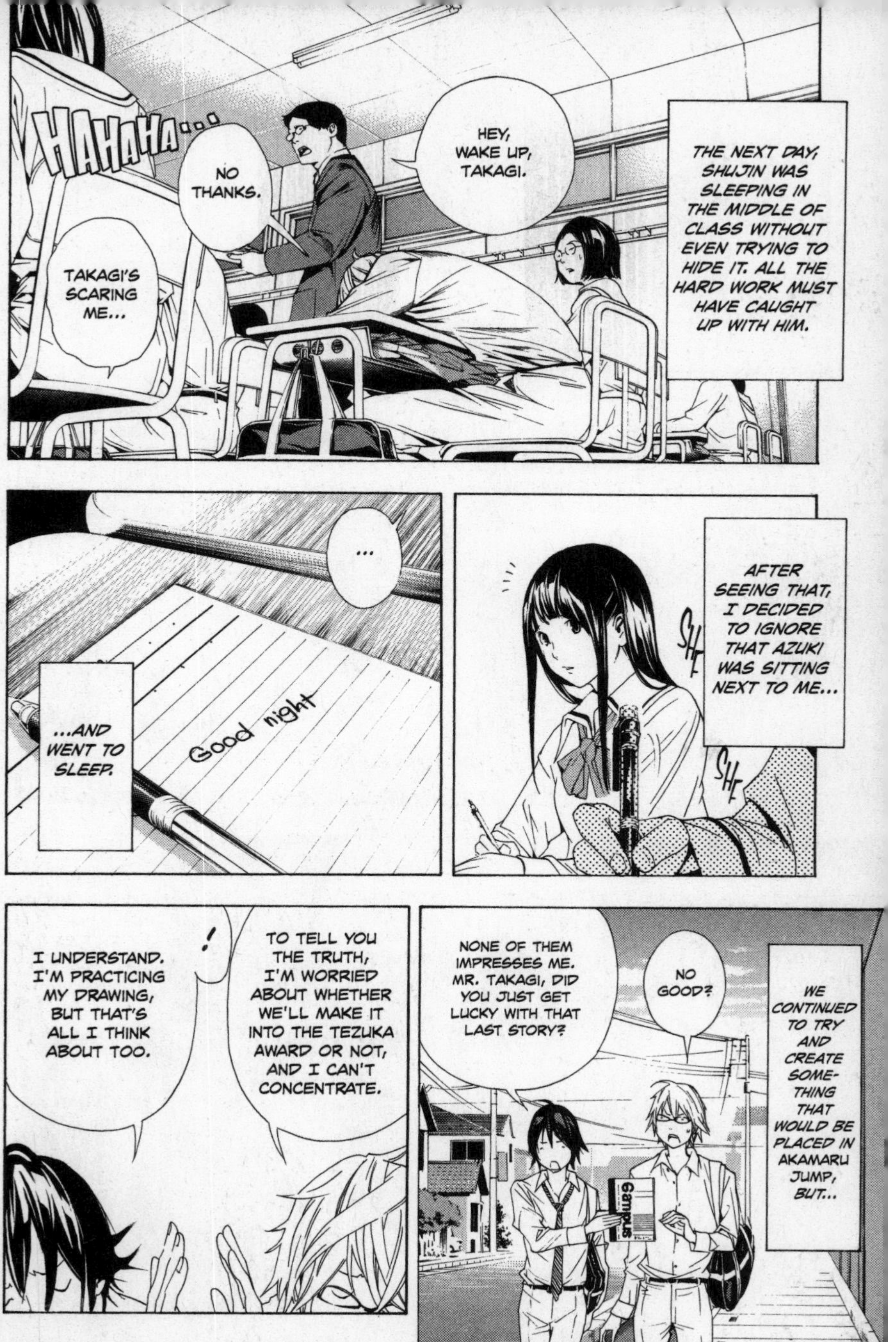
THE NEXT DAY, SHUJIN WAS SLEEPING IN THE MIDDLE OF CLASS WITHOUT EVEN TRYING TO HIDE IT. ALL THE HARD WORK MUST HAVE CAUGHT UP WITH HIM.
HEY, WAKE UP, TAKAGI.
NO THANKS.
HAHAHA...
TAKAGI'S SCARING ME...
AFTER SEEING THAT, I DECIDED TO IGNORE THAT AZUKI WAS SITTING NEXT TO ME...
SHF
SHF
...
Good night
...AND WENT TO SLEEP.
WE CONTINUED TO TRY AND CREATE SOME-THING THAT WOULD BE PLACED IN AKAMARU JUMP, BUT...
NO GOOD?
NONE OF THEM IMPRESSES ME. MR. TAKAGI, DID YOU JUST GET LUCKY WITH THAT LAST STORY?
TO TELL YOU THE TRUTH, I'M WORRIED ABOUT WHETHER WE'LL MAKE IT INTO THE TEZUKA AWARD OR NOT, AND I CAN'T CONCENTRATE.
!
I UNDERSTAND. I'M PRACTICING MY DRAWING, BUT THAT'S ALL I THINK ABOUT TOO.

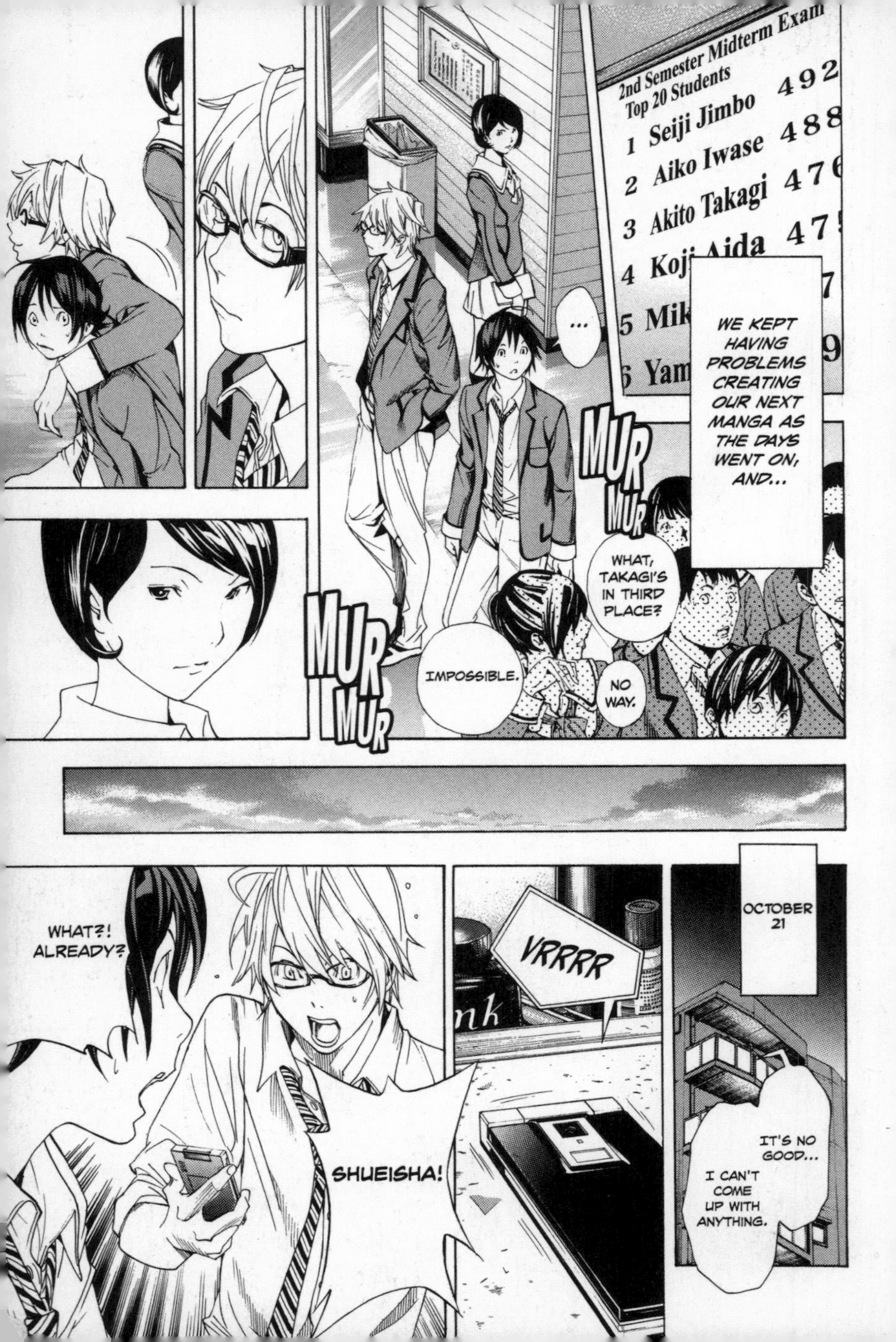
2nd Semester Midterm Exam
Top 20 Students
1 Seiji Jimbo 492
2 Aiko Iwase 488
3 Akito Takagi 476
...
WE KEPT HAVING PROBLEMS CREATING OUR NEXT MANGA AS THE DAYS WENT ON, AND...
MUR MUR
WHAT, TAKAGI'S IN THIRD PLACE?
NO WAY.
IMPOSSIBLE.
MUR MUR
OCTOBER 21
IT'S NO GOOD...
I CAN'T COME UP WITH ANYTHING.
VRRRR
SHUEISHA!
WHAT?! ALREADY?

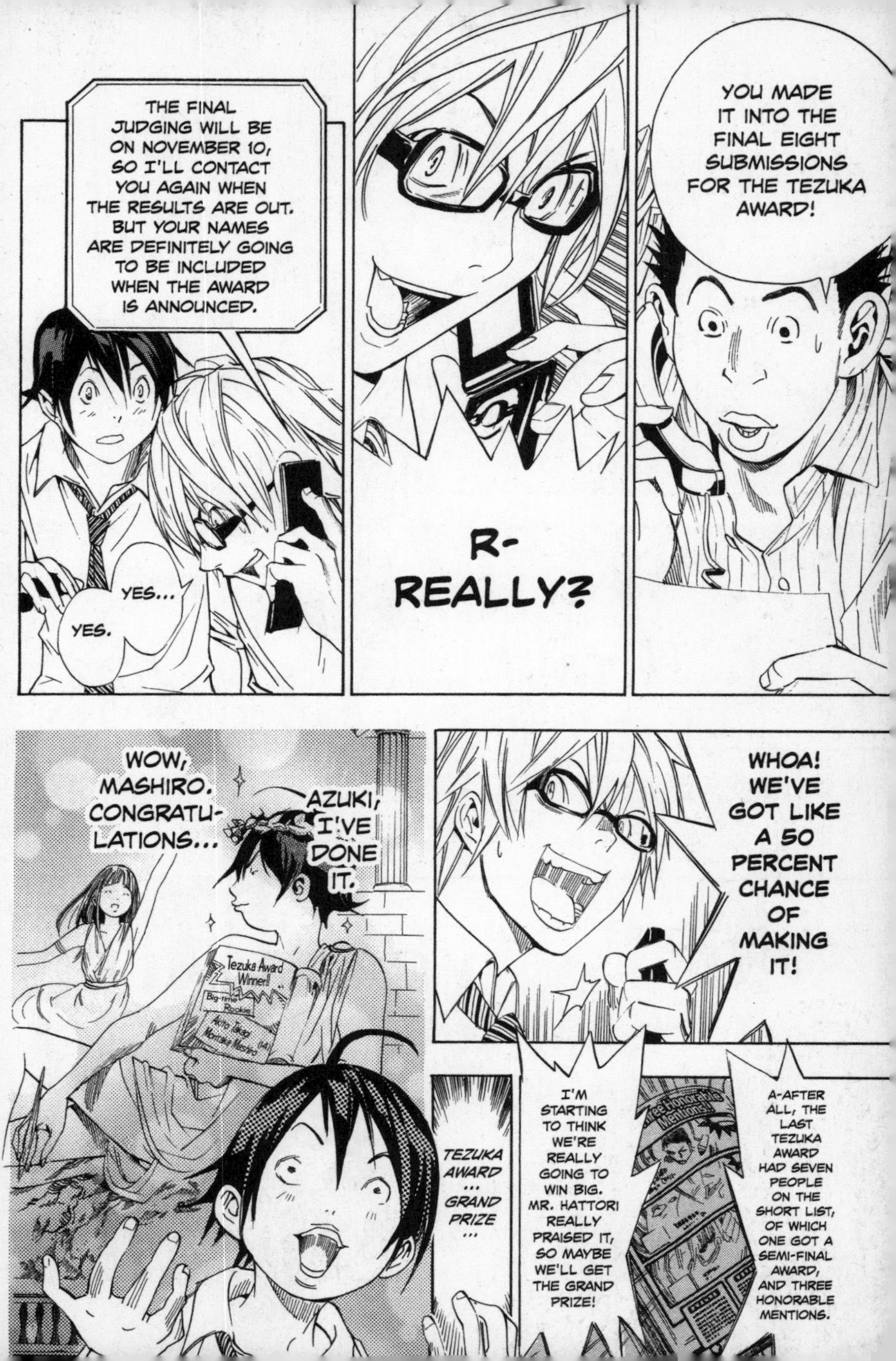
YOU MADE IT INTO THE FINAL EIGHT SUBMISSIONS FOR THE TEZUKA AWARD!
R-REALLY?
THE FINAL JUDGING WILL BE ON NOVEMBER 10, SO I'LL CONTACT YOU AGAIN WHEN THE RESULTS ARE OUT. BUT YOUR NAMES ARE DEFINITELY GOING TO BE INCLUDED WHEN THE AWARD IS ANNOUNCED.
YES...
YES.
WHOA! WE'VE GOT LIKE A 50 PERCENT CHANCE OF MAKING IT!
A-AFTER ALL, THE LAST TEZUKA AWARD HAD SEVEN PEOPLE ON THE SHORT LIST, OF WHICH ONE GOT A SEMI-FINAL AWARD, AND THREE HONORABLE MENTIONS.
I'M STARTING TO THINK WE'RE REALLY GOING TO WIN BIG. MR. HATTORI REALLY PRAISED IT, SO MAYBE WE'LL GET THE GRAND PRIZE!
TEZUKA AWARD ... GRAND PRIZE ...
AZUKI, I'VE DONE IT.
WOW, MASHIRO. CONGRATULATIONS...
Tezuka Award Winner!!
Big-time Rookie

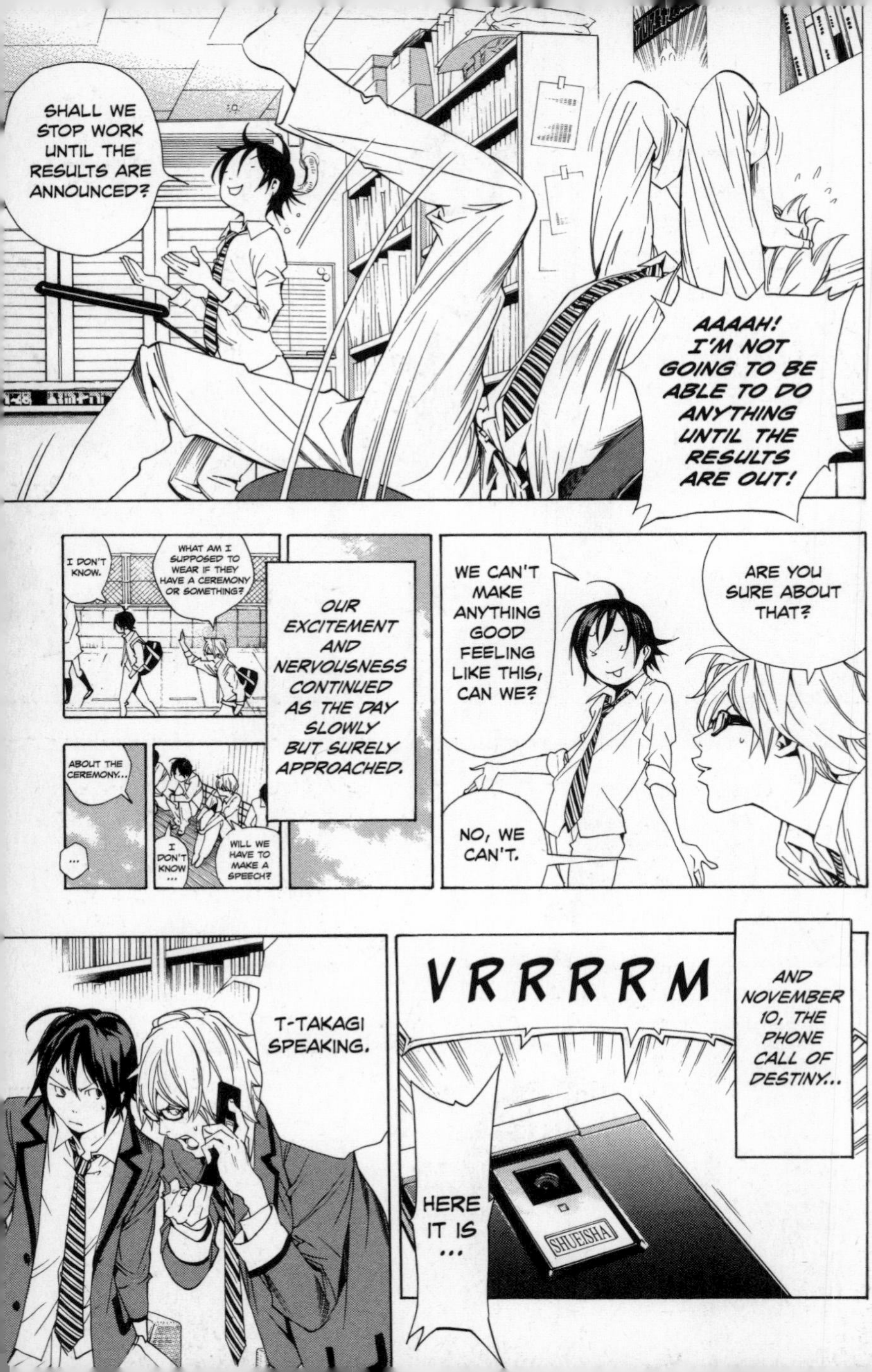
AAAAH! I'M NOT GOING TO BE ABLE TO DO ANYTHING UNTIL THE RESULTS ARE OUT!
SHALL WE STOP WORK UNTIL THE RESULTS ARE ANNOUNCED?
ARE YOU SURE ABOUT THAT?
WE CAN'T MAKE ANYTHING GOOD FEELING LIKE THIS, CAN WE?
NO, WE CAN'T.
OUR EXCITEMENT AND NERVOUSNESS CONTINUED AS THE DAY SLOWLY BUT SURELY APPROACHED.
WHAT AM I SUPPOSED TO WEAR IF THEY HAVE A CEREMONY OR SOMETHING?
I DON'T KNOW.
WILL WE HAVE TO MAKE A SPEECH?
I DON'T KNOW...
ABOUT THE CEREMONY...
...
AND NOVEMBER 10, THE PHONE CALL OF DESTINY...
VRRRRM
HERE IT IS...
SHUEISHA
T-TAKAGI SPEAKING.

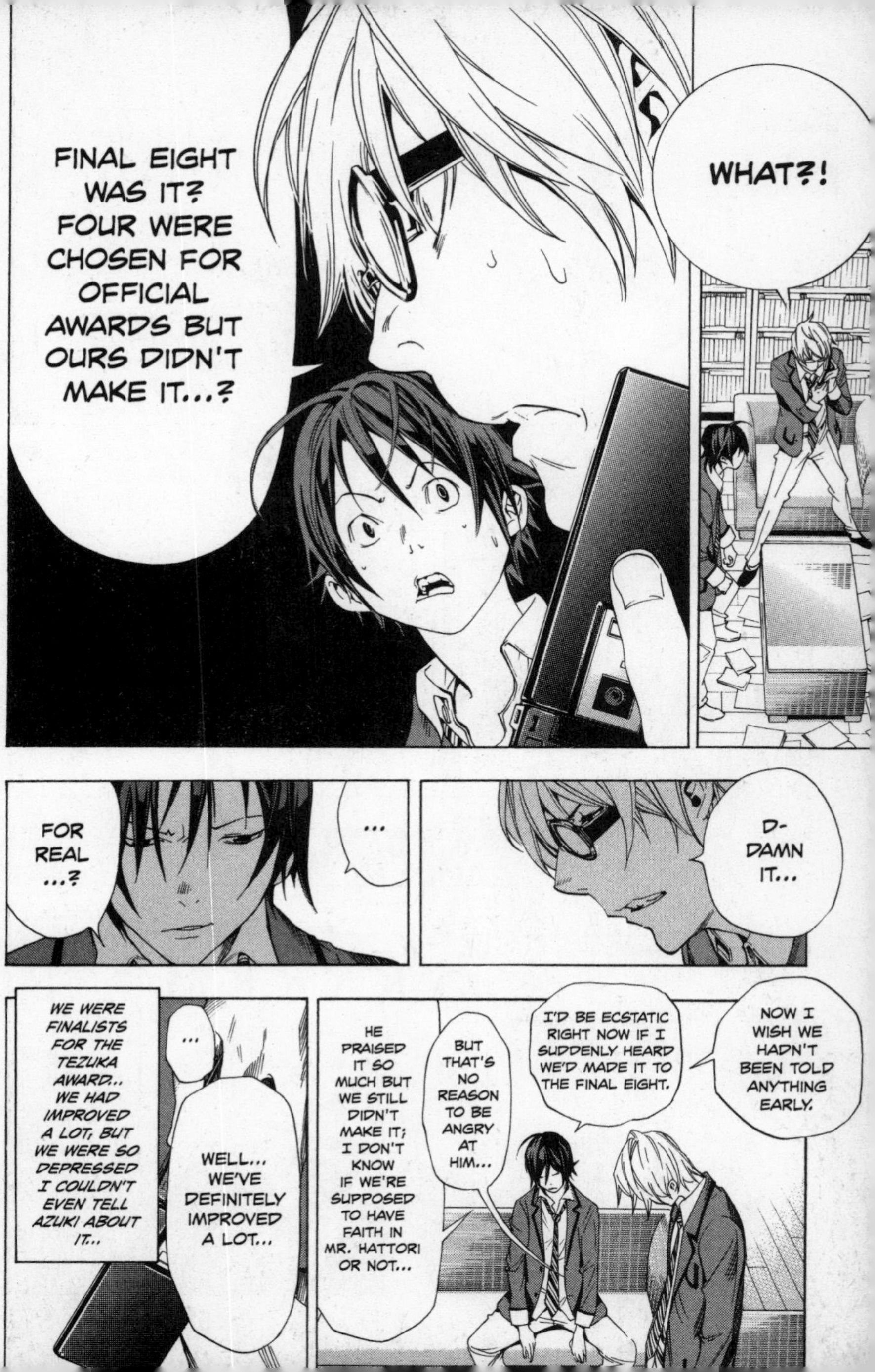
WHAT?!
FINAL EIGHT WAS IT? FOUR WERE CHOSEN FOR OFFICIAL AWARDS BUT OURS DIDN'T MAKE IT...?
D-DAMN IT...
...
FOR REAL...?
NOW I WISH WE HADN'T BEEN TOLD ANYTHING EARLY.
I'D BE ECSTATIC RIGHT NOW IF I SUDDENLY HEARD WE'D MADE IT TO THE FINAL EIGHT.
BUT THAT'S NO REASON TO BE ANGRY AT HIM...
HE PRAISED IT SO MUCH BUT WE STILL DIDN'T MAKE IT; I DON'T KNOW IF WE'RE SUPPOSED TO HAVE FAITH IN MR. HATTORI OR NOT...
...
WELL... WE'VE DEFINITELY IMPROVED A LOT...
WE WERE FINALISTS FOR THE TEZUKA AWARD... WE HAD IMPROVED A LOT, BUT WE WERE SO DEPRESSED I COULDN'T EVEN TELL AZUKI ABOUT IT...

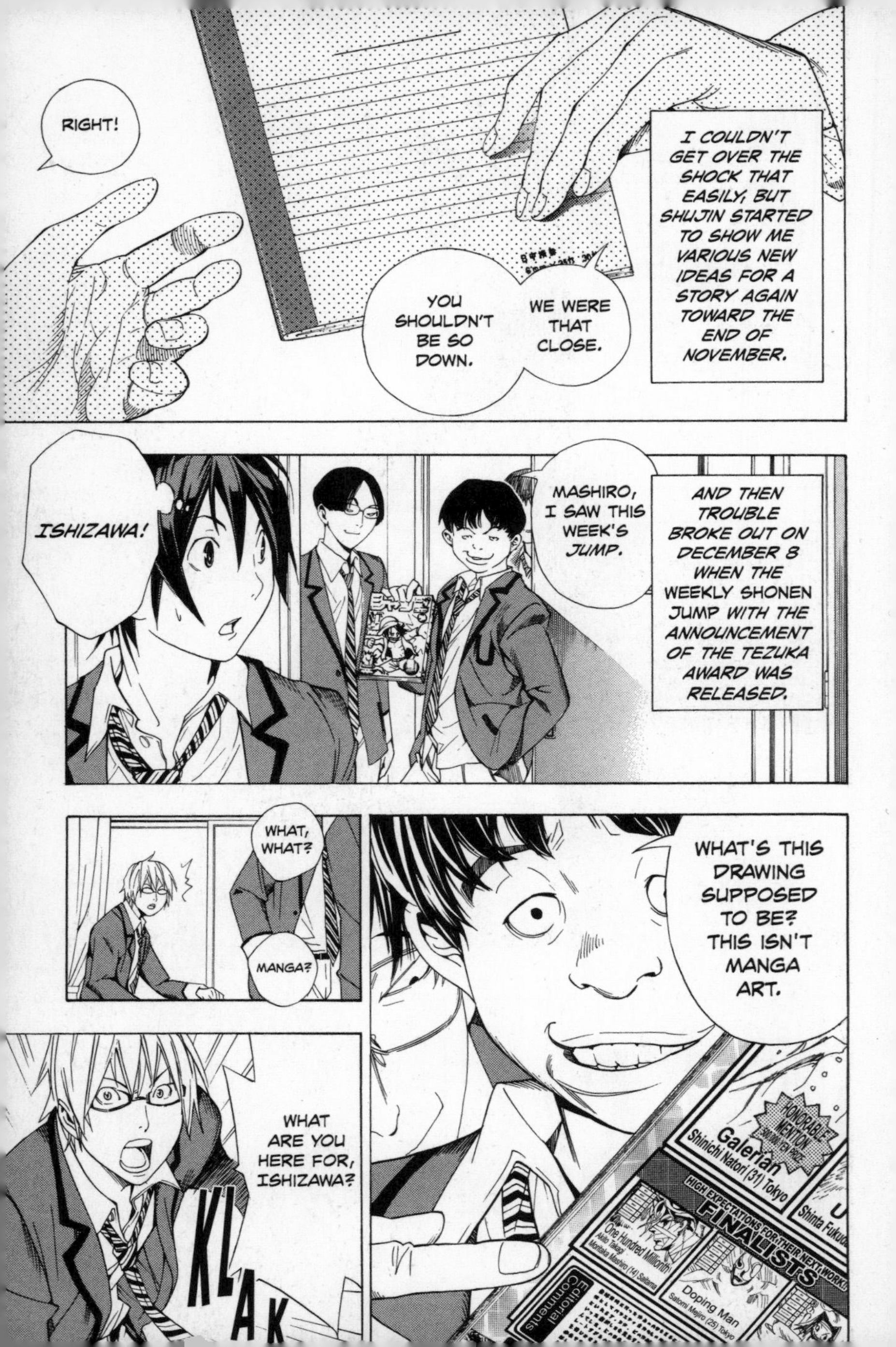
I COULDN'T GET OVER THE SHOCK THAT EASILY, BUT SHUJIN STARTED TO SHOW ME VARIOUS NEW IDEAS FOR A STORY AGAIN TOWARD THE END OF NOVEMBER.
WE WERE THAT CLOSE.
YOU SHOULDN'T BE SO DOWN.
RIGHT!
AND THEN TROUBLE BROKE OUT ON DECEMBER 8 WHEN THE WEEKLY SHONEN JUMP WITH THE ANNOUNCEMENT OF THE TEZUKA AWARD WAS RELEASED.
MASHIRO, I SAW THIS WEEK'S JUMP.
ISHIZAWA!
WHAT'S THIS DRAWING SUPPOSED TO BE? THIS ISN'T MANGA ART.
HONORABLE MENTION
Galerian
Shinichi Natori (31) Tokyo
HIGH EXPECTATIONS FOR THEIR NEXT WORK!
FINALISTS
One Hundred Million
Doping Man
Satomi Mejiro (25) Tokyo
Editorial Comments
WHAT, WHAT?
MANGA?
WHAT ARE YOU HERE FOR, ISHIZAWA?
KLAK

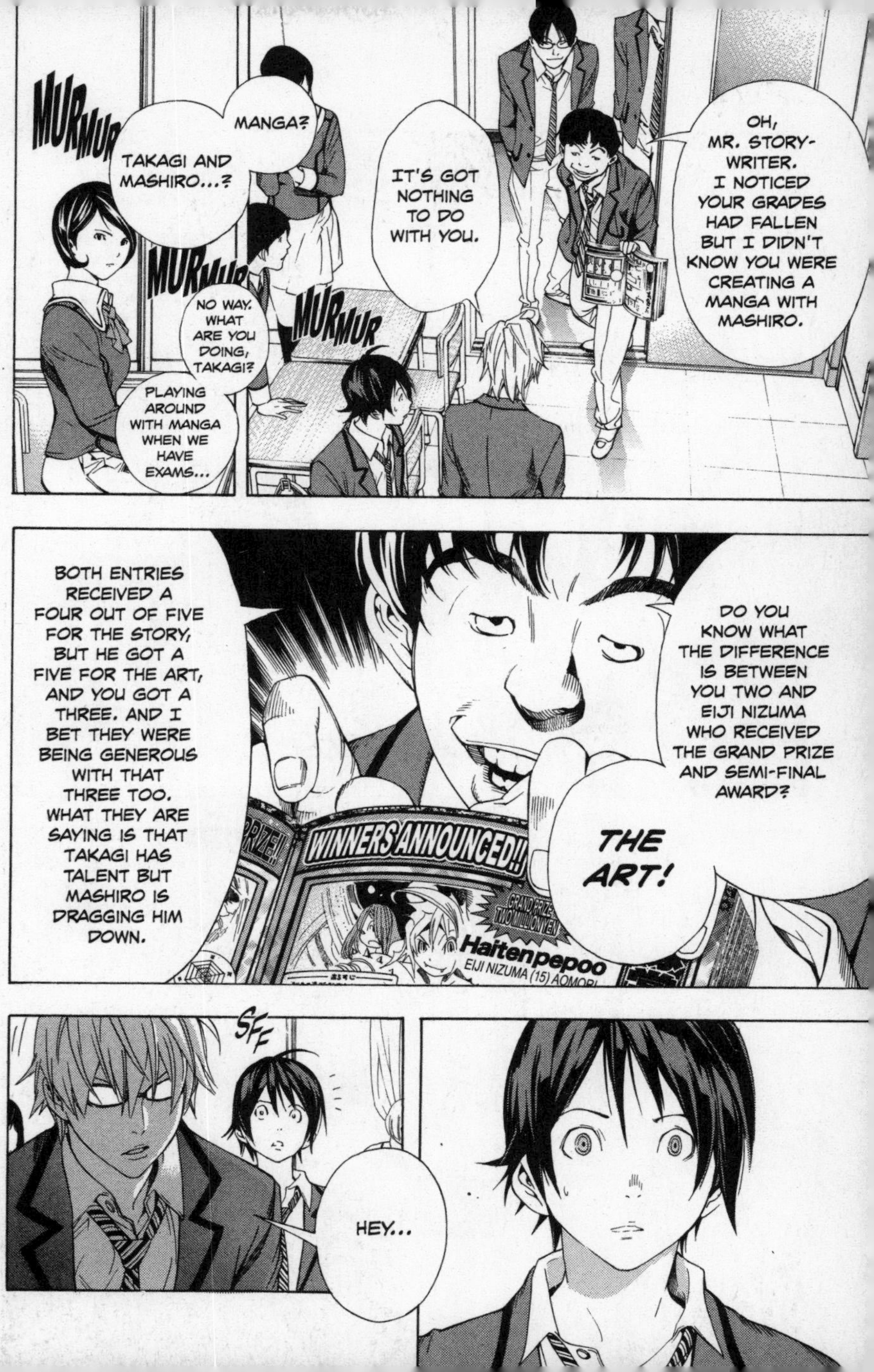
OH, MR. STORY-WRITER. I NOTICED YOUR GRADES HAD FALLEN BUT I DIDN'T KNOW YOU WERE CREATING A MANGA WITH MASHIRO.
IT'S GOT NOTHING TO DO WITH YOU.
MURMUR
MANGA?
TAKAGI AND MASHIRO...?
MURMUR
MURMUR
NO WAY. WHAT ARE YOU DOING, TAKAGI?
PLAYING AROUND WITH MANGA WHEN WE HAVE EXAMS...
DO YOU KNOW WHAT THE DIFFERENCE IS BETWEEN YOU TWO AND EIJI NIZUMA WHO RECEIVED THE GRAND PRIZE AND SEMI-FINAL AWARD?
THE ART!
WINNERS ANNOUNCED!!
GRAND PRIZE TWO MILLION YEN
Haitenpepoo
EIJI NIZUMA (15) AOMORI
BOTH ENTRIES RECEIVED A FOUR OUT OF FIVE FOR THE STORY, BUT HE GOT A FIVE FOR THE ART, AND YOU GOT A THREE. AND I BET THEY WERE BEING GENEROUS WITH THAT THREE TOO. WHAT THEY ARE SAYING IS THAT TAKAGI HAS TALENT BUT MASHIRO IS DRAGGING HIM DOWN.
SFF
HEY...

READ THIS WAY

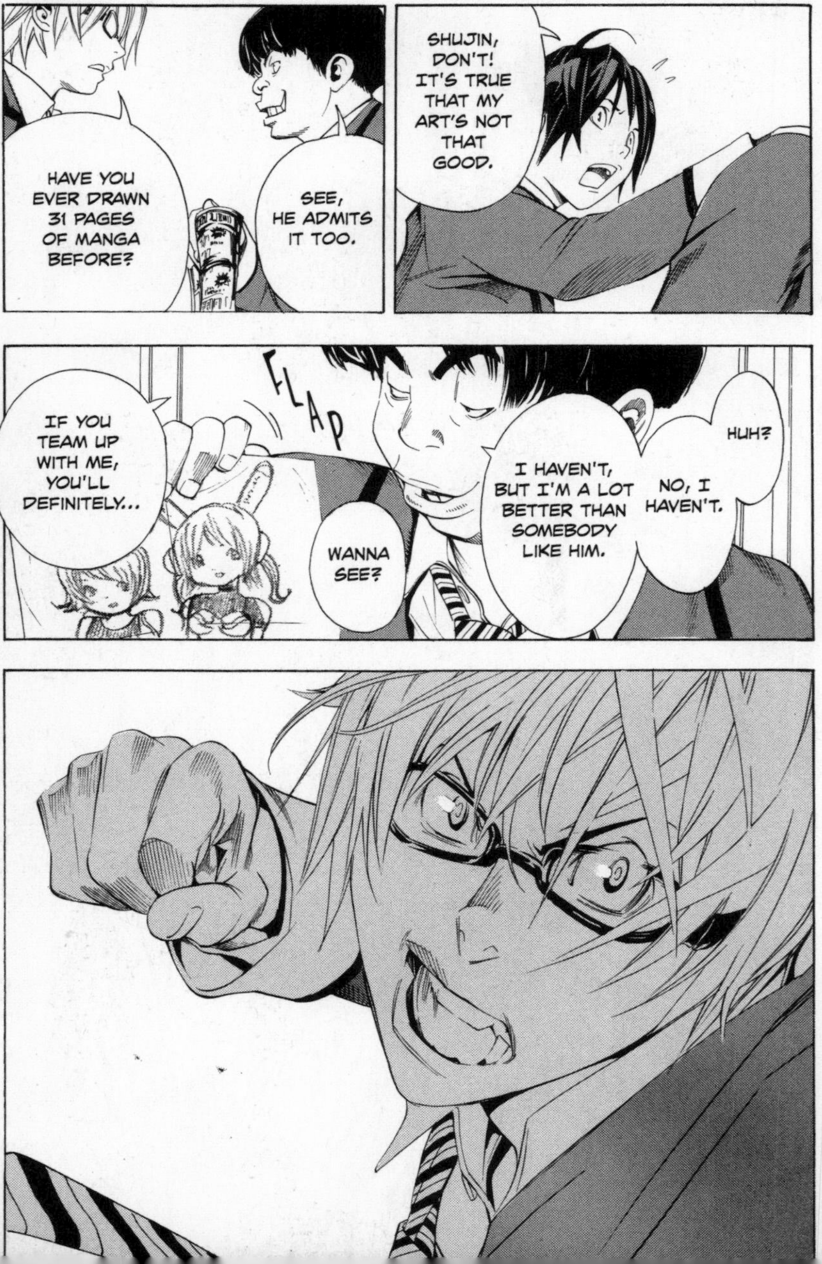
SHUJIN, DON'T! IT'S TRUE THAT MY ART'S NOT THAT GOOD.
SEE, HE ADMITS IT TOO.
HAVE YOU EVER DRAWN 31 PAGES OF MANGA BEFORE?
HUH?
NO, I HAVEN'T.
I HAVEN'T, BUT I'M A LOT BETTER THAN SOMEBODY LIKE HIM.
FLAP
WANNA SEE?
IF YOU TEAM UP WITH ME, YOU'LL DEFINITELY...

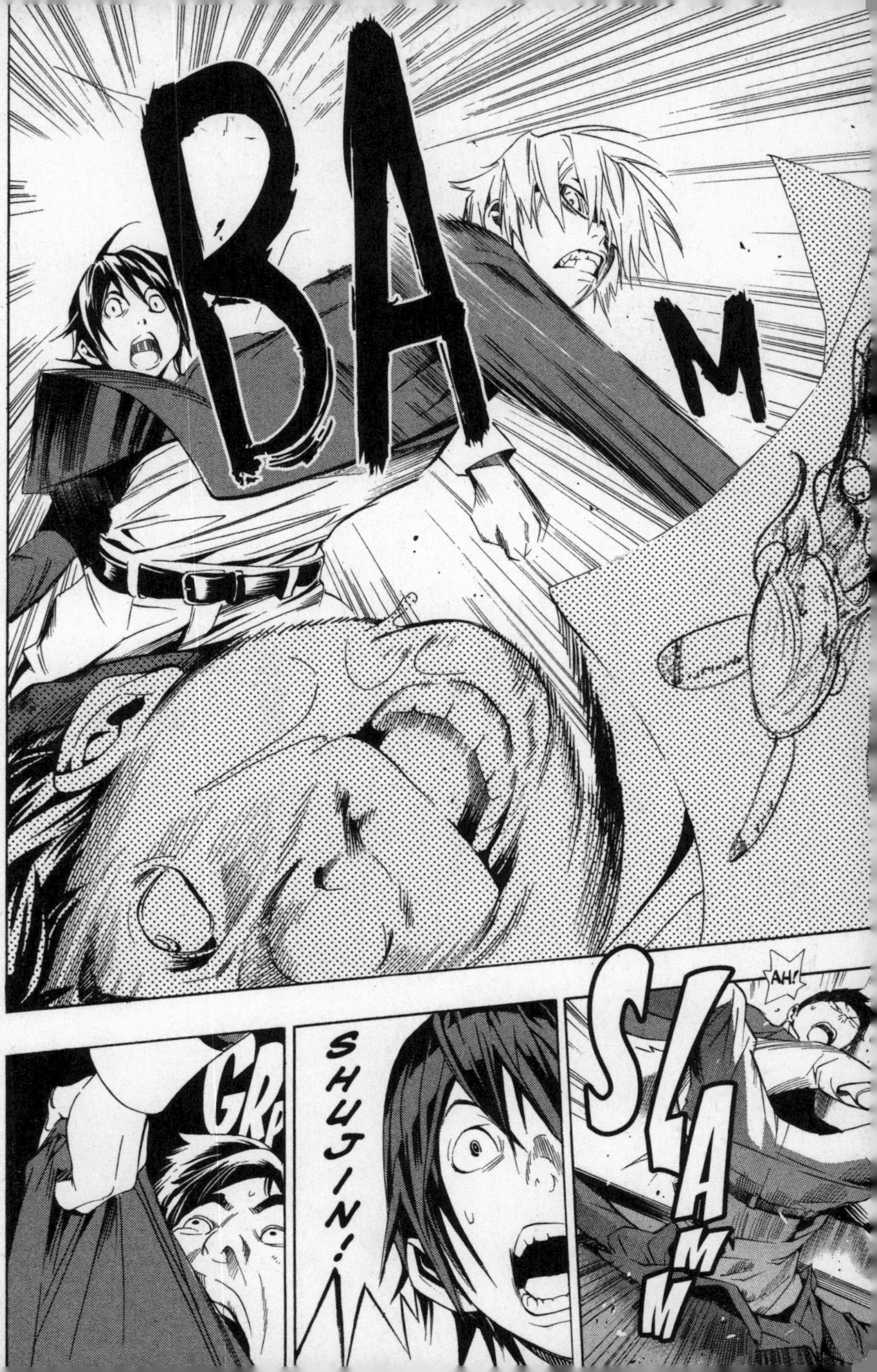
BAM
SLAMM
AH!
SHUJIN!
GR

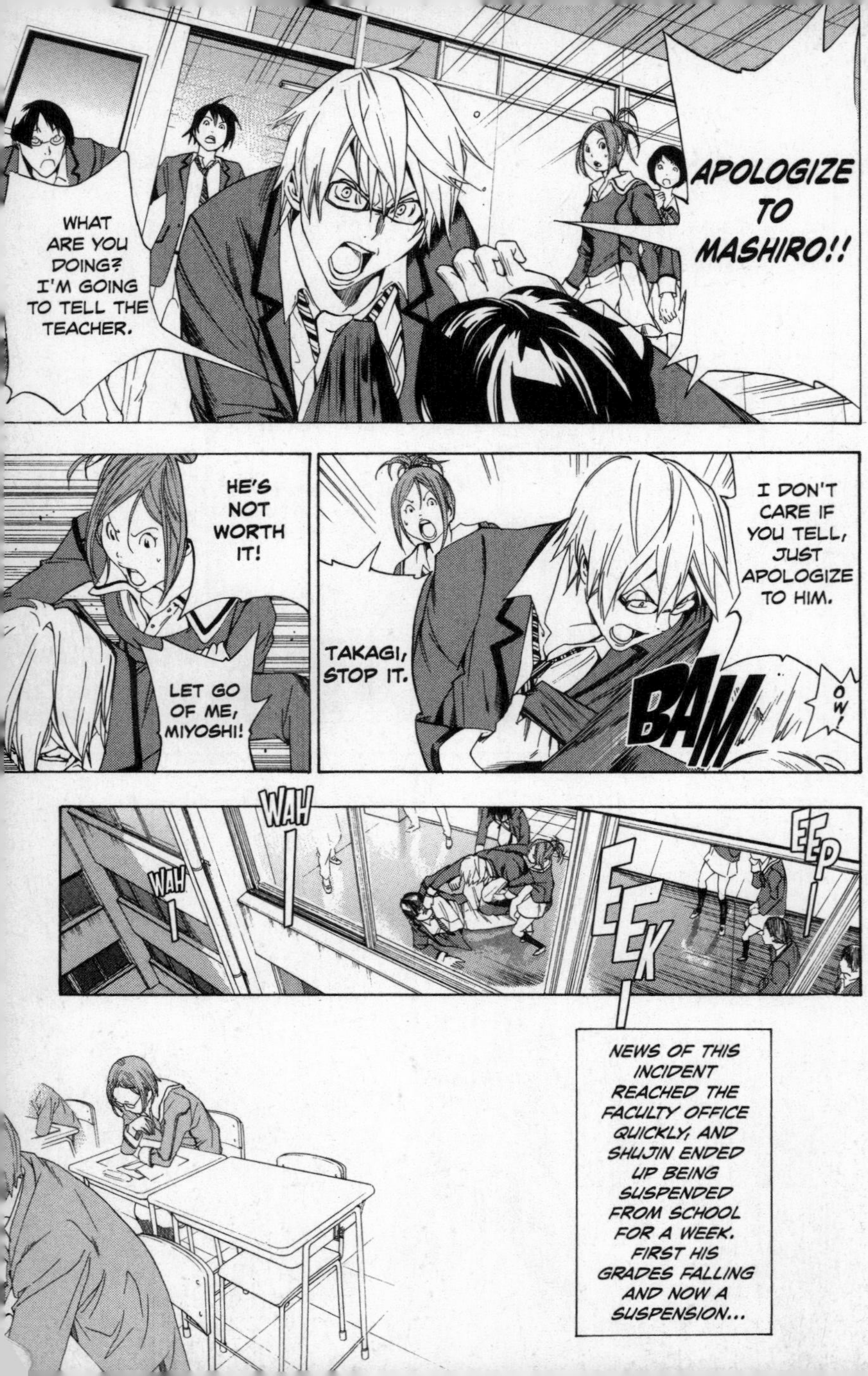
APOLOGIZE TO MASHIRO!!
WHAT ARE YOU DOING? I'M GOING TO TELL THE TEACHER.
I DON'T CARE IF YOU TELL, JUST APOLOGIZE TO HIM.
TAKAGI, STOP IT.
BAM
OW!
HE'S NOT WORTH IT!
LET GO OF ME, MIYOSHI!
EEP
EEK
WAH
WAH
NEWS OF THIS INCIDENT REACHED THE FACULTY OFFICE QUICKLY, AND SHUJIN ENDED UP BEING SUSPENDED FROM SCHOOL FOR A WEEK. FIRST HIS GRADES FALLING AND NOW A SUSPENSION...

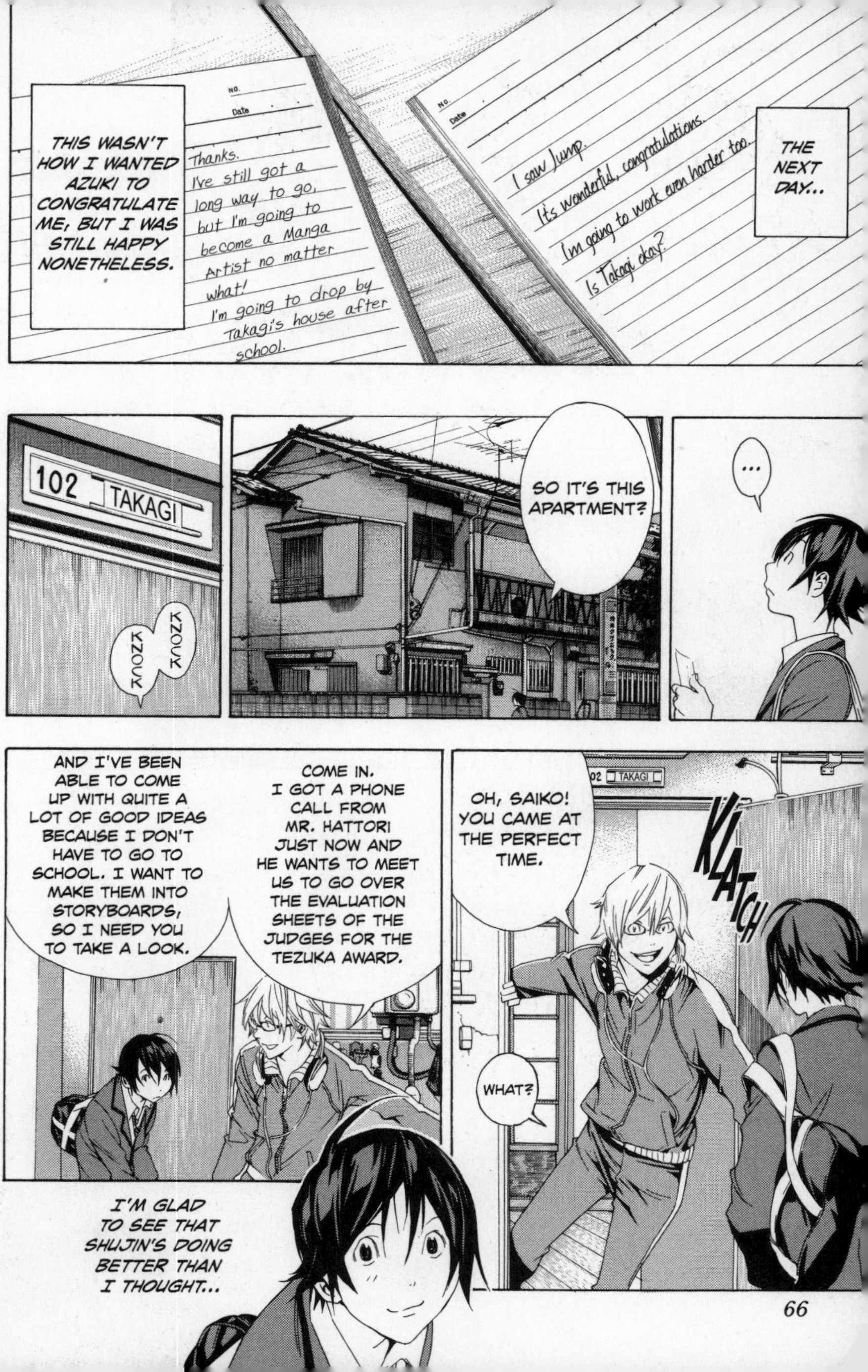
THE NEXT DAY...
No.
Date
I saw Jump.
It's wonderful, congratulations.
I'm going to work even harder too.
Is Takagi okay?
No.
Date
Thanks.
I've still got a long way to go, but I'm going to become a Manga Artist no matter what!
I'm going to drop by Takagi's house after school.
THIS WASN'T HOW I WANTED AZUKI TO CONGRATULATE ME, BUT I WAS STILL HAPPY NONETHELESS.
...
SO IT'S THIS APARTMENT?
102 TAKAGI
KNOCK KNOCK
102 TAKAGI
KLATCH
OH, SAIKO! YOU CAME AT THE PERFECT TIME.
WHAT?
COME IN. I GOT A PHONE CALL FROM MR. HATTORI JUST NOW AND HE WANTS TO MEET US TO GO OVER THE EVALUATION SHEETS OF THE JUDGES FOR THE TEZUKA AWARD.
AND I'VE BEEN ABLE TO COME UP WITH QUITE A LOT OF GOOD IDEAS BECAUSE I DON'T HAVE TO GO TO SCHOOL. I WANT TO MAKE THEM INTO STORYBOARDS, SO I NEED YOU TO TAKE A LOOK.
I'M GLAD TO SEE THAT SHUJIN'S DOING BETTER THAN I THOUGHT...

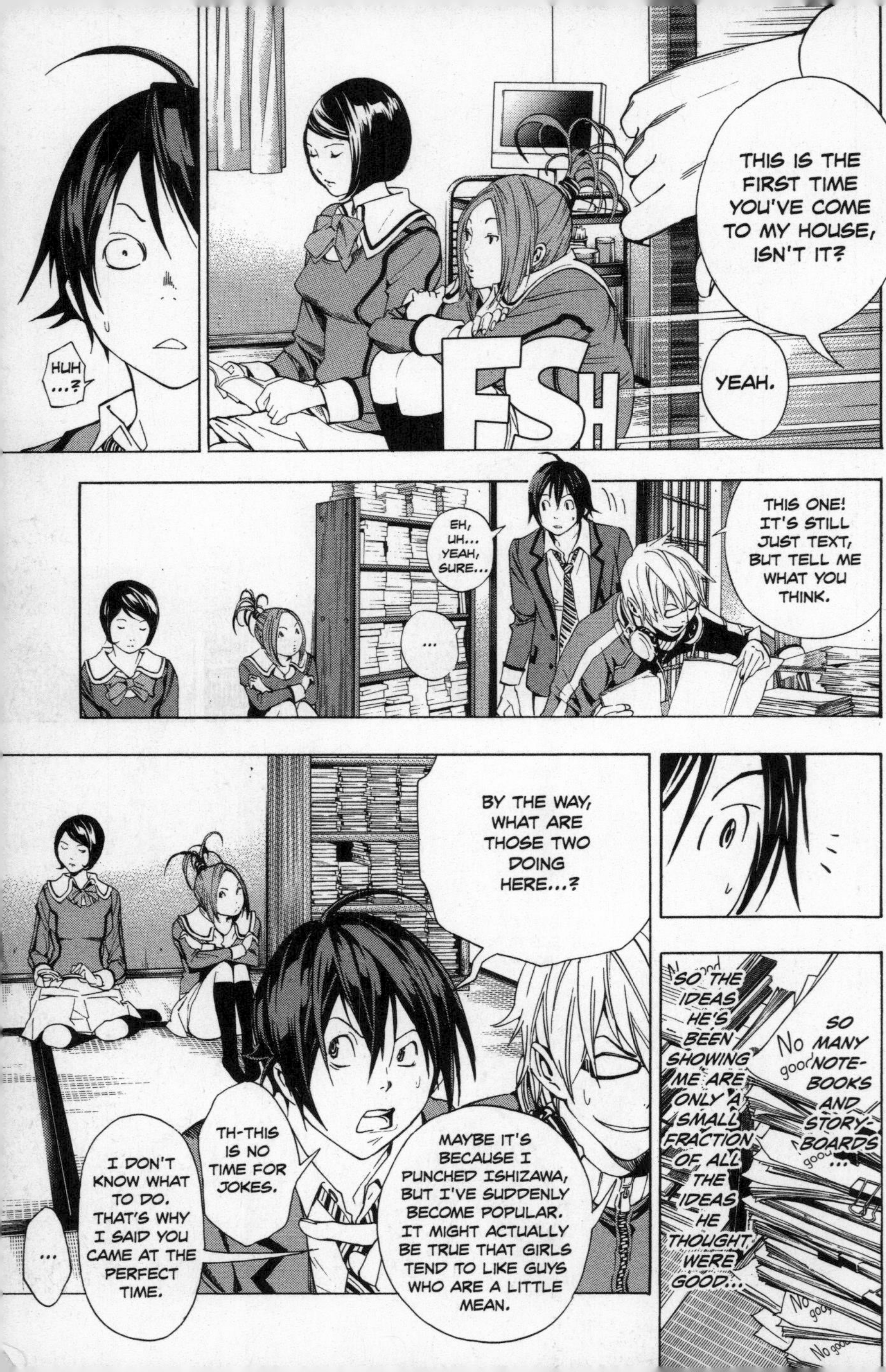
THIS IS THE FIRST TIME YOU'VE COME TO MY HOUSE, ISN'T IT?
YEAH.
FSH
HUH ...?
THIS ONE! IT'S STILL JUST TEXT, BUT TELL ME WHAT YOU THINK.
EH, UH... YEAH, SURE...
...
SO MANY NOTE-BOOKS AND STORY-BOARDS...
SO THE IDEAS HE'S BEEN SHOWING ME ARE ONLY A SMALL FRACTION OF ALL THE IDEAS HE THOUGHT WERE GOOD...
No good
BY THE WAY, WHAT ARE THOSE TWO DOING HERE...?
MAYBE IT'S BECAUSE I PUNCHED ISHIZAWA, BUT I'VE SUDDENLY BECOME POPULAR. IT MIGHT ACTUALLY BE TRUE THAT GIRLS TEND TO LIKE GUYS WHO ARE A LITTLE MEAN.
TH-THIS IS NO TIME FOR JOKES.
I DON'T KNOW WHAT TO DO. THAT'S WHY I SAID YOU CAME AT THE PERFECT TIME.
...

OHBA'S STORYBOARD

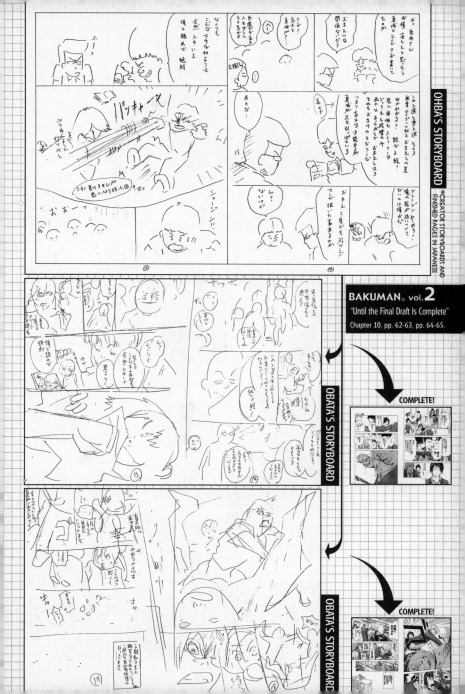

※CREATOR STORYBOARDS AND FINISHED PAGES IN JAPANESE

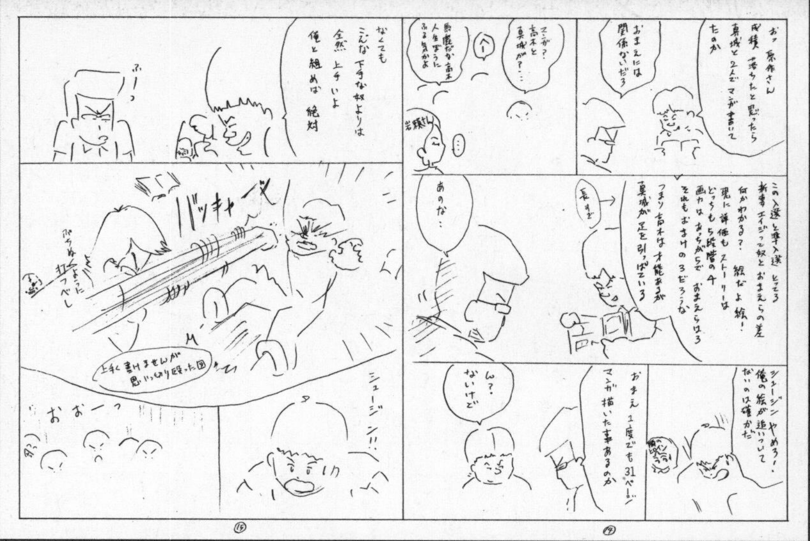
おっ 亜作さん 成績落ちたと思ったら 真城と2人でマンガ書いてたのか
おまえには関係ないだろ
マンガ? 高木と真城が?…
へー
馬鹿だな高木 人生ぼうにふる気かよ
岩瀬さん
…
この入選と準入選とってる新妻エイジって奴とおまえらの差 何かわかる?
絵だよ絵!
現に評価もストーリーはどっちも5段階の4 画力はおっちがらでおまえらは3 それもおまけの3だろうな
つまり高木は才能あるが真城が足を引っぱっている
長すぎ
あのな…
シュージンやめろ! 俺の絵が追いついてないのは確かだ
おまえ1度でも31ページマンガ描いた事あるのか
ん? ないけど
なくても こんな下手な奴よりは 全然上手いよ 俺と組めば絶対
ふーっ
バッキャー
上手く書けませんが思いっきり殴った図
ぶちぬくように打つべし
シュージン!!
おおーっ

BAKUMAN。vol.2

"Until the Final Draft Is Complete"

Chapter 10, pp. 62-63, pp. 64-65.

OBATA'S STORYBOARD

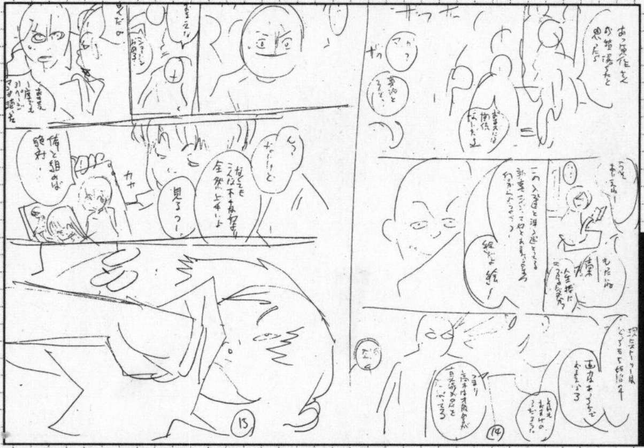

COMPLETE!

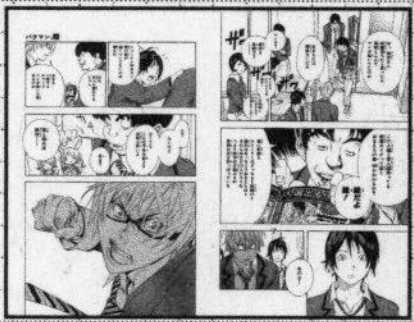

OBATA'S STORYBOARD

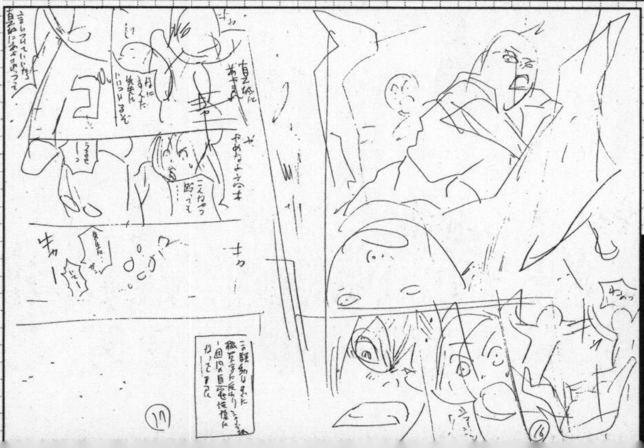

COMPLETE!

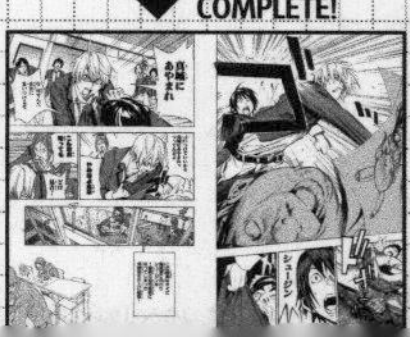

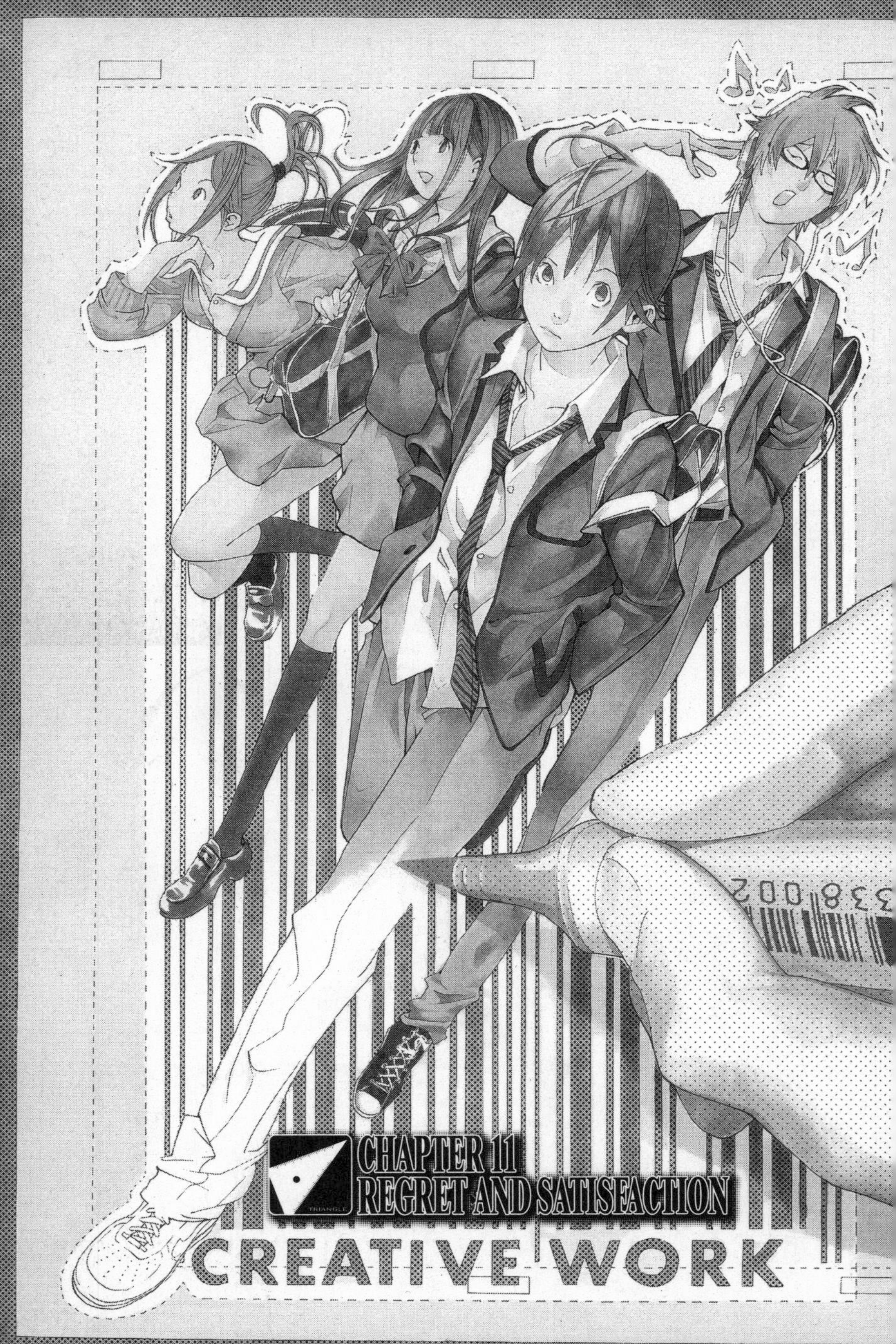
CHAPTER 11
REGRET AND SATISFACTION
CREATIVE WORK

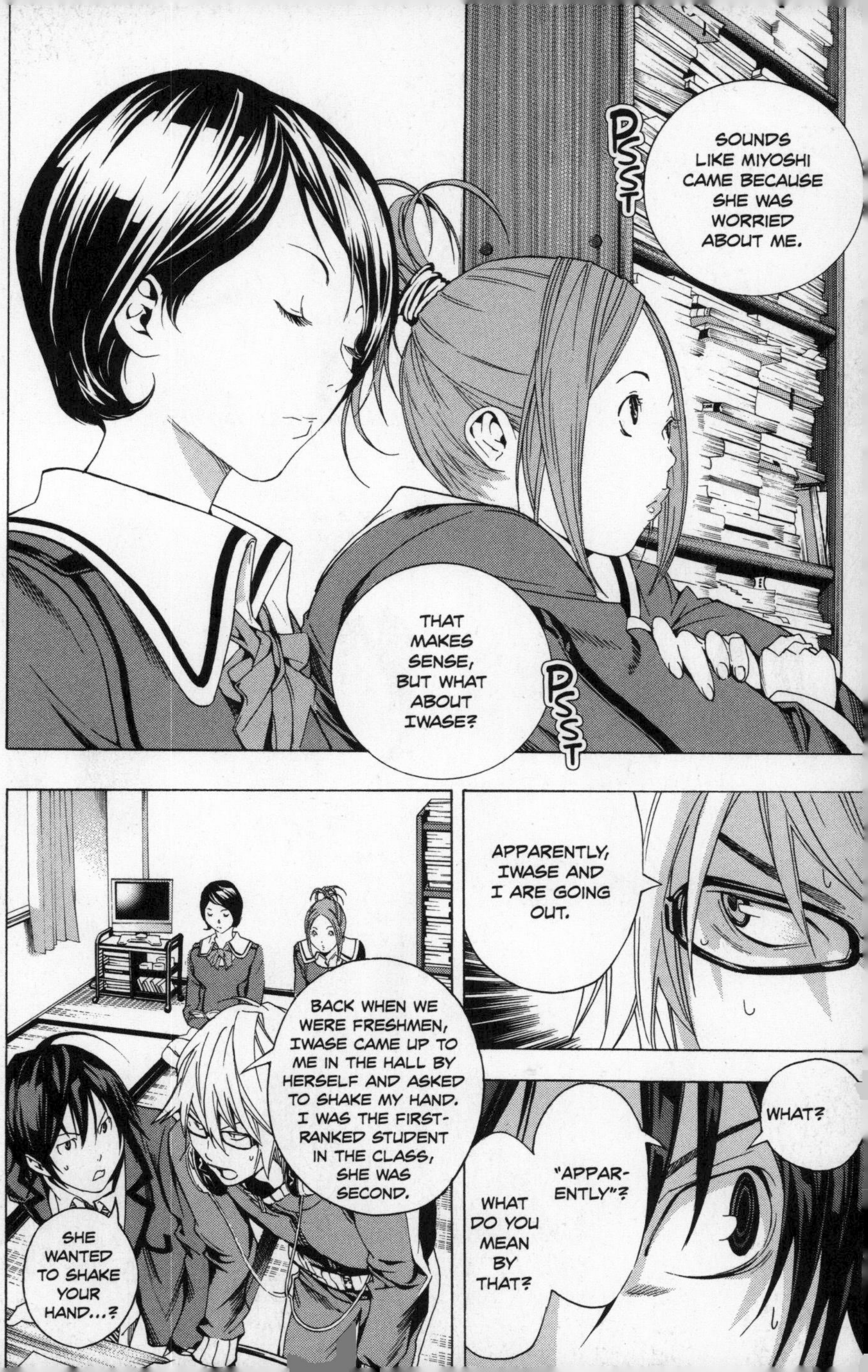
PSST
SOUNDS LIKE MIYOSHI CAME BECAUSE SHE WAS WORRIED ABOUT ME.
THAT MAKES SENSE, BUT WHAT ABOUT IWASE?
PSST
APPARENTLY, IWASE AND I ARE GOING OUT.
WHAT?
"APPAR-ENTLY"?
WHAT DO YOU MEAN BY THAT?
BACK WHEN WE WERE FRESHMEN, IWASE CAME UP TO ME IN THE HALL BY HERSELF AND ASKED TO SHAKE MY HAND. I WAS THE FIRST-RANKED STUDENT IN THE CLASS, SHE WAS SECOND.
SHE WANTED TO SHAKE YOUR HAND...?

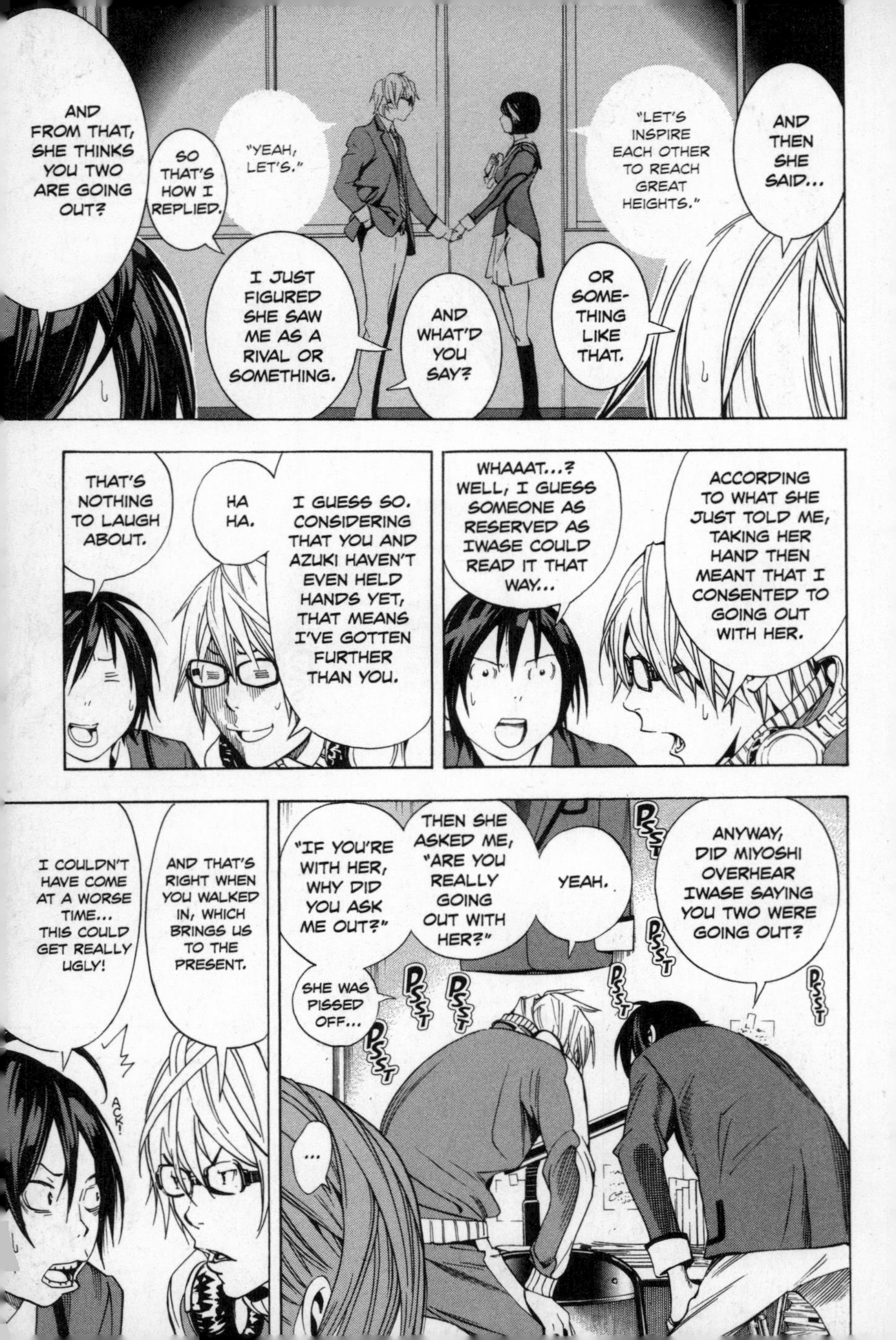
AND THEN SHE SAID...
"LET'S INSPIRE EACH OTHER TO REACH GREAT HEIGHTS."
OR SOMETHING LIKE THAT.
AND WHAT'D YOU SAY?
"YEAH, LET'S."
SO THAT'S HOW I REPLIED.
I JUST FIGURED SHE SAW ME AS A RIVAL OR SOMETHING.
AND FROM THAT, SHE THINKS YOU TWO ARE GOING OUT?
ACCORDING TO WHAT SHE JUST TOLD ME, TAKING HER HAND THEN MEANT THAT I CONSENTED TO GOING OUT WITH HER.
WHAAAT...? WELL, I GUESS SOMEONE AS RESERVED AS IWASE COULD READ IT THAT WAY...
I GUESS SO. CONSIDERING THAT YOU AND AZUKI HAVEN'T EVEN HELD HANDS YET, THAT MEANS I'VE GOTTEN FURTHER THAN YOU.
HA HA.
THAT'S NOTHING TO LAUGH ABOUT.
ANYWAY, DID MIYOSHI OVERHEAR IWASE SAYING YOU TWO WERE GOING OUT?
PSST
YEAH.
THEN SHE ASKED ME, "ARE YOU REALLY GOING OUT WITH HER?"
"IF YOU'RE WITH HER, WHY DID YOU ASK ME OUT?"
PSST
PSST
SHE WAS PISSED OFF...
PSST
PSST
PSST
PSST
...
AND THAT'S RIGHT WHEN YOU WALKED IN, WHICH BRINGS US TO THE PRESENT.
I COULDN'T HAVE COME AT A WORSE TIME... THIS COULD GET REALLY UGLY!
ACK!

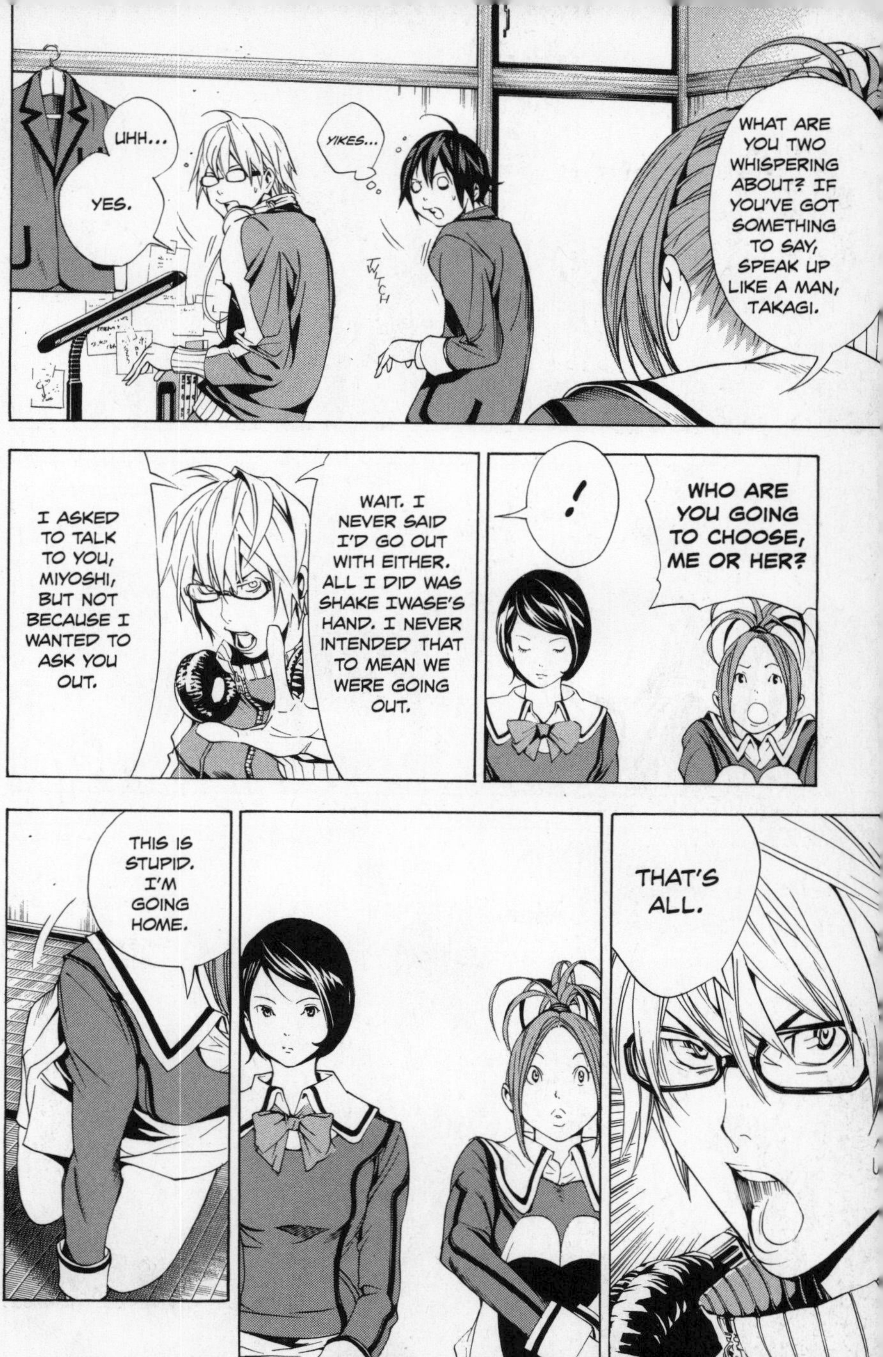
WHAT ARE YOU TWO WHISPERING ABOUT? IF YOU'VE GOT SOMETHING TO SAY, SPEAK UP LIKE A MAN, TAKAGI.
YIKES...
TWITCH
UHH...
YES.
WHO ARE YOU GOING TO CHOOSE, ME OR HER?
!
WAIT. I NEVER SAID I'D GO OUT WITH EITHER. ALL I DID WAS SHAKE IWASE'S HAND. I NEVER INTENDED THAT TO MEAN WE WERE GOING OUT.
I ASKED TO TALK TO YOU, MIYOSHI, BUT NOT BECAUSE I WANTED TO ASK YOU OUT.
THAT'S ALL.
THIS IS STUPID. I'M GOING HOME.

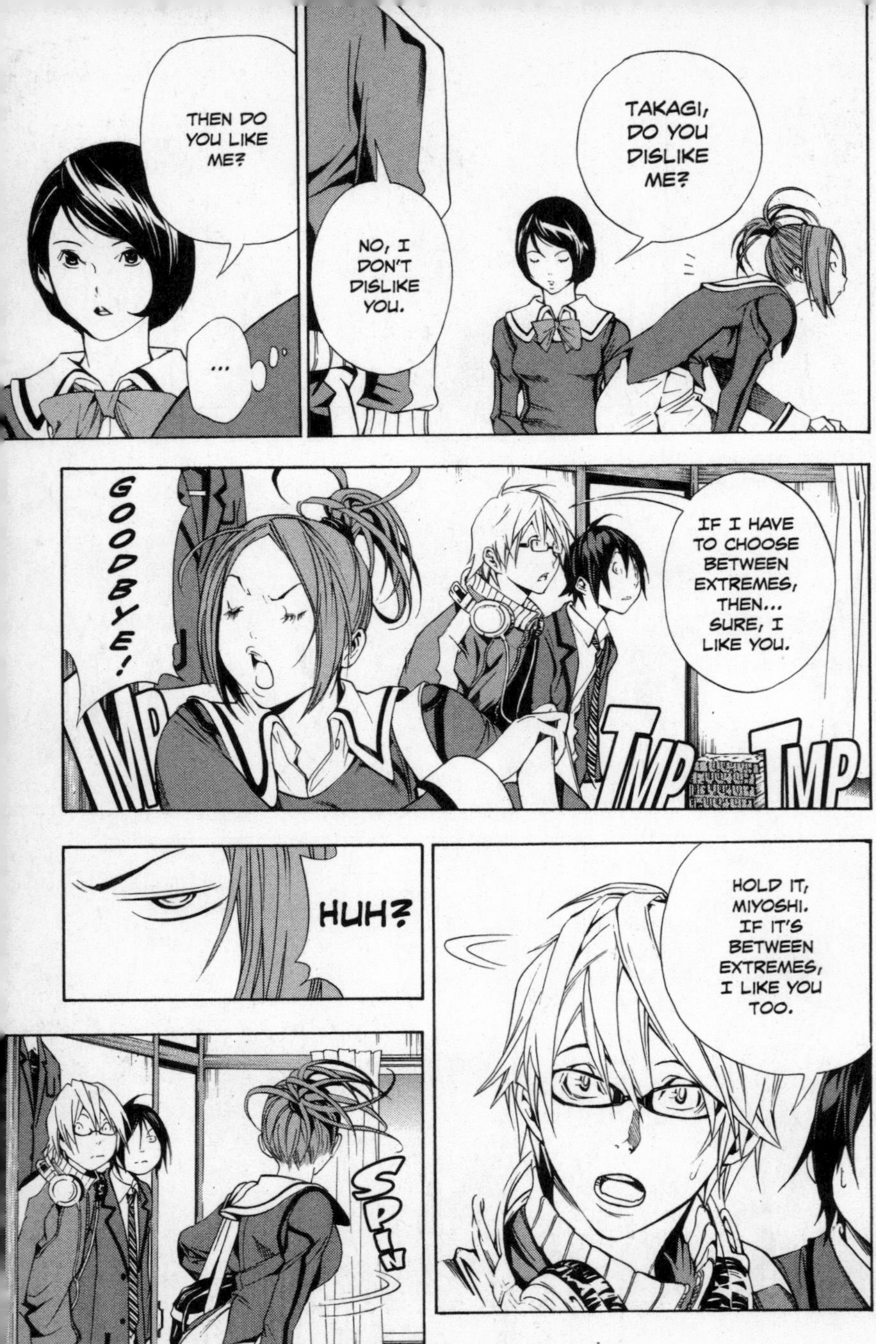
TAKAGI, DO YOU DISLIKE ME?
NO, I DON'T DISLIKE YOU.
THEN DO YOU LIKE ME?
...
IF I HAVE TO CHOOSE BETWEEN EXTREMES, THEN... SURE, I LIKE YOU.
TMP
TMP
GOODBYE!
TMP
HOLD IT, MIYOSHI. IF IT'S BETWEEN EXTREMES, I LIKE YOU TOO.
HUH?
SPIN

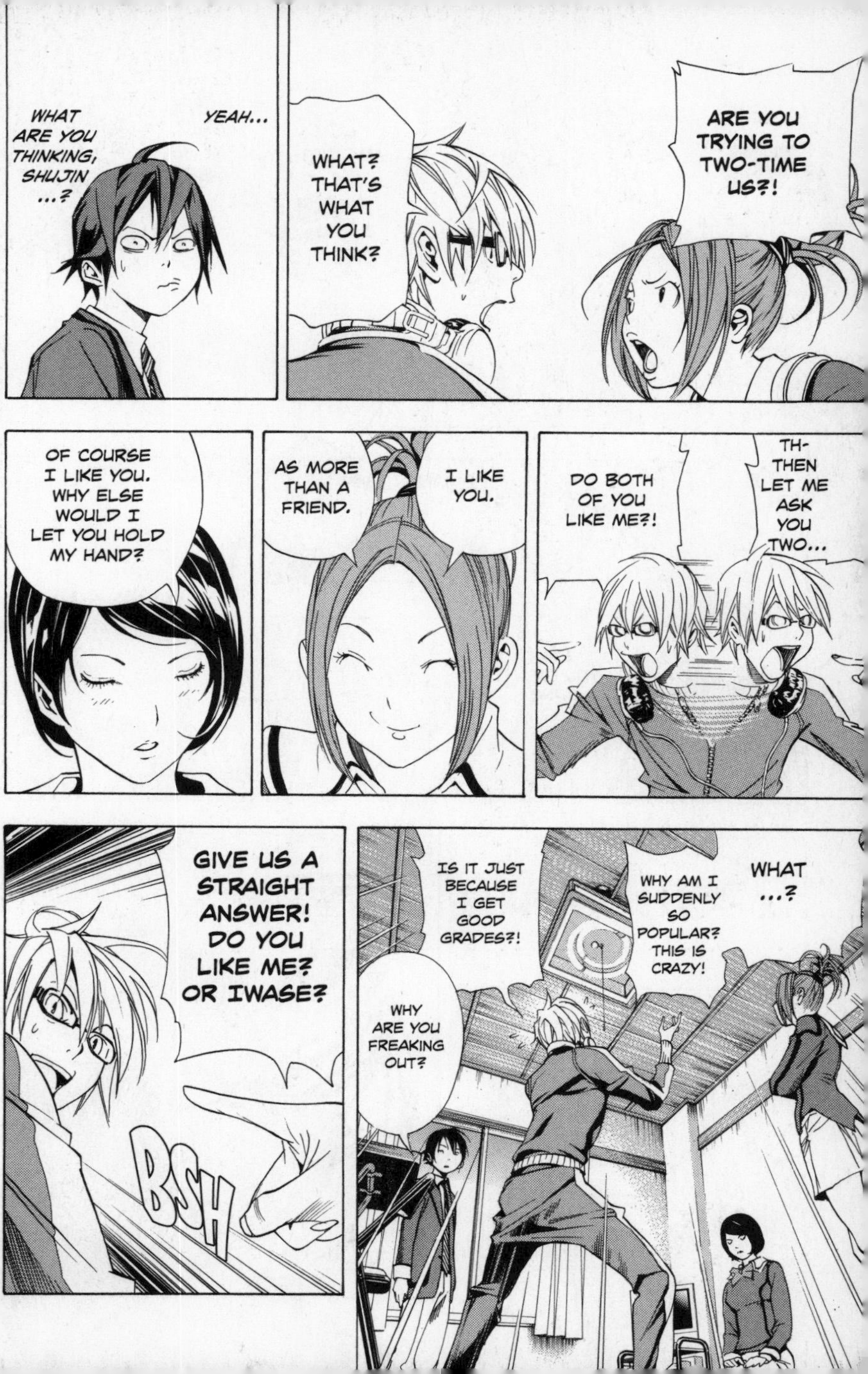
ARE YOU TRYING TO TWO-TIME US?!
WHAT? THAT'S WHAT YOU THINK?
YEAH...
WHAT ARE YOU THINKING, SHUJIN ...?
TH- THEN LET ME ASK YOU TWO...
DO BOTH OF YOU LIKE ME?!
I LIKE YOU.
AS MORE THAN A FRIEND.
OF COURSE I LIKE YOU. WHY ELSE WOULD I LET YOU HOLD MY HAND?
WHAT ...?
WHY AM I SUDDENLY SO POPULAR? THIS IS CRAZY!
IS IT JUST BECAUSE I GET GOOD GRADES?!
WHY ARE YOU FREAKING OUT?
GIVE US A STRAIGHT ANSWER! DO YOU LIKE ME? OR IWASE?
BSH

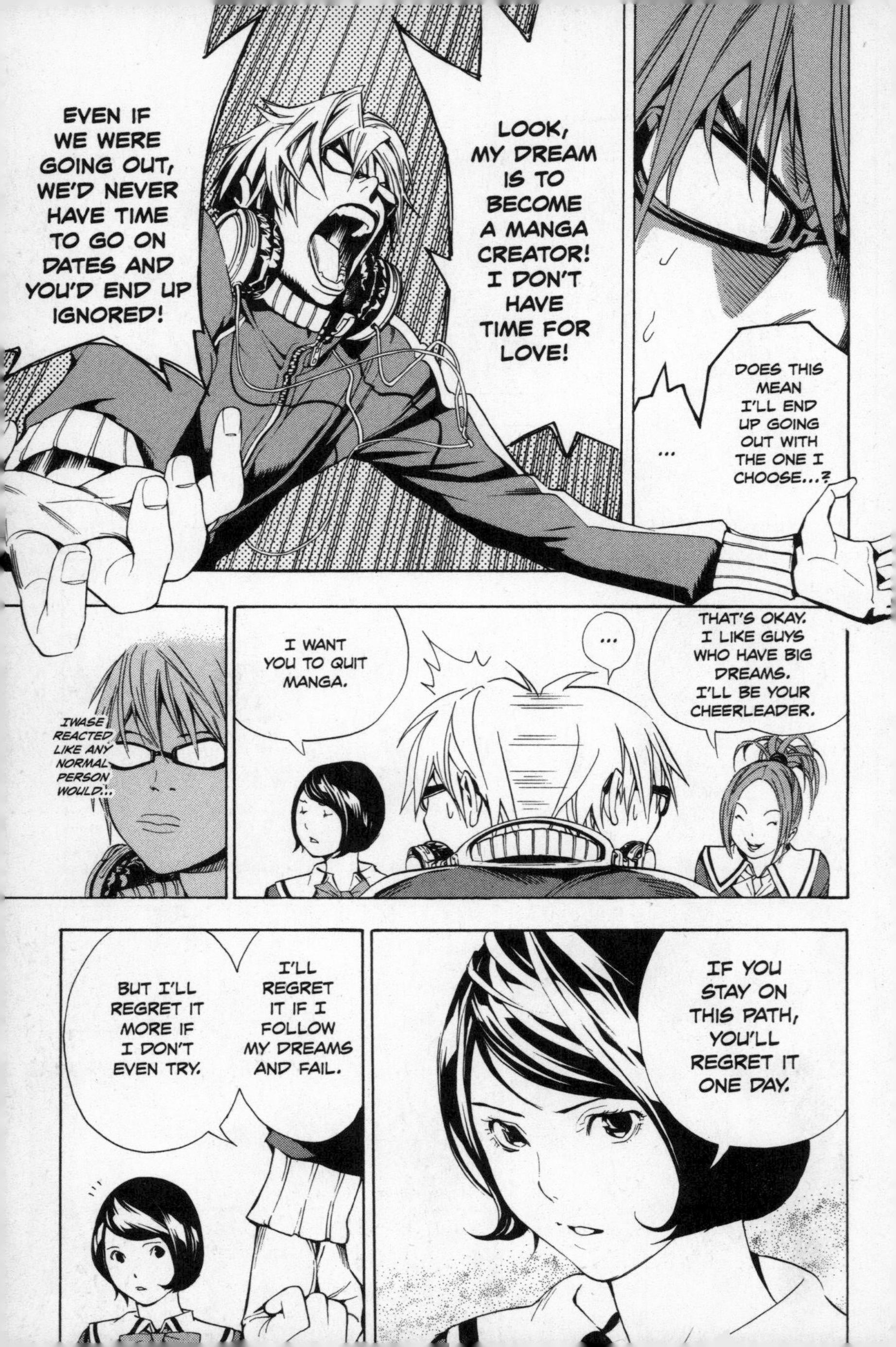
...
DOES THIS MEAN I'LL END UP GOING OUT WITH THE ONE I CHOOSE...?
LOOK, MY DREAM IS TO BECOME A MANGA CREATOR! I DON'T HAVE TIME FOR LOVE!
EVEN IF WE WERE GOING OUT, WE'D NEVER HAVE TIME TO GO ON DATES AND YOU'D END UP IGNORED!
THAT'S OKAY. I LIKE GUYS WHO HAVE BIG DREAMS. I'LL BE YOUR CHEERLEADER.
...
I WANT YOU TO QUIT MANGA.
IWASE REACTED LIKE ANY NORMAL PERSON WOULD...
IF YOU STAY ON THIS PATH, YOU'LL REGRET IT ONE DAY.
I'LL REGRET IT IF I FOLLOW MY DREAMS AND FAIL.
BUT I'LL REGRET IT MORE IF I DON'T EVEN TRY.

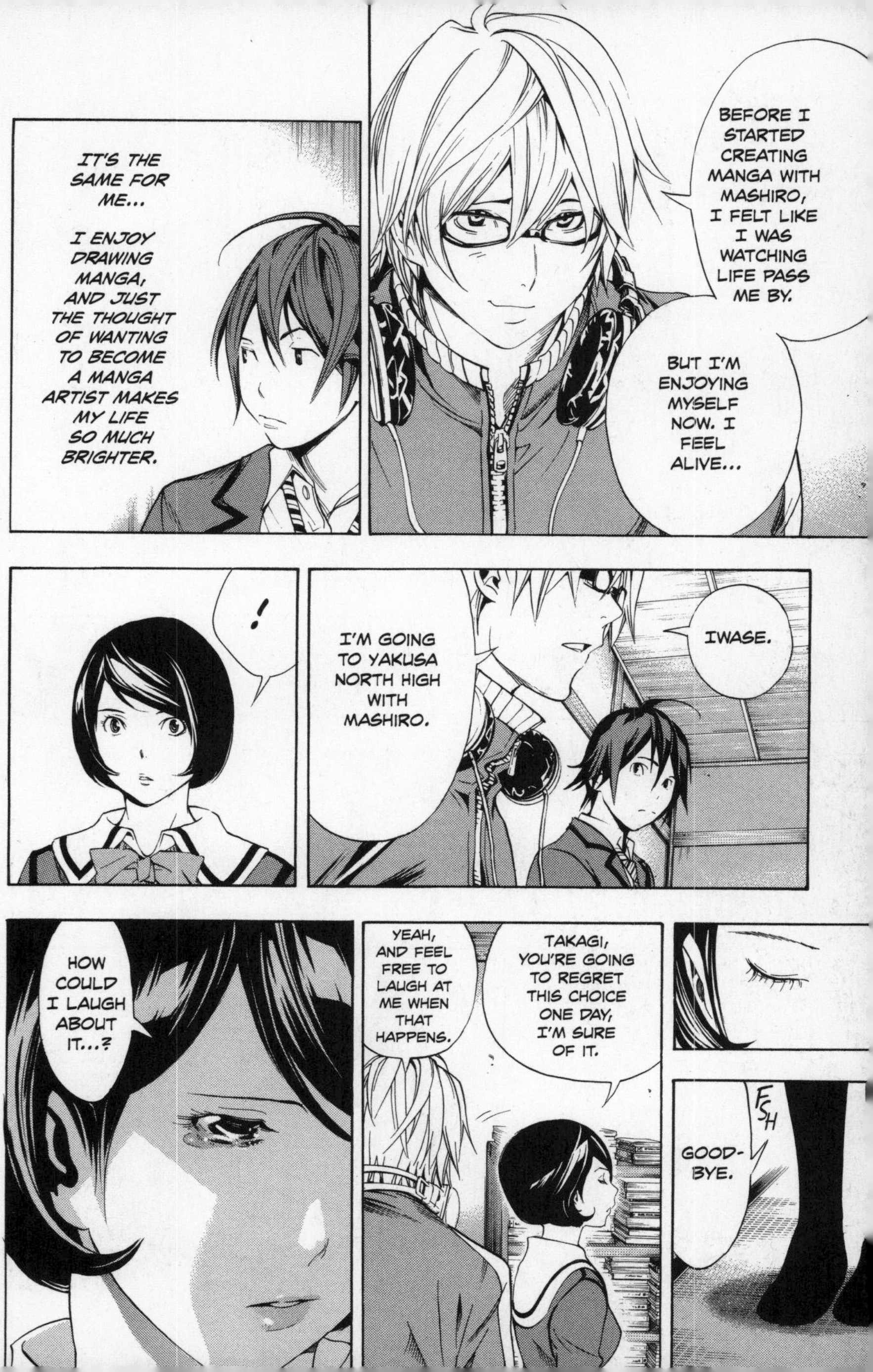
BEFORE I STARTED CREATING MANGA WITH MASHIRO, I FELT LIKE I WAS WATCHING LIFE PASS ME BY.
BUT I'M ENJOYING MYSELF NOW. I FEEL ALIVE...
IT'S THE SAME FOR ME...
I ENJOY DRAWING MANGA, AND JUST THE THOUGHT OF WANTING TO BECOME A MANGA ARTIST MAKES MY LIFE SO MUCH BRIGHTER.
IWASE.
I'M GOING TO YAKUSA NORTH HIGH WITH MASHIRO.
!
FSH
GOOD-BYE.
TAKAGI, YOU'RE GOING TO REGRET THIS CHOICE ONE DAY, I'M SURE OF IT.
YEAH, AND FEEL FREE TO LAUGH AT ME WHEN THAT HAPPENS.
HOW COULD I LAUGH ABOUT IT...?

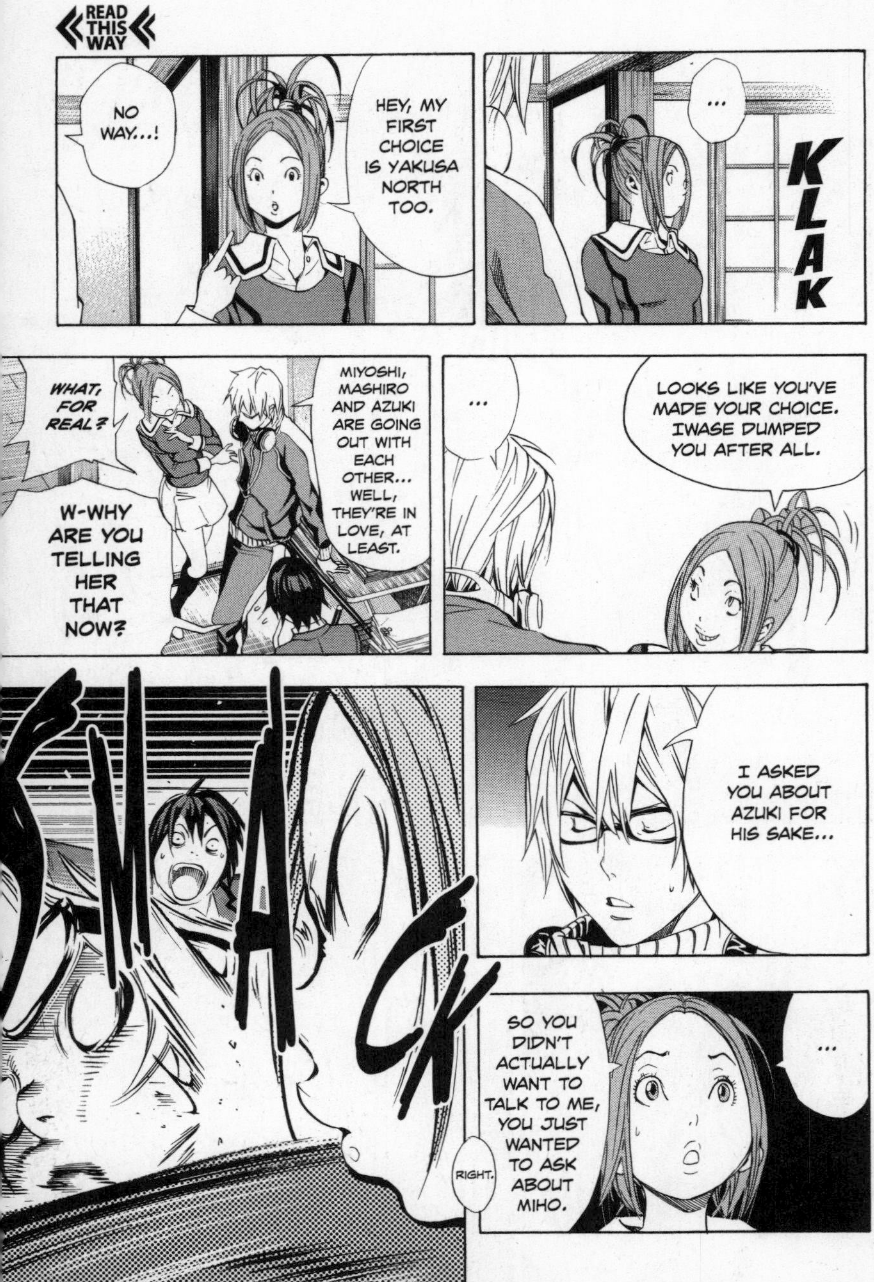
READ THIS WAY
...
KLAK
HEY, MY FIRST CHOICE IS YAKUSA NORTH TOO.
NO WAY...!
LOOKS LIKE YOU'VE MADE YOUR CHOICE. IWASE DUMPED YOU AFTER ALL.
...
MIYOSHI, MASHIRO AND AZUKI ARE GOING OUT WITH EACH OTHER... WELL, THEY'RE IN LOVE, AT LEAST.
WHAT, FOR REAL?
W-WHY ARE YOU TELLING HER THAT NOW?
I ASKED YOU ABOUT AZUKI FOR HIS SAKE...
...
SO YOU DIDN'T ACTUALLY WANT TO TALK TO ME, YOU JUST WANTED TO ASK ABOUT MIHO.
RIGHT.
SMACK

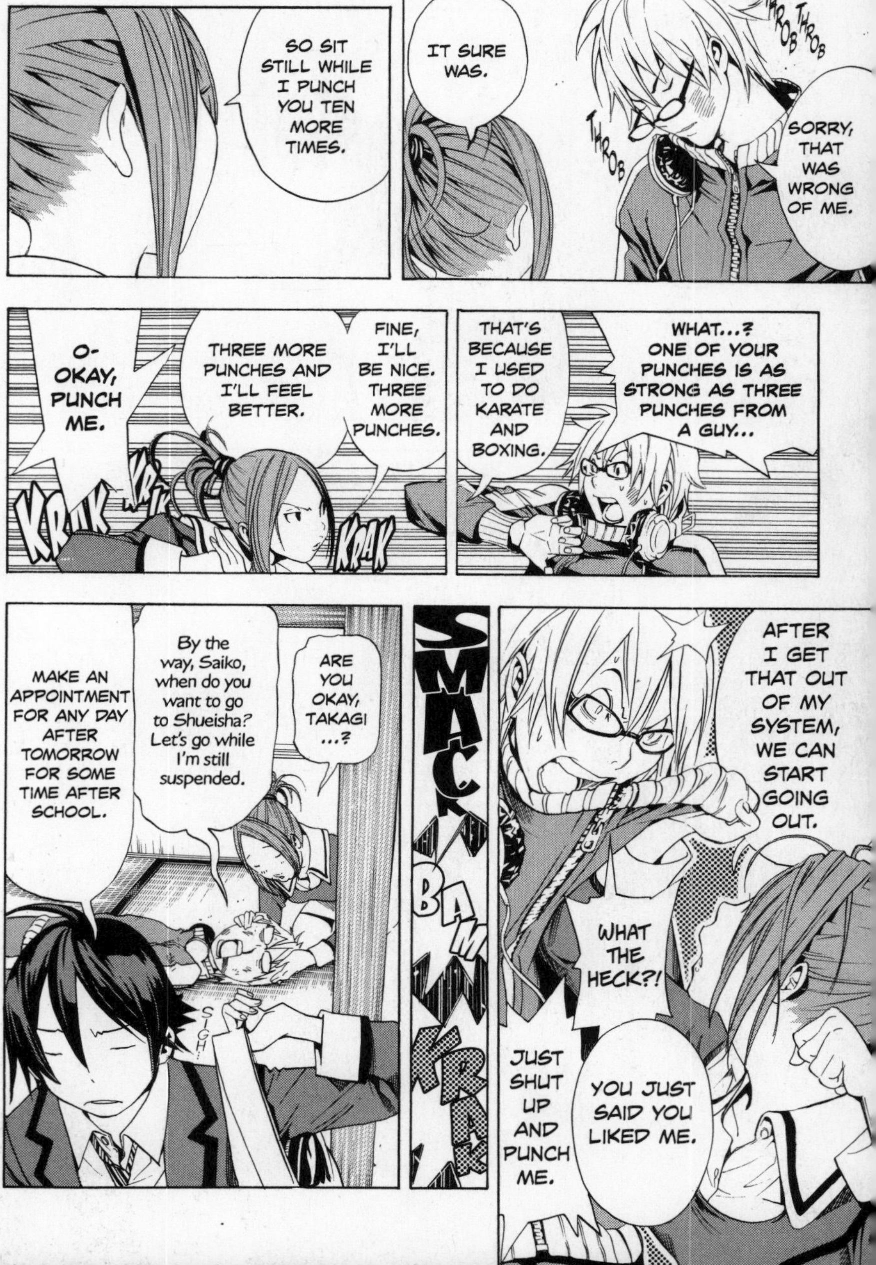
SORRY, THAT WAS WRONG OF ME.
THROB THROB
THROB
IT SURE WAS.
SO SIT STILL WHILE I PUNCH YOU TEN MORE TIMES.
WHAT...? ONE OF YOUR PUNCHES IS AS STRONG AS THREE PUNCHES FROM A GUY...
THAT'S BECAUSE I USED TO DO KARATE AND BOXING.
FINE, I'LL BE NICE. THREE MORE PUNCHES.
KRAK
THREE MORE PUNCHES AND I'LL FEEL BETTER.
O-OKAY, PUNCH ME.
KRIK
KRAK
AFTER I GET THAT OUT OF MY SYSTEM, WE CAN START GOING OUT.
WHAT THE HECK?!
YOU JUST SAID YOU LIKED ME.
JUST SHUT UP AND PUNCH ME.
SMACK
BAM
KRAK
ARE YOU OKAY, TAKAGI...?
By the way, Saiko, when do you want to go to Shueisha? Let's go while I'm still suspended.
MAKE AN APPOINTMENT FOR ANY DAY AFTER TOMORROW FOR SOME TIME AFTER SCHOOL.
SIGH...

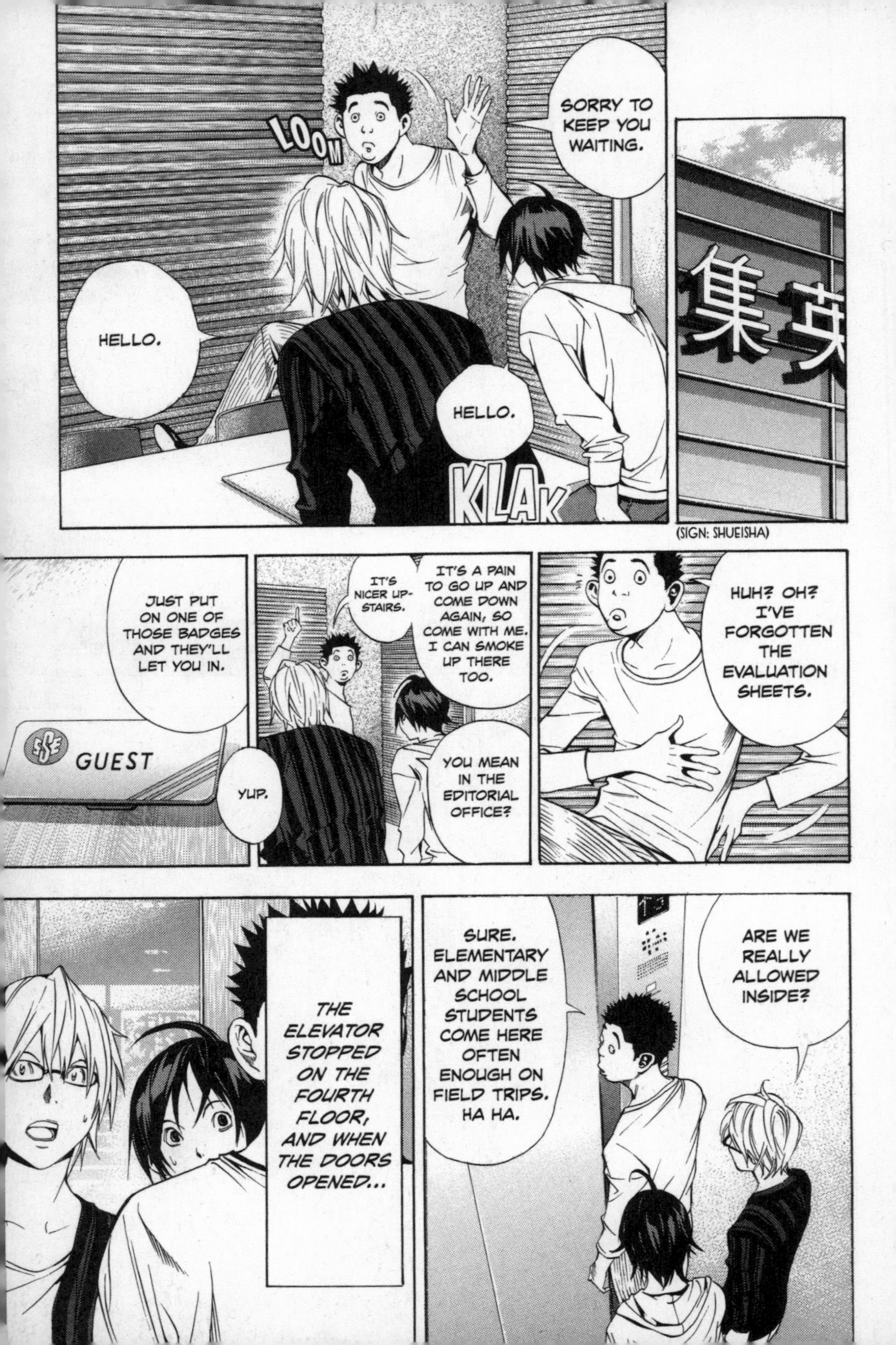
集英
(SIGN: SHUEISHA)
SORRY TO KEEP YOU WAITING.
LOOM
HELLO.
HELLO.
KLAK
HUH? OH? I'VE FORGOTTEN THE EVALUATION SHEETS.
IT'S A PAIN TO GO UP AND COME DOWN AGAIN, SO COME WITH ME. I CAN SMOKE UP THERE TOO.
IT'S NICER UPSTAIRS.
YOU MEAN IN THE EDITORIAL OFFICE?
YUP.
JUST PUT ON ONE OF THOSE BADGES AND THEY'LL LET YOU IN.
GUEST
ARE WE REALLY ALLOWED INSIDE?
SURE. ELEMENTARY AND MIDDLE SCHOOL STUDENTS COME HERE OFTEN ENOUGH ON FIELD TRIPS. HA HA.
THE ELEVATOR STOPPED ON THE FOURTH FLOOR, AND WHEN THE DOORS OPENED...

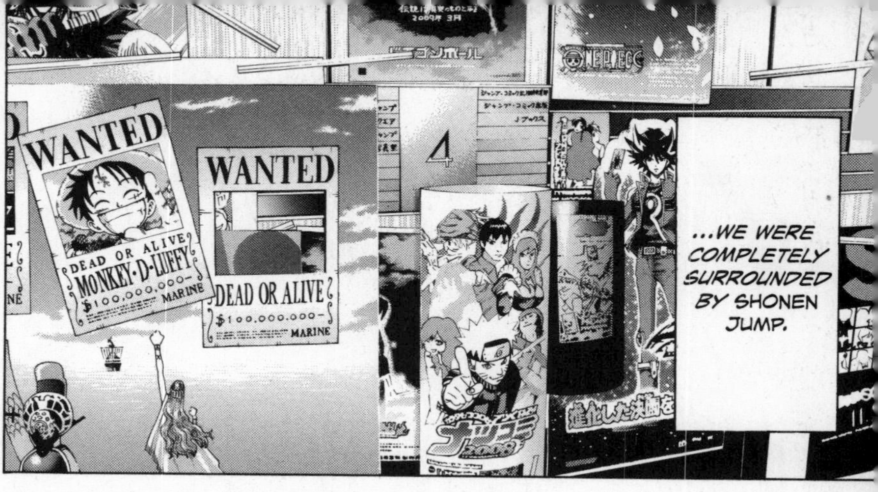
...WE WERE COMPLETELY SURROUNDED BY SHONEN JUMP.
ONE PIECE
2009年 3月
WANTED
DEAD OR ALIVE
$100.000.000-
MARINE
WANTED
DEAD OR ALIVE
MONKEY・D・LUFFY
$100,000,000-
MARINE
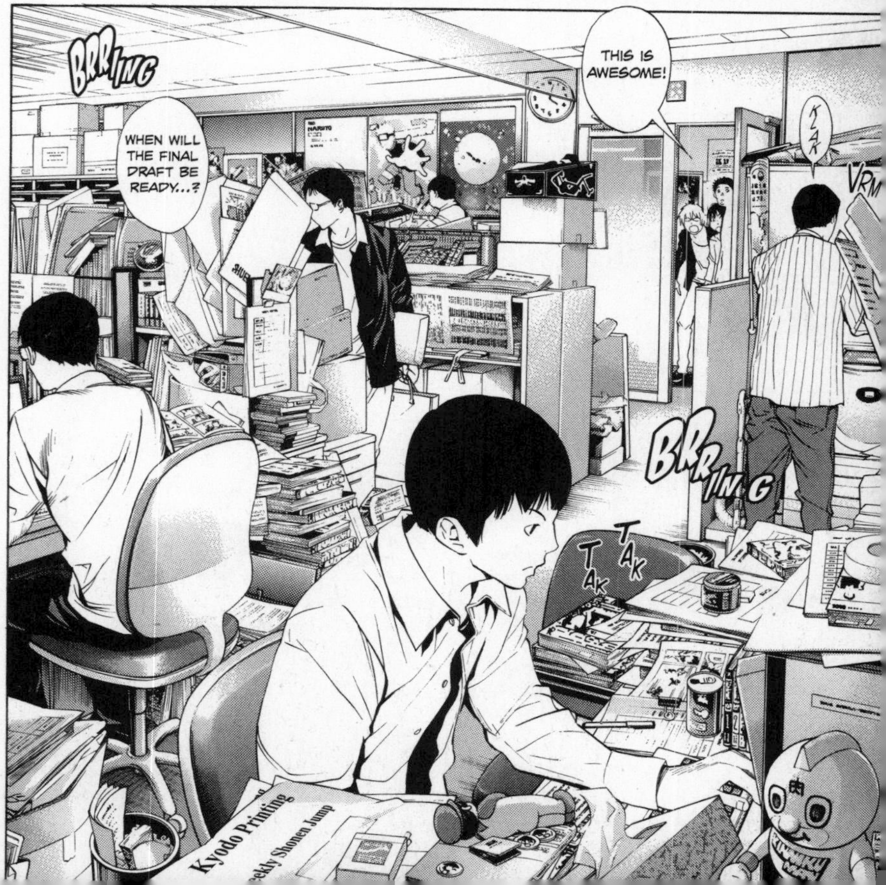
VRM
KLAK
THIS IS AWESOME!
WHEN WILL THE FINAL DRAFT BE READY...?
BRRING
BRRING
TAK TAK
Kyodo Printing
eekly Shonen Jump

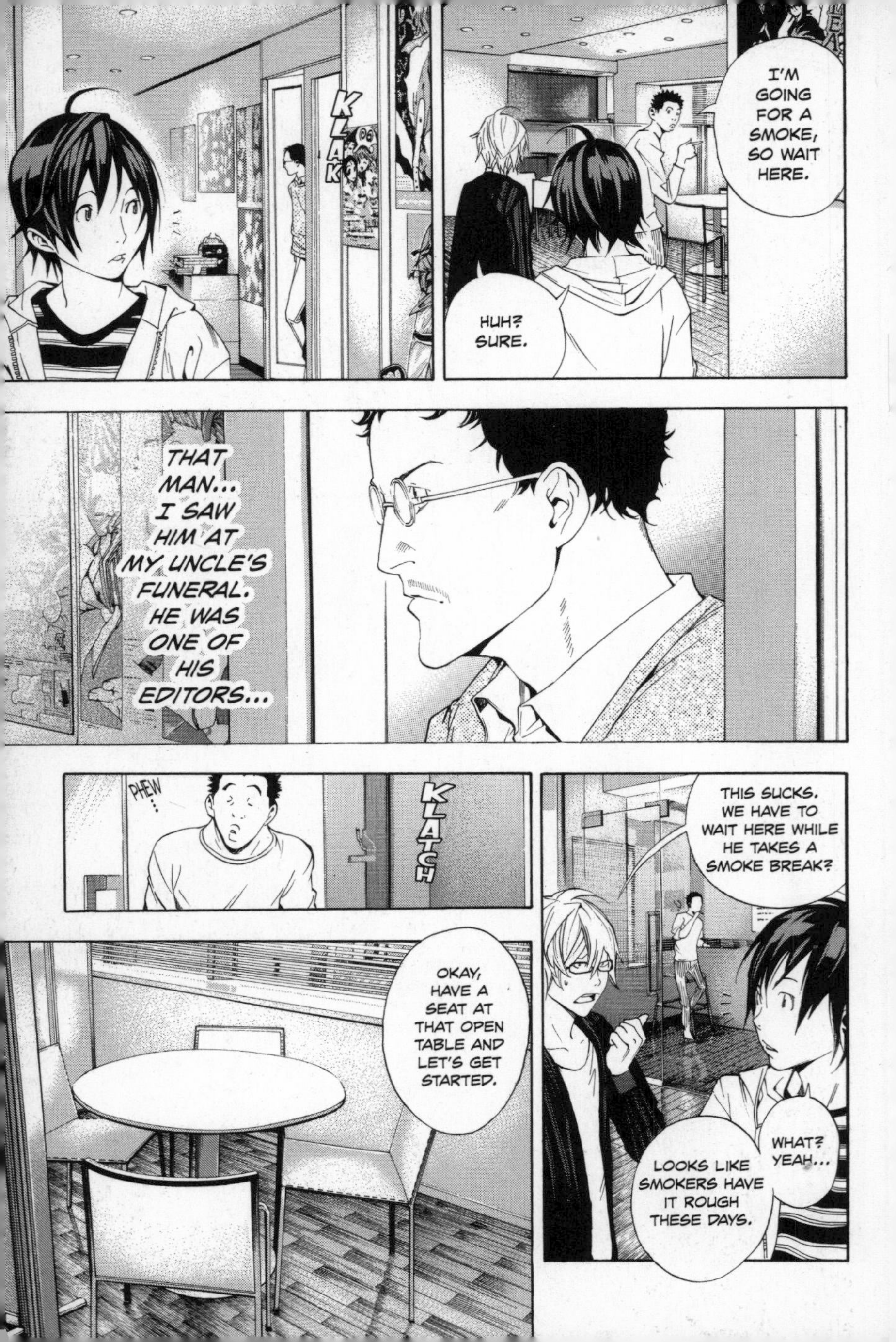
I'M GOING FOR A SMOKE, SO WAIT HERE.
HUH? SURE.
KLAK
THAT MAN... I SAW HIM AT MY UNCLE'S FUNERAL. HE WAS ONE OF HIS EDITORS...
THIS SUCKS. WE HAVE TO WAIT HERE WHILE HE TAKES A SMOKE BREAK?
LOOKS LIKE SMOKERS HAVE IT ROUGH THESE DAYS.
WHAT? YEAH...
PHEW...
KLATCH
OKAY, HAVE A SEAT AT THAT OPEN TABLE AND LET'S GET STARTED.

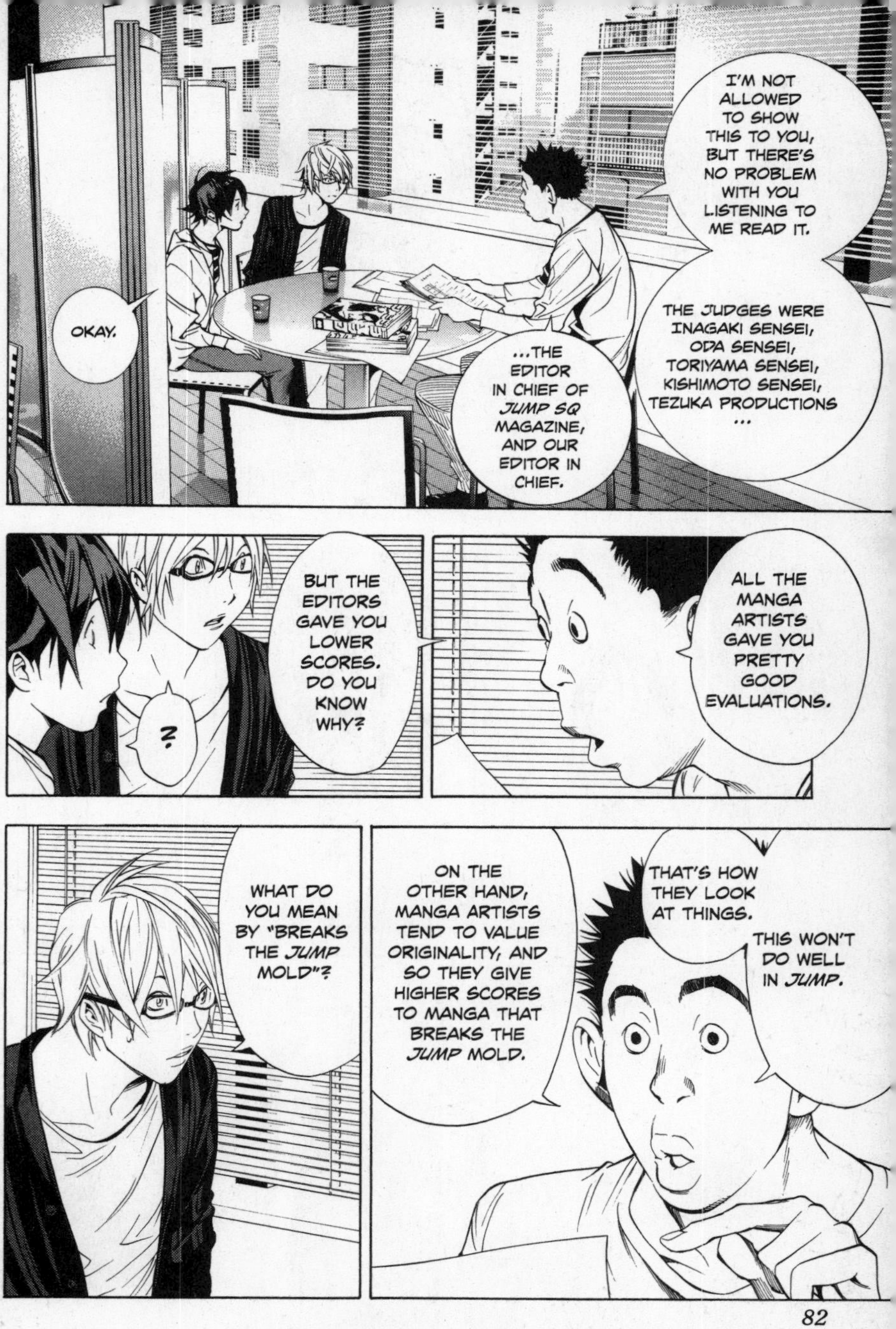
I'M NOT ALLOWED TO SHOW THIS TO YOU, BUT THERE'S NO PROBLEM WITH YOU LISTENING TO ME READ IT.
OKAY.
THE JUDGES WERE INAGAKI SENSEI, ODA SENSEI, TORIYAMA SENSEI, KISHIMOTO SENSEI, TEZUKA PRODUCTIONS ...
...THE EDITOR IN CHIEF OF *JUMP SQ* MAGAZINE, AND OUR EDITOR IN CHIEF.
ALL THE MANGA ARTISTS GAVE YOU PRETTY GOOD EVALUATIONS.
BUT THE EDITORS GAVE YOU LOWER SCORES. DO YOU KNOW WHY?
?
THIS WON'T DO WELL IN *JUMP*.
THAT'S HOW THEY LOOK AT THINGS.
ON THE OTHER HAND, MANGA ARTISTS TEND TO VALUE ORIGINALITY, AND SO THEY GIVE HIGHER SCORES TO MANGA THAT BREAKS THE *JUMP* MOLD.
WHAT DO YOU MEAN BY "BREAKS THE *JUMP* MOLD"?

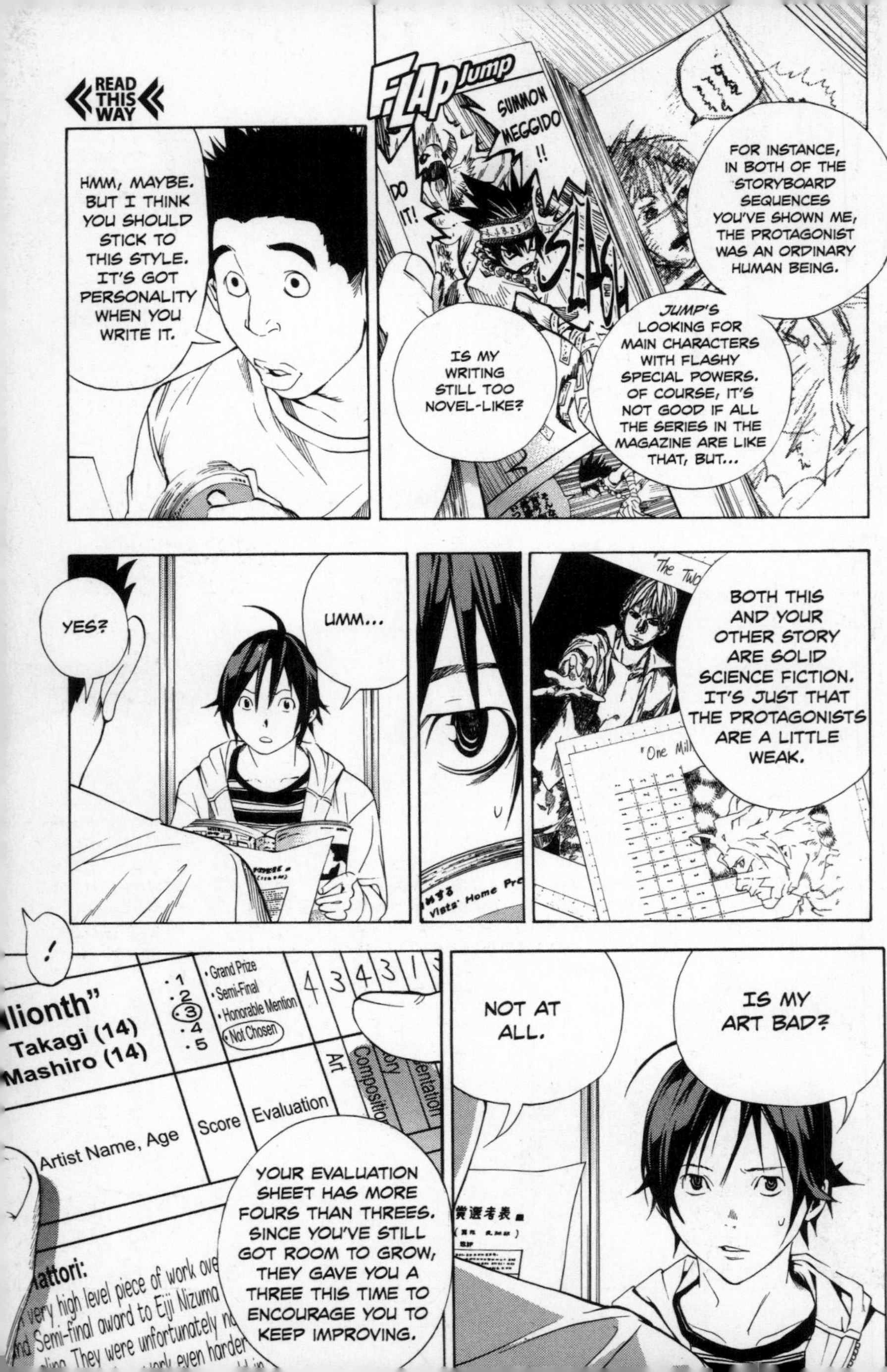
READ THIS WAY
FLAP
Jump
SUMMON MEGGIDO !!
DO IT!
FOR INSTANCE, IN BOTH OF THE STORYBOARD SEQUENCES YOU'VE SHOWN ME, THE PROTAGONIST WAS AN ORDINARY HUMAN BEING.
JUMP'S LOOKING FOR MAIN CHARACTERS WITH FLASHY SPECIAL POWERS. OF COURSE, IT'S NOT GOOD IF ALL THE SERIES IN THE MAGAZINE ARE LIKE THAT, BUT...
IS MY WRITING STILL TOO NOVEL-LIKE?
HMM, MAYBE. BUT I THINK YOU SHOULD STICK TO THIS STYLE. IT'S GOT PERSONALITY WHEN YOU WRITE IT.
The Two
"One Mill
BOTH THIS AND YOUR OTHER STORY ARE SOLID SCIENCE FICTION. IT'S JUST THAT THE PROTAGONISTS ARE A LITTLE WEAK.
Visits' Home Pro
UMM...
YES?
IS MY ART BAD?
NOT AT ALL.
!
llionth"
Takagi (14)
Mashiro (14)
1 2 3 4 5
Grand Prize
Semi-Final
Honorable Mention
Not Chosen
4 3 4 3 1
Art
Composition
Artist Name, Age
Score
Evaluation
Hattori:
very high level piece of work ove
Semi-final award to Eiji Nizuma
They were unfortunately no
YOUR EVALUATION SHEET HAS MORE FOURS THAN THREES. SINCE YOU'VE STILL GOT ROOM TO GROW, THEY GAVE YOU A THREE THIS TIME TO ENCOURAGE YOU TO KEEP IMPROVING.

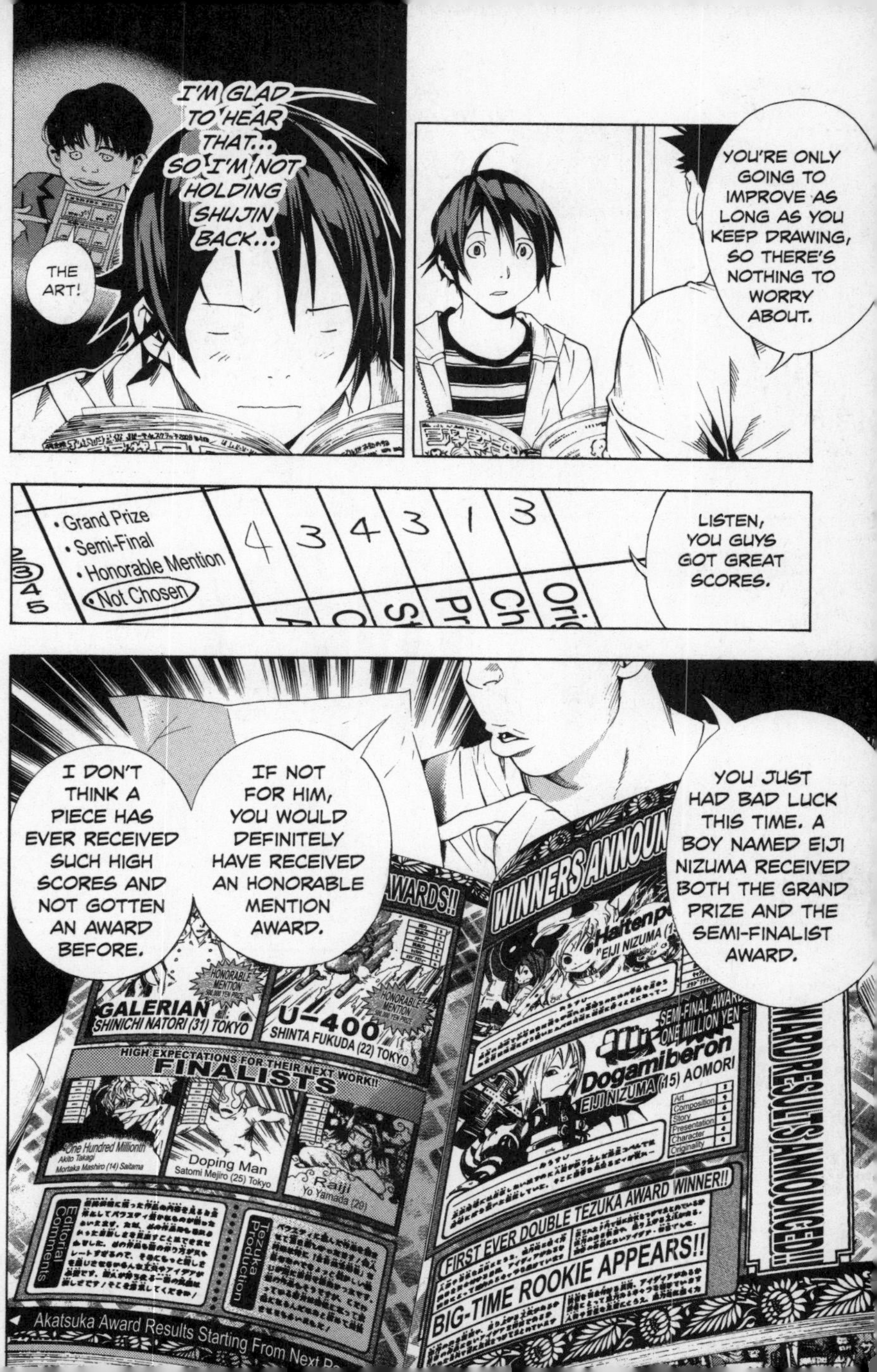
YOU'RE ONLY GOING TO IMPROVE AS LONG AS YOU KEEP DRAWING, SO THERE'S NOTHING TO WORRY ABOUT.
I'M GLAD TO HEAR THAT... SO I'M NOT HOLDING SHUJIN BACK...
THE ART!
LISTEN, YOU GUYS GOT GREAT SCORES.
• Grand Prize
• Semi-Final
• Honorable Mention
• Not Chosen
4 3 4 3 1 3
YOU JUST HAD BAD LUCK THIS TIME. A BOY NAMED EIJI NIZUMA RECEIVED BOTH THE GRAND PRIZE AND THE SEMI-FINALIST AWARD.
IF NOT FOR HIM, YOU WOULD DEFINITELY HAVE RECEIVED AN HONORABLE MENTION AWARD.
I DON'T THINK A PIECE HAS EVER RECEIVED SUCH HIGH SCORES AND NOT GOTTEN AN AWARD BEFORE.
WINNERS ANNOUN
Haitenpo
EIJI NIZUMA
SEMI-FINAL AWARD ONE MILLION YEN
Dogamiberon
EIJI NIZUMA (15) AOMORI
Art
Composition
Story
Presentation
Character
Originality
FIRST EVER DOUBLE TEZUKA AWARD WINNER!!
BIG-TIME ROOKIE APPEARS!!
AWARD RESULTS ANNOUNCED!!
AWARDS!!
HONORABLE MENTION
GALERIAN
SHINICHI NATORI (31) TOKYO
U-400
SHINTA FUKUDA (22) TOKYO
HIGH EXPECTATIONS FOR THEIR NEXT WORK!!
FINALISTS
One Hundred Millionth
Akito Takagi
Moritaka Mashiro (14) Saitama
Doping Man
Satomi Mejiro (25) Tokyo
Raiji
Yo Yamada (29)
Editorial Comments
Tezuka Production
Akatsuka Award Results Starting From Next Page

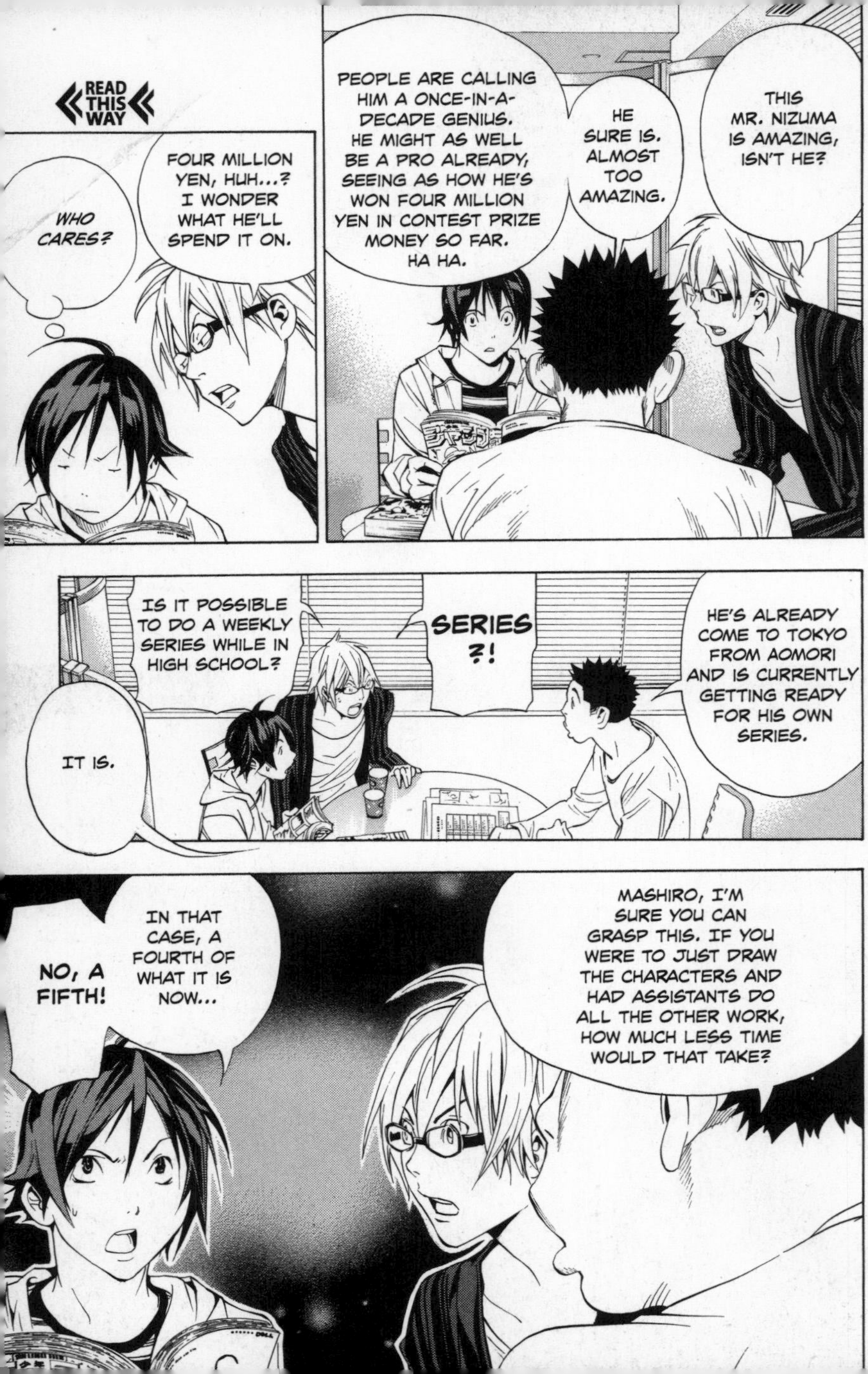
READ THIS WAY
THIS MR. NIZUMA IS AMAZING, ISN'T HE?
HE SURE IS. ALMOST TOO AMAZING.
PEOPLE ARE CALLING HIM A ONCE-IN-A-DECADE GENIUS. HE MIGHT AS WELL BE A PRO ALREADY, SEEING AS HOW HE'S WON FOUR MILLION YEN IN CONTEST PRIZE MONEY SO FAR. HA HA.
FOUR MILLION YEN, HUH...? I WONDER WHAT HE'LL SPEND IT ON.
WHO CARES?
HE'S ALREADY COME TO TOKYO FROM AOMORI AND IS CURRENTLY GETTING READY FOR HIS OWN SERIES.
SERIES ?!
IS IT POSSIBLE TO DO A WEEKLY SERIES WHILE IN HIGH SCHOOL?
IT IS.
MASHIRO, I'M SURE YOU CAN GRASP THIS. IF YOU WERE TO JUST DRAW THE CHARACTERS AND HAD ASSISTANTS DO ALL THE OTHER WORK, HOW MUCH LESS TIME WOULD THAT TAKE?
IN THAT CASE, A FOURTH OF WHAT IT IS NOW...
NO, A FIFTH!

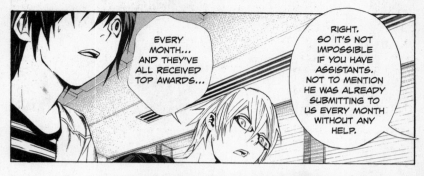

RIGHT. SO IT'S NOT IMPOSSIBLE IF YOU HAVE ASSISTANTS. NOT TO MENTION HE WAS ALREADY SUBMITTING TO US EVERY MONTH WITHOUT ANY HELP.
EVERY MONTH... AND THEY'VE ALL RECEIVED TOP AWARDS...
MAINLY BECAUSE OF THE ART, THE HARDEST TIME FOR A MANGA CREATOR IS BEFORE YOU MAKE YOUR DEBUT. THAT'S WHEN YOU HAVE TO DRAW ALL THE PAGES YOU SHOW TO A PUBLISHER OR SUBMIT TO AN AWARD BY YOURSELF.
MOST PEOPLE START HAVING TROUBLE FURTHERING THE STORY ONCE THEY GET A SERIES, WHICH CUTS INTO THEIR DRAWING TIME. BUT AT THE SAME TIME, THE QUALITY OF PAGES AND PACE PICKS UP BECAUSE YOU'RE DRAWING EVERY WEEK.
SORRY, I GOT OFF TRACK. JUDGING FROM THESE EVALUATION SHEETS AND MY OPINION...
...WHAT YOU'RE MISSING IS A MORE *JUMP*-LIKE MAIN CHARACTER.
THE STORY CAN BE SCIENCE FICTION OR ANYTHING ELSE. IF YOU'RE ABLE TO CREATE AN APPEALING CHARACTER, I PROMISE YOU THAT YOU WILL BE ABLE TO WIN AN AWARD NEXT TIME.
PLUS NIZUMA WON'T BE ENTERING THESE CONTESTS ANYMORE. HA HA.
OOO

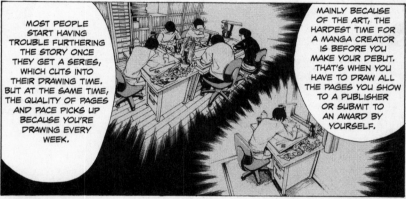

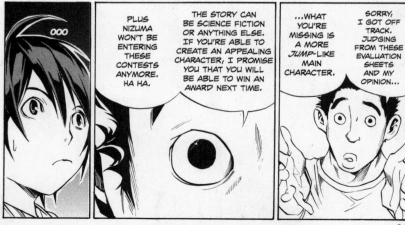

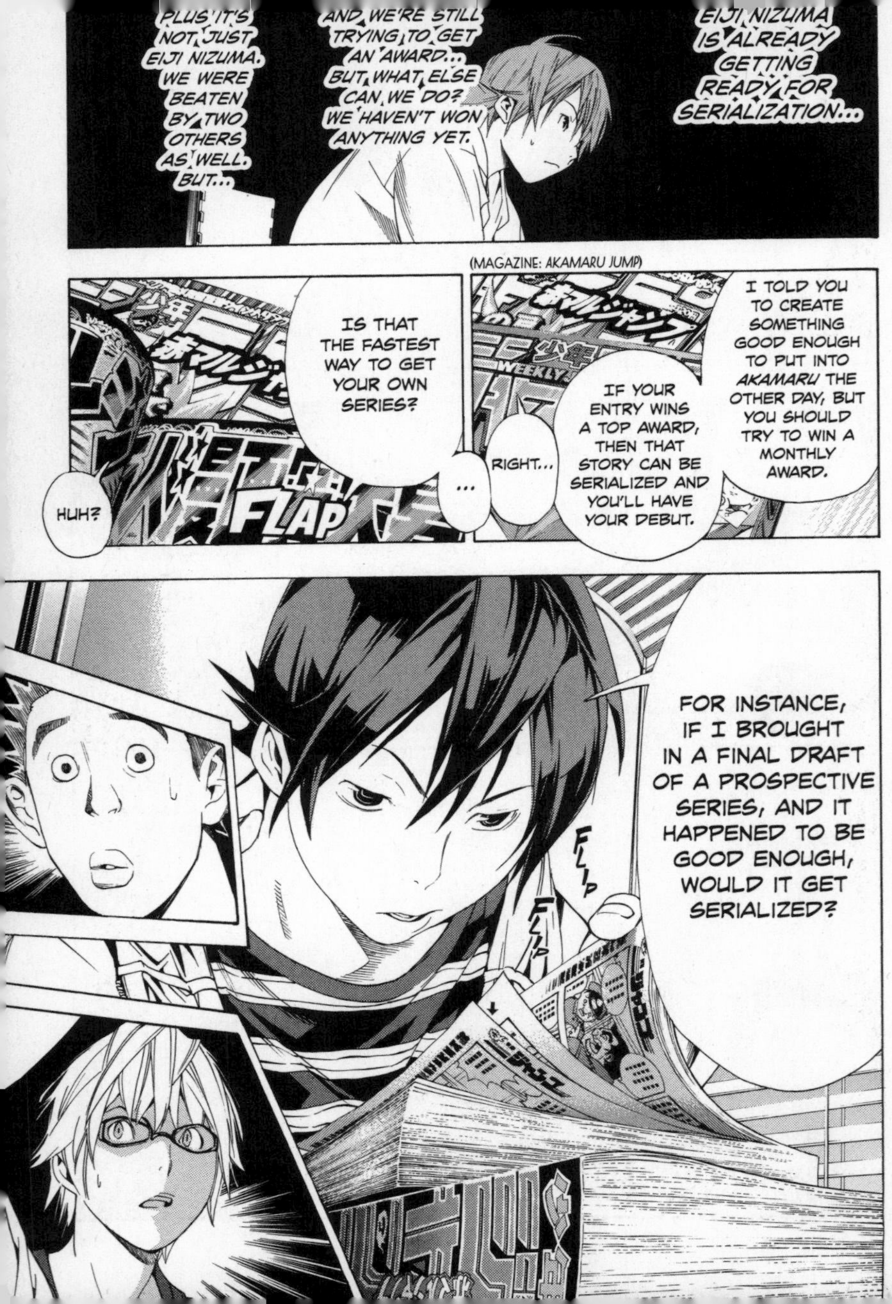
EIJI NIZUMA IS ALREADY GETTING READY FOR SERIALIZATION...
AND WE'RE STILL TRYING TO GET AN AWARD... BUT WHAT ELSE CAN WE DO? WE HAVEN'T WON ANYTHING YET.
PLUS IT'S NOT JUST EIJI NIZUMA. WE WERE BEATEN BY TWO OTHERS AS WELL. BUT...
(MAGAZINE: AKAMARU JUMP)
I TOLD YOU TO CREATE SOMETHING GOOD ENOUGH TO PUT INTO AKAMARU THE OTHER DAY, BUT YOU SHOULD TRY TO WIN A MONTHLY AWARD.
IF YOUR ENTRY WINS A TOP AWARD, THEN THAT STORY CAN BE SERIALIZED AND YOU'LL HAVE YOUR DEBUT.
RIGHT...
IS THAT THE FASTEST WAY TO GET YOUR OWN SERIES?
...
FLAP
HUH?
FOR INSTANCE, IF I BROUGHT IN A FINAL DRAFT OF A PROSPECTIVE SERIES, AND IT HAPPENED TO BE GOOD ENOUGH, WOULD IT GET SERIALIZED?
FLIP
FLIP

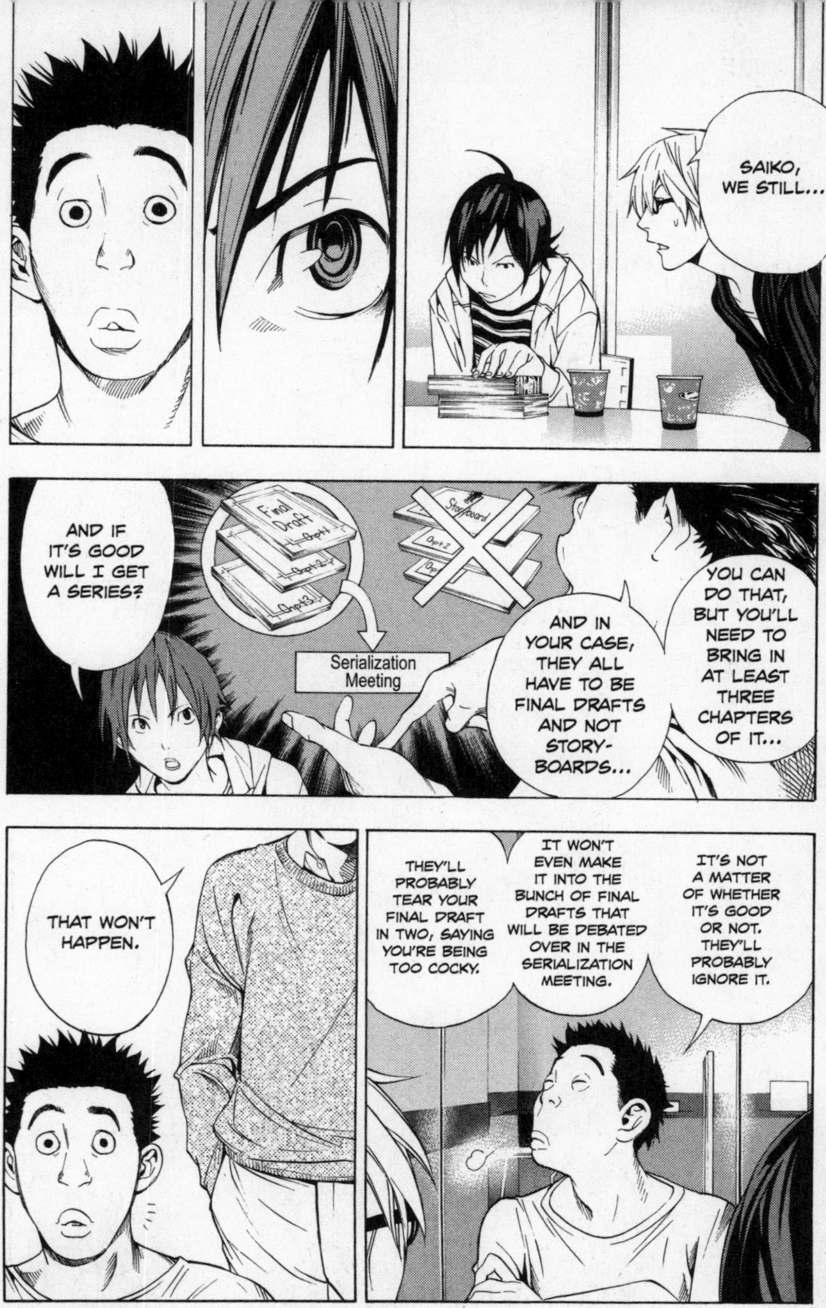
SAIKO, WE STILL...
YOU CAN DO THAT, BUT YOU'LL NEED TO BRING IN AT LEAST THREE CHAPTERS OF IT...
Storyboard
AND IN YOUR CASE, THEY ALL HAVE TO BE FINAL DRAFTS AND NOT STORY-BOARDS...
Final Draft
Serialization Meeting
AND IF IT'S GOOD WILL I GET A SERIES?
IT'S NOT A MATTER OF WHETHER IT'S GOOD OR NOT. THEY'LL PROBABLY IGNORE IT.
IT WON'T EVEN MAKE IT INTO THE BUNCH OF FINAL DRAFTS THAT WILL BE DEBATED OVER IN THE SERIALIZATION MEETING.
THEY'LL PROBABLY TEAR YOUR FINAL DRAFT IN TWO, SAYING YOU'RE BEING TOO COCKY.
THAT WON'T HAPPEN.

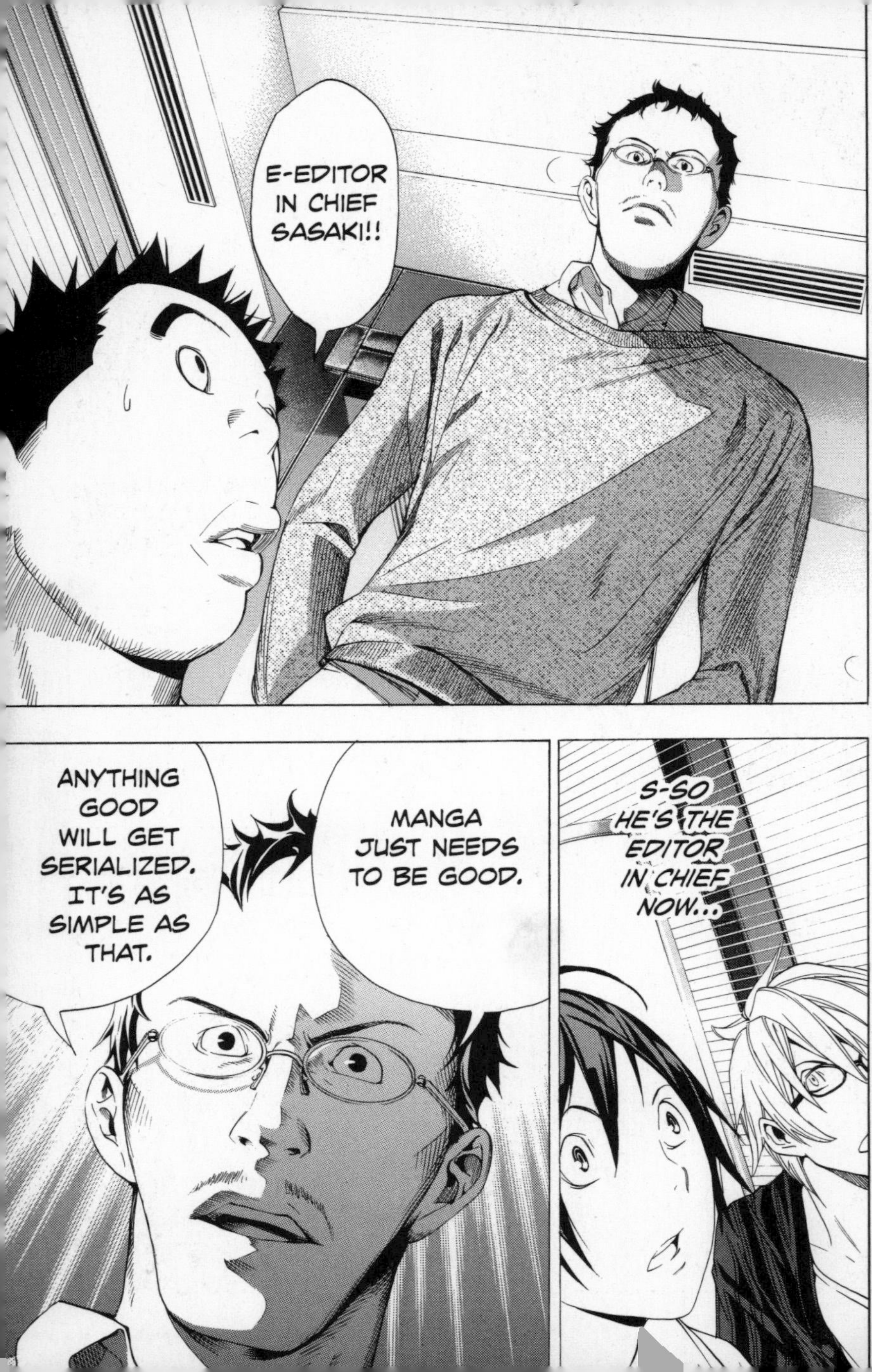
E-EDITOR IN CHIEF SASAKI!!
S-SO HE'S THE EDITOR IN CHIEF NOW...
MANGA JUST NEEDS TO BE GOOD.
ANYTHING GOOD WILL GET SERIALIZED. IT'S AS SIMPLE AS THAT.

OHBA'S STORYBOARD

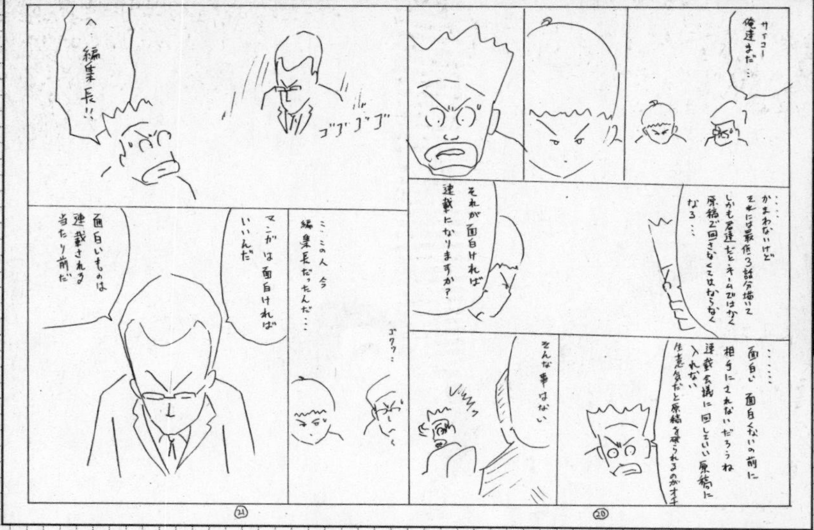
サイコー 俺達まだ・・・
・・・かまわないけど それには最低3話分描いて しかも君達だとネームではなく原稿で回さなくてはならなくなる・・・
それが面白ければ連載になりますか?
・・・・・・面白い 面白くないの前に 相手にされないだろうね 連載会議に回していい原稿に入れない 生意気だと原稿を破られるのがオチ
そんな事はない
20
ゴゴゴゴ
へ・・・編集長!!
ゴクッ・・・
こ・・・この人 今 編集長だったんだ・・・
マンガは面白ければいいんだ
面白いものは連載される 当たり前だ
21

OBATA'S STORYBOARD

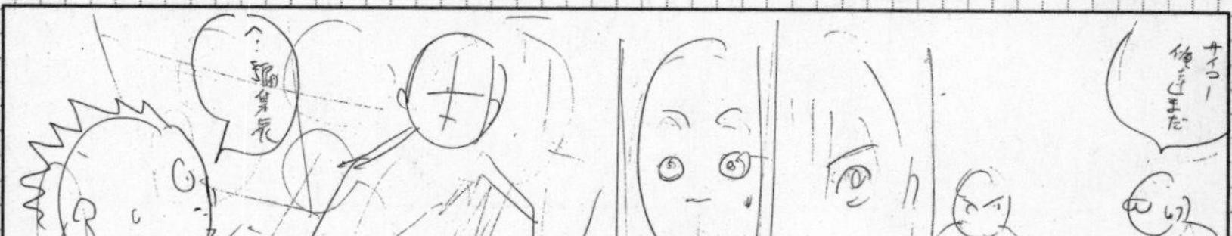
サイコー 俺達まだ
3話分
連載会議
それが面白ければ連載になりますか
そんな事はない
20
へ・・・編集長
こ・・・この人 今 編集長だったんだ
マンガは面白ければいいんだ
面白いものは連載される 当たり前だ
21

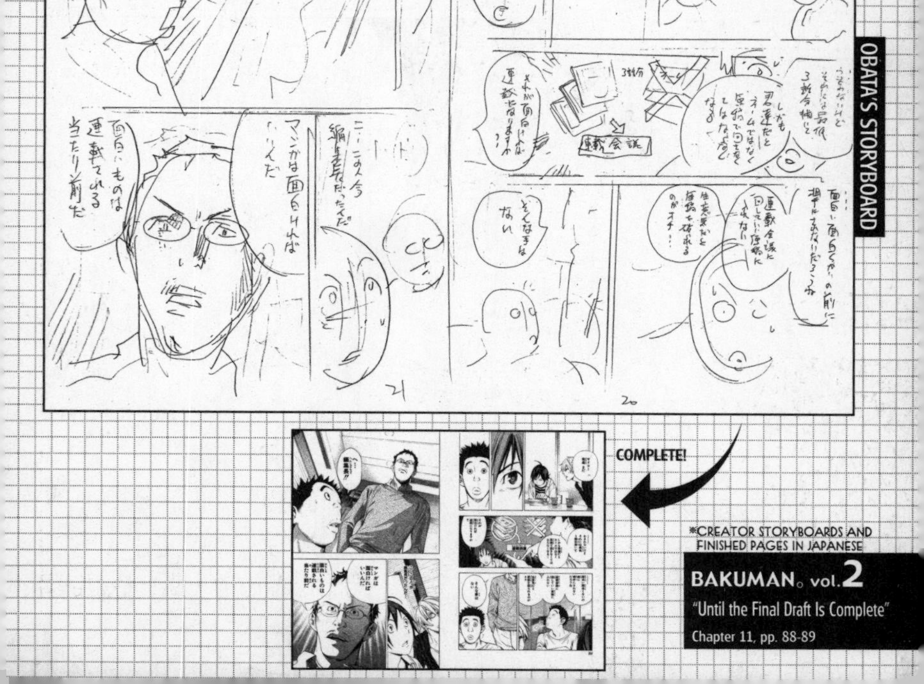

COMPLETE!

*CREATOR STORYBOARDS AND FINISHED PAGES IN JAPANESE

**BAKUMAN。 vol.2**

“Until the Final Draft Is Complete”

Chapter 11, pp. 88-89

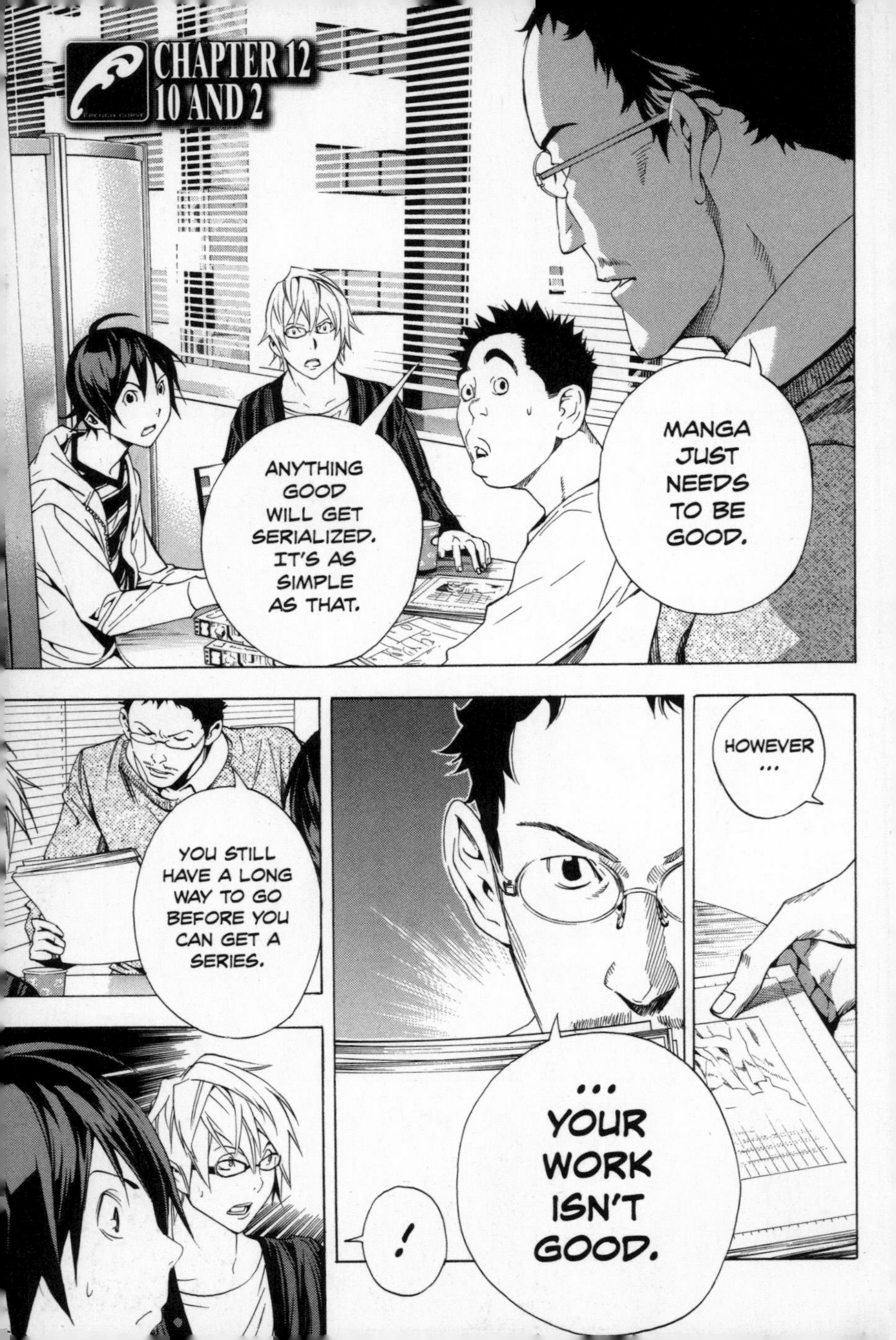
CHAPTER 12
10 AND 2
FRENCH CURVE
MANGA JUST NEEDS TO BE GOOD.
ANYTHING GOOD WILL GET SERIALIZED. IT'S AS SIMPLE AS THAT.
HOWEVER ...
... YOUR WORK ISN'T GOOD.
YOU STILL HAVE A LONG WAY TO GO BEFORE YOU CAN GET A SERIES.
!

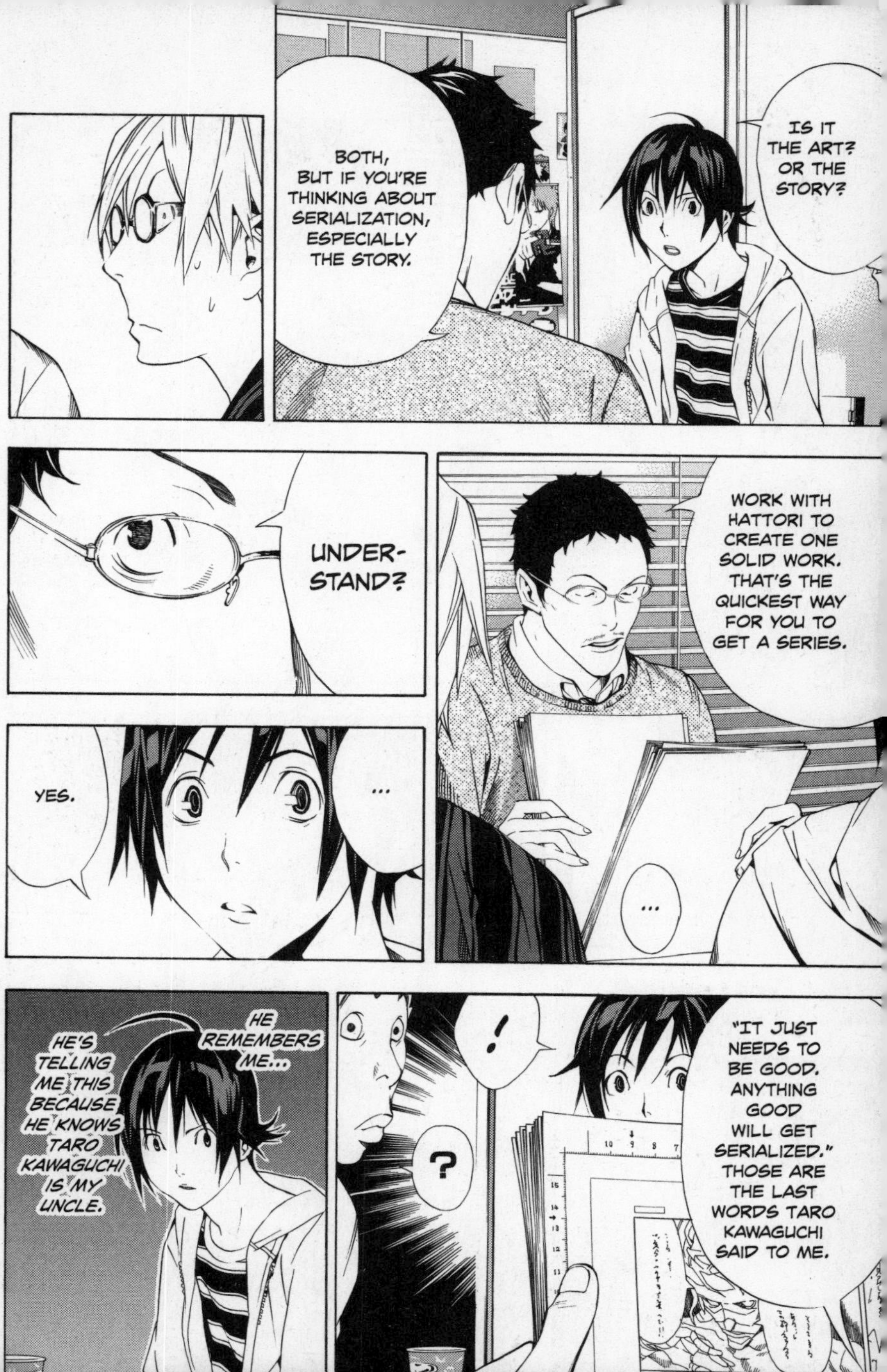
IS IT THE ART? OR THE STORY?
BOTH, BUT IF YOU'RE THINKING ABOUT SERIALIZATION, ESPECIALLY THE STORY.
WORK WITH HATTORI TO CREATE ONE SOLID WORK. THAT'S THE QUICKEST WAY FOR YOU TO GET A SERIES.
...
UNDER-STAND?
...
YES.
"IT JUST NEEDS TO BE GOOD. ANYTHING GOOD WILL GET SERIALIZED." THOSE ARE THE LAST WORDS TARO KAWAGUCHI SAID TO ME.
!
?
HE REMEMBERS ME...
HE'S TELLING ME THIS BECAUSE HE KNOWS TARO KAWAGUCHI IS MY UNCLE.

READ THIS WAY

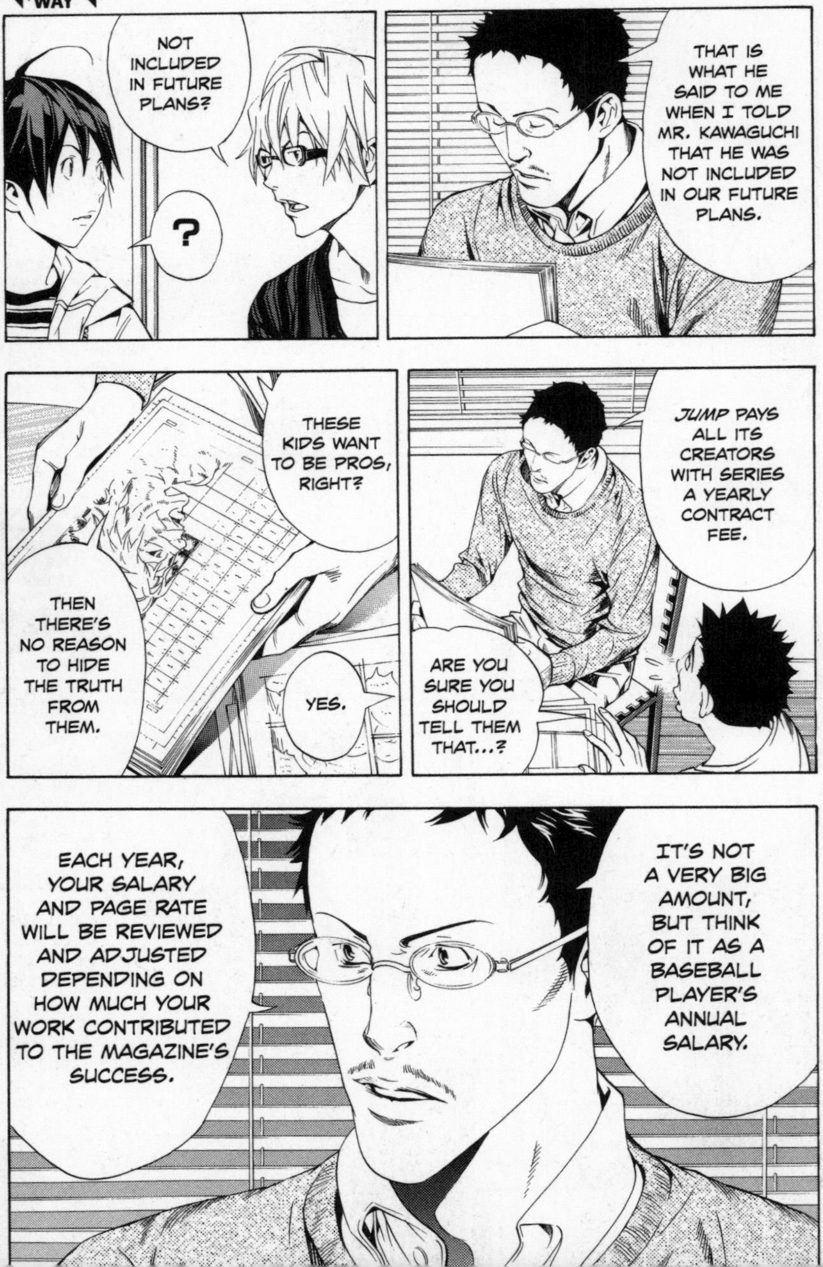

THAT IS WHAT HE SAID TO ME WHEN I TOLD MR. KAWAGUCHI THAT HE WAS NOT INCLUDED IN OUR FUTURE PLANS.
NOT INCLUDED IN FUTURE PLANS?
?
JUMP PAYS ALL ITS CREATORS WITH SERIES A YEARLY CONTRACT FEE.
ARE YOU SURE YOU SHOULD TELL THEM THAT...?
THESE KIDS WANT TO BE PROS, RIGHT?
YES.
THEN THERE'S NO REASON TO HIDE THE TRUTH FROM THEM.
IT'S NOT A VERY BIG AMOUNT, BUT THINK OF IT AS A BASEBALL PLAYER'S ANNUAL SALARY.
EACH YEAR, YOUR SALARY AND PAGE RATE WILL BE REVIEWED AND ADJUSTED DEPENDING ON HOW MUCH YOUR WORK CONTRIBUTED TO THE MAGAZINE'S SUCCESS.

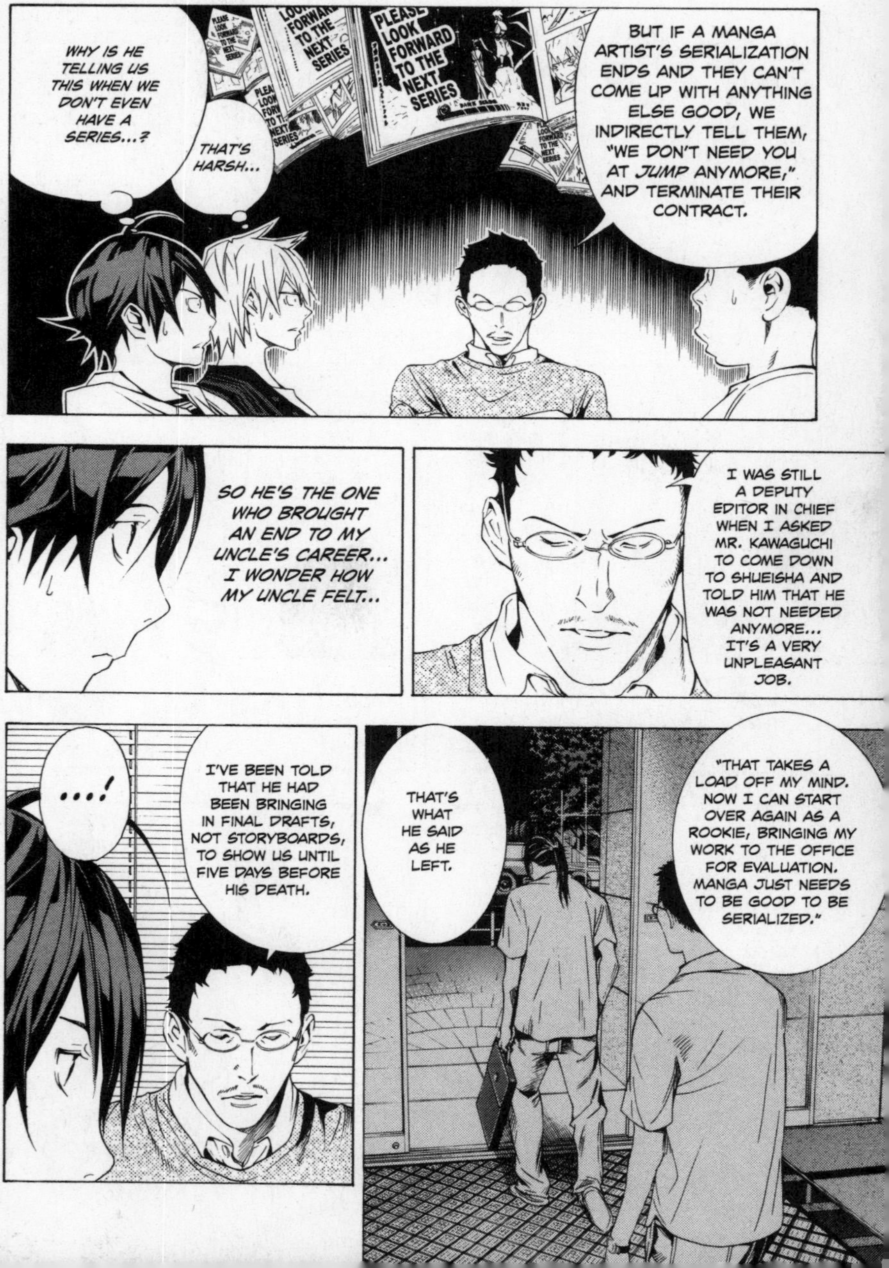
PLEASE LOOK FORWARD TO THE NEXT SERIES
BUT IF A MANGA ARTIST'S SERIALIZATION ENDS AND THEY CAN'T COME UP WITH ANYTHING ELSE GOOD, WE INDIRECTLY TELL THEM, "WE DON'T NEED YOU AT *JUMP* ANYMORE," AND TERMINATE THEIR CONTRACT.
THAT'S HARSH...
*WHY IS HE TELLING US THIS WHEN WE DON'T EVEN HAVE A SERIES...?*
I WAS STILL A DEPUTY EDITOR IN CHIEF WHEN I ASKED MR. KAWAGUCHI TO COME DOWN TO SHUEISHA AND TOLD HIM THAT HE WAS NOT NEEDED ANYMORE... IT'S A VERY UNPLEASANT JOB.
*SO HE'S THE ONE WHO BROUGHT AN END TO MY UNCLE'S CAREER... I WONDER HOW MY UNCLE FELT...*
"THAT TAKES A LOAD OFF MY MIND. NOW I CAN START OVER AGAIN AS A ROOKIE, BRINGING MY WORK TO THE OFFICE FOR EVALUATION. MANGA JUST NEEDS TO BE GOOD TO BE SERIALIZED."
THAT'S WHAT HE SAID AS HE LEFT.
I'VE BEEN TOLD THAT HE HAD BEEN BRINGING IN FINAL DRAFTS, NOT STORYBOARDS, TO SHOW US UNTIL FIVE DAYS BEFORE HIS DEATH.
...!

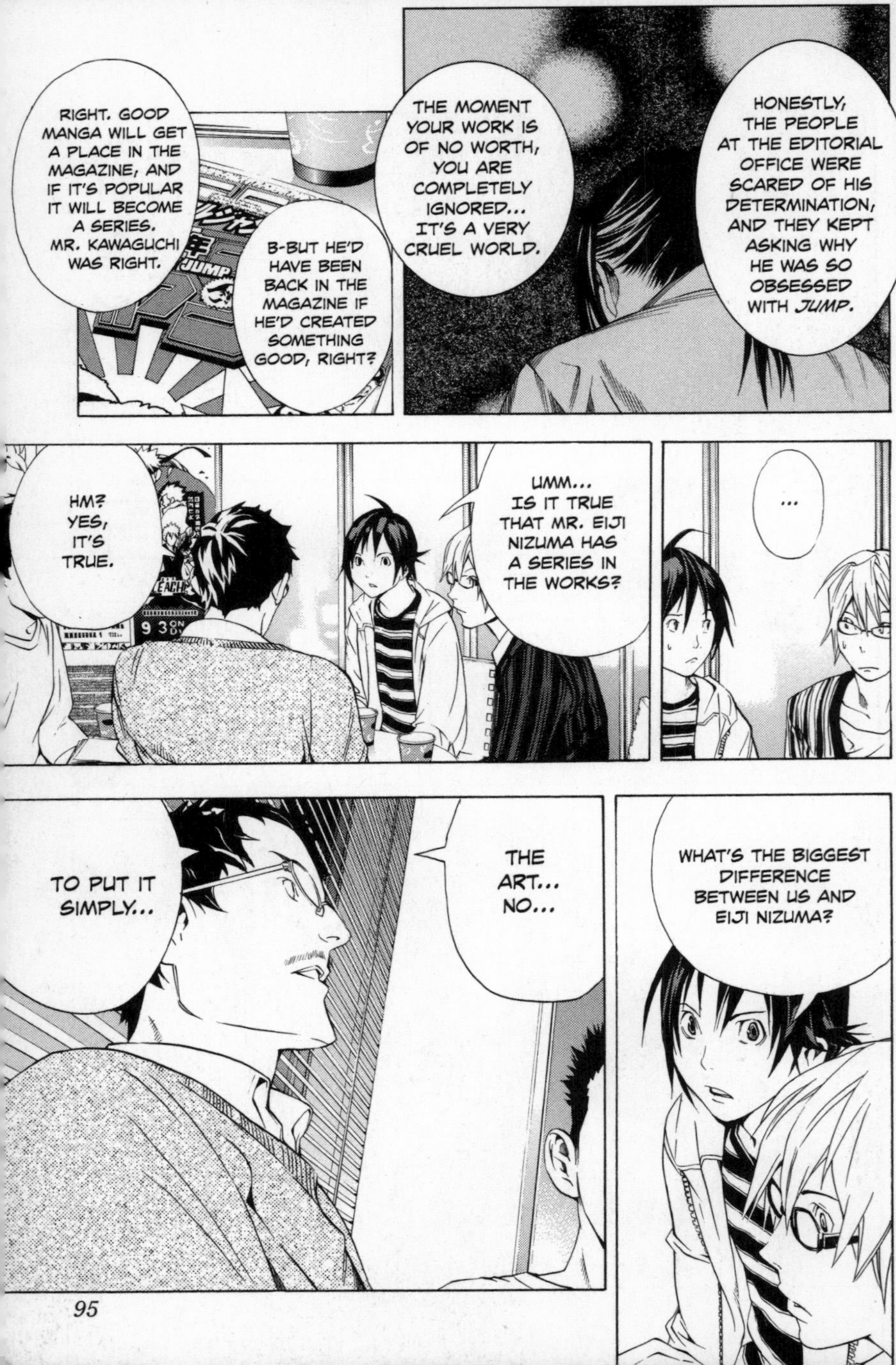
HONESTLY, THE PEOPLE AT THE EDITORIAL OFFICE WERE SCARED OF HIS DETERMINATION, AND THEY KEPT ASKING WHY HE WAS SO OBSESSED WITH *JUMP*.
THE MOMENT YOUR WORK IS OF NO WORTH, YOU ARE COMPLETELY IGNORED... IT'S A VERY CRUEL WORLD.
B-BUT HE'D HAVE BEEN BACK IN THE MAGAZINE IF HE'D CREATED SOMETHING GOOD, RIGHT?
RIGHT. GOOD MANGA WILL GET A PLACE IN THE MAGAZINE, AND IF IT'S POPULAR IT WILL BECOME A SERIES. MR. KAWAGUCHI WAS RIGHT.
...
UMM... IS IT TRUE THAT MR. EIJI NIZUMA HAS A SERIES IN THE WORKS?
HM? YES, IT'S TRUE.
WHAT'S THE BIGGEST DIFFERENCE BETWEEN US AND EIJI NIZUMA?
THE ART... NO...
TO PUT IT SIMPLY...

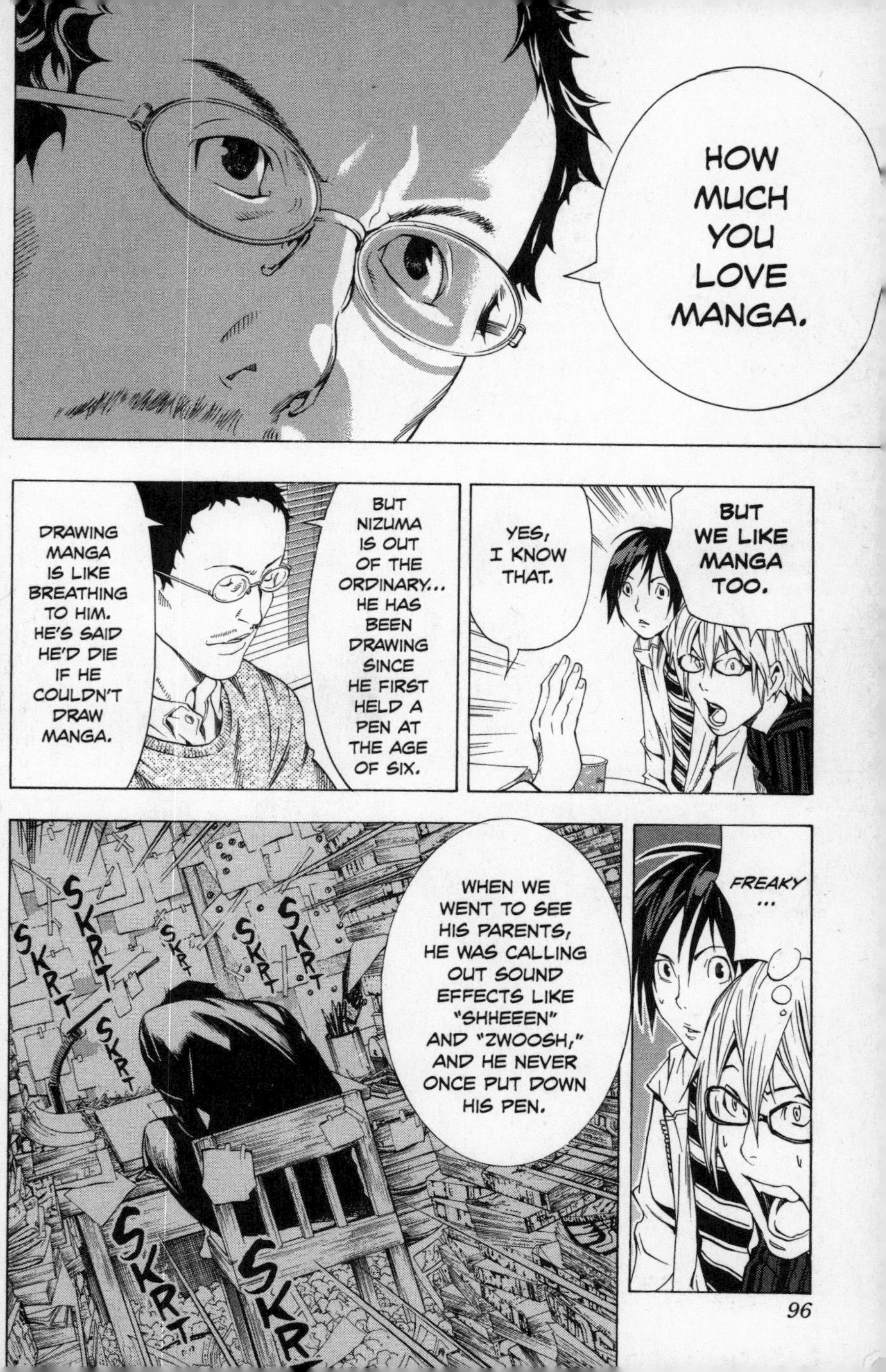
HOW MUCH YOU LOVE MANGA.
BUT WE LIKE MANGA TOO.
YES, I KNOW THAT.
BUT NIZUMA IS OUT OF THE ORDINARY... HE HAS BEEN DRAWING SINCE HE FIRST HELD A PEN AT THE AGE OF SIX.
DRAWING MANGA IS LIKE BREATHING TO HIM. HE'S SAID HE'D DIE IF HE COULDN'T DRAW MANGA.
FREAKY ...
WHEN WE WENT TO SEE HIS PARENTS, HE WAS CALLING OUT SOUND EFFECTS LIKE "SHHEEEN" AND "ZWOOSH," AND HE NEVER ONCE PUT DOWN HIS PEN.
SKRT
SKRT
SKRT
SKRT
SKRT
SKRT
SKRT
SKRT
SKR

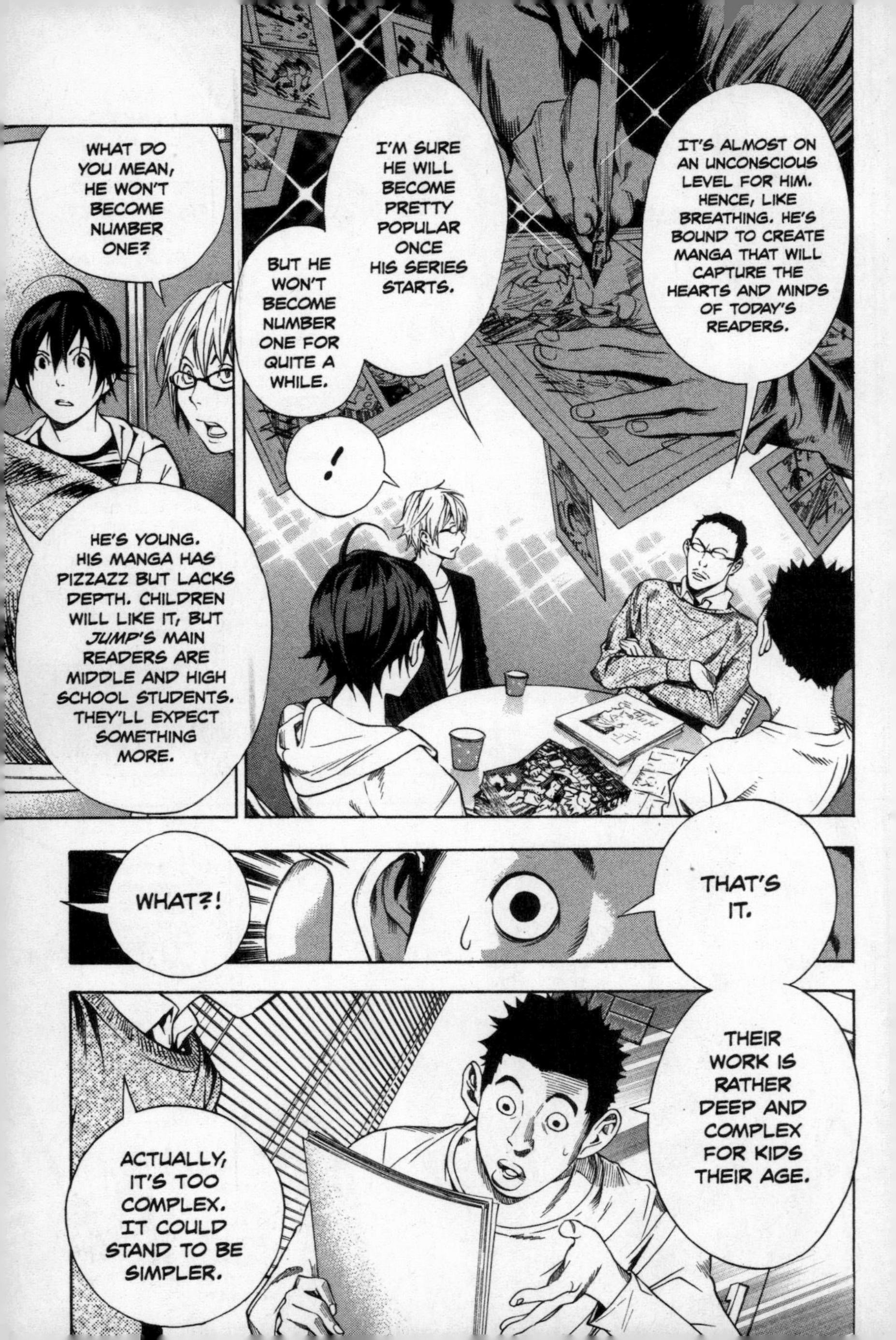
IT'S ALMOST ON AN UNCONSCIOUS LEVEL FOR HIM. HENCE, LIKE BREATHING. HE'S BOUND TO CREATE MANGA THAT WILL CAPTURE THE HEARTS AND MINDS OF TODAY'S READERS.
I'M SURE HE WILL BECOME PRETTY POPULAR ONCE HIS SERIES STARTS.
BUT HE WON'T BECOME NUMBER ONE FOR QUITE A WHILE.
!
WHAT DO YOU MEAN, HE WON'T BECOME NUMBER ONE?
HE'S YOUNG. HIS MANGA HAS PIZZAZZ BUT LACKS DEPTH. CHILDREN WILL LIKE IT, BUT *JUMP*'S MAIN READERS ARE MIDDLE AND HIGH SCHOOL STUDENTS. THEY'LL EXPECT SOMETHING MORE.
THAT'S IT.
WHAT?!
THEIR WORK IS RATHER DEEP AND COMPLEX FOR KIDS THEIR AGE.
ACTUALLY, IT'S TOO COMPLEX. IT COULD STAND TO BE SIMPLER.

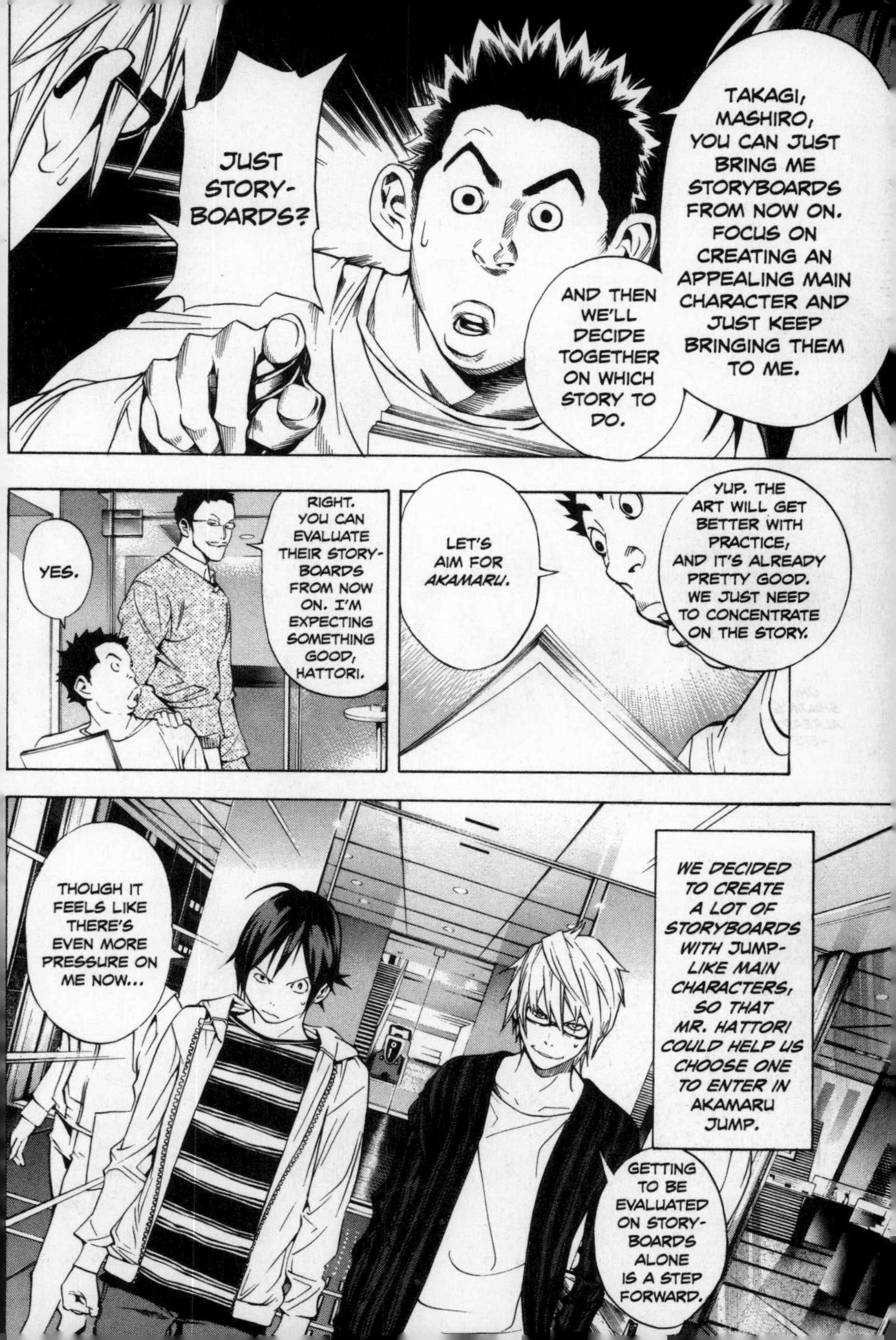
TAKAGI, MASHIRO, YOU CAN JUST BRING ME STORYBOARDS FROM NOW ON. FOCUS ON CREATING AN APPEALING MAIN CHARACTER AND JUST KEEP BRINGING THEM TO ME.
AND THEN WE'LL DECIDE TOGETHER ON WHICH STORY TO DO.
JUST STORY-BOARDS?
YUP. THE ART WILL GET BETTER WITH PRACTICE, AND IT'S ALREADY PRETTY GOOD. WE JUST NEED TO CONCENTRATE ON THE STORY.
LET'S AIM FOR *AKAMARU*.
RIGHT. YOU CAN EVALUATE THEIR STORY-BOARDS FROM NOW ON. I'M EXPECTING SOMETHING GOOD, HATTORI.
YES.
*WE DECIDED TO CREATE A LOT OF STORYBOARDS WITH JUMP-LIKE MAIN CHARACTERS, SO THAT MR. HATTORI COULD HELP US CHOOSE ONE TO ENTER IN AKAMARU JUMP.*
GETTING TO BE EVALUATED ON STORY-BOARDS ALONE IS A STEP FORWARD.
THOUGH IT FEELS LIKE THERE'S EVEN MORE PRESSURE ON ME NOW...

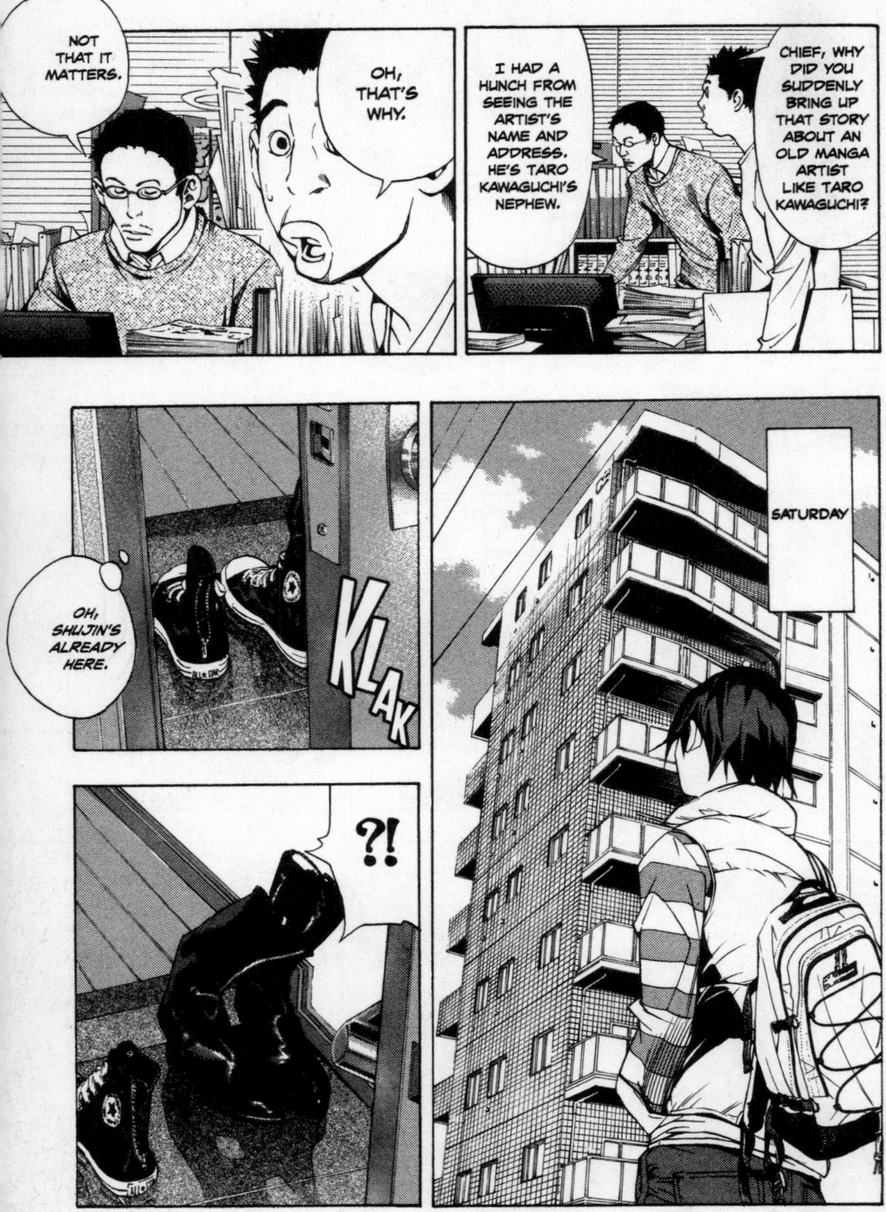
CHIEF, WHY DID YOU SUDDENLY BRING UP THAT STORY ABOUT AN OLD MANGA ARTIST LIKE TARO KAWAGUCHI?
I HAD A HUNCH FROM SEEING THE ARTIST'S NAME AND ADDRESS. HE'S TARO KAWAGUCHI'S NEPHEW.
OH, THAT'S WHY.
NOT THAT IT MATTERS.
SATURDAY
OH, SHUJIN'S ALREADY HERE.
KLAK
?!

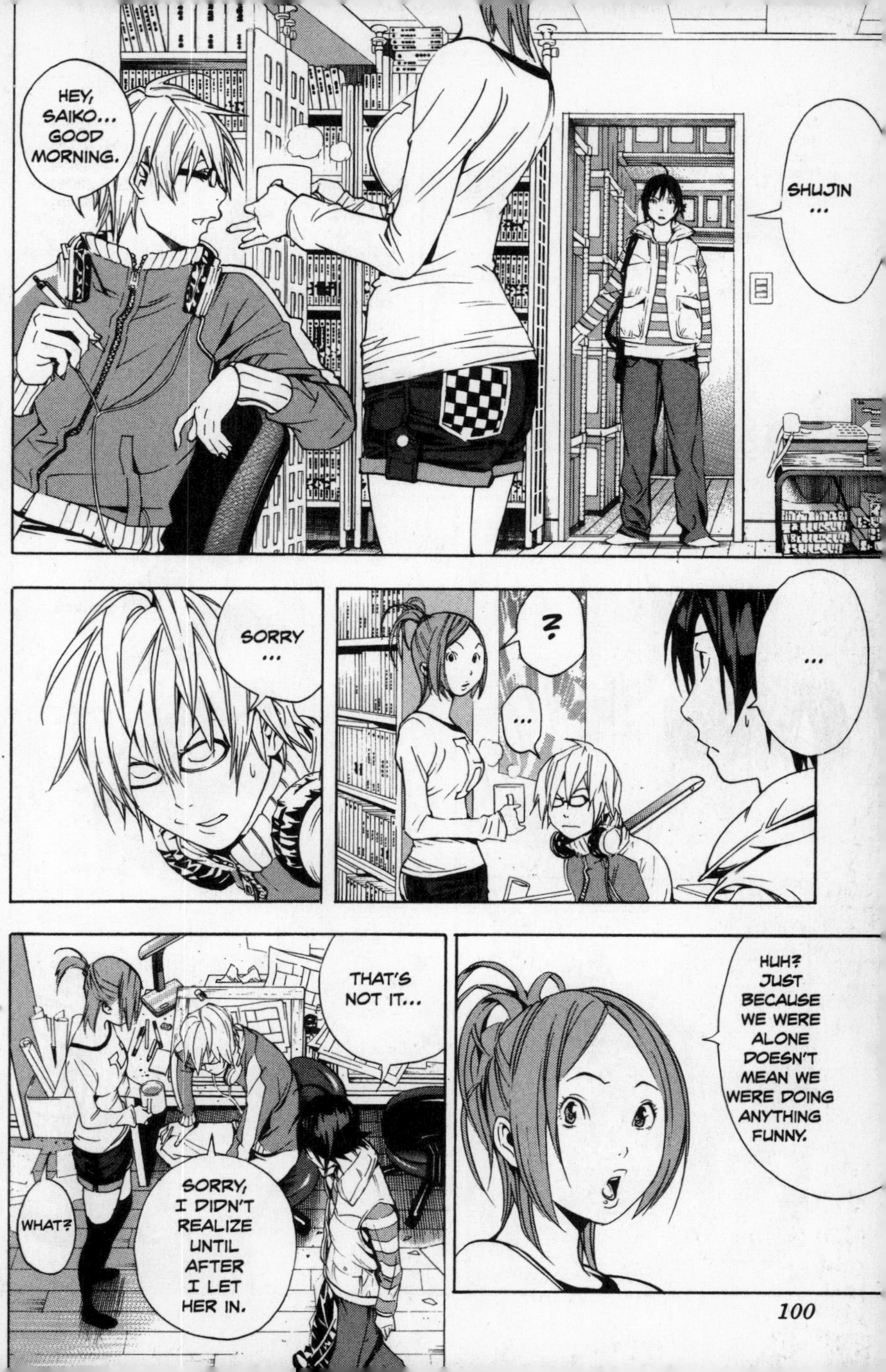
SHUJIN ...
HEY, SAIKO... GOOD MORNING.
...
?
...
SORRY ...
HUH? JUST BECAUSE WE WERE ALONE DOESN'T MEAN WE WERE DOING ANYTHING FUNNY.
THAT'S NOT IT...
SORRY, I DIDN'T REALIZE UNTIL AFTER I LET HER IN.
WHAT?

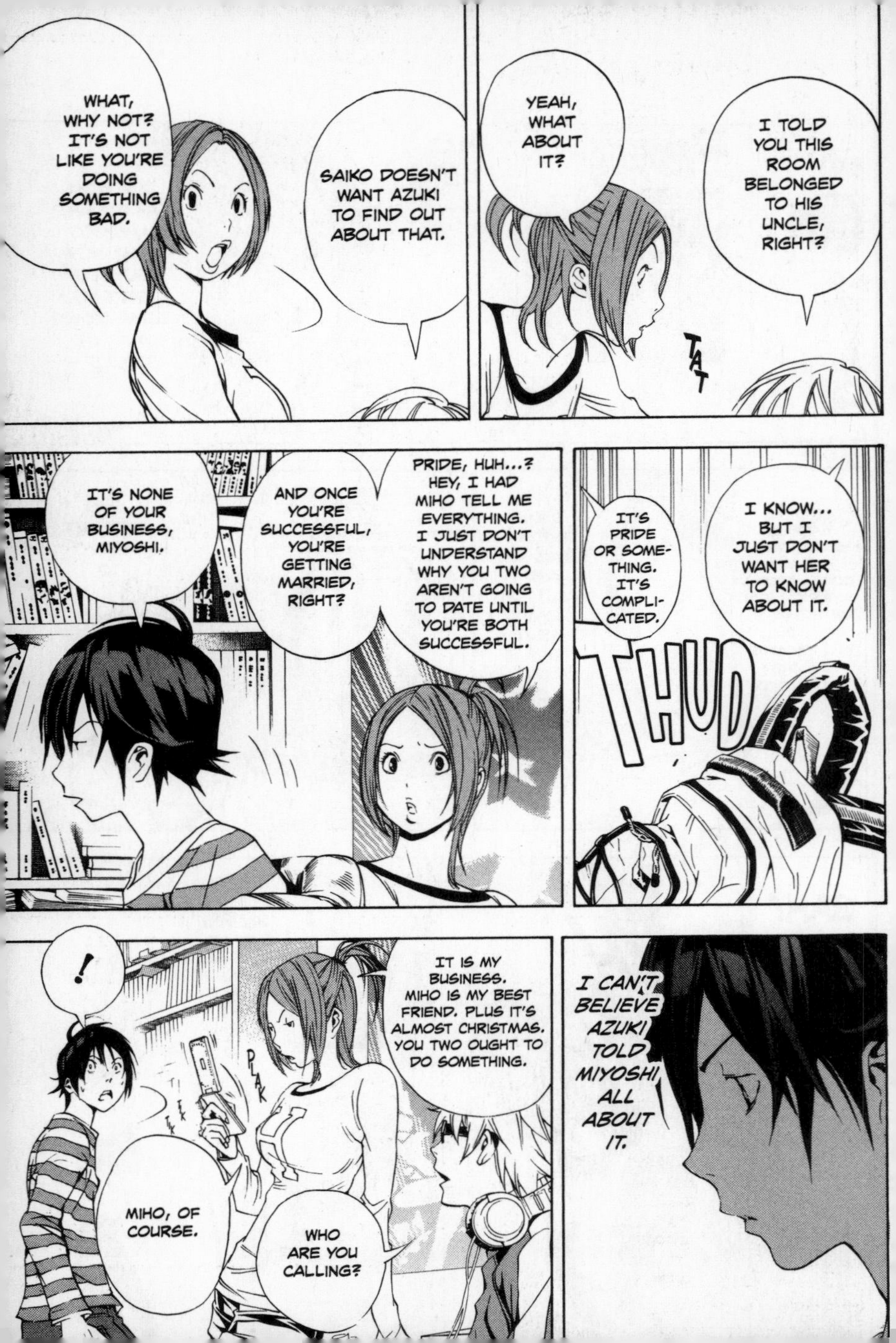
I TOLD YOU THIS ROOM BELONGED TO HIS UNCLE, RIGHT?
YEAH, WHAT ABOUT IT?
TAT
SAIKO DOESN'T WANT AZUKI TO FIND OUT ABOUT THAT.
WHAT, WHY NOT? IT'S NOT LIKE YOU'RE DOING SOMETHING BAD.
I KNOW... BUT I JUST DON'T WANT HER TO KNOW ABOUT IT.
IT'S PRIDE OR SOME-THING. IT'S COMPLI-CATED.
THUD
PRIDE, HUH...? HEY, I HAD MIHO TELL ME EVERYTHING. I JUST DON'T UNDERSTAND WHY YOU TWO AREN'T GOING TO DATE UNTIL YOU'RE BOTH SUCCESSFUL.
AND ONCE YOU'RE SUCCESSFUL, YOU'RE GETTING MARRIED, RIGHT?
IT'S NONE OF YOUR BUSINESS, MIYOSHI.
I CAN'T BELIEVE AZUKI TOLD MIYOSHI ALL ABOUT IT.
IT IS MY BUSINESS. MIHO IS MY BEST FRIEND. PLUS IT'S ALMOST CHRISTMAS. YOU TWO OUGHT TO DO SOMETHING.
PLAK
!
WHO ARE YOU CALLING?
MIHO, OF COURSE.

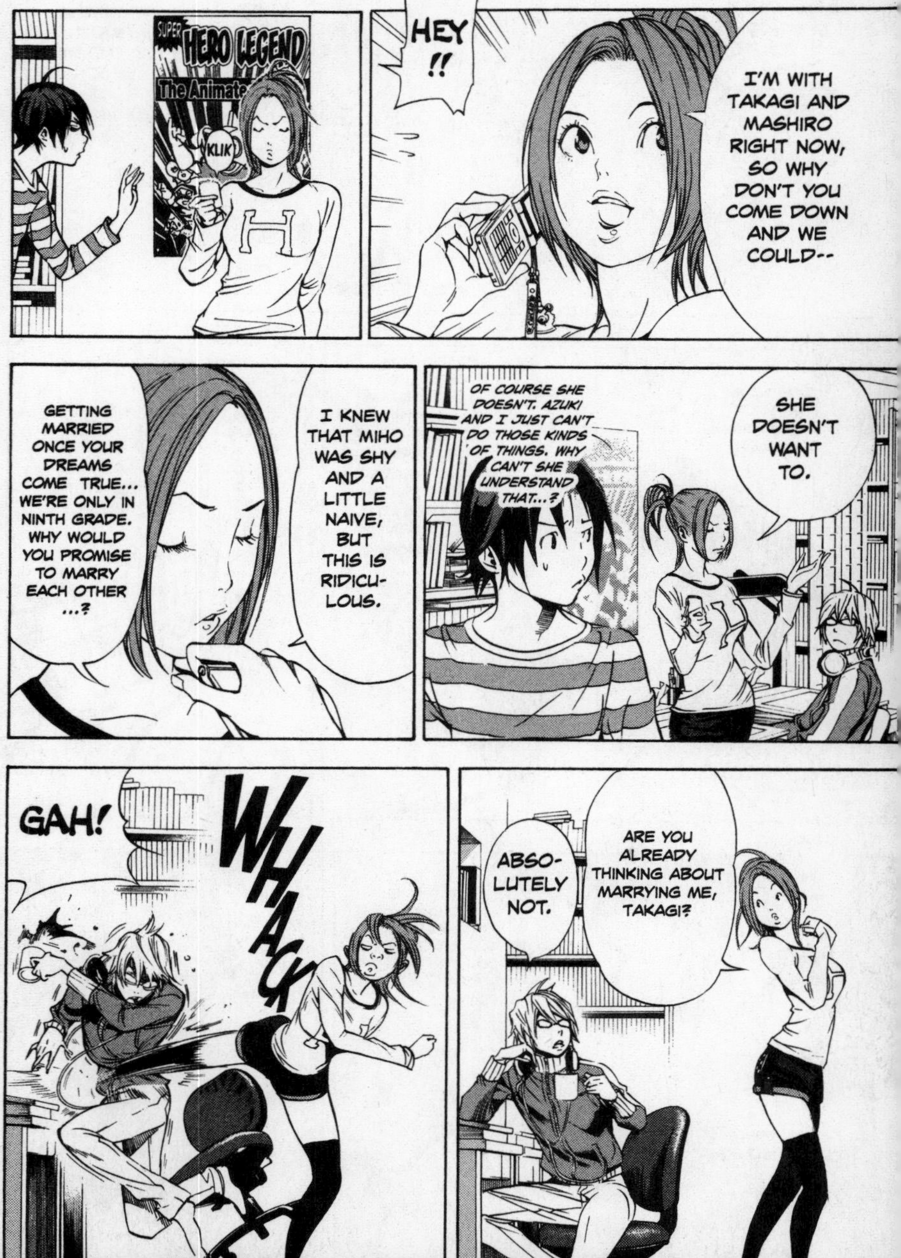
HEY !!
I'M WITH TAKAGI AND MASHIRO RIGHT NOW, SO WHY DON'T YOU COME DOWN AND WE COULD--
SUPER HERO LEGEND
KLIK
SHE DOESN'T WANT TO.
OF COURSE SHE DOESN'T. AZUKI AND I JUST CAN'T DO THOSE KINDS OF THINGS. WHY CAN'T SHE UNDERSTAND THAT...?
I KNEW THAT MIHO WAS SHY AND A LITTLE NAIVE, BUT THIS IS RIDICU-LOUS.
GETTING MARRIED ONCE YOUR DREAMS COME TRUE... WE'RE ONLY IN NINTH GRADE. WHY WOULD YOU PROMISE TO MARRY EACH OTHER ...?
ARE YOU ALREADY THINKING ABOUT MARRYING ME, TAKAGI?
ABSO-LUTELY NOT.
WHACK
GAH!

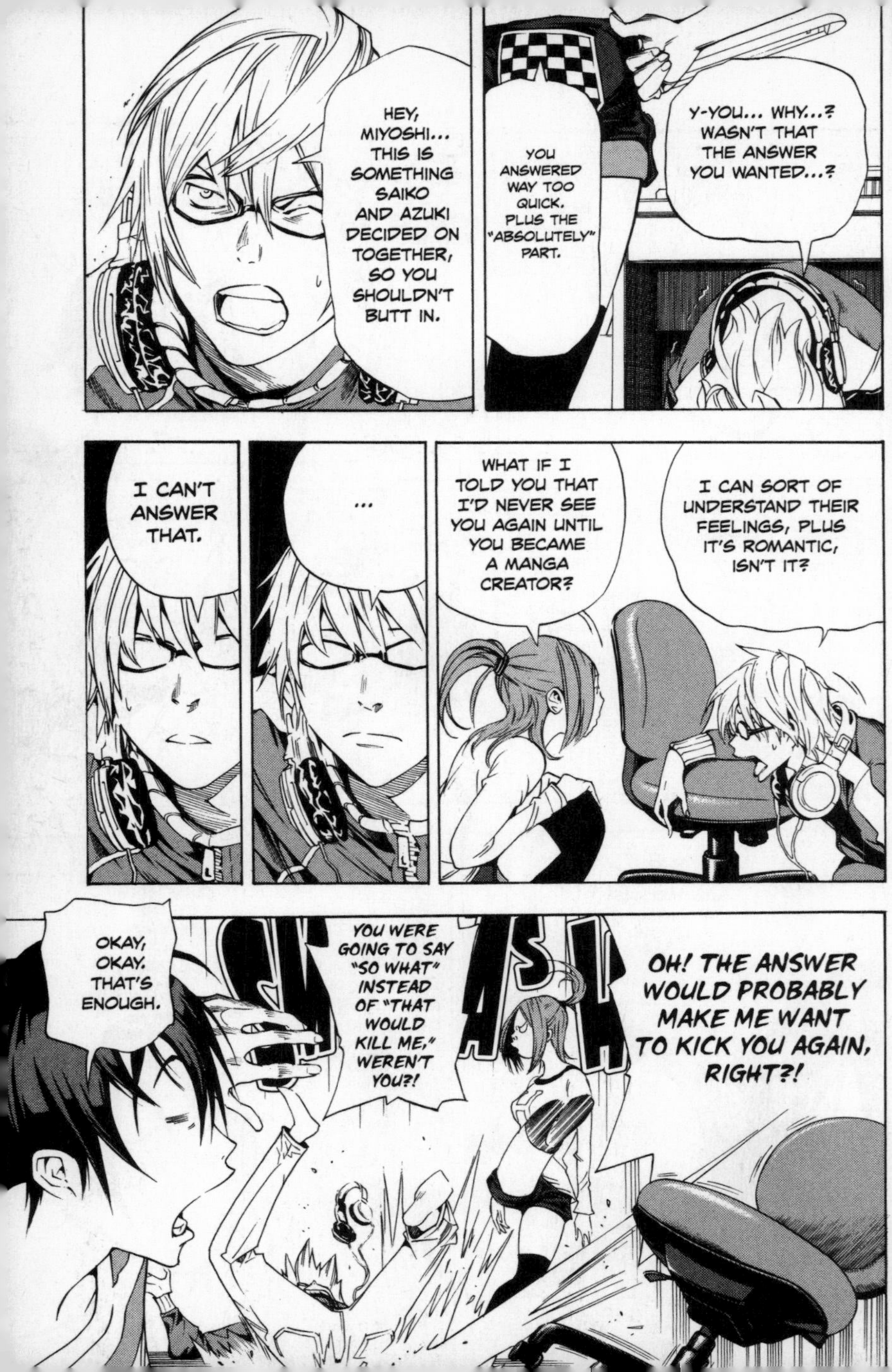
Y-YOU... WHY...? WASN'T THAT THE ANSWER YOU WANTED...?
YOU ANSWERED WAY TOO QUICK. PLUS THE "ABSOLUTELY" PART.
HEY, MIYOSHI... THIS IS SOMETHING SAIKO AND AZUKI DECIDED ON TOGETHER, SO YOU SHOULDN'T BUTT IN.
I CAN SORT OF UNDERSTAND THEIR FEELINGS, PLUS IT'S ROMANTIC, ISN'T IT?
WHAT IF I TOLD YOU THAT I'D NEVER SEE YOU AGAIN UNTIL YOU BECAME A MANGA CREATOR?
...
I CAN'T ANSWER THAT.
OH! THE ANSWER WOULD PROBABLY MAKE ME WANT TO KICK YOU AGAIN, RIGHT?!
YOU WERE GOING TO SAY "SO WHAT" INSTEAD OF "THAT WOULD KILL ME," WEREN'T YOU?!
OKAY, OKAY. THAT'S ENOUGH.

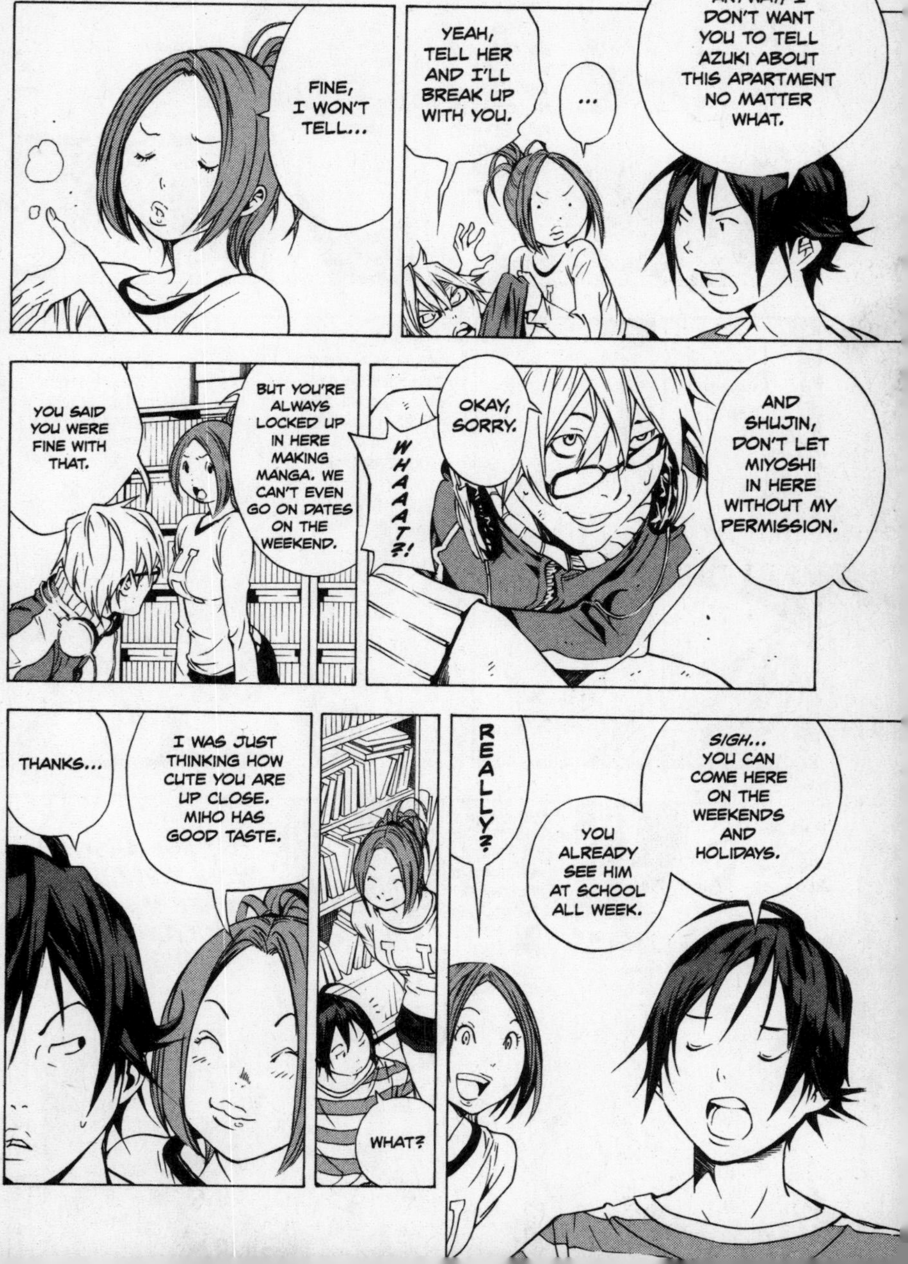
ANYWAY, I DON'T WANT YOU TO TELL AZUKI ABOUT THIS APARTMENT NO MATTER WHAT.
...
YEAH, TELL HER AND I'LL BREAK UP WITH YOU.
FINE, I WON'T TELL...
AND SHUJIN, DON'T LET MIYOSHI IN HERE WITHOUT MY PERMISSION.
OKAY, SORRY.
WHAAAAT?!
BUT YOU'RE ALWAYS LOCKED UP IN HERE MAKING MANGA. WE CAN'T EVEN GO ON DATES ON THE WEEKEND.
YOU SAID YOU WERE FINE WITH THAT.
*SIGH...* YOU CAN COME HERE ON THE WEEKENDS AND HOLIDAYS.
YOU ALREADY SEE HIM AT SCHOOL ALL WEEK.
REALLY?
WHAT?
I WAS JUST THINKING HOW CUTE YOU ARE UP CLOSE. MIHO HAS GOOD TASTE.
THANKS...

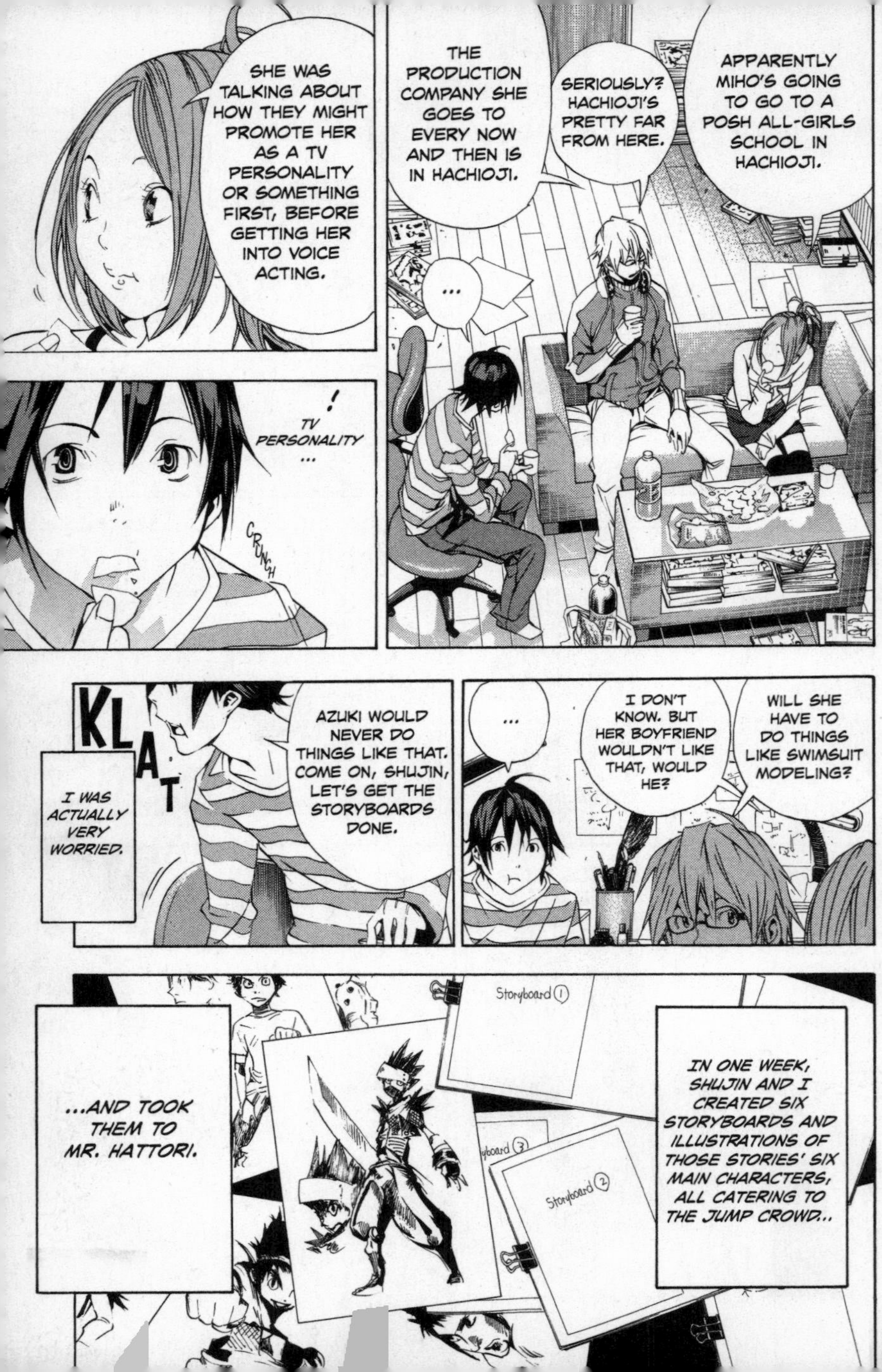
APPARENTLY MIHO'S GOING TO GO TO A POSH ALL-GIRLS SCHOOL IN HACHIOJI.
SERIOUSLY? HACHIOJI'S PRETTY FAR FROM HERE.
THE PRODUCTION COMPANY SHE GOES TO EVERY NOW AND THEN IS IN HACHIOJI.
...
SHE WAS TALKING ABOUT HOW THEY MIGHT PROMOTE HER AS A TV PERSONALITY OR SOMETHING FIRST, BEFORE GETTING HER INTO VOICE ACTING.
!
TV PERSONALITY ...
CRUNCH
WILL SHE HAVE TO DO THINGS LIKE SWIMSUIT MODELING?
I DON'T KNOW. BUT HER BOYFRIEND WOULDN'T LIKE THAT, WOULD HE?
...
KLAT
AZUKI WOULD NEVER DO THINGS LIKE THAT. COME ON, SHUJIN, LET'S GET THE STORYBOARDS DONE.
I WAS ACTUALLY VERY WORRIED.
IN ONE WEEK, SHUJIN AND I CREATED SIX STORYBOARDS AND ILLUSTRATIONS OF THOSE STORIES' SIX MAIN CHARACTERS, ALL CATERING TO THE JUMP CROWD...
Storyboard ①
Storyboard ②
...AND TOOK THEM TO MR. HATTORI.

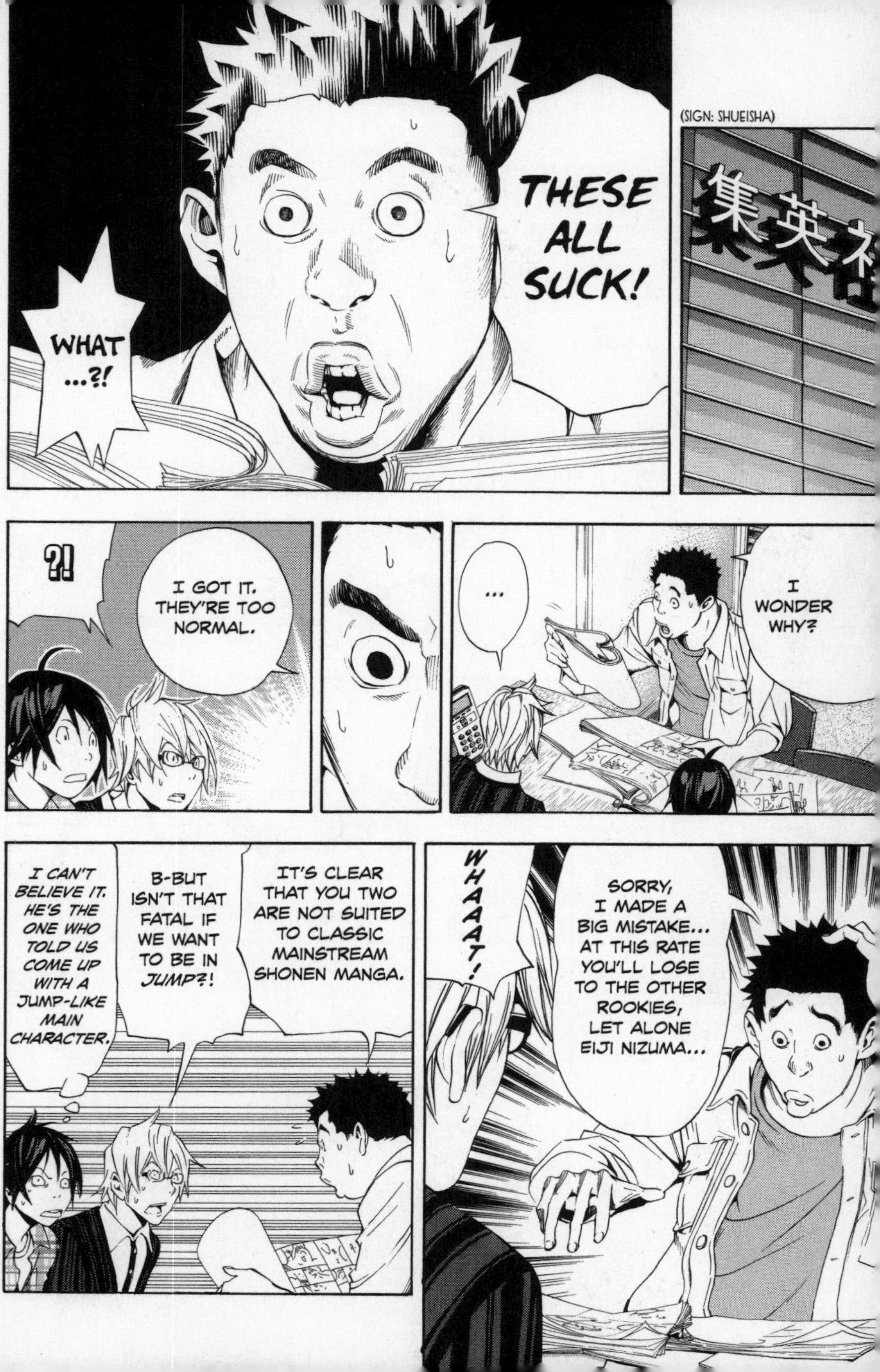
(SIGN: SHUEISHA)
THESE ALL SUCK!
WHAT ...?!
I WONDER WHY?
...
I GOT IT. THEY'RE TOO NORMAL.
?!
SORRY, I MADE A BIG MISTAKE... AT THIS RATE YOU'LL LOSE TO THE OTHER ROOKIES, LET ALONE EIJI NIZUMA...
WHAAAAT!
IT'S CLEAR THAT YOU TWO ARE NOT SUITED TO CLASSIC MAINSTREAM SHONEN MANGA.
B-BUT ISN'T THAT FATAL IF WE WANT TO BE IN *JUMP*?!
*I CAN'T BELIEVE IT. HE'S THE ONE WHO TOLD US COME UP WITH A JUMP-LIKE MAIN CHARACTER.*

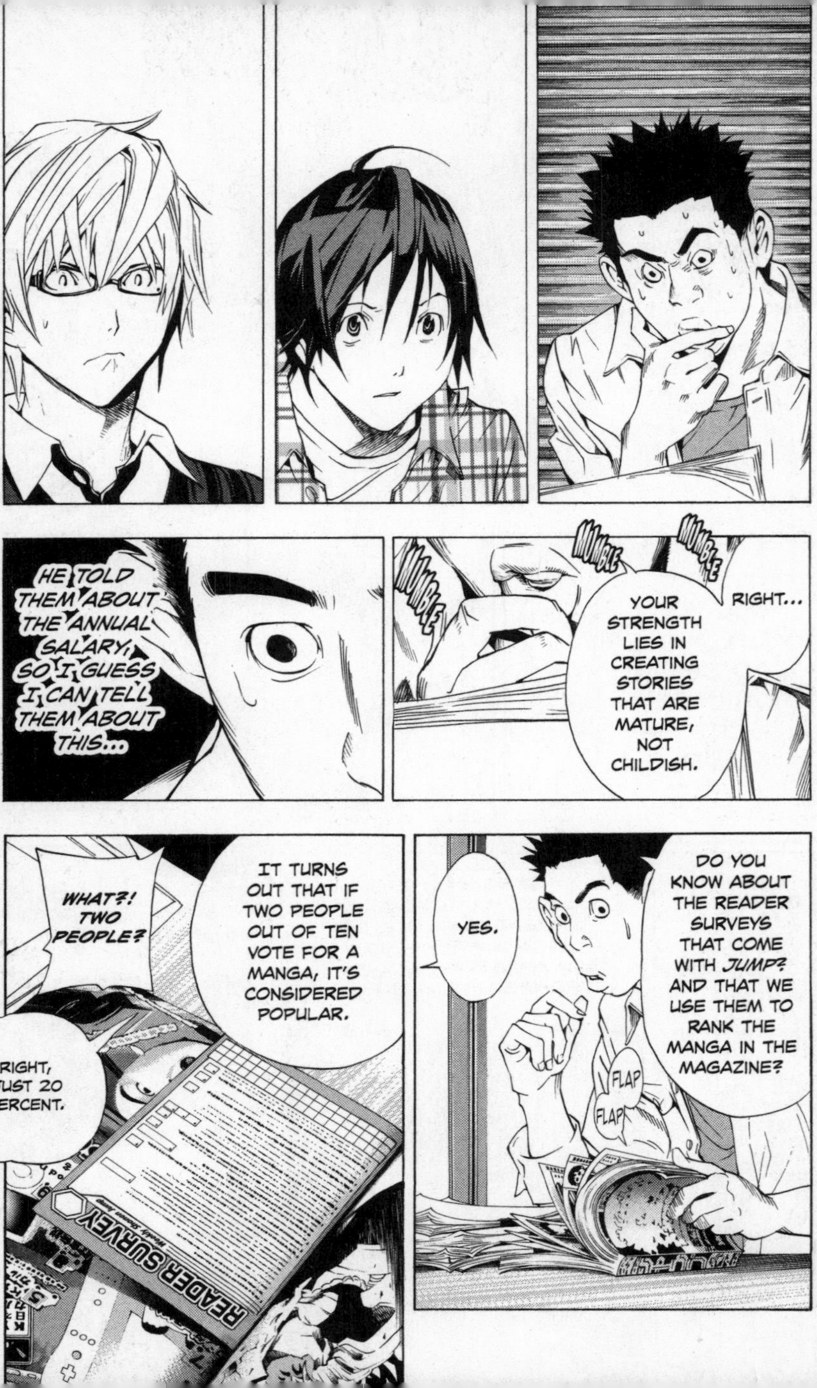
MUMBLE
MUMBLE
MUMBLE
RIGHT...
YOUR STRENGTH LIES IN CREATING STORIES THAT ARE MATURE, NOT CHILDISH.
HE TOLD THEM ABOUT THE ANNUAL SALARY, SO I GUESS I CAN TELL THEM ABOUT THIS...
DO YOU KNOW ABOUT THE READER SURVEYS THAT COME WITH *JUMP*? AND THAT WE USE THEM TO RANK THE MANGA IN THE MAGAZINE?
YES.
FLAP
FLAP
IT TURNS OUT THAT IF TWO PEOPLE OUT OF TEN VOTE FOR A MANGA, IT'S CONSIDERED POPULAR.
*WHAT?! TWO PEOPLE?*
RIGHT, JUST 20 PERCENT.
READER SURVEY

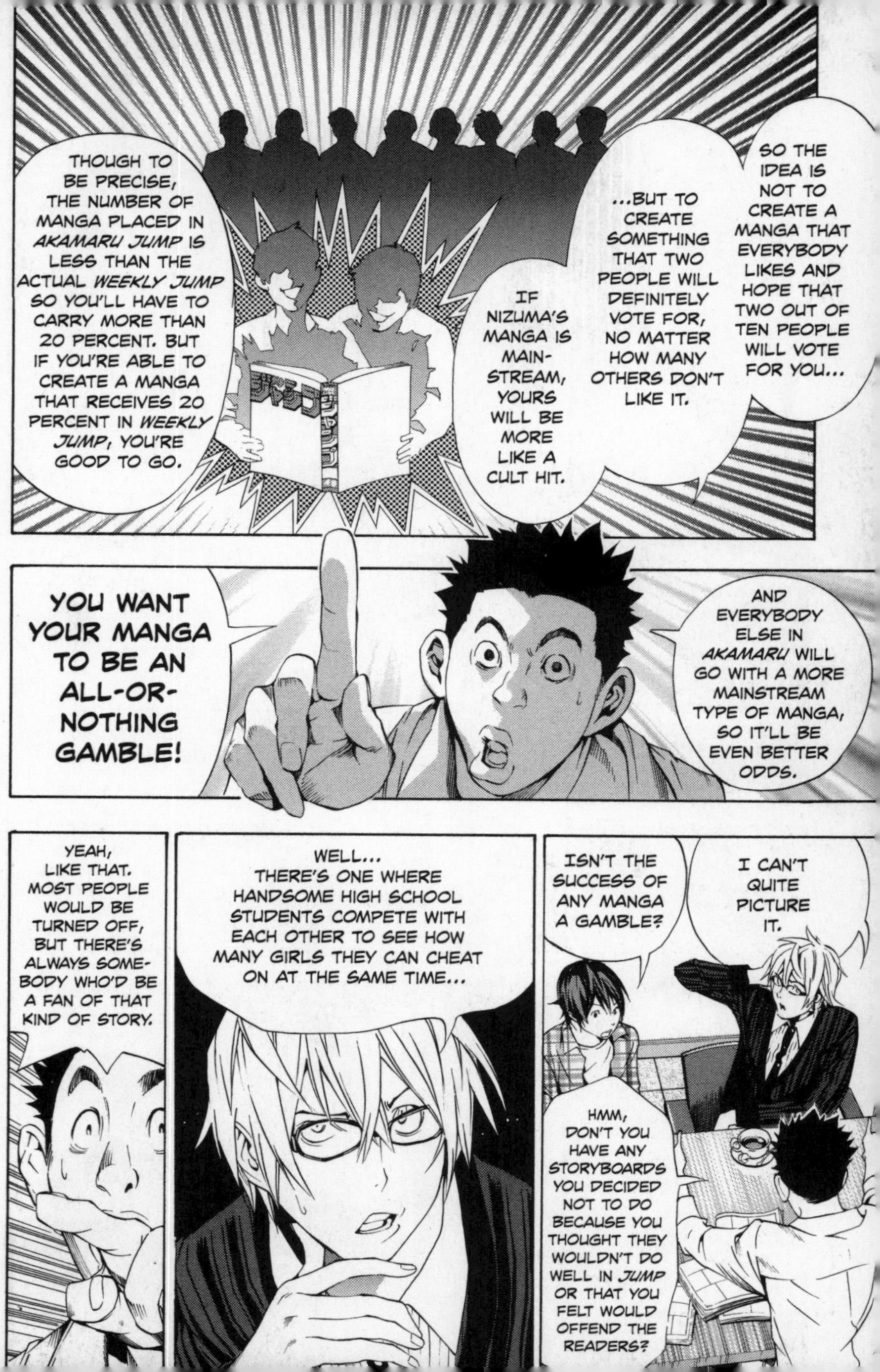
SO THE IDEA IS NOT TO CREATE A MANGA THAT EVERYBODY LIKES AND HOPE THAT TWO OUT OF TEN PEOPLE WILL VOTE FOR YOU...
...BUT TO CREATE SOMETHING THAT TWO PEOPLE WILL DEFINITELY VOTE FOR, NO MATTER HOW MANY OTHERS DON'T LIKE IT.
IF NIZUMA'S MANGA IS MAIN-STREAM, YOURS WILL BE MORE LIKE A CULT HIT.
THOUGH TO BE PRECISE, THE NUMBER OF MANGA PLACED IN *AKAMARU JUMP* IS LESS THAN THE ACTUAL *WEEKLY JUMP* SO YOU'LL HAVE TO CARRY MORE THAN 20 PERCENT. BUT IF YOU'RE ABLE TO CREATE A MANGA THAT RECEIVES 20 PERCENT IN *WEEKLY JUMP*, YOU'RE GOOD TO GO.
AND EVERYBODY ELSE IN *AKAMARU* WILL GO WITH A MORE MAINSTREAM TYPE OF MANGA, SO IT'LL BE EVEN BETTER ODDS.
YOU WANT YOUR MANGA TO BE AN ALL-OR-NOTHING GAMBLE!
I CAN'T QUITE PICTURE IT.
ISN'T THE SUCCESS OF ANY MANGA A GAMBLE?
HMM, DON'T YOU HAVE ANY STORYBOARDS YOU DECIDED NOT TO DO BECAUSE YOU THOUGHT THEY WOULDN'T DO WELL IN *JUMP* OR THAT YOU FELT WOULD OFFEND THE READERS?
WELL... THERE'S ONE WHERE HANDSOME HIGH SCHOOL STUDENTS COMPETE WITH EACH OTHER TO SEE HOW MANY GIRLS THEY CAN CHEAT ON AT THE SAME TIME...
YEAH, LIKE THAT. MOST PEOPLE WOULD BE TURNED OFF, BUT THERE'S ALWAYS SOME-BODY WHO'D BE A FAN OF THAT KIND OF STORY.

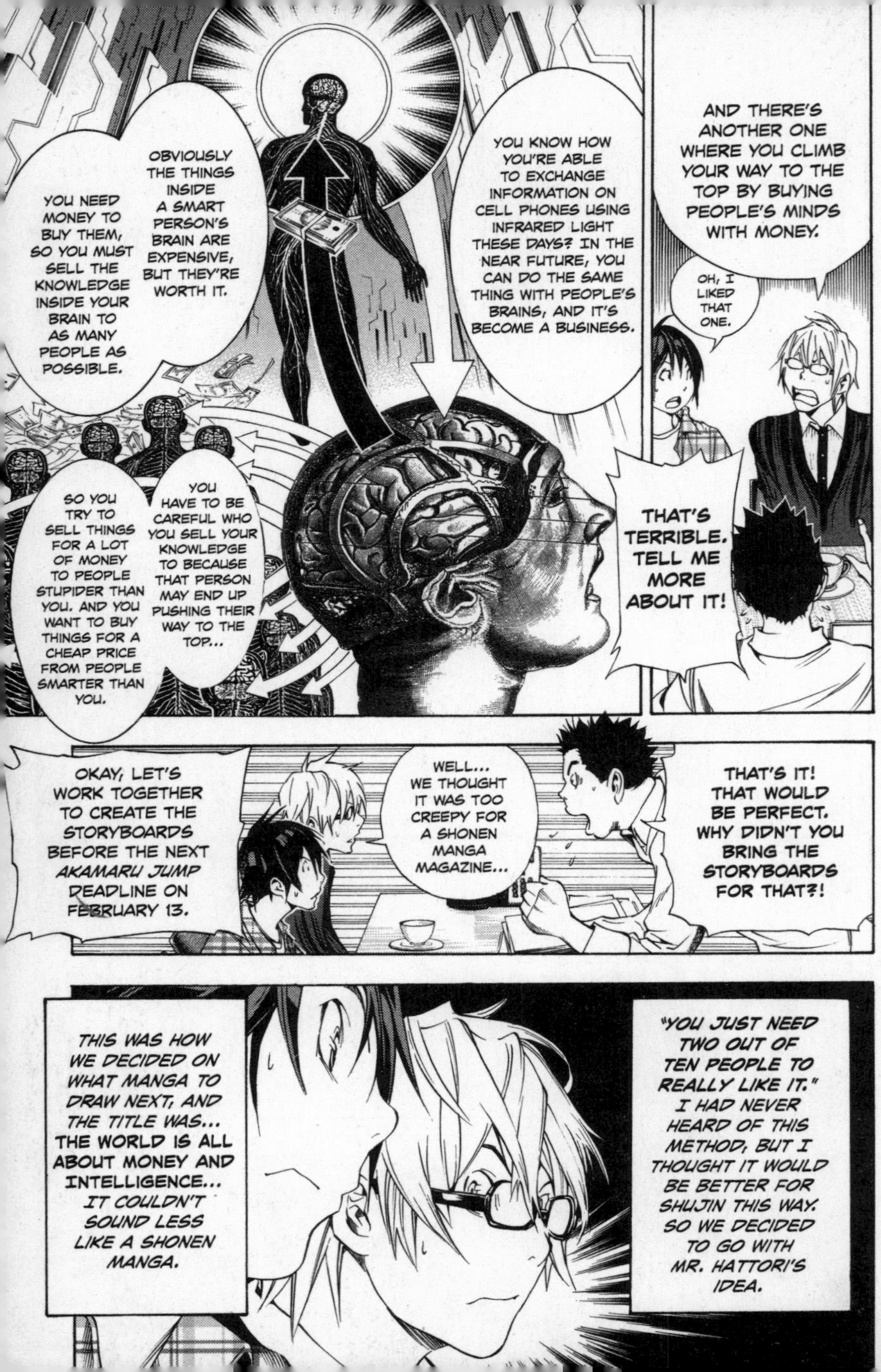
AND THERE'S ANOTHER ONE WHERE YOU CLIMB YOUR WAY TO THE TOP BY BUYING PEOPLE'S MINDS WITH MONEY.
OH, I LIKED THAT ONE.
THAT'S TERRIBLE. TELL ME MORE ABOUT IT!
YOU KNOW HOW YOU'RE ABLE TO EXCHANGE INFORMATION ON CELL PHONES USING INFRARED LIGHT THESE DAYS? IN THE NEAR FUTURE, YOU CAN DO THE SAME THING WITH PEOPLE'S BRAINS, AND IT'S BECOME A BUSINESS.
OBVIOUSLY THE THINGS INSIDE A SMART PERSON'S BRAIN ARE EXPENSIVE, BUT THEY'RE WORTH IT.
YOU NEED MONEY TO BUY THEM, SO YOU MUST SELL THE KNOWLEDGE INSIDE YOUR BRAIN TO AS MANY PEOPLE AS POSSIBLE.
YOU HAVE TO BE CAREFUL WHO YOU SELL YOUR KNOWLEDGE TO BECAUSE THAT PERSON MAY END UP PUSHING THEIR WAY TO THE TOP...
SO YOU TRY TO SELL THINGS FOR A LOT OF MONEY TO PEOPLE STUPIDER THAN YOU. AND YOU WANT TO BUY THINGS FOR A CHEAP PRICE FROM PEOPLE SMARTER THAN YOU.
THAT'S IT! THAT WOULD BE PERFECT. WHY DIDN'T YOU BRING THE STORYBOARDS FOR THAT?!
WELL... WE THOUGHT IT WAS TOO CREEPY FOR A SHONEN MANGA MAGAZINE...
OKAY, LET'S WORK TOGETHER TO CREATE THE STORYBOARDS BEFORE THE NEXT *AKAMARU JUMP* DEADLINE ON FEBRUARY 13.
*"YOU JUST NEED TWO OUT OF TEN PEOPLE TO REALLY LIKE IT." I HAD NEVER HEARD OF THIS METHOD, BUT I THOUGHT IT WOULD BE BETTER FOR SHUJIN THIS WAY. SO WE DECIDED TO GO WITH MR. HATTORI'S IDEA.*
*THIS WAS HOW WE DECIDED ON WHAT MANGA TO DRAW NEXT, AND THE TITLE WAS...* THE WORLD IS ALL ABOUT MONEY AND INTELLIGENCE... *IT COULDN'T SOUND LESS LIKE A SHONEN MANGA.*

OHBA'S STORYBOARD

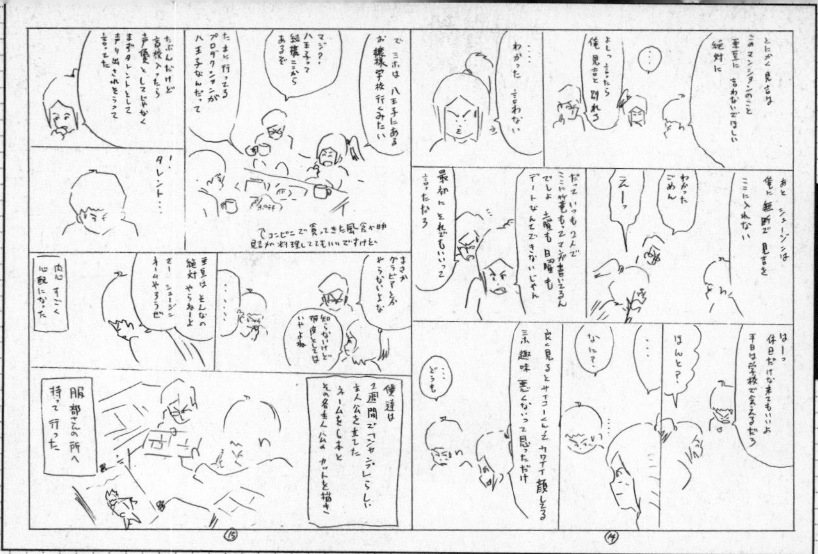
とにかく見吉は このマンションのこと 亜豆に 言わないでほしい 絶対に
…
よしっ 言ったら 俺見吉と 別れる
…わかった 言わない
あと シュージンは 俺に無断で 見吉を ここに入れない
わかった ごめん
えーっ
だっていつも2人で ここで マンガ書いてるん でしょ 土曜も 日曜も デートなんてできないじゃん
最初に それでもいいって 言ったろ
ほんと？
…
なに？
…どうも
で 三ホは 八王子にある お嬢様学校 行くみたい
マジ？ 八王子って 結構ここから あるぞ
たまに行ってる プロダクションが 八王子なんだって
タレント…
亜豆は そんなの 絶対やらねーよ
…
さーシュージン ネームやろうぜ
内心 すごく 心配になった
服部さんの所へ 持って行った

OBATA'S STORYBOARD

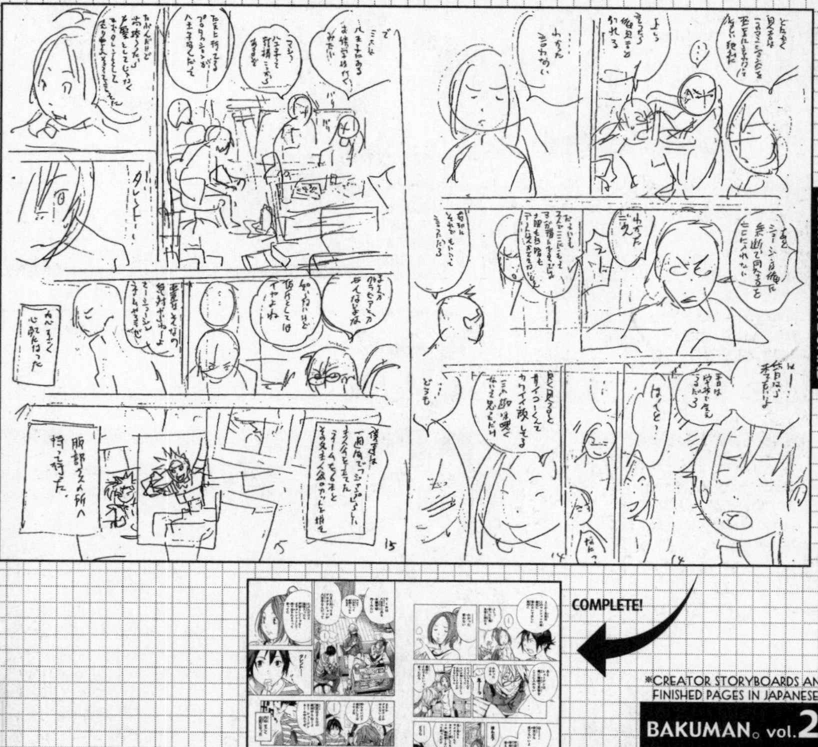

COMPLETE!

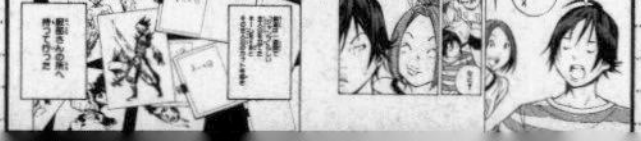

※CREATOR STORYBOARDS AND FINISHED PAGES IN JAPANESE

**BAKUMAN。 vol. 2**

"Until the Final Draft Is Complete"

Chapter 12, pp. 104-105

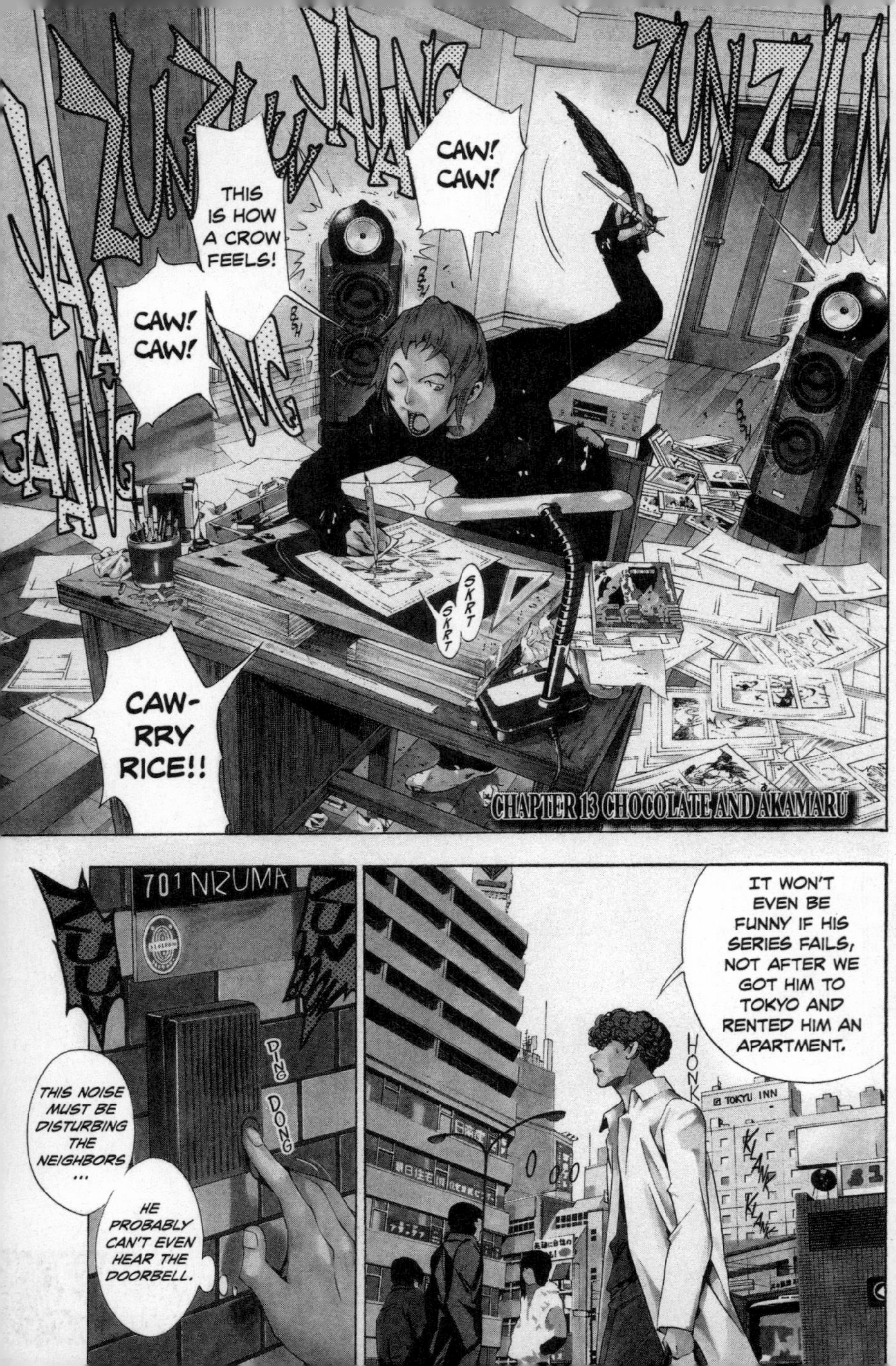
ZUN ZUN
CAW! CAW!
THIS IS HOW A CROW FEELS!
CAW! CAW!
SKRT SKRT
CAW-RRY RICE!!
CHAPTER 13 CHOCOLATE AND AKAMARU
IT WON'T EVEN BE FUNNY IF HIS SERIES FAILS, NOT AFTER WE GOT HIM TO TOKYO AND RENTED HIM AN APARTMENT.
HONK
TOKYU INN
KLANK KLANK
701 NIZUMA
DING DONG
THIS NOISE MUST BE DISTURBING THE NEIGHBORS...
HE PROBABLY CAN'T EVEN HEAR THE DOORBELL.

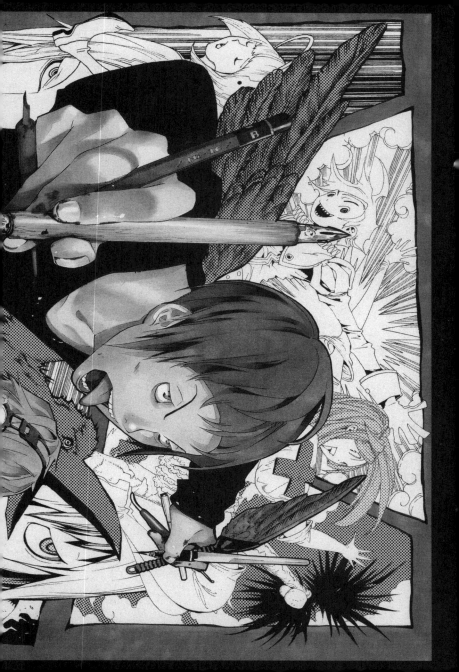

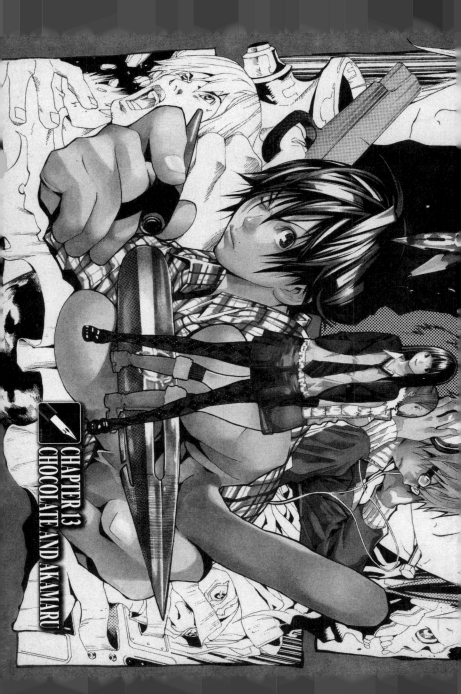

CHAPTER 13
CHOCOLATE AND AKAMARU

BAKUMAN。

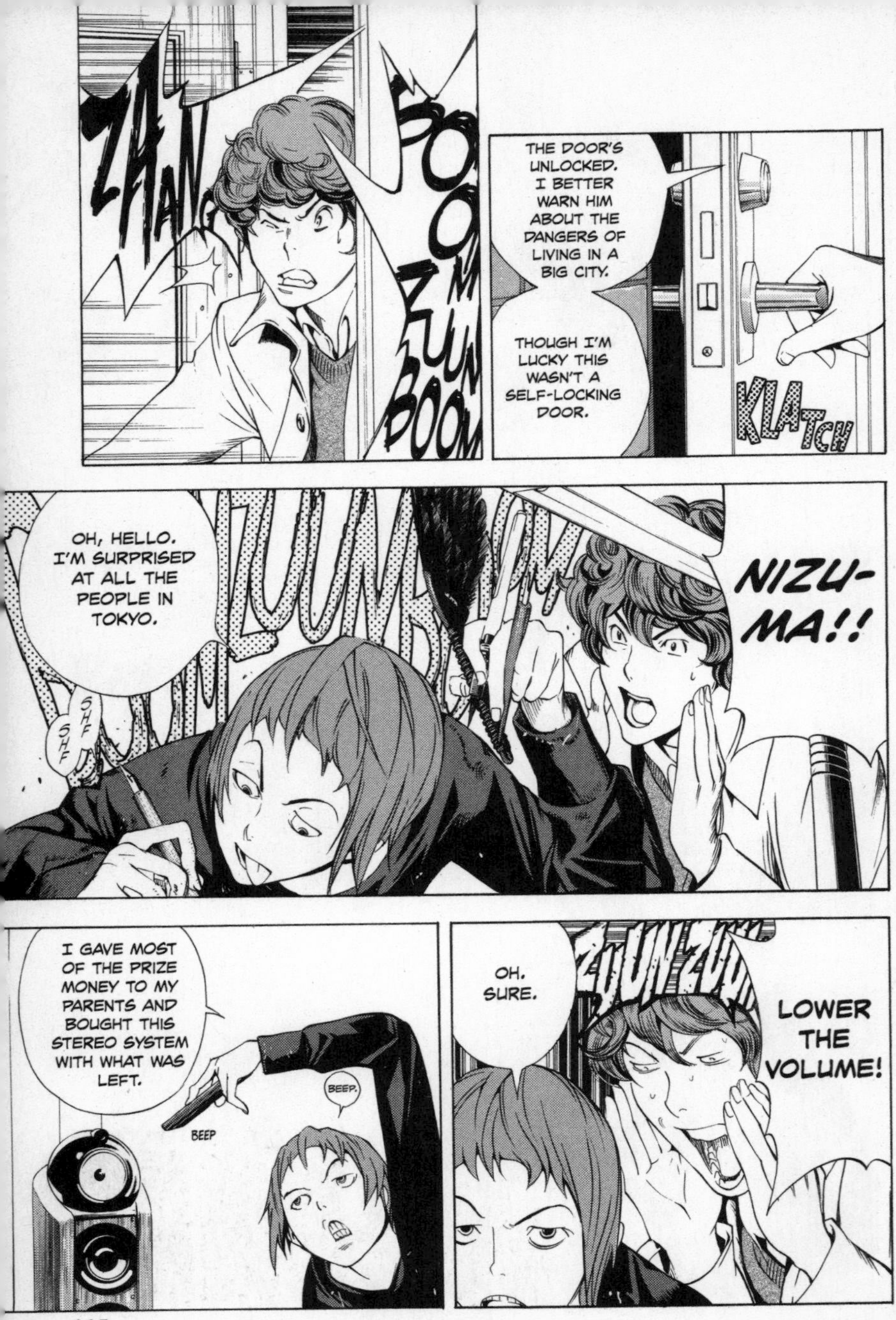
THE DOOR'S UNLOCKED. I BETTER WARN HIM ABOUT THE DANGERS OF LIVING IN A BIG CITY.
THOUGH I'M LUCKY THIS WASN'T A SELF-LOCKING DOOR.
KLATCH
ZAHAN
POOM
ZUUN
BOOM
NIZUMA!!
OH, HELLO. I'M SURPRISED AT ALL THE PEOPLE IN TOKYO.
SHF
SHF
LOWER THE VOLUME!
OH. SURE.
I GAVE MOST OF THE PRIZE MONEY TO MY PARENTS AND BOUGHT THIS STEREO SYSTEM WITH WHAT WAS LEFT.
BEEP.
BEEP

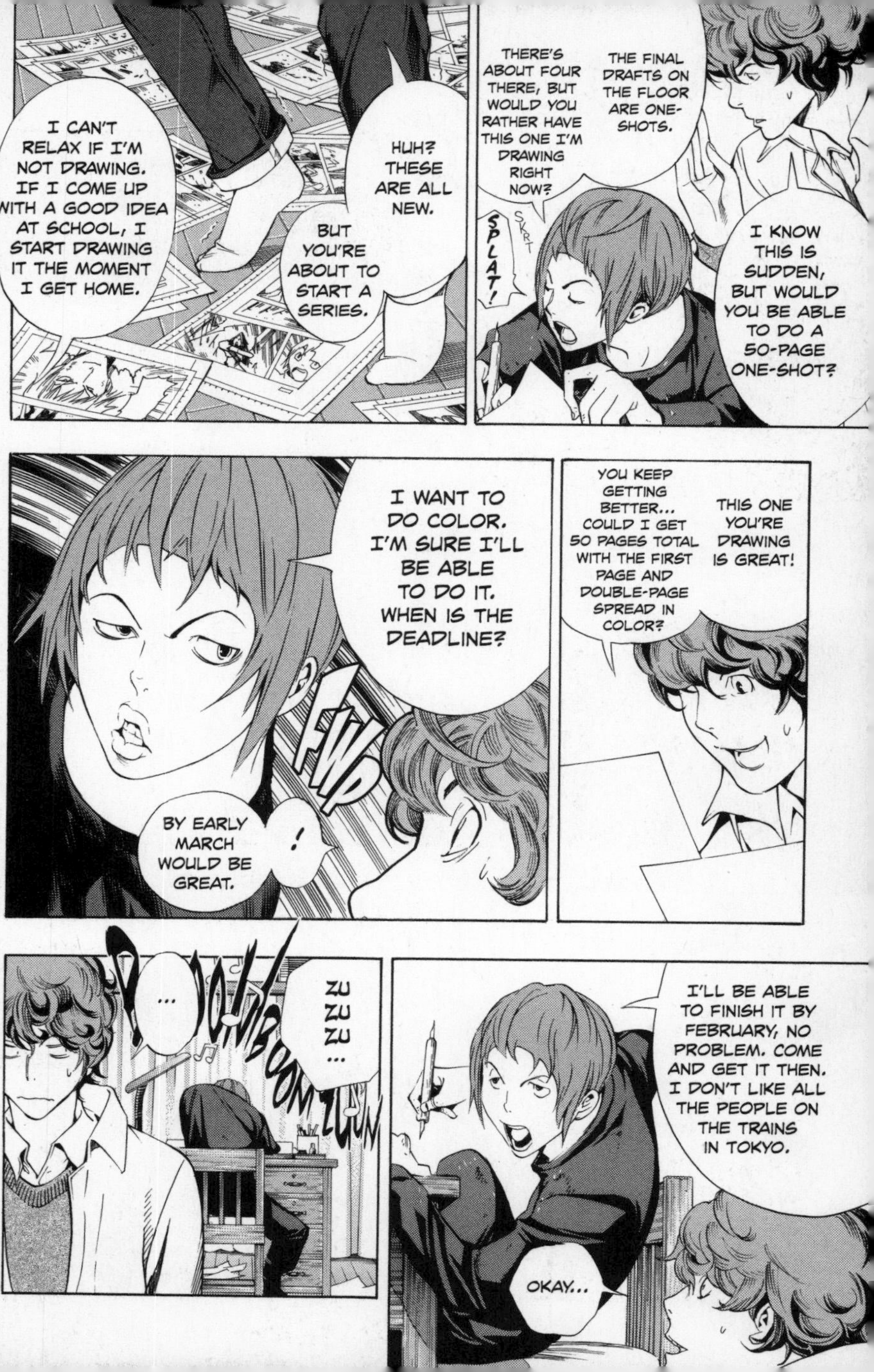
I KNOW THIS IS SUDDEN, BUT WOULD YOU BE ABLE TO DO A 50-PAGE ONE-SHOT?
THE FINAL DRAFTS ON THE FLOOR ARE ONE-SHOTS.
THERE'S ABOUT FOUR THERE, BUT WOULD YOU RATHER HAVE THIS ONE I'M DRAWING RIGHT NOW?
SPLAT!
SKRT
HUH? THESE ARE ALL NEW.
BUT YOU'RE ABOUT TO START A SERIES.
I CAN'T RELAX IF I'M NOT DRAWING. IF I COME UP WITH A GOOD IDEA AT SCHOOL, I START DRAWING IT THE MOMENT I GET HOME.
THIS ONE YOU'RE DRAWING IS GREAT!
YOU KEEP GETTING BETTER... COULD I GET 50 PAGES TOTAL WITH THE FIRST PAGE AND DOUBLE-PAGE SPREAD IN COLOR?
I WANT TO DO COLOR. I'M SURE I'LL BE ABLE TO DO IT. WHEN IS THE DEADLINE?
FWIP
!
BY EARLY MARCH WOULD BE GREAT.
I'LL BE ABLE TO FINISH IT BY FEBRUARY, NO PROBLEM. COME AND GET IT THEN. I DON'T LIKE ALL THE PEOPLE ON THE TRAINS IN TOKYO.
OKAY...
ZU ZU ZU...
...

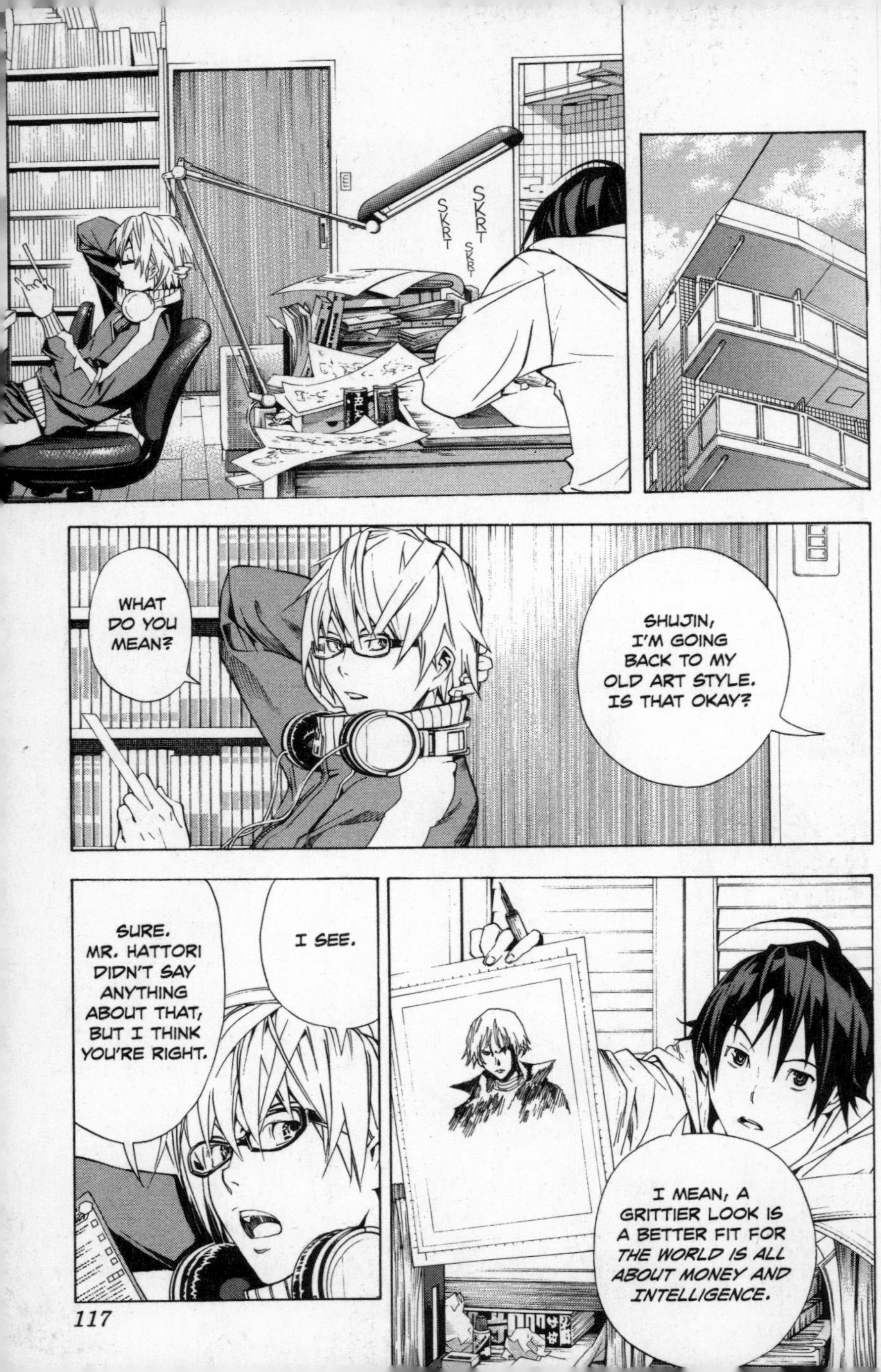
SKRT SKRT
SKRT SKRT
SHUJIN, I'M GOING BACK TO MY OLD ART STYLE. IS THAT OKAY?
WHAT DO YOU MEAN?
I MEAN, A GRITTIER LOOK IS A BETTER FIT FOR THE WORLD IS ALL ABOUT MONEY AND INTELLIGENCE.
I SEE.
SURE. MR. HATTORI DIDN'T SAY ANYTHING ABOUT THAT, BUT I THINK YOU'RE RIGHT.

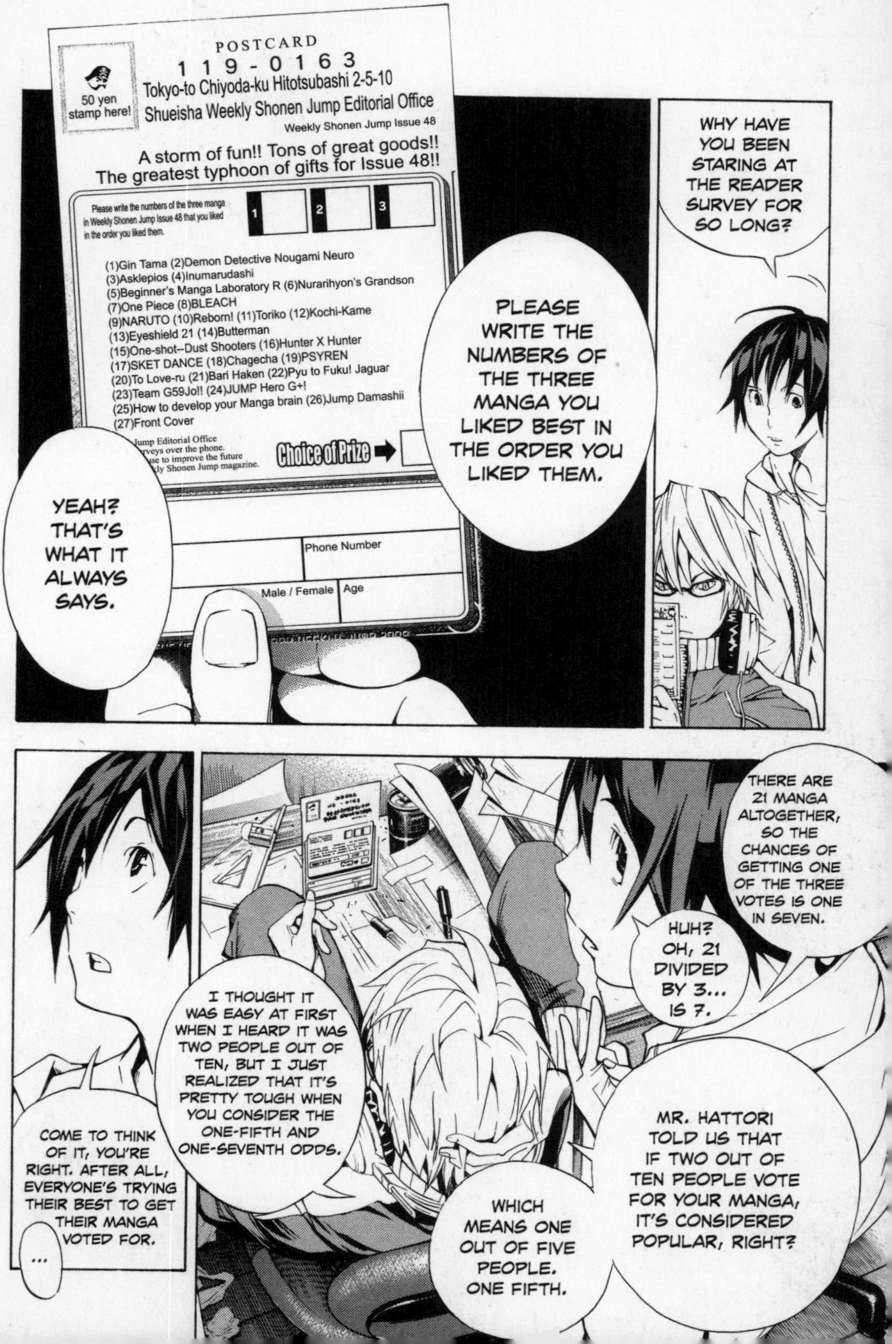
WHY HAVE YOU BEEN STARING AT THE READER SURVEY FOR SO LONG?
POSTCARD
119-0163
Tokyo-to Chiyoda-ku Hitotsubashi 2-5-10
Shueisha Weekly Shonen Jump Editorial Office
Weekly Shonen Jump Issue 48
50 yen stamp here!
A storm of fun!! Tons of great goods!!
The greatest typhoon of gifts for Issue 48!!
Please write the numbers of the three manga in Weekly Shonen Jump Issue 48 that you liked in the order you liked them.
1 2 3
(1)Gin Tama (2)Demon Detective Nougami Neuro
(3)Asklepios (4)Inumarudashi
(5)Beginner's Manga Laboratory R (6)Nurarihyon's Grandson
(7)One Piece (8)BLEACH
(9)NARUTO (10)Reborn! (11)Toriko (12)Kochi-Kame
(13)Eyeshield 21 (14)Butterman
(15)One-shot--Dust Shooters (16)Hunter X Hunter
(17)SKET DANCE (18)Chagecha (19)PSYREN
(20)To Love-ru (21)Bari Haken (22)Pyu to Fuku! Jaguar
(23)Team G59Jo!! (24)JUMP Hero G+!
(25)How to develop your Manga brain (26)Jump Damashii
(27)Front Cover
Choice of Prize
Phone Number
Male / Female
Age
PLEASE WRITE THE NUMBERS OF THE THREE MANGA YOU LIKED BEST IN THE ORDER YOU LIKED THEM.
YEAH? THAT'S WHAT IT ALWAYS SAYS.
THERE ARE 21 MANGA ALTOGETHER, SO THE CHANCES OF GETTING ONE OF THE THREE VOTES IS ONE IN SEVEN.
HUH? OH, 21 DIVIDED BY 3... IS 7.
MR. HATTORI TOLD US THAT IF TWO OUT OF TEN PEOPLE VOTE FOR YOUR MANGA, IT'S CONSIDERED POPULAR, RIGHT?
WHICH MEANS ONE OUT OF FIVE PEOPLE. ONE FIFTH.
I THOUGHT IT WAS EASY AT FIRST WHEN I HEARD IT WAS TWO PEOPLE OUT OF TEN, BUT I JUST REALIZED THAT IT'S PRETTY TOUGH WHEN YOU CONSIDER THE ONE-FIFTH AND ONE-SEVENTH ODDS.
COME TO THINK OF IT, YOU'RE RIGHT. AFTER ALL, EVERYONE'S TRYING THEIR BEST TO GET THEIR MANGA VOTED FOR.
...

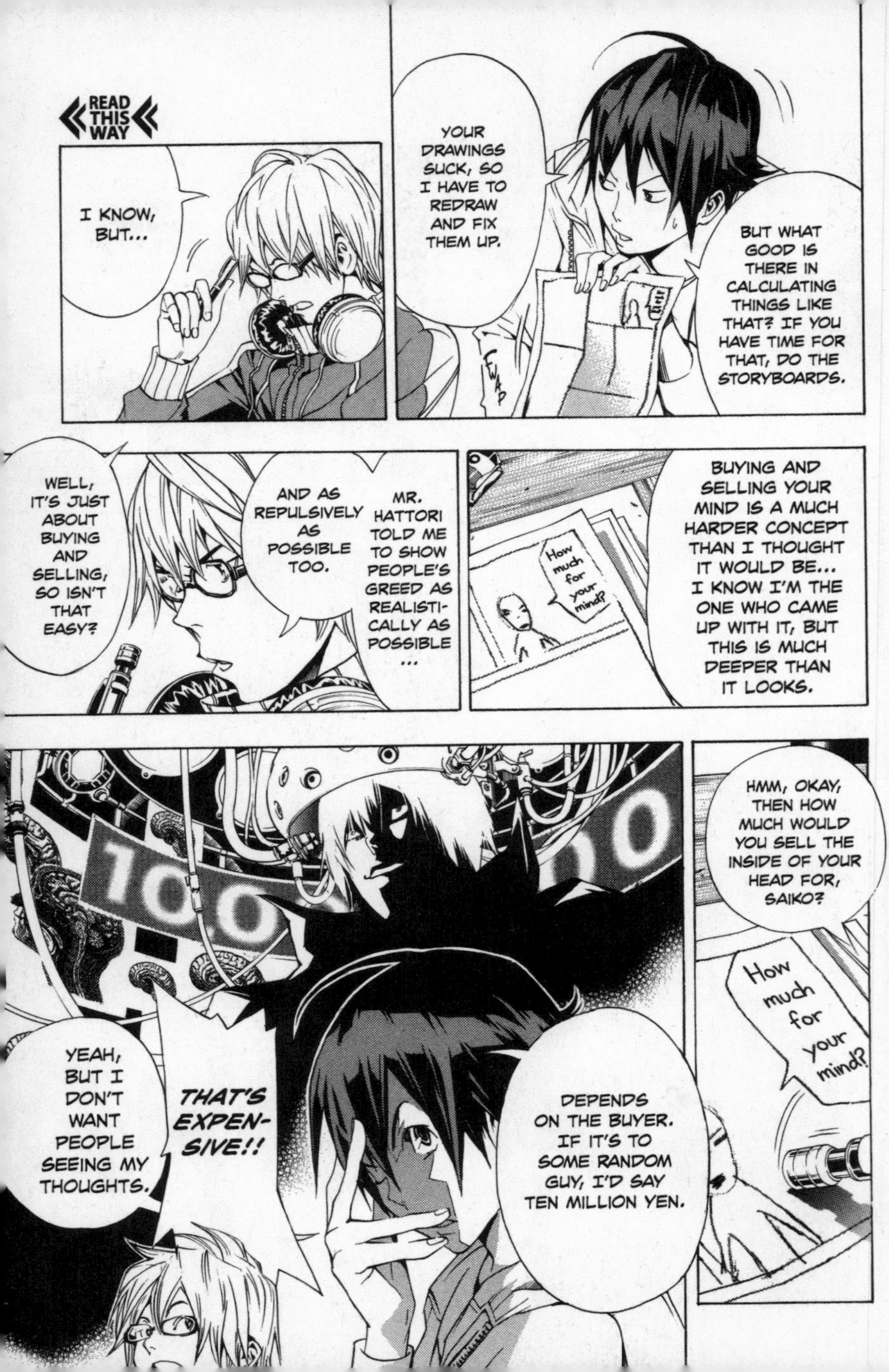
READ THIS WAY
YOUR DRAWINGS SUCK, SO I HAVE TO REDRAW AND FIX THEM UP.
BUT WHAT GOOD IS THERE IN CALCULATING THINGS LIKE THAT? IF YOU HAVE TIME FOR THAT, DO THE STORYBOARDS.
FWAP
I KNOW, BUT...
BUYING AND SELLING YOUR MIND IS A MUCH HARDER CONCEPT THAN I THOUGHT IT WOULD BE... I KNOW I'M THE ONE WHO CAME UP WITH IT, BUT THIS IS MUCH DEEPER THAN IT LOOKS.
How much for your mind?
MR. HATTORI TOLD ME TO SHOW PEOPLE'S GREED AS REALISTICALLY AS POSSIBLE...
AND AS REPULSIVELY AS POSSIBLE TOO.
WELL, IT'S JUST ABOUT BUYING AND SELLING, SO ISN'T THAT EASY?
HMM, OKAY, THEN HOW MUCH WOULD YOU SELL THE INSIDE OF YOUR HEAD FOR, SAIKO?
How much for your mind?
DEPENDS ON THE BUYER. IF IT'S TO SOME RANDOM GUY, I'D SAY TEN MILLION YEN.
THAT'S EXPENSIVE!!
YEAH, BUT I DON'T WANT PEOPLE SEEING MY THOUGHTS.

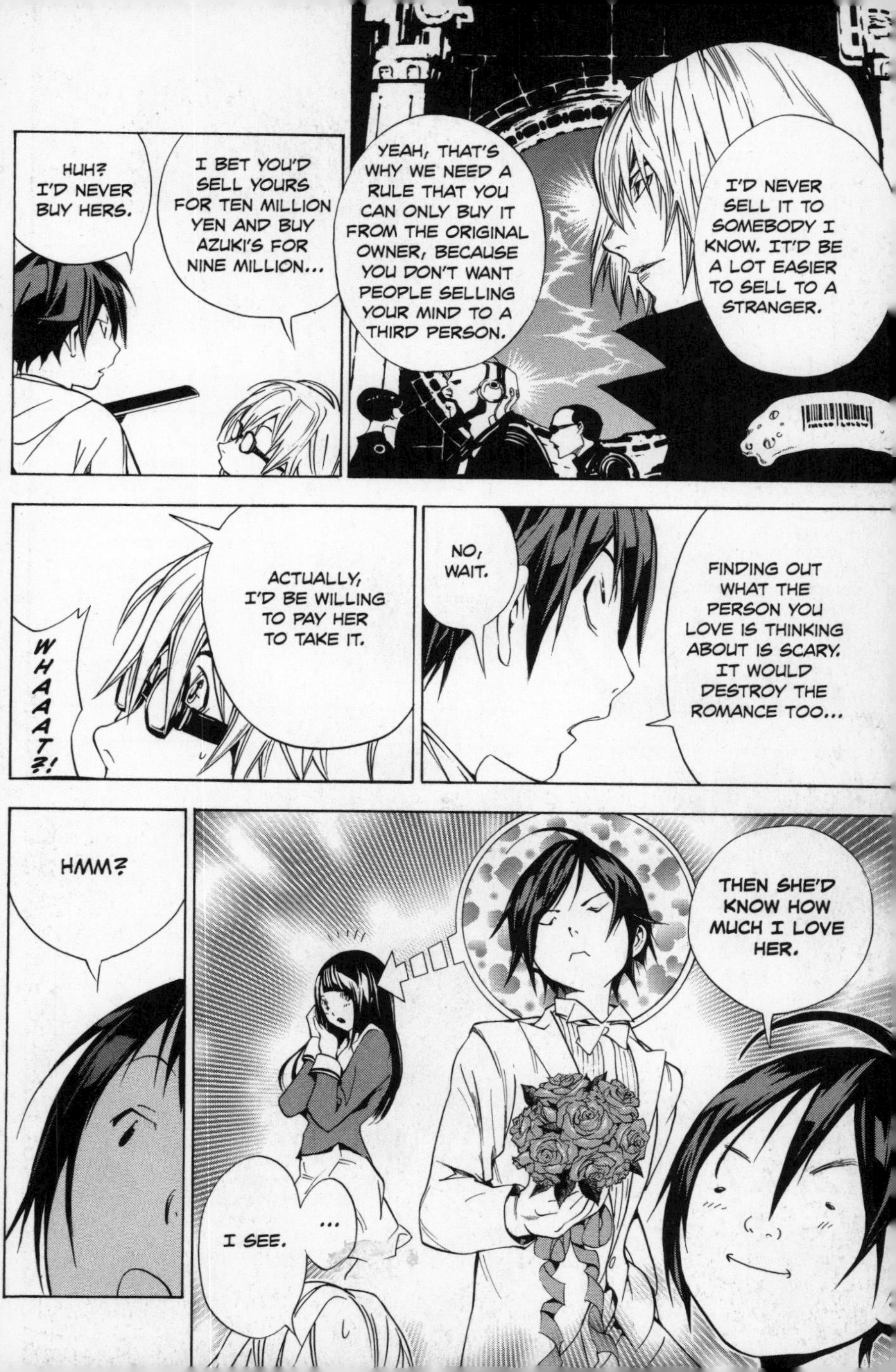
I'D NEVER SELL IT TO SOMEBODY I KNOW. IT'D BE A LOT EASIER TO SELL TO A STRANGER.
YEAH, THAT'S WHY WE NEED A RULE THAT YOU CAN ONLY BUY IT FROM THE ORIGINAL OWNER, BECAUSE YOU DON'T WANT PEOPLE SELLING YOUR MIND TO A THIRD PERSON.
I BET YOU'D SELL YOURS FOR TEN MILLION YEN AND BUY AZUKI'S FOR NINE MILLION...
HUH? I'D NEVER BUY HERS.
FINDING OUT WHAT THE PERSON YOU LOVE IS THINKING ABOUT IS SCARY. IT WOULD DESTROY THE ROMANCE TOO...
NO, WAIT.
ACTUALLY, I'D BE WILLING TO PAY HER TO TAKE IT.
WHAAAAT?!
THEN SHE'D KNOW HOW MUCH I LOVE HER.
... I SEE.
HMM?

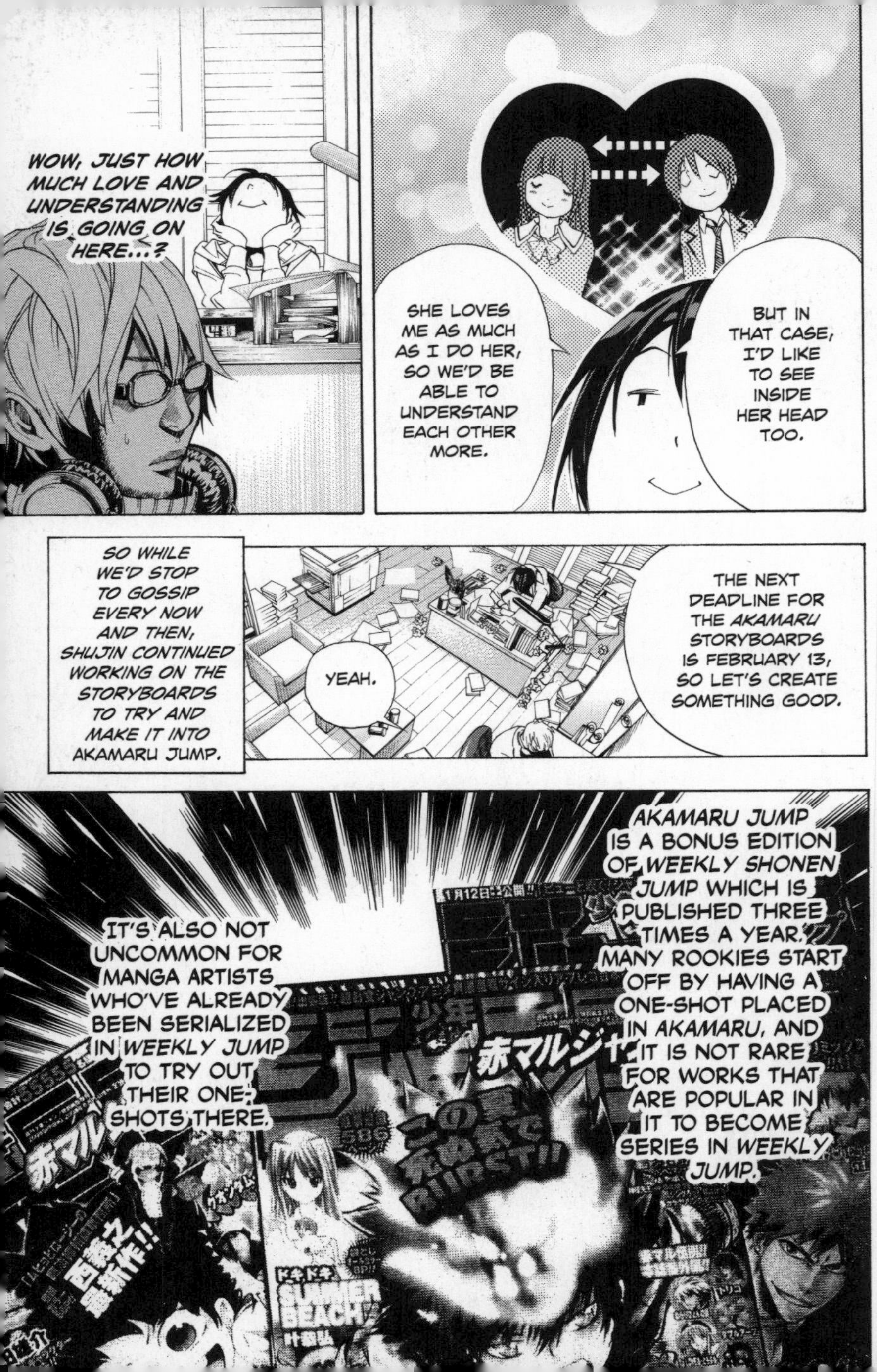
SHE LOVES ME AS MUCH AS I DO HER, SO WE'D BE ABLE TO UNDERSTAND EACH OTHER MORE.
BUT IN THAT CASE, I'D LIKE TO SEE INSIDE HER HEAD TOO.
WOW, JUST HOW MUCH LOVE AND UNDERSTANDING IS GOING ON HERE...?
THE NEXT DEADLINE FOR THE *AKAMARU* STORYBOARDS IS FEBRUARY 13, SO LET'S CREATE SOMETHING GOOD.
YEAH.
SO WHILE WE'D STOP TO GOSSIP EVERY NOW AND THEN, SHUJIN CONTINUED WORKING ON THE STORYBOARDS TO TRY AND MAKE IT INTO AKAMARU JUMP.
AKAMARU JUMP IS A BONUS EDITION OF *WEEKLY SHONEN JUMP* WHICH IS PUBLISHED THREE TIMES A YEAR. MANY ROOKIES START OFF BY HAVING A ONE-SHOT PLACED IN *AKAMARU*, AND IT IS NOT RARE FOR WORKS THAT ARE POPULAR IN IT TO BECOME SERIES IN *WEEKLY JUMP*.
IT'S ALSO NOT UNCOMMON FOR MANGA ARTISTS WHO'VE ALREADY BEEN SERIALIZED IN *WEEKLY JUMP* TO TRY OUT THEIR ONE-SHOTS THERE.
赤マルジャ
SUMMER BEACH

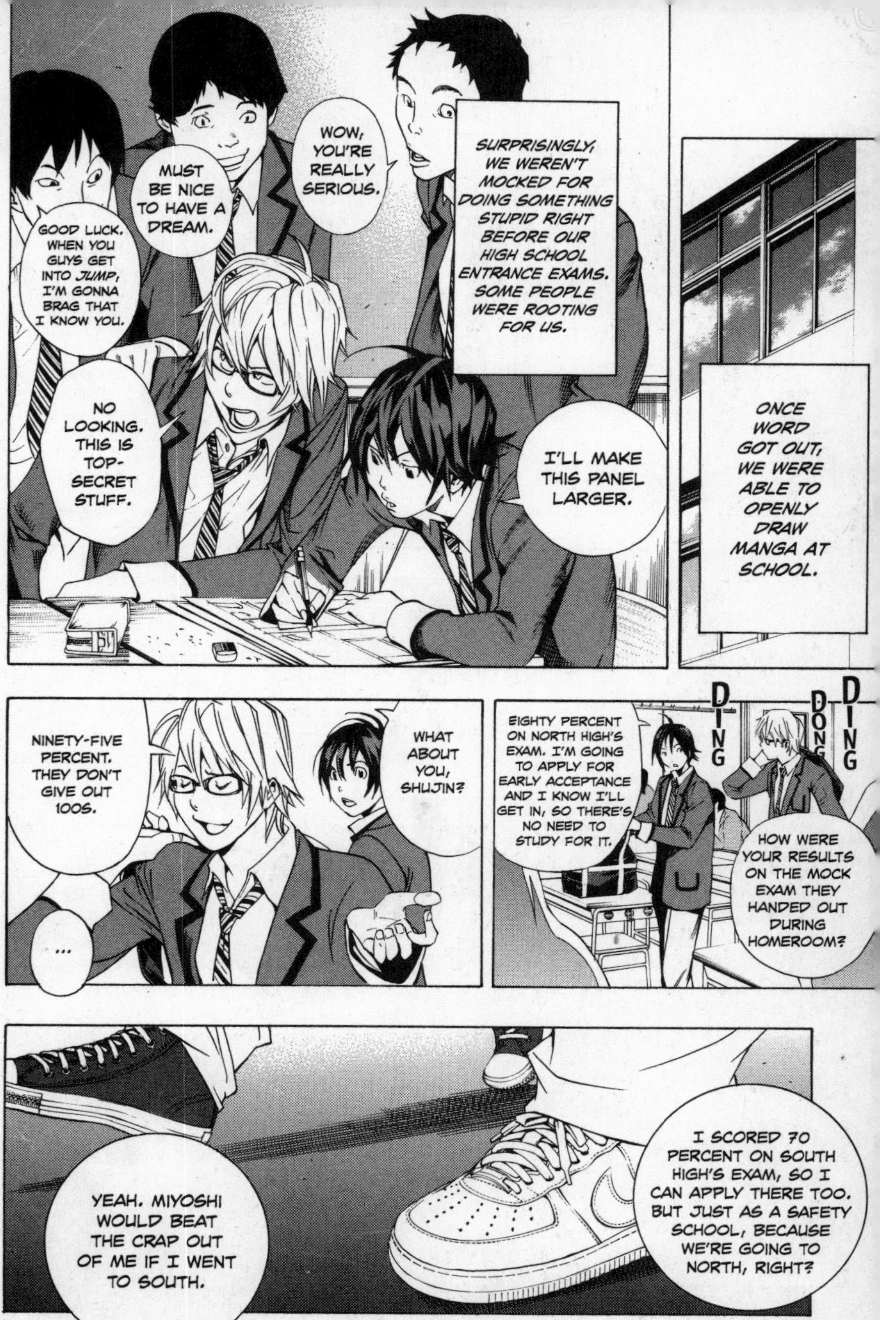
ONCE WORD GOT OUT, WE WERE ABLE TO OPENLY DRAW MANGA AT SCHOOL.
SURPRISINGLY, WE WEREN'T MOCKED FOR DOING SOMETHING STUPID RIGHT BEFORE OUR HIGH SCHOOL ENTRANCE EXAMS. SOME PEOPLE WERE ROOTING FOR US.
WOW, YOU'RE REALLY SERIOUS.
MUST BE NICE TO HAVE A DREAM.
GOOD LUCK. WHEN YOU GUYS GET INTO *JUMP*, I'M GONNA BRAG THAT I KNOW YOU.
I'LL MAKE THIS PANEL LARGER.
NO LOOKING. THIS IS TOP-SECRET STUFF.
DING DONG DING
HOW WERE YOUR RESULTS ON THE MOCK EXAM THEY HANDED OUT DURING HOMEROOM?
EIGHTY PERCENT ON NORTH HIGH'S EXAM. I'M GOING TO APPLY FOR EARLY ACCEPTANCE AND I KNOW I'LL GET IN, SO THERE'S NO NEED TO STUDY FOR IT.
WHAT ABOUT YOU, SHUJIN?
NINETY-FIVE PERCENT. THEY DON'T GIVE OUT 100S.
...
I SCORED 70 PERCENT ON SOUTH HIGH'S EXAM, SO I CAN APPLY THERE TOO. BUT JUST AS A SAFETY SCHOOL, BECAUSE WE'RE GOING TO NORTH, RIGHT?
YEAH. MIYOSHI WOULD BEAT THE CRAP OUT OF ME IF I WENT TO SOUTH.

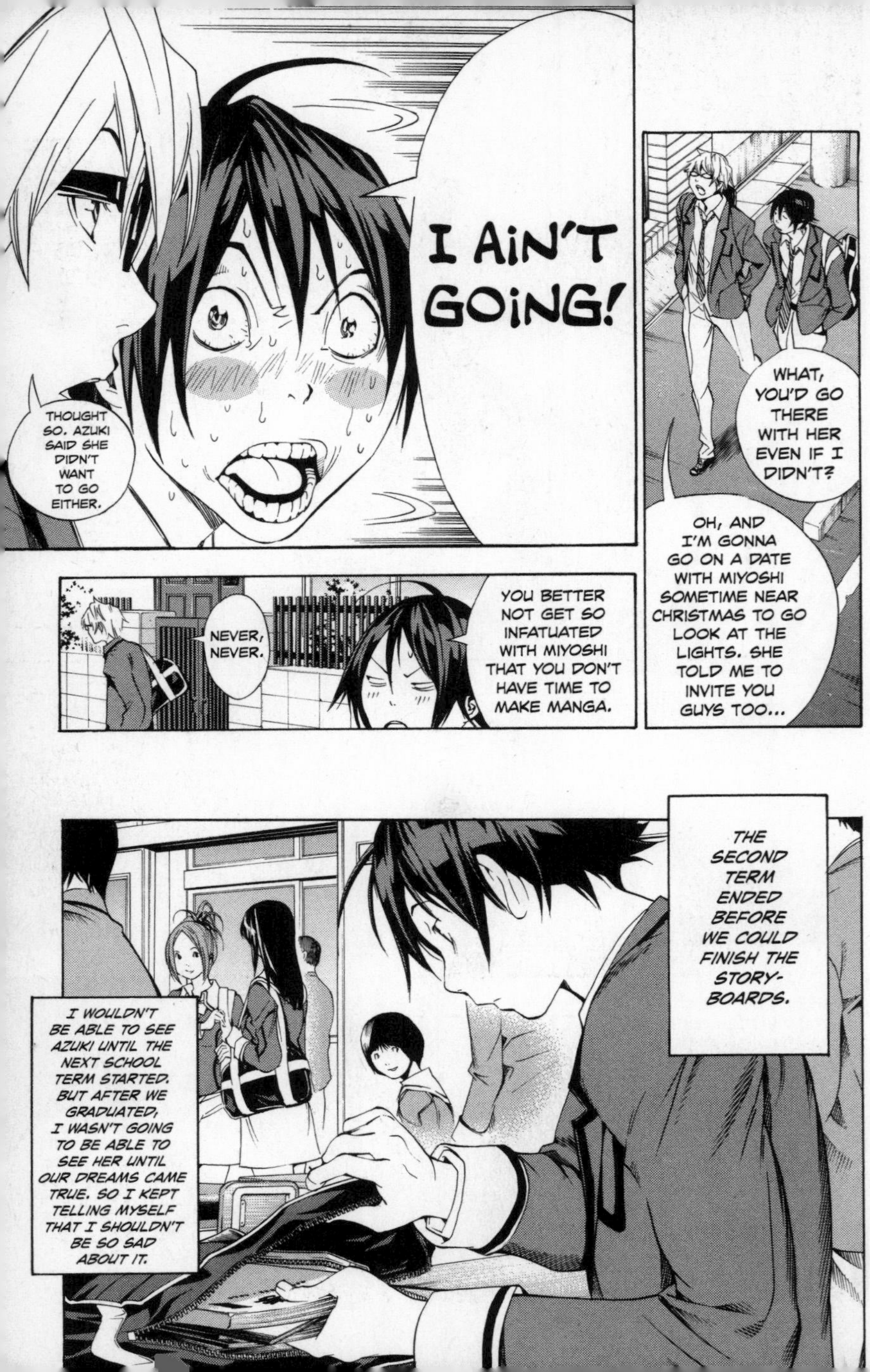
WHAT, YOU'D GO THERE WITH HER EVEN IF I DIDN'T?
OH, AND I'M GONNA GO ON A DATE WITH MIYOSHI SOMETIME NEAR CHRISTMAS TO GO LOOK AT THE LIGHTS. SHE TOLD ME TO INVITE YOU GUYS TOO...
I AIN'T GOING!
THOUGHT SO. AZUKI SAID SHE DIDN'T WANT TO GO EITHER.
YOU BETTER NOT GET SO INFATUATED WITH MIYOSHI THAT YOU DON'T HAVE TIME TO MAKE MANGA.
NEVER, NEVER.
THE SECOND TERM ENDED BEFORE WE COULD FINISH THE STORY-BOARDS.
I WOULDN'T BE ABLE TO SEE AZUKI UNTIL THE NEXT SCHOOL TERM STARTED. BUT AFTER WE GRADUATED, I WASN'T GOING TO BE ABLE TO SEE HER UNTIL OUR DREAMS CAME TRUE. SO I KEPT TELLING MYSELF THAT I SHOULDN'T BE SO SAD ABOUT IT.

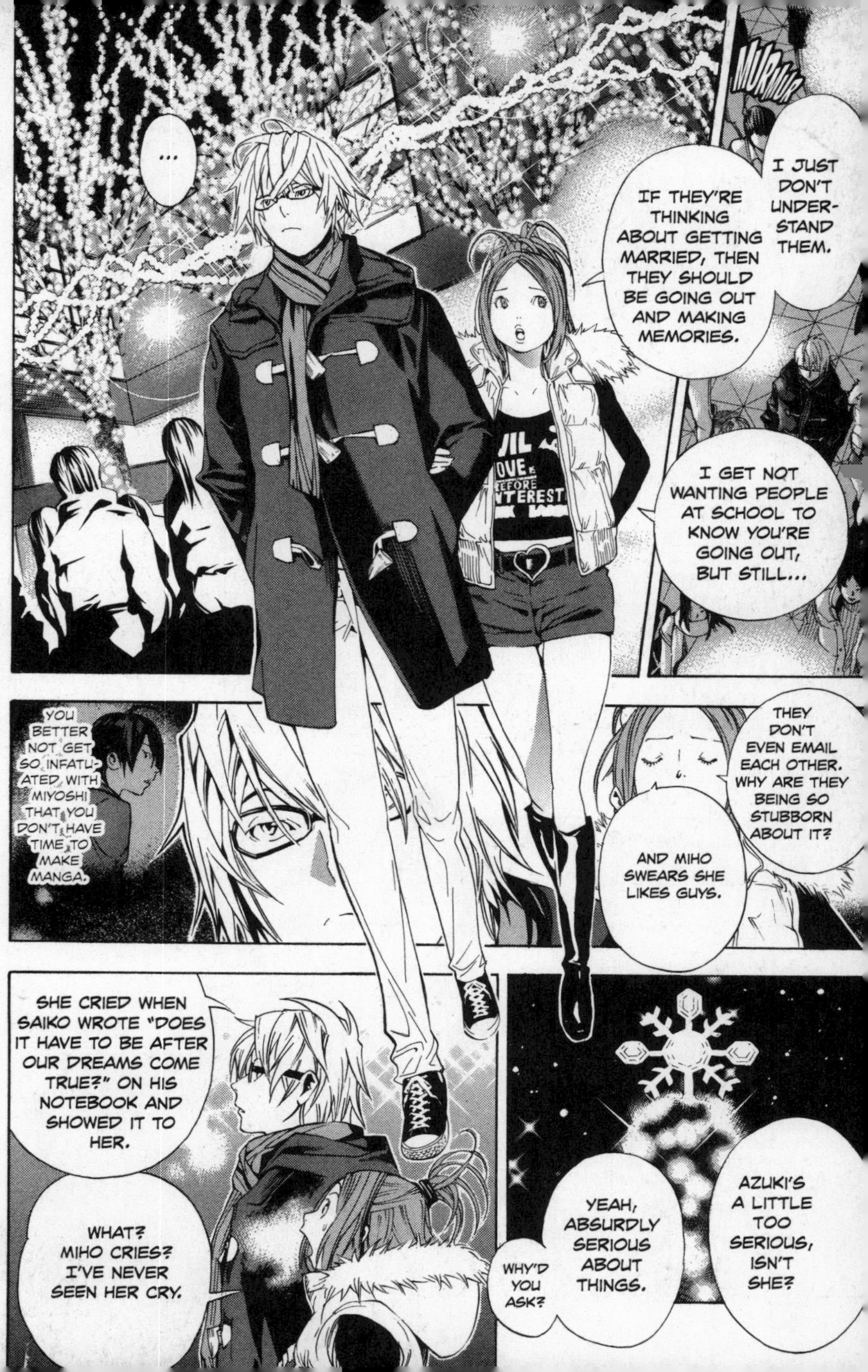
MURMUR
I JUST DON'T UNDERSTAND THEM.
IF THEY'RE THINKING ABOUT GETTING MARRIED, THEN THEY SHOULD BE GOING OUT AND MAKING MEMORIES.
I GET NOT WANTING PEOPLE AT SCHOOL TO KNOW YOU'RE GOING OUT, BUT STILL...
...
THEY DON'T EVEN EMAIL EACH OTHER. WHY ARE THEY BEING SO STUBBORN ABOUT IT?
AND MIHO SWEARS SHE LIKES GUYS.
YOU BETTER NOT GET SO INFATUATED WITH MIYOSHI THAT YOU DON'T HAVE TIME TO MAKE MANGA.
AZUKI'S A LITTLE TOO SERIOUS, ISN'T SHE?
YEAH, ABSURDLY SERIOUS ABOUT THINGS.
WHY'D YOU ASK?
SHE CRIED WHEN SAIKO WROTE "DOES IT HAVE TO BE AFTER OUR DREAMS COME TRUE?" ON HIS NOTEBOOK AND SHOWED IT TO HER.
WHAT? MIHO CRIES? I'VE NEVER SEEN HER CRY.

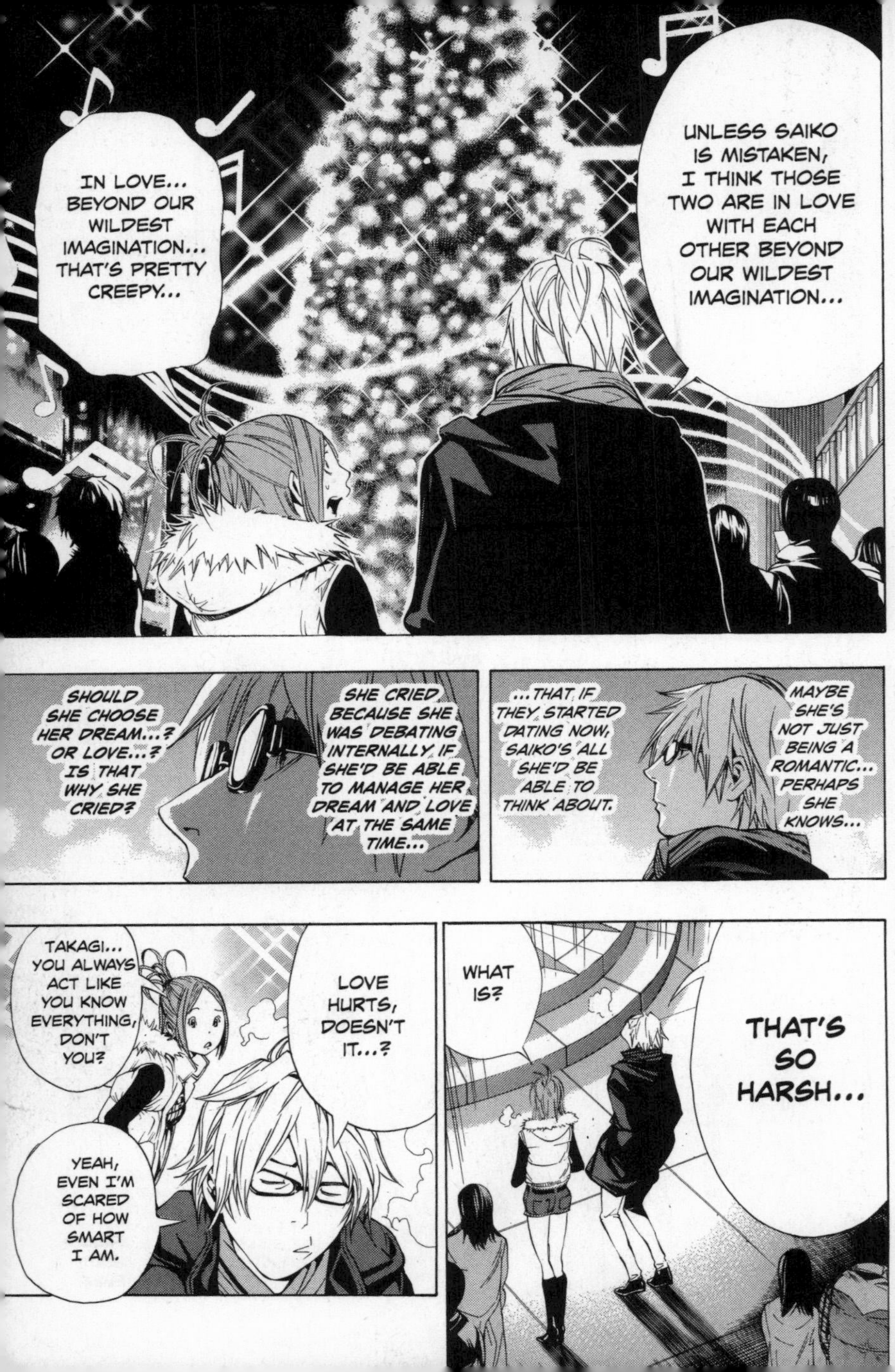
UNLESS SAIKO IS MISTAKEN, I THINK THOSE TWO ARE IN LOVE WITH EACH OTHER BEYOND OUR WILDEST IMAGINATION...
IN LOVE... BEYOND OUR WILDEST IMAGINATION... THAT'S PRETTY CREEPY...
MAYBE SHE'S NOT JUST BEING A ROMANTIC... PERHAPS SHE KNOWS...
...THAT IF THEY STARTED DATING NOW, SAIKO'S ALL SHE'D BE ABLE TO THINK ABOUT.
SHE CRIED BECAUSE SHE WAS DEBATING INTERNALLY IF SHE'D BE ABLE TO MANAGE HER DREAM AND LOVE AT THE SAME TIME...
SHOULD SHE CHOOSE HER DREAM...? OR LOVE...? IS THAT WHY SHE CRIED?
THAT'S SO HARSH...
WHAT IS?
LOVE HURTS, DOESN'T IT...?
TAKAGI... YOU ALWAYS ACT LIKE YOU KNOW EVERYTHING, DON'T YOU?
YEAH, EVEN I'M SCARED OF HOW SMART I AM.

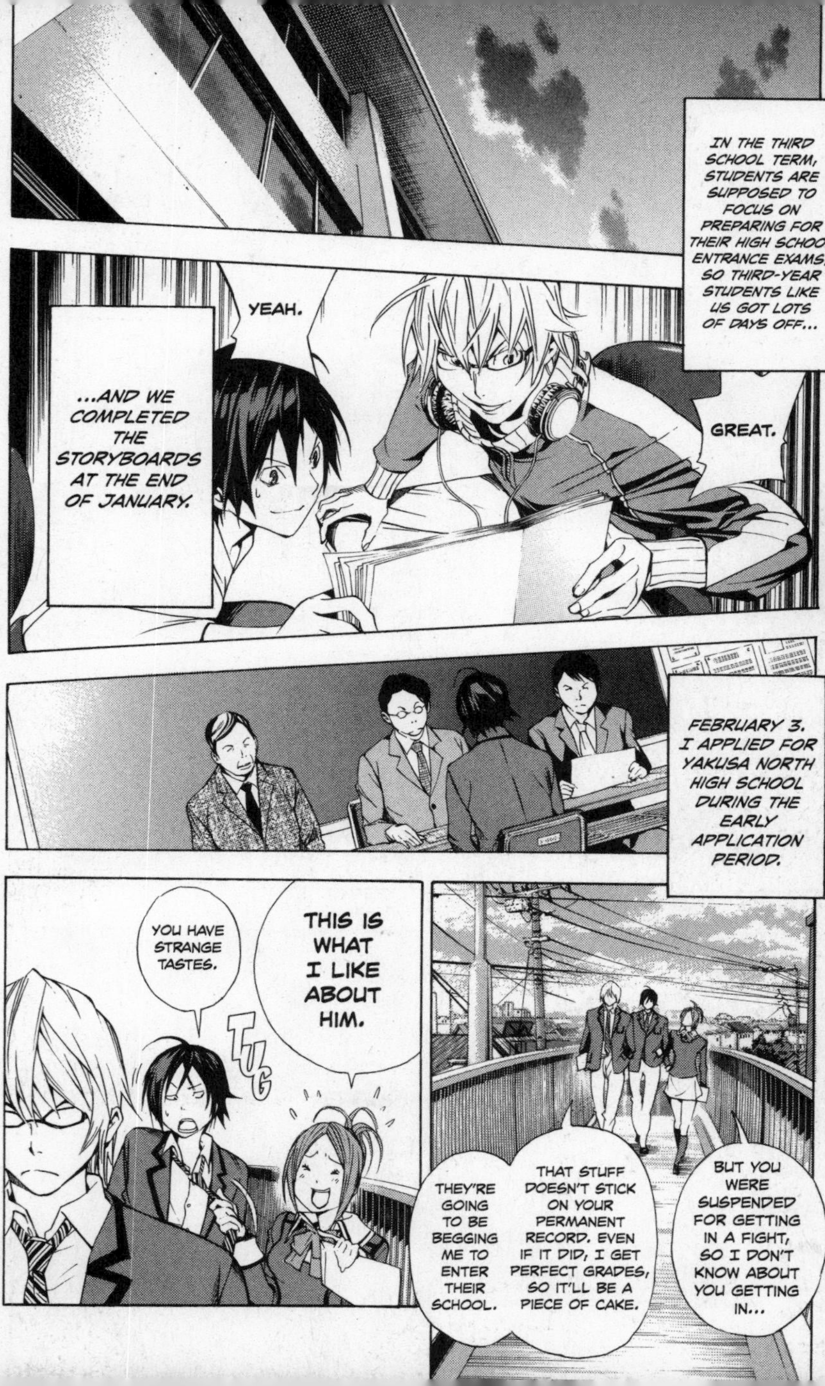
IN THE THIRD SCHOOL TERM, STUDENTS ARE SUPPOSED TO FOCUS ON PREPARING FOR THEIR HIGH SCHOOL ENTRANCE EXAMS, SO THIRD-YEAR STUDENTS LIKE US GOT LOTS OF DAYS OFF...
GREAT.
YEAH.
...AND WE COMPLETED THE STORYBOARDS AT THE END OF JANUARY.
FEBRUARY 3. I APPLIED FOR YAKUSA NORTH HIGH SCHOOL DURING THE EARLY APPLICATION PERIOD.
BUT YOU WERE SUSPENDED FOR GETTING IN A FIGHT, SO I DON'T KNOW ABOUT YOU GETTING IN...
THAT STUFF DOESN'T STICK ON YOUR PERMANENT RECORD. EVEN IF IT DID, I GET PERFECT GRADES, SO IT'LL BE A PIECE OF CAKE.
THEY'RE GOING TO BE BEGGING ME TO ENTER THEIR SCHOOL.
THIS IS WHAT I LIKE ABOUT HIM.
TUG
YOU HAVE STRANGE TASTES.

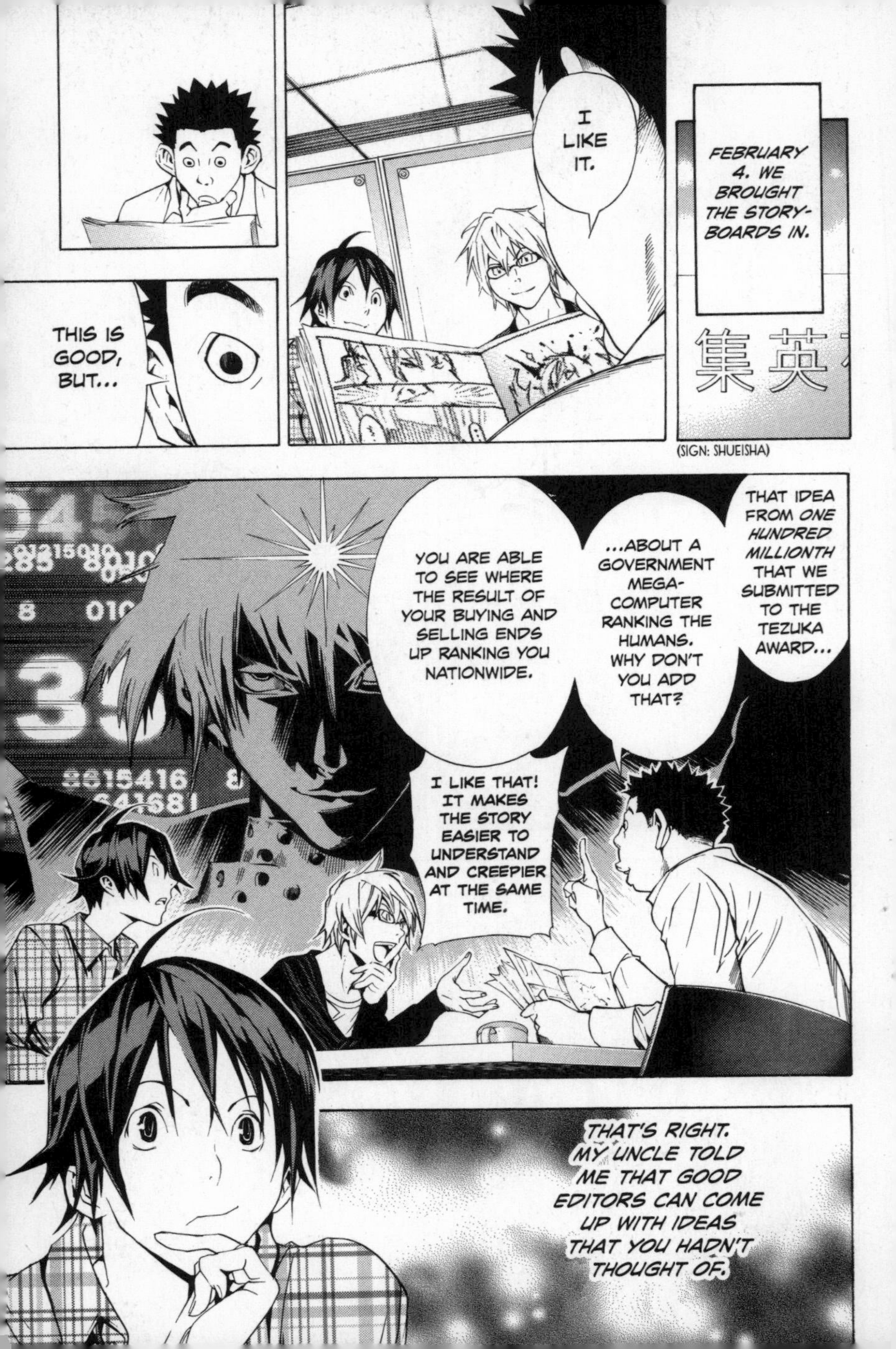
FEBRUARY 4. WE BROUGHT THE STORY-BOARDS IN.
集英
(SIGN: SHUEISHA)
I LIKE IT.
THIS IS GOOD, BUT...
THAT IDEA FROM *ONE HUNDRED MILLIONTH* THAT WE SUBMITTED TO THE TEZUKA AWARD...
...ABOUT A GOVERNMENT MEGA-COMPUTER RANKING THE HUMANS. WHY DON'T YOU ADD THAT?
YOU ARE ABLE TO SEE WHERE THE RESULT OF YOUR BUYING AND SELLING ENDS UP RANKING YOU NATIONWIDE.
I LIKE THAT! IT MAKES THE STORY EASIER TO UNDERSTAND AND CREEPIER AT THE SAME TIME.
THAT'S RIGHT. MY UNCLE TOLD ME THAT GOOD EDITORS CAN COME UP WITH IDEAS THAT YOU HADN'T THOUGHT OF.

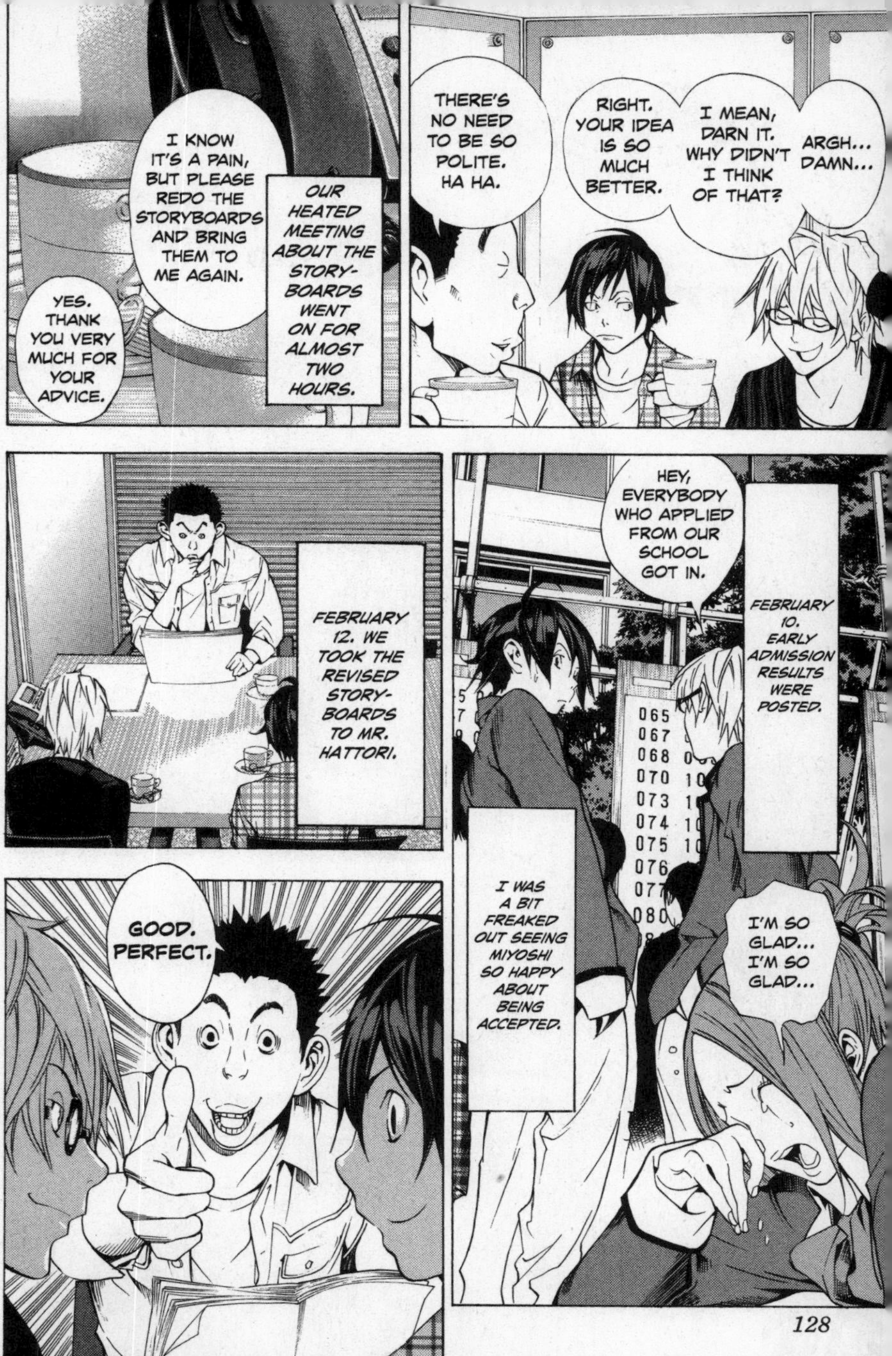
ARGH... DAMN...
I MEAN, DARN IT. WHY DIDN'T I THINK OF THAT?
RIGHT. YOUR IDEA IS SO MUCH BETTER.
THERE'S NO NEED TO BE SO POLITE. HA HA.
OUR HEATED MEETING ABOUT THE STORY-BOARDS WENT ON FOR ALMOST TWO HOURS.
I KNOW IT'S A PAIN, BUT PLEASE REDO THE STORYBOARDS AND BRING THEM TO ME AGAIN.
YES. THANK YOU VERY MUCH FOR YOUR ADVICE.
HEY, EVERYBODY WHO APPLIED FROM OUR SCHOOL GOT IN.
FEBRUARY 10. EARLY ADMISSION RESULTS WERE POSTED.
065 067 068 070 073 074 075 076
I'M SO GLAD... I'M SO GLAD...
I WAS A BIT FREAKED OUT SEEING MIYOSHI SO HAPPY ABOUT BEING ACCEPTED.
FEBRUARY 12. WE TOOK THE REVISED STORY-BOARDS TO MR. HATTORI.
GOOD. PERFECT.

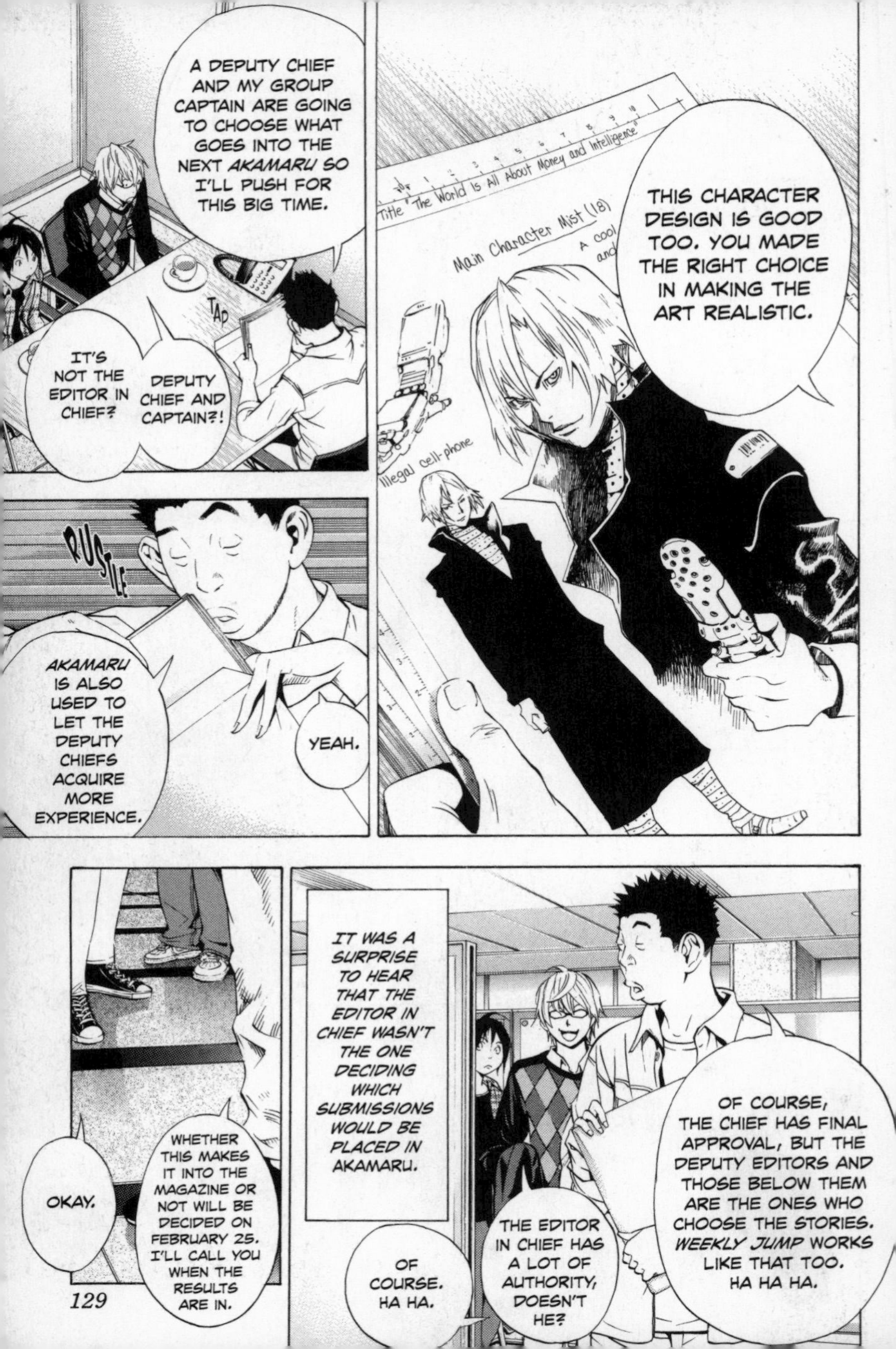
Title "The World Is All About Money and Intelligence"
Main Character Mist (18)
A cool and
Illegal cell-phone
THIS CHARACTER DESIGN IS GOOD TOO. YOU MADE THE RIGHT CHOICE IN MAKING THE ART REALISTIC.
A DEPUTY CHIEF AND MY GROUP CAPTAIN ARE GOING TO CHOOSE WHAT GOES INTO THE NEXT *AKAMARU* SO I'LL PUSH FOR THIS BIG TIME.
TAP
DEPUTY CHIEF AND CAPTAIN?!
IT'S NOT THE EDITOR IN CHIEF?
RUSTLE
*AKAMARU* IS ALSO USED TO LET THE DEPUTY CHIEFS ACQUIRE MORE EXPERIENCE.
YEAH.
*IT WAS A SURPRISE TO HEAR THAT THE EDITOR IN CHIEF WASN'T THE ONE DECIDING WHICH SUBMISSIONS WOULD BE PLACED IN* AKAMARU.
THE EDITOR IN CHIEF HAS A LOT OF AUTHORITY, DOESN'T HE?
OF COURSE. HA HA.
OF COURSE, THE CHIEF HAS FINAL APPROVAL, BUT THE DEPUTY EDITORS AND THOSE BELOW THEM ARE THE ONES WHO CHOOSE THE STORIES. *WEEKLY JUMP* WORKS LIKE THAT TOO. HA HA HA.
WHETHER THIS MAKES IT INTO THE MAGAZINE OR NOT WILL BE DECIDED ON FEBRUARY 25. I'LL CALL YOU WHEN THE RESULTS ARE IN.
OKAY.

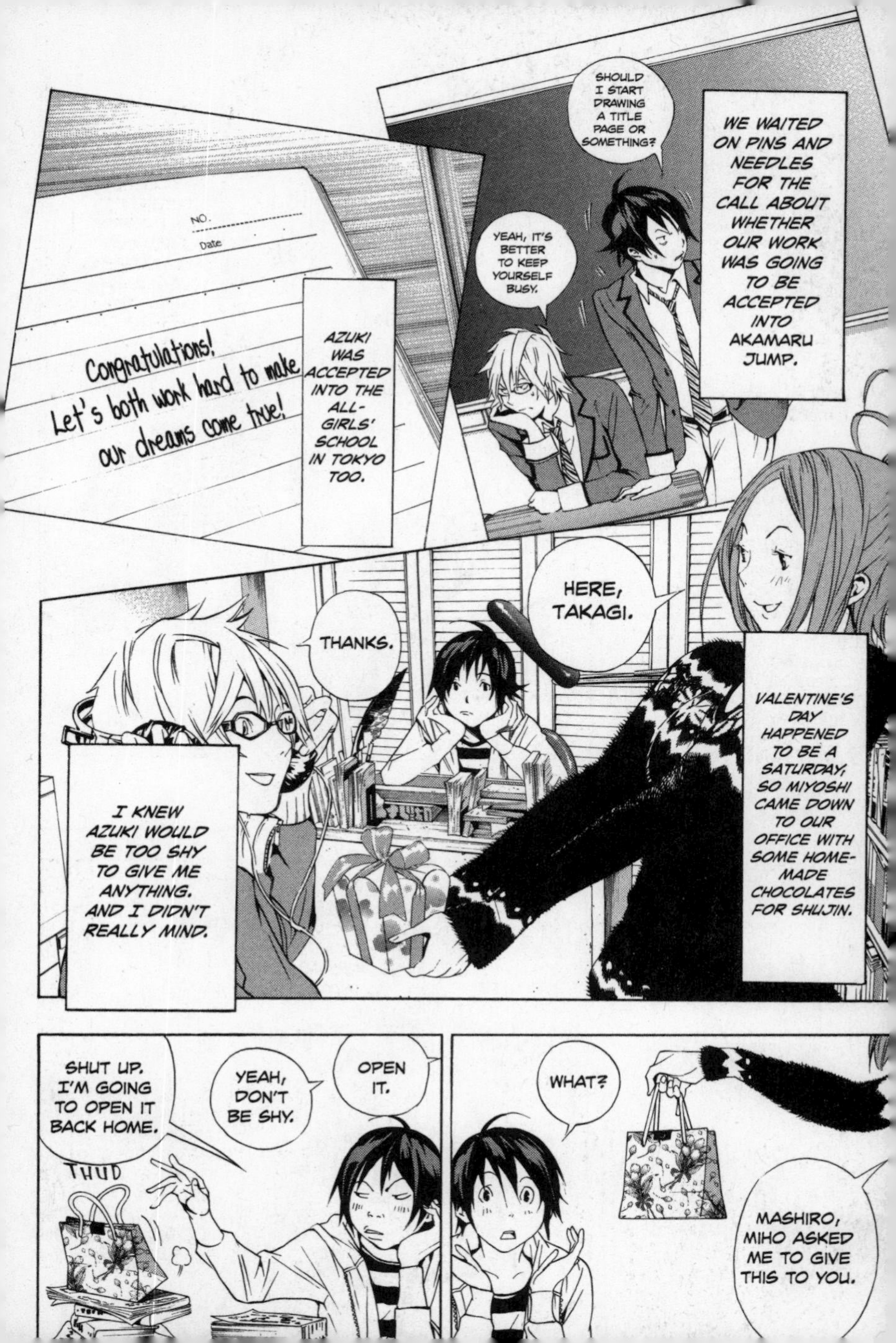
WE WAITED ON PINS AND NEEDLES FOR THE CALL ABOUT WHETHER OUR WORK WAS GOING TO BE ACCEPTED INTO AKAMARU JUMP.
SHOULD I START DRAWING A TITLE PAGE OR SOMETHING?
YEAH, IT'S BETTER TO KEEP YOURSELF BUSY.
AZUKI WAS ACCEPTED INTO THE ALL-GIRLS' SCHOOL IN TOKYO TOO.
NO.
Date
Congratulations!
Let's both work hard to make our dreams come true!
VALENTINE'S DAY HAPPENED TO BE A SATURDAY, SO MIYOSHI CAME DOWN TO OUR OFFICE WITH SOME HOME-MADE CHOCOLATES FOR SHUJIN.
HERE, TAKAGI.
THANKS.
I KNEW AZUKI WOULD BE TOO SHY TO GIVE ME ANYTHING. AND I DIDN'T REALLY MIND.
MASHIRO, MIHO ASKED ME TO GIVE THIS TO YOU.
WHAT?
OPEN IT.
YEAH, DON'T BE SHY.
SHUT UP. I'M GOING TO OPEN IT BACK HOME.
THUD

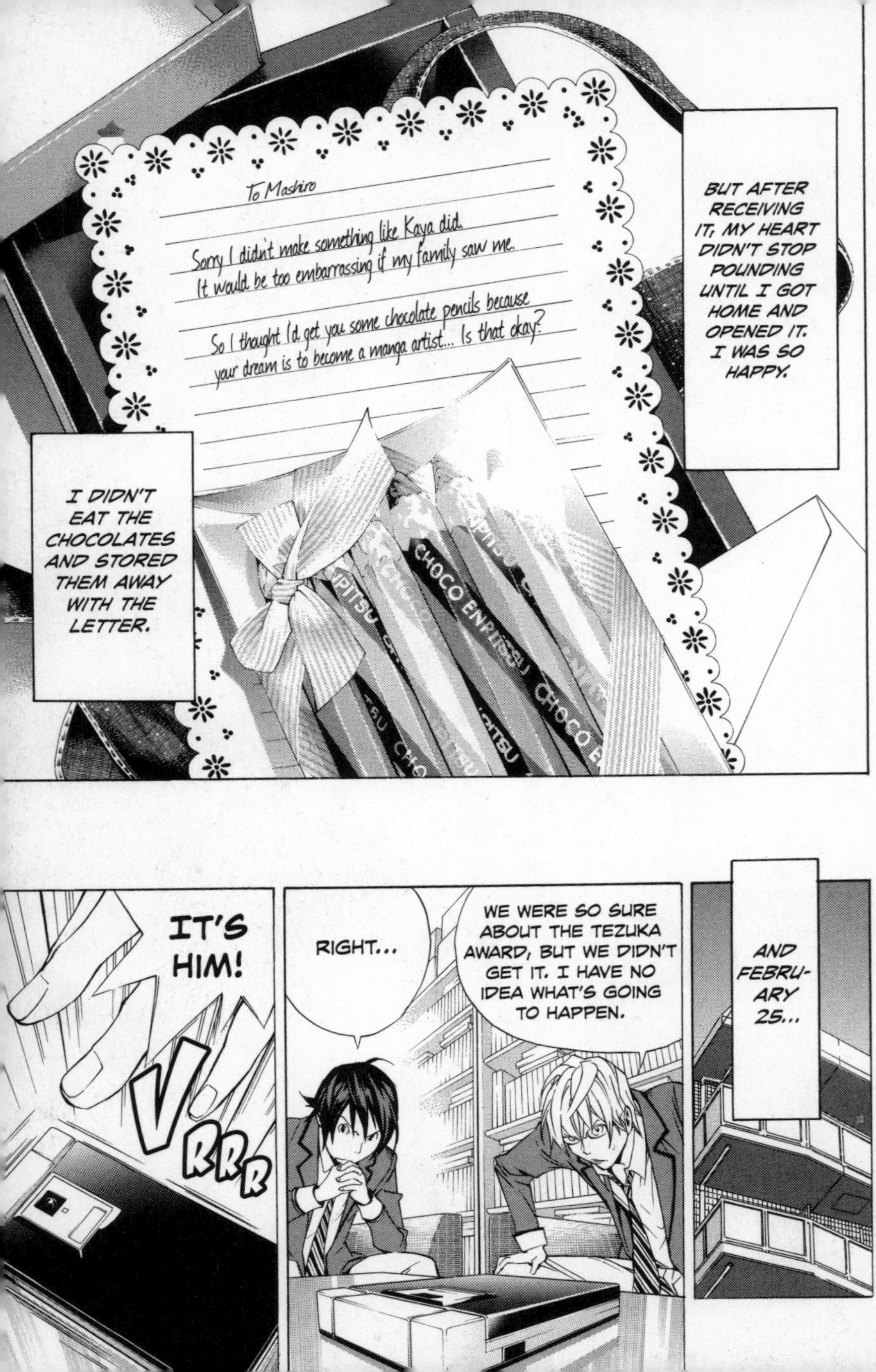
BUT AFTER RECEIVING IT, MY HEART DIDN'T STOP POUNDING UNTIL I GOT HOME AND OPENED IT. I WAS SO HAPPY.
To Mashiro
Sorry I didn't make something like Kaya did.
It would be too embarrassing if my family saw me.
So I thought I'd get you some chocolate pencils because your dream is to become a manga artist... Is that okay?
CHOCO ENPITSU
I DIDN'T EAT THE CHOCOLATES AND STORED THEM AWAY WITH THE LETTER.
AND FEBRUARY 25...
WE WERE SO SURE ABOUT THE TEZUKA AWARD, BUT WE DIDN'T GET IT. I HAVE NO IDEA WHAT'S GOING TO HAPPEN.
RIGHT...
IT'S HIM!
VRRR

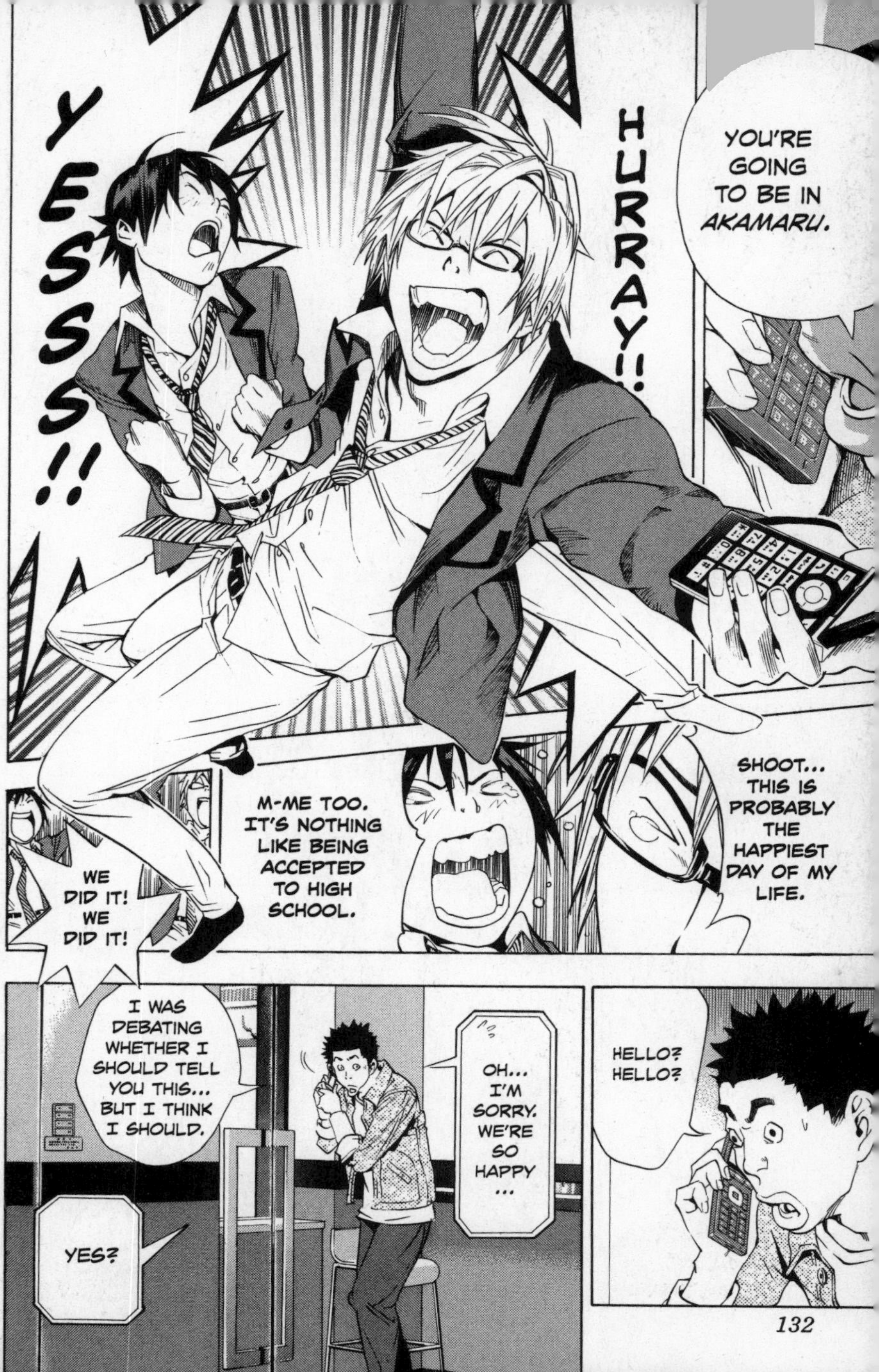
YOU'RE GOING TO BE IN *AKAMARU*.
HURRAY!!
YESSS!!
SHOOT... THIS IS PROBABLY THE HAPPIEST DAY OF MY LIFE.
M-ME TOO. IT'S NOTHING LIKE BEING ACCEPTED TO HIGH SCHOOL.
WE DID IT! WE DID IT!
HELLO? HELLO?
OH... I'M SORRY. WE'RE SO HAPPY ...
I WAS DEBATING WHETHER I SHOULD TELL YOU THIS... BUT I THINK I SHOULD.
YES?

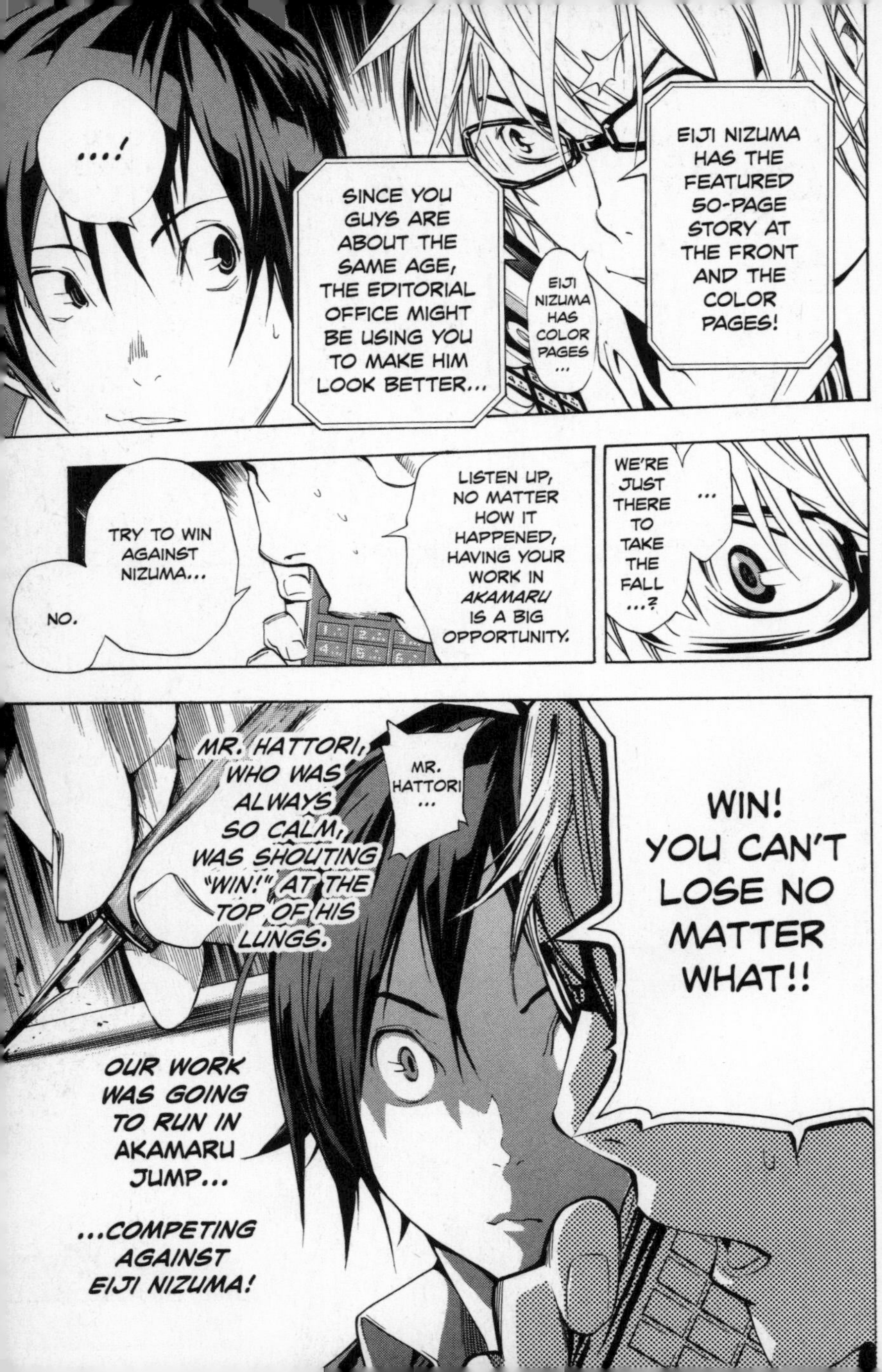
EIJI NIZUMA HAS THE FEATURED 50-PAGE STORY AT THE FRONT AND THE COLOR PAGES!
EIJI NIZUMA HAS COLOR PAGES ...
SINCE YOU GUYS ARE ABOUT THE SAME AGE, THE EDITORIAL OFFICE MIGHT BE USING YOU TO MAKE HIM LOOK BETTER...
...!
...
WE'RE JUST THERE TO TAKE THE FALL ...?
LISTEN UP, NO MATTER HOW IT HAPPENED, HAVING YOUR WORK IN AKAMARU IS A BIG OPPORTUNITY.
TRY TO WIN AGAINST NIZUMA...
NO.
WIN! YOU CAN'T LOSE NO MATTER WHAT!!
MR. HATTORI ...
MR. HATTORI, WHO WAS ALWAYS SO CALM, WAS SHOUTING "WIN!" AT THE TOP OF HIS LUNGS.
OUR WORK WAS GOING TO RUN IN AKAMARU JUMP...
...COMPETING AGAINST EIJI NIZUMA!

OHBA'S STORYBOARD

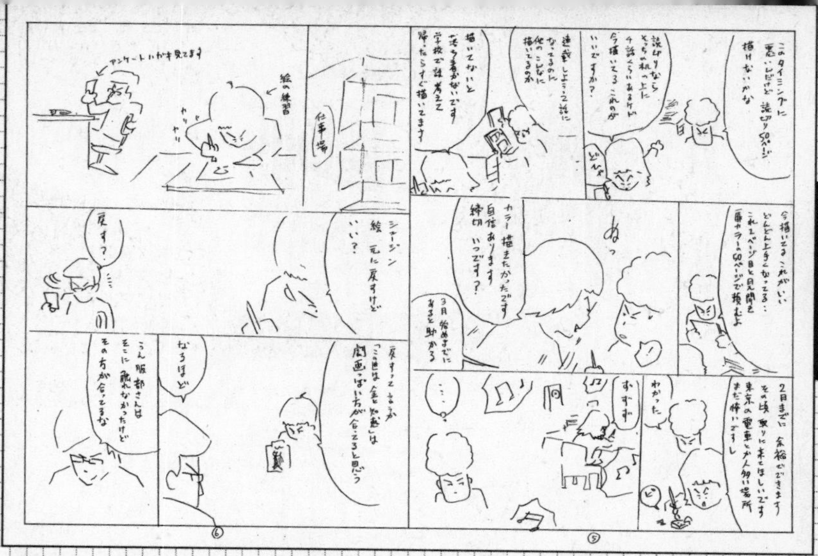
このタイミングに悪いんだけど読切り50ページ描けないかな
読切りならそっちの机の上に4話ぐらいあるけど今描いてるこれのがいいですか？
どんっ
連載しようと話になってるのに他のこんなに描いてるのか
描いてないと落ち着かないです学校で話考えて帰ったらすぐ描いてます
仕事場
絵の練習
カリカリ
アンケートハガキ見てます
今描いてるこれがいいどんどん上手くなってる…これ2ページ目と見開きと扉カラーの50ページで頼むよ
ぬっ
カラー描きたかったです自信あります締切いつです？
3月始めまでにあると助かる
シュージン絵元に戻すけどいい？
戻す？
2月までに余裕でできますその頃取りに来てほしいです東京の電車とか人多い場所まだ怖いですし
わかった
…
戻すっていうか「この世は金と知恵」は劇画っぽい方が合ってると思う
なるほど
うん服部さんはそこに触れなかったけどその方が合ってるな

OBATA'S STORYBOARD

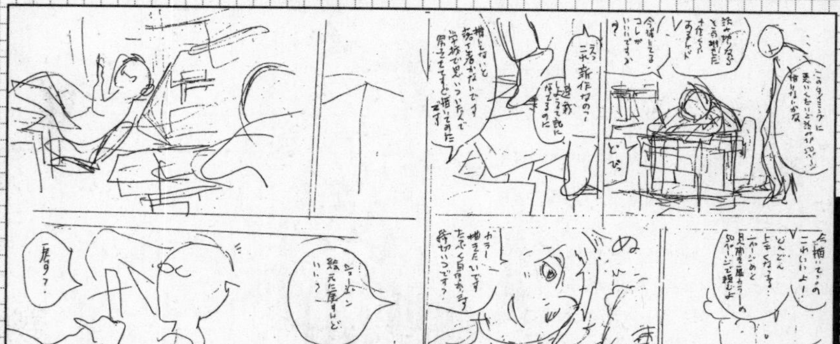

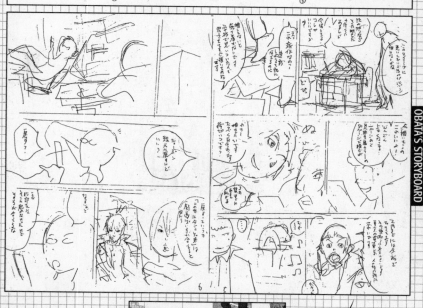

COMPLETE!

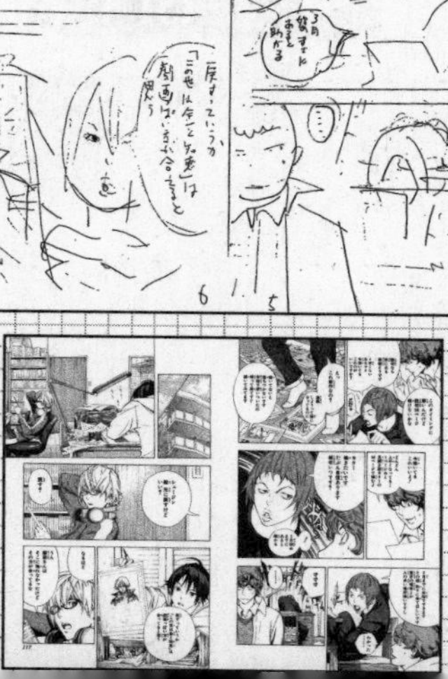

※CREATOR STORYBOARDS AND FINISHED PAGES IN JAPANESE

**BAKUMAN。vol.2**

"Until the Final Draft Is Complete"

Chapter 13, pp. 116-117

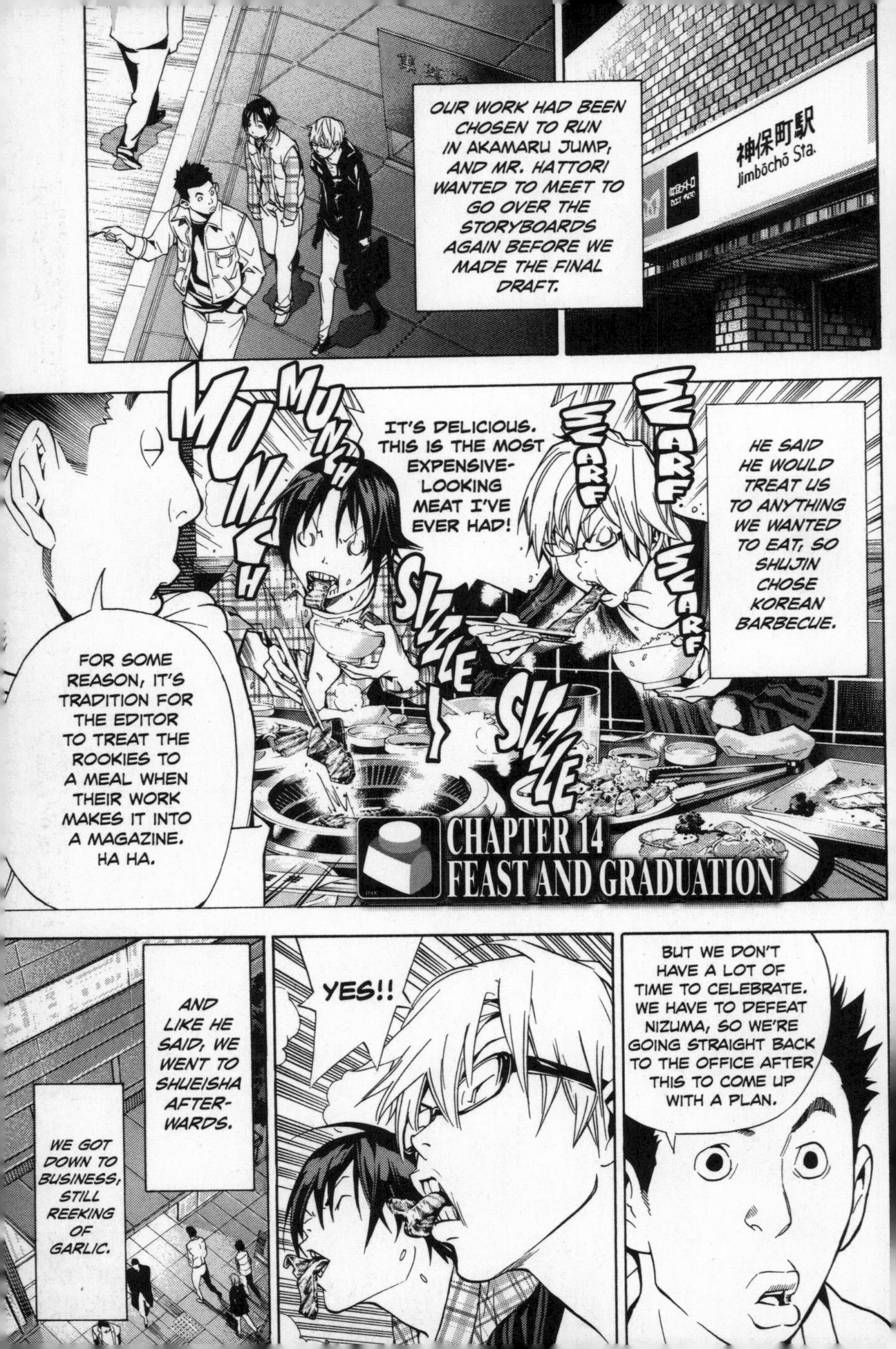
神保町駅
Jimbōchō Sta.
OUR WORK HAD BEEN CHOSEN TO RUN IN AKAMARU JUMP, AND MR. HATTORI WANTED TO MEET TO GO OVER THE STORYBOARDS AGAIN BEFORE WE MADE THE FINAL DRAFT.
HE SAID HE WOULD TREAT US TO ANYTHING WE WANTED TO EAT, SO SHUJIN CHOSE KOREAN BARBECUE.
SCARF SCARF
SCARF SCARF
IT'S DELICIOUS. THIS IS THE MOST EXPENSIVE-LOOKING MEAT I'VE EVER HAD!
MUNCH MUNCH
SIZZLE SIZZLE
FOR SOME REASON, IT'S TRADITION FOR THE EDITOR TO TREAT THE ROOKIES TO A MEAL WHEN THEIR WORK MAKES IT INTO A MAGAZINE. HA HA.
CHAPTER 14
FEAST AND GRADUATION
BUT WE DON'T HAVE A LOT OF TIME TO CELEBRATE. WE HAVE TO DEFEAT NIZUMA, SO WE'RE GOING STRAIGHT BACK TO THE OFFICE AFTER THIS TO COME UP WITH A PLAN.
YES!!
AND LIKE HE SAID, WE WENT TO SHUEISHA AFTER-WARDS.
WE GOT DOWN TO BUSINESS, STILL REEKING OF GARLIC.

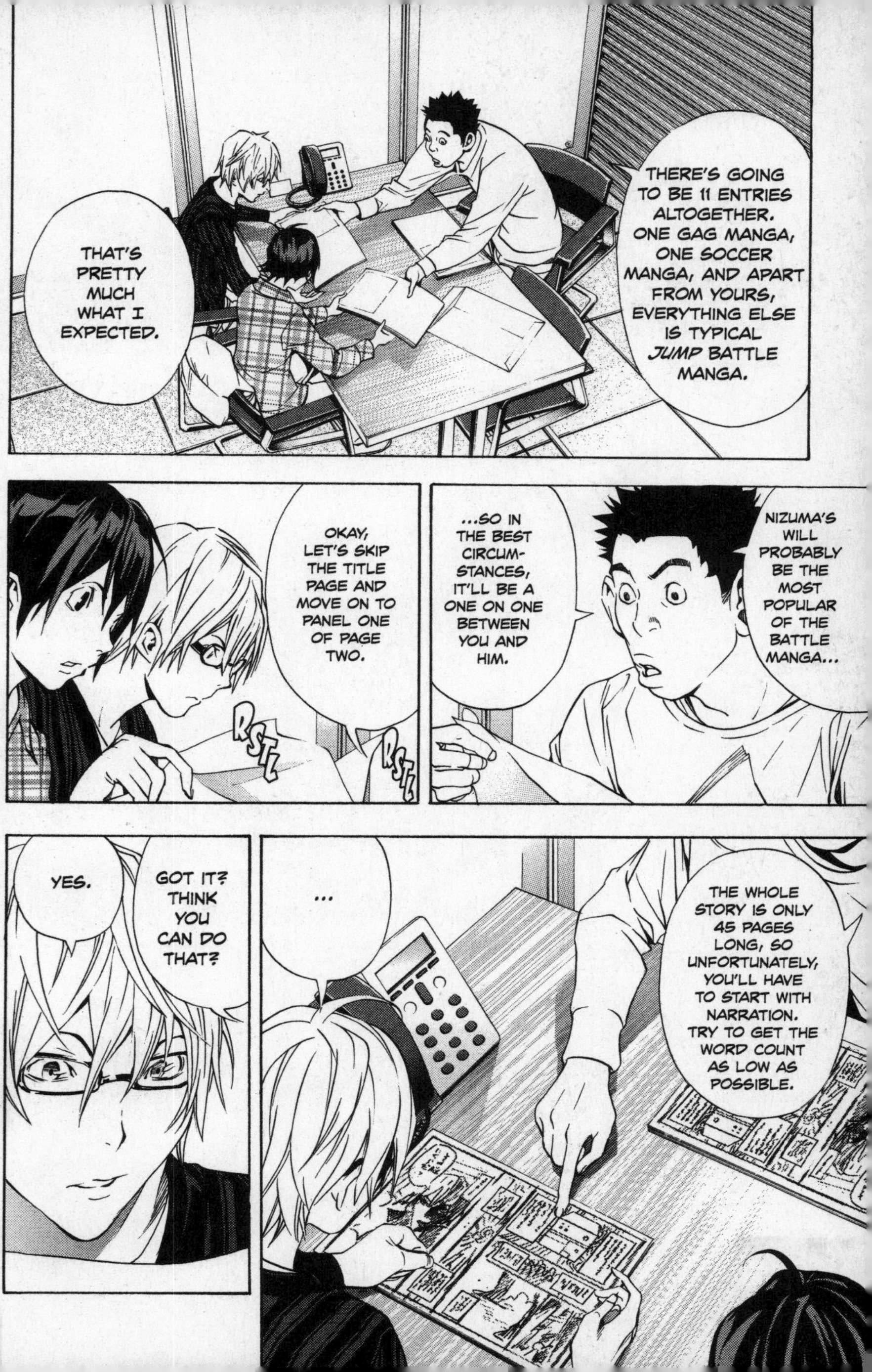

THERE'S GOING TO BE 11 ENTRIES ALTOGETHER. ONE GAG MANGA, ONE SOCCER MANGA, AND APART FROM YOURS, EVERYTHING ELSE IS TYPICAL *JUMP* BATTLE MANGA.
THAT'S PRETTY MUCH WHAT I EXPECTED.
NIZUMA'S WILL PROBABLY BE THE MOST POPULAR OF THE BATTLE MANGA...
...SO IN THE BEST CIRCUM-STANCES, IT'LL BE A ONE ON ONE BETWEEN YOU AND HIM.
OKAY, LET'S SKIP THE TITLE PAGE AND MOVE ON TO PANEL ONE OF PAGE TWO.
RSTL
RSTL
THE WHOLE STORY IS ONLY 45 PAGES LONG, SO UNFORTUNATELY, YOU'LL HAVE TO START WITH NARRATION. TRY TO GET THE WORD COUNT AS LOW AS POSSIBLE.
...
GOT IT? THINK YOU CAN DO THAT?
YES.

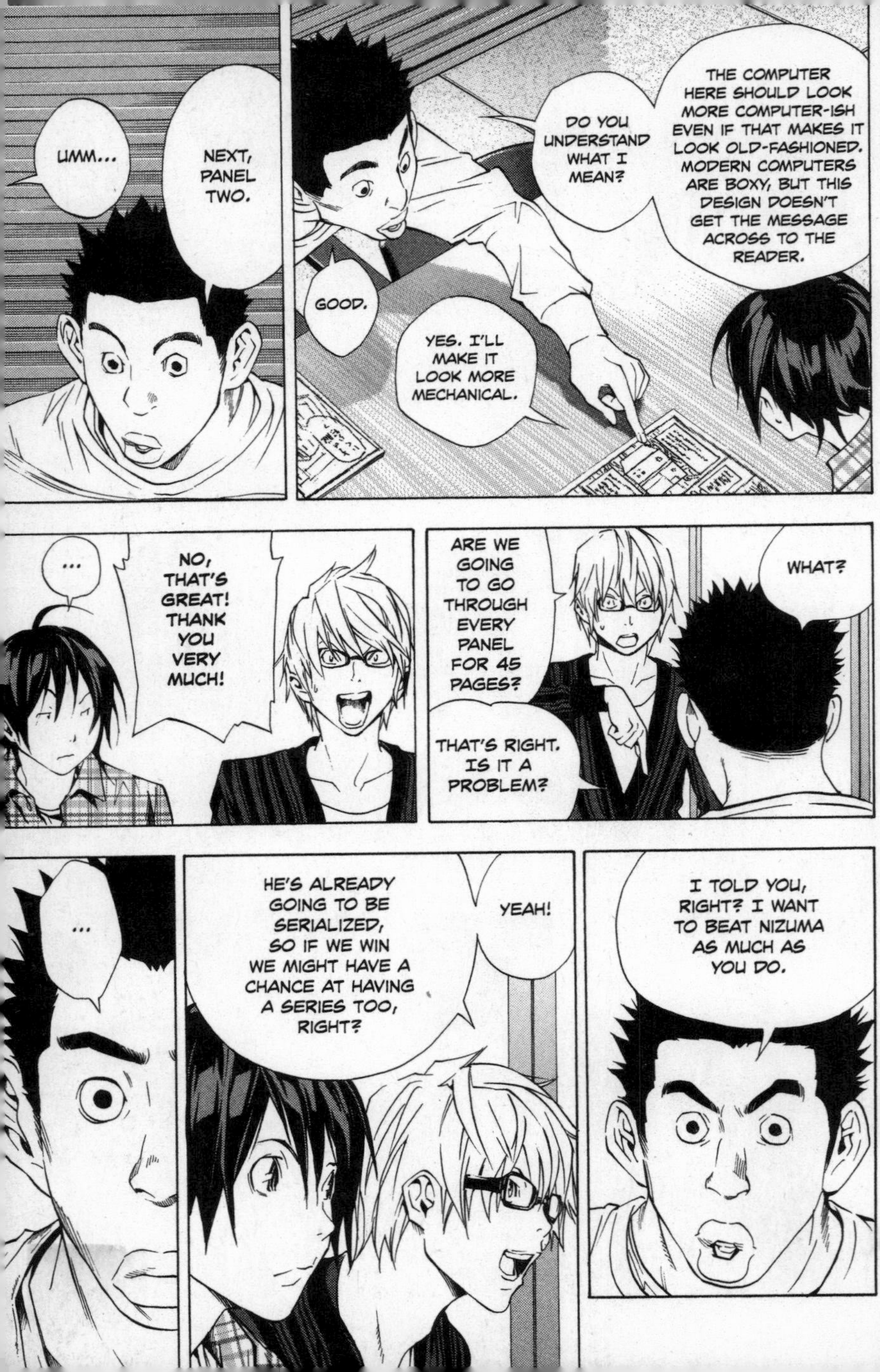
THE COMPUTER HERE SHOULD LOOK MORE COMPUTER-ISH EVEN IF THAT MAKES IT LOOK OLD-FASHIONED. MODERN COMPUTERS ARE BOXY, BUT THIS DESIGN DOESN'T GET THE MESSAGE ACROSS TO THE READER.
DO YOU UNDERSTAND WHAT I MEAN?
YES. I'LL MAKE IT LOOK MORE MECHANICAL.
GOOD.
NEXT, PANEL TWO.
UMM...
WHAT?
ARE WE GOING TO GO THROUGH EVERY PANEL FOR 45 PAGES?
THAT'S RIGHT. IS IT A PROBLEM?
NO, THAT'S GREAT! THANK YOU VERY MUCH!
...
I TOLD YOU, RIGHT? I WANT TO BEAT NIZUMA AS MUCH AS YOU DO.
YEAH!
HE'S ALREADY GOING TO BE SERIALIZED, SO IF WE WIN WE MIGHT HAVE A CHANCE AT HAVING A SERIES TOO, RIGHT?
...

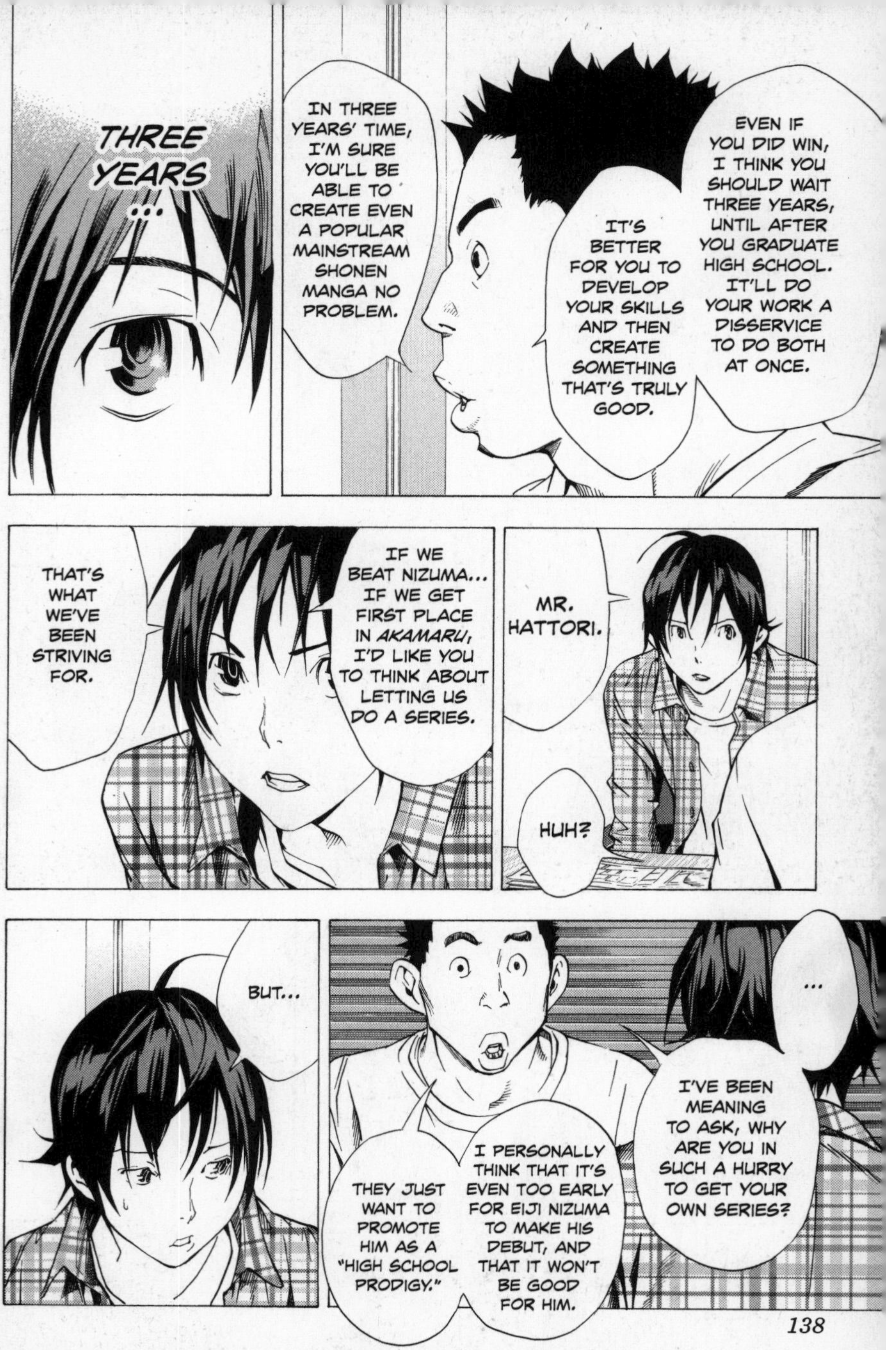
EVEN IF YOU DID WIN, I THINK YOU SHOULD WAIT THREE YEARS, UNTIL AFTER YOU GRADUATE HIGH SCHOOL. IT'LL DO YOUR WORK A DISSERVICE TO DO BOTH AT ONCE.
IT'S BETTER FOR YOU TO DEVELOP YOUR SKILLS AND THEN CREATE SOMETHING THAT'S TRULY GOOD.
IN THREE YEARS' TIME, I'M SURE YOU'LL BE ABLE TO CREATE EVEN A POPULAR MAINSTREAM SHONEN MANGA NO PROBLEM.
THREE YEARS ...
MR. HATTORI.
HUH?
IF WE BEAT NIZUMA... IF WE GET FIRST PLACE IN *AKAMARU*, I'D LIKE YOU TO THINK ABOUT LETTING US DO A SERIES.
THAT'S WHAT WE'VE BEEN STRIVING FOR.
...
I'VE BEEN MEANING TO ASK, WHY ARE YOU IN SUCH A HURRY TO GET YOUR OWN SERIES?
I PERSONALLY THINK THAT IT'S EVEN TOO EARLY FOR EIJI NIZUMA TO MAKE HIS DEBUT, AND THAT IT WON'T BE GOOD FOR HIM.
THEY JUST WANT TO PROMOTE HIM AS A "HIGH SCHOOL PRODIGY."
BUT...

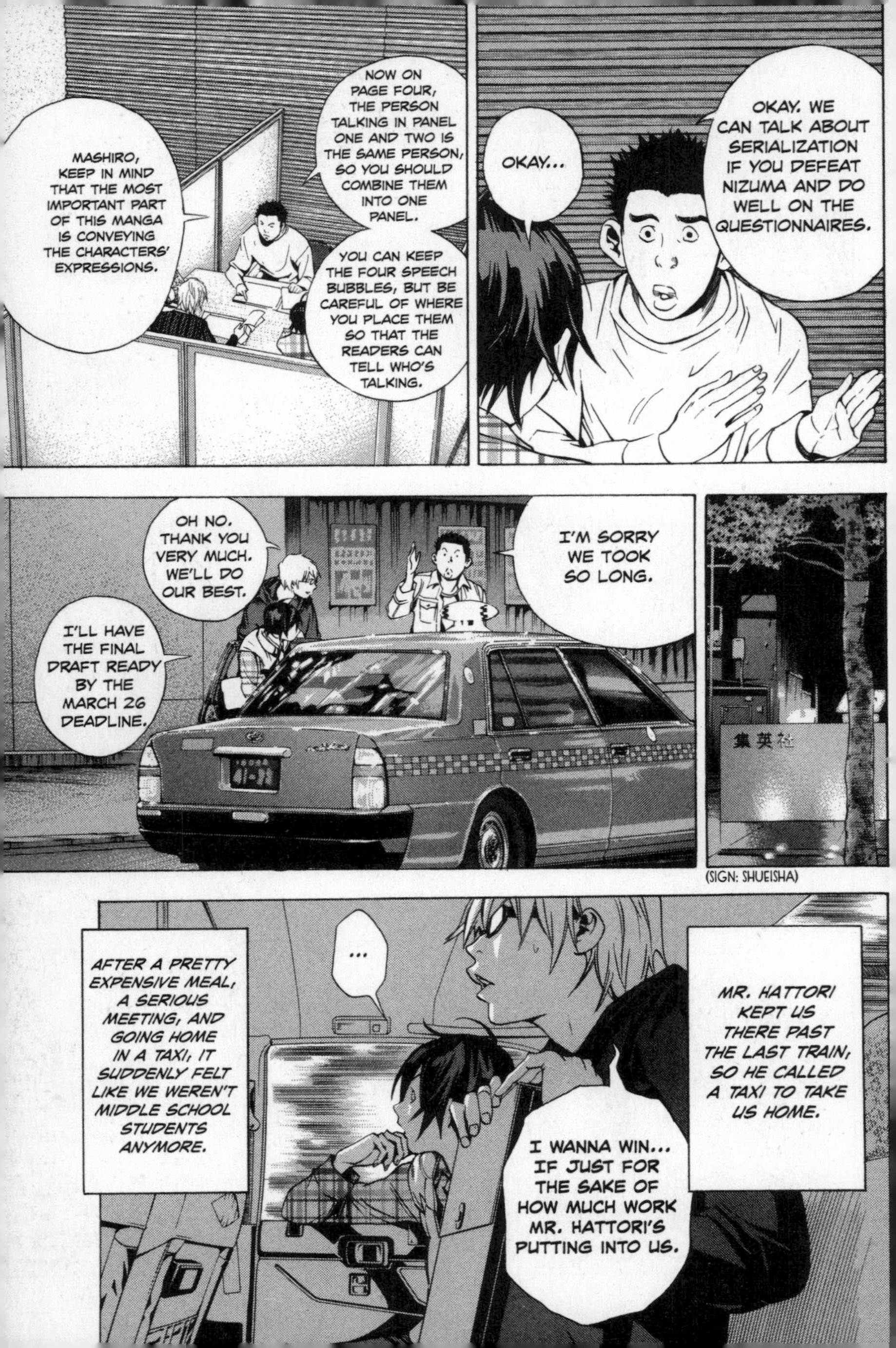
OKAY. WE CAN TALK ABOUT SERIALIZATION IF YOU DEFEAT NIZUMA AND DO WELL ON THE QUESTIONNAIRES.
OKAY...
NOW ON PAGE FOUR, THE PERSON TALKING IN PANEL ONE AND TWO IS THE SAME PERSON, SO YOU SHOULD COMBINE THEM INTO ONE PANEL.
YOU CAN KEEP THE FOUR SPEECH BUBBLES, BUT BE CAREFUL OF WHERE YOU PLACE THEM SO THAT THE READERS CAN TELL WHO'S TALKING.
MASHIRO, KEEP IN MIND THAT THE MOST IMPORTANT PART OF THIS MANGA IS CONVEYING THE CHARACTERS' EXPRESSIONS.
集英社
I'M SORRY WE TOOK SO LONG.
OH NO. THANK YOU VERY MUCH. WE'LL DO OUR BEST.
I'LL HAVE THE FINAL DRAFT READY BY THE MARCH 26 DEADLINE.
MR. HATTORI KEPT US THERE PAST THE LAST TRAIN, SO HE CALLED A TAXI TO TAKE US HOME.
...
AFTER A PRETTY EXPENSIVE MEAL, A SERIOUS MEETING, AND GOING HOME IN A TAXI, IT SUDDENLY FELT LIKE WE WEREN'T MIDDLE SCHOOL STUDENTS ANYMORE.
I WANNA WIN... IF JUST FOR THE SAKE OF HOW MUCH WORK MR. HATTORI'S PUTTING INTO US.
(SIGN: SHUEISHA)

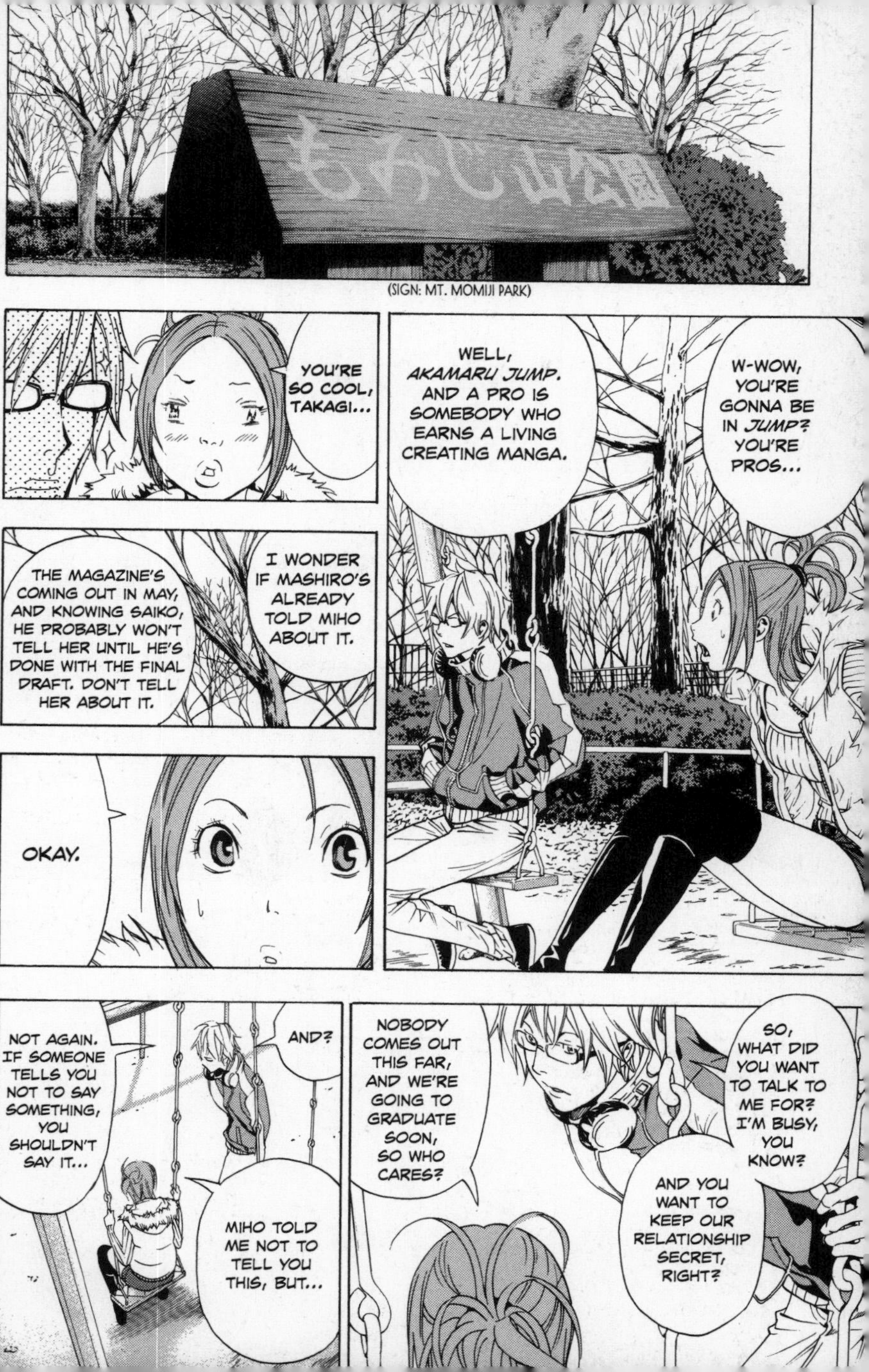
(SIGN: MT. MOMIJI PARK)
W-WOW, YOU'RE GONNA BE IN JUMP? YOU'RE PROS...
WELL, AKAMARU JUMP. AND A PRO IS SOMEBODY WHO EARNS A LIVING CREATING MANGA.
YOU'RE SO COOL, TAKAGI...
I WONDER IF MASHIRO'S ALREADY TOLD MIHO ABOUT IT.
THE MAGAZINE'S COMING OUT IN MAY, AND KNOWING SAIKO, HE PROBABLY WON'T TELL HER UNTIL HE'S DONE WITH THE FINAL DRAFT. DON'T TELL HER ABOUT IT.
OKAY.
SO, WHAT DID YOU WANT TO TALK TO ME FOR? I'M BUSY, YOU KNOW?
NOBODY COMES OUT THIS FAR, AND WE'RE GOING TO GRADUATE SOON, SO WHO CARES?
AND YOU WANT TO KEEP OUR RELATIONSHIP SECRET, RIGHT?
AND?
NOT AGAIN. IF SOMEONE TELLS YOU NOT TO SAY SOMETHING, YOU SHOULDN'T SAY IT...
MIHO TOLD ME NOT TO TELL YOU THIS, BUT...

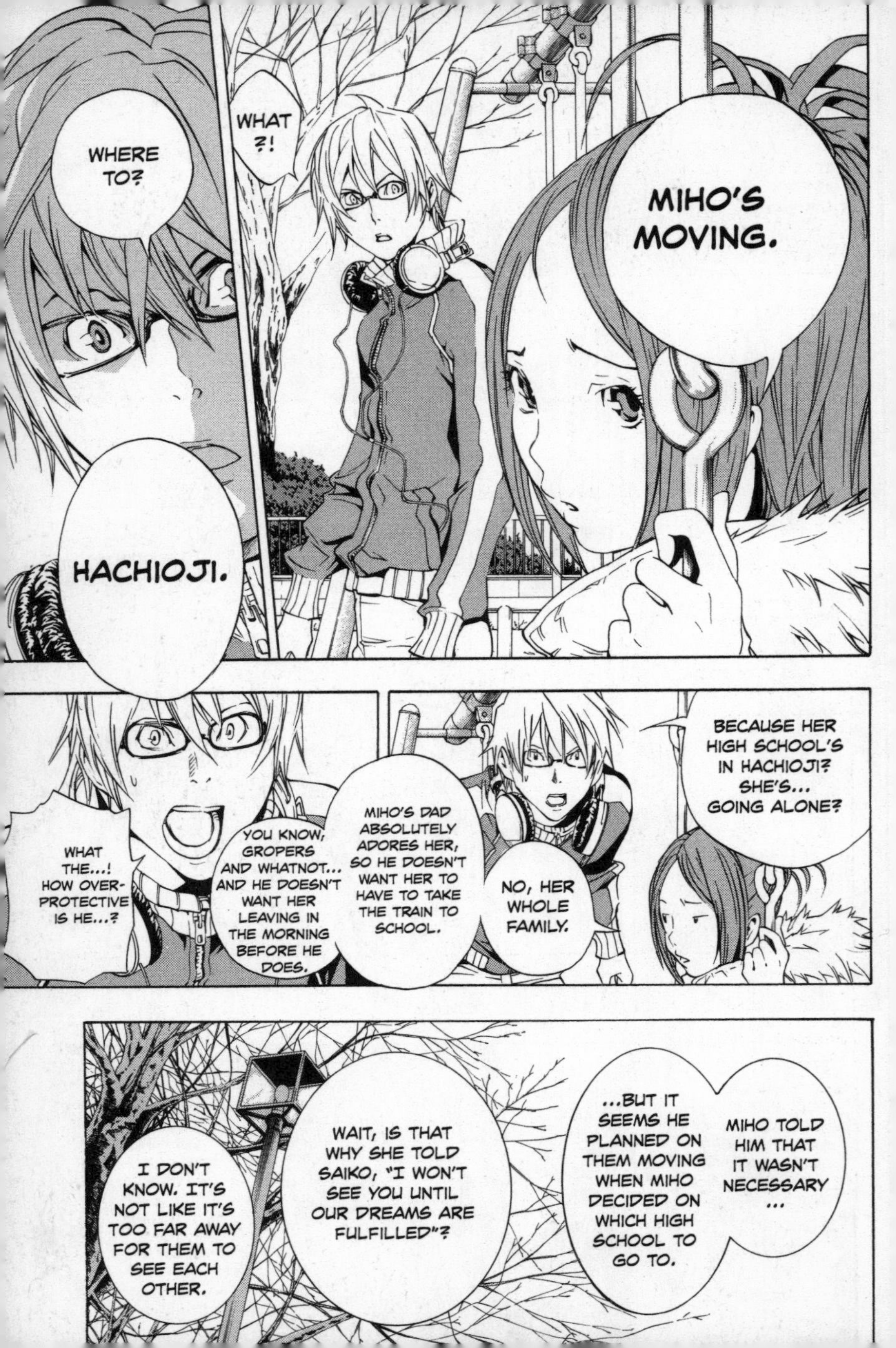
MIHO'S MOVING.
WHAT ?!
WHERE TO?
HACHIOJI.
BECAUSE HER HIGH SCHOOL'S IN HACHIOJI? SHE'S... GOING ALONE?
NO, HER WHOLE FAMILY.
MIHO'S DAD ABSOLUTELY ADORES HER, SO HE DOESN'T WANT HER TO HAVE TO TAKE THE TRAIN TO SCHOOL.
YOU KNOW, GROPERS AND WHATNOT... AND HE DOESN'T WANT HER LEAVING IN THE MORNING BEFORE HE DOES.
WHAT THE...! HOW OVER-PROTECTIVE IS HE...?
MIHO TOLD HIM THAT IT WASN'T NECESSARY...
...BUT IT SEEMS HE PLANNED ON THEM MOVING WHEN MIHO DECIDED ON WHICH HIGH SCHOOL TO GO TO.
WAIT, IS THAT WHY SHE TOLD SAIKO, "I WON'T SEE YOU UNTIL OUR DREAMS ARE FULFILLED"?
I DON'T KNOW. IT'S NOT LIKE IT'S TOO FAR AWAY FOR THEM TO SEE EACH OTHER.

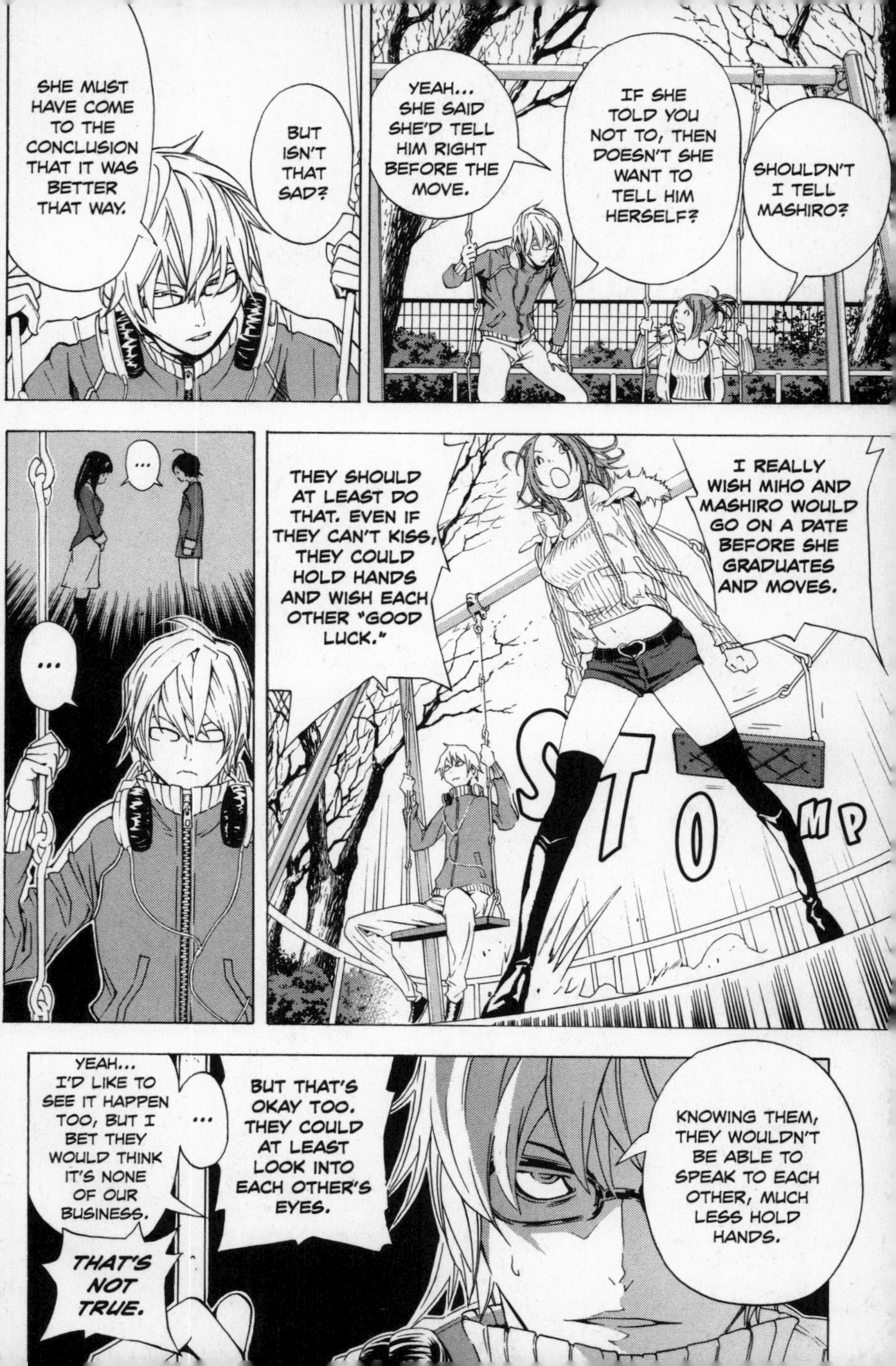
SHOULDN'T I TELL MASHIRO?
IF SHE TOLD YOU NOT TO, THEN DOESN'T SHE WANT TO TELL HIM HERSELF?
YEAH... SHE SAID SHE'D TELL HIM RIGHT BEFORE THE MOVE.
BUT ISN'T THAT SAD?
SHE MUST HAVE COME TO THE CONCLUSION THAT IT WAS BETTER THAT WAY.
I REALLY WISH MIHO AND MASHIRO WOULD GO ON A DATE BEFORE SHE GRADUATES AND MOVES.
THEY SHOULD AT LEAST DO THAT. EVEN IF THEY CAN'T KISS, THEY COULD HOLD HANDS AND WISH EACH OTHER "GOOD LUCK."
STOMP
...
...
KNOWING THEM, THEY WOULDN'T BE ABLE TO SPEAK TO EACH OTHER, MUCH LESS HOLD HANDS.
BUT THAT'S OKAY TOO. THEY COULD AT LEAST LOOK INTO EACH OTHER'S EYES.
...
YEAH... I'D LIKE TO SEE IT HAPPEN TOO, BUT I BET THEY WOULD THINK IT'S NONE OF OUR BUSINESS.
THAT'S NOT TRUE.

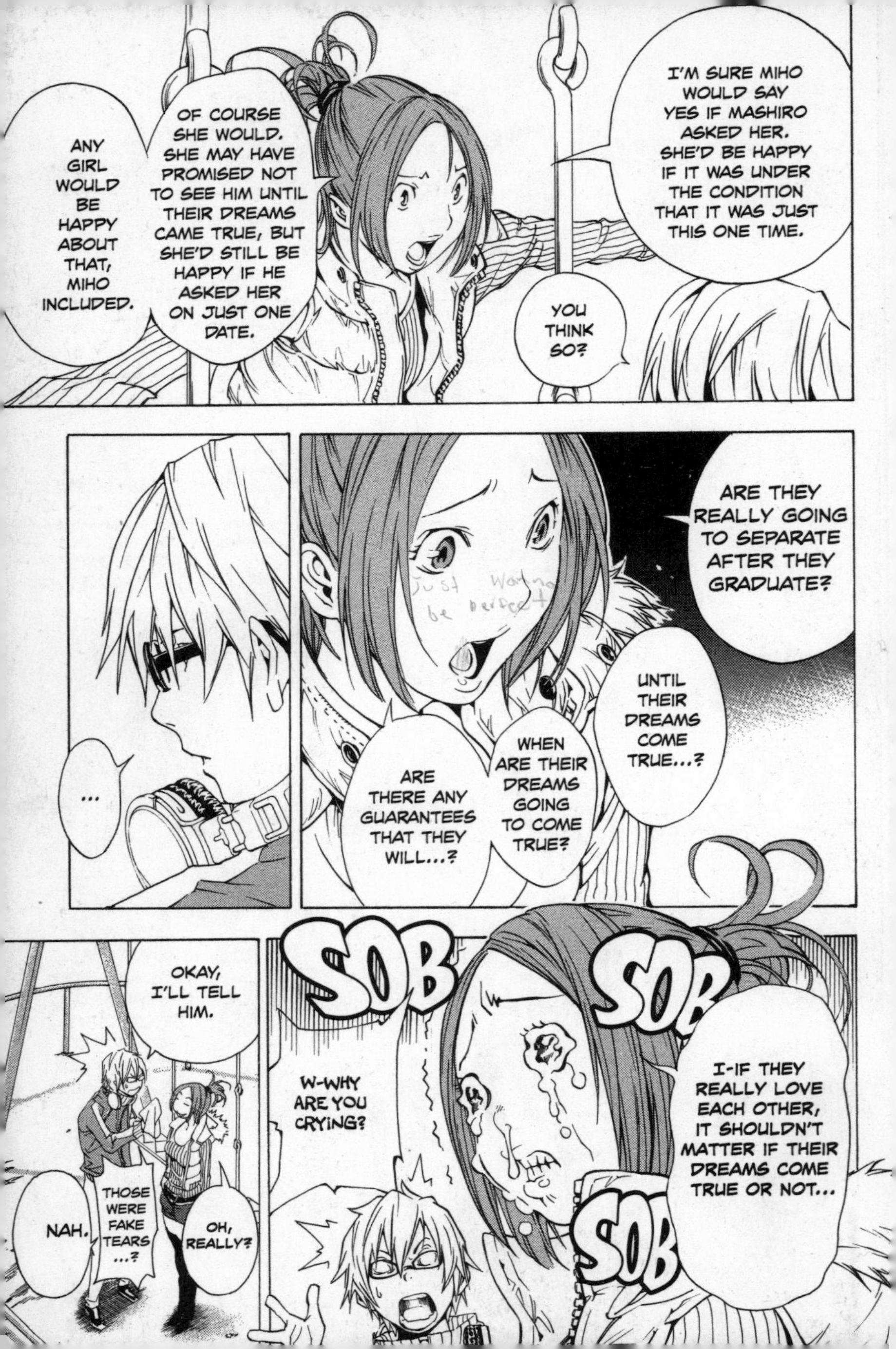
I'M SURE MIHO WOULD SAY YES IF MASHIRO ASKED HER. SHE'D BE HAPPY IF IT WAS UNDER THE CONDITION THAT IT WAS JUST THIS ONE TIME.
YOU THINK SO?
OF COURSE SHE WOULD. SHE MAY HAVE PROMISED NOT TO SEE HIM UNTIL THEIR DREAMS CAME TRUE, BUT SHE'D STILL BE HAPPY IF HE ASKED HER ON JUST ONE DATE.
ANY GIRL WOULD BE HAPPY ABOUT THAT, MIHO INCLUDED.
ARE THEY REALLY GOING TO SEPARATE AFTER THEY GRADUATE?
UNTIL THEIR DREAMS COME TRUE...?
WHEN ARE THEIR DREAMS GOING TO COME TRUE?
ARE THERE ANY GUARANTEES THAT THEY WILL...?
...
SOB
SOB
SOB
I-IF THEY REALLY LOVE EACH OTHER, IT SHOULDN'T MATTER IF THEIR DREAMS COME TRUE OR NOT...
W-WHY ARE YOU CRYING?
OKAY, I'LL TELL HIM.
OH, REALLY?
THOSE WERE FAKE TEARS...?
NAH.

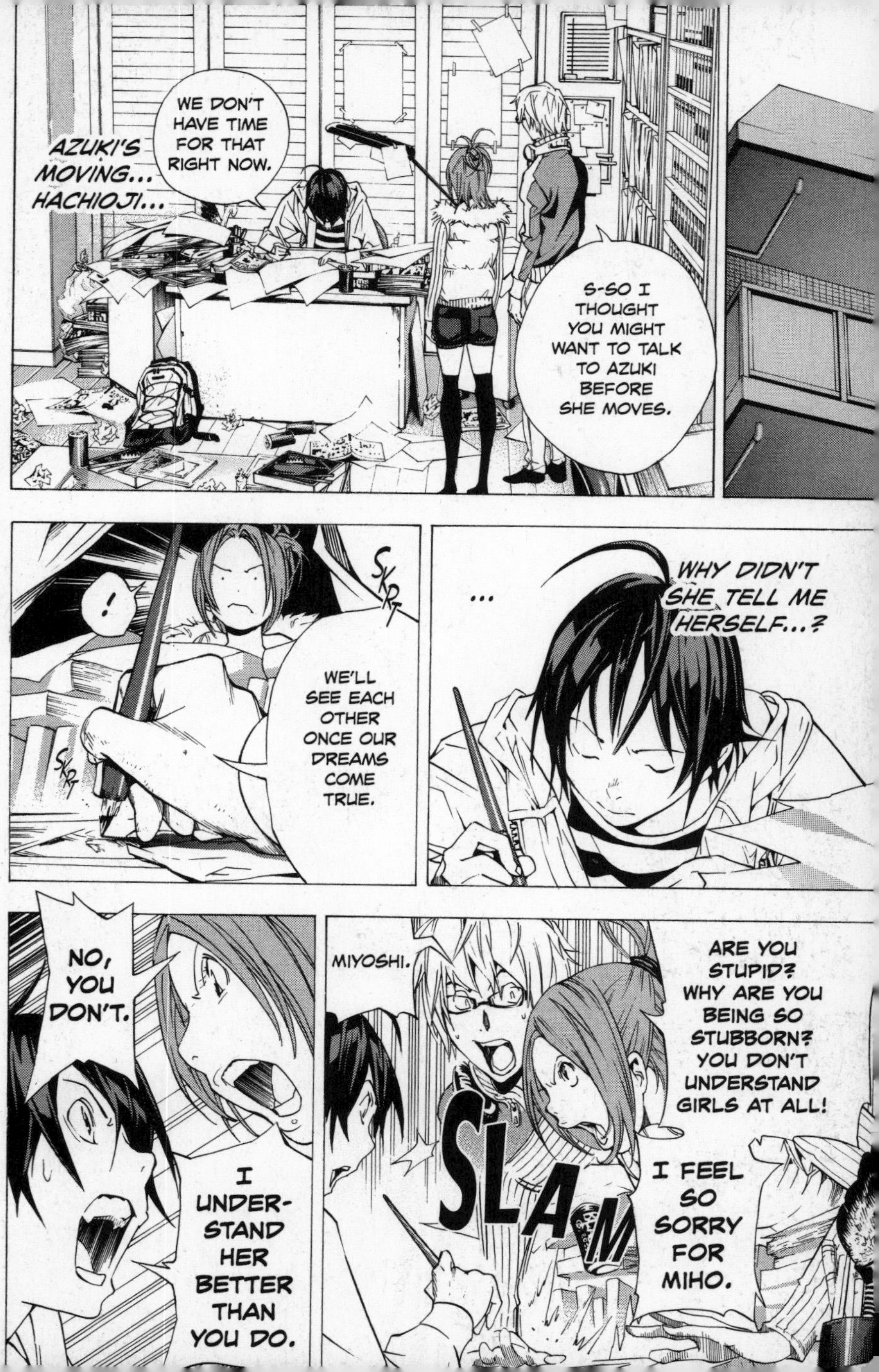
S-SO I THOUGHT YOU MIGHT WANT TO TALK TO AZUKI BEFORE SHE MOVES.
WE DON'T HAVE TIME FOR THAT RIGHT NOW.
AZUKI'S MOVING... HACHIOJI...
...
WHY DIDN'T SHE TELL ME HERSELF...?
!
SKRT
WE'LL SEE EACH OTHER ONCE OUR DREAMS COME TRUE.
SKRT
ARE YOU STUPID? WHY ARE YOU BEING SO STUBBORN? YOU DON'T UNDERSTAND GIRLS AT ALL!
MIYOSHI.
I FEEL SO SORRY FOR MIHO.
SLAM
NO, YOU DON'T.
I UNDER-STAND HER BETTER THAN YOU DO.

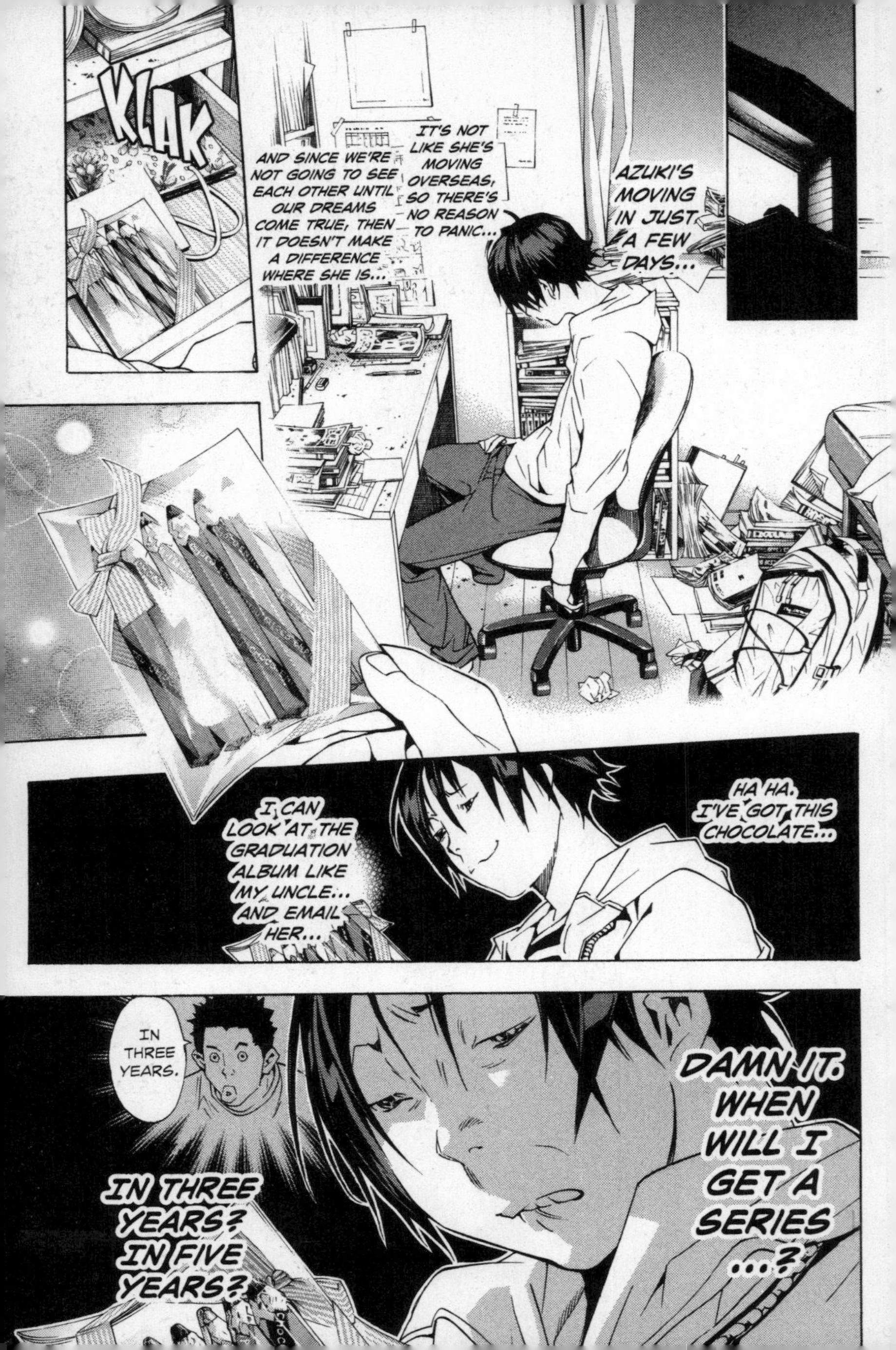
AZUKI'S MOVING IN JUST A FEW DAYS...
IT'S NOT LIKE SHE'S MOVING OVERSEAS, SO THERE'S NO REASON TO PANIC...
AND SINCE WE'RE NOT GOING TO SEE EACH OTHER UNTIL OUR DREAMS COME TRUE, THEN IT DOESN'T MAKE A DIFFERENCE WHERE SHE IS...
KLAK
HA HA. I'VE GOT THIS CHOCOLATE...
I CAN LOOK AT THE GRADUATION ALBUM LIKE MY UNCLE... AND EMAIL HER...
DAMN IT. WHEN WILL I GET A SERIES ...?
IN THREE YEARS.
IN THREE YEARS? IN FIVE YEARS?

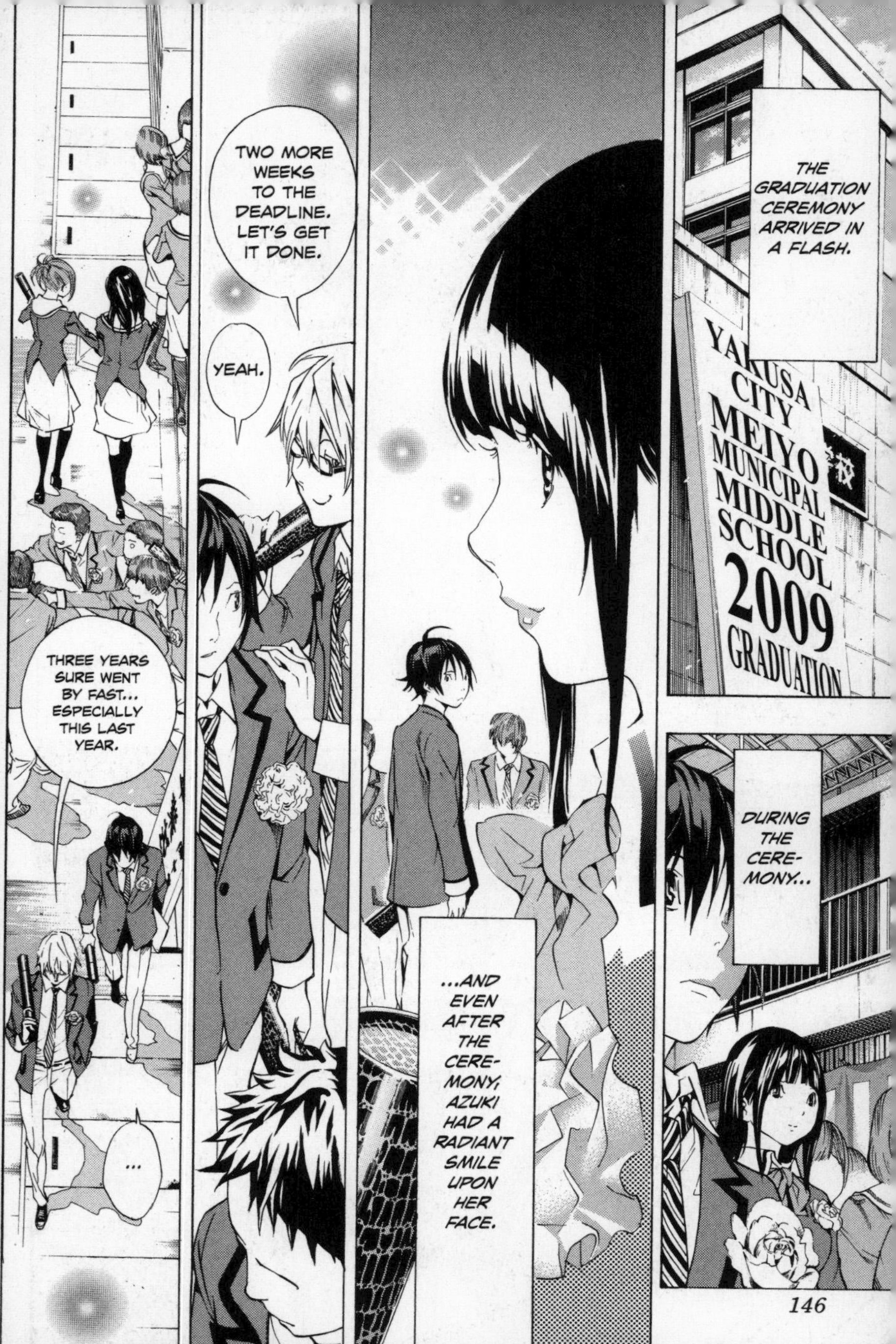
YAKUSA CITY MEIYO MUNICIPAL MIDDLE SCHOOL 2009 GRADUATION
THE GRADUATION CEREMONY ARRIVED IN A FLASH.
DURING THE CEREMONY...
...AND EVEN AFTER THE CEREMONY, AZUKI HAD A RADIANT SMILE UPON HER FACE.
TWO MORE WEEKS TO THE DEADLINE. LET'S GET IT DONE.
YEAH.
THREE YEARS SURE WENT BY FAST... ESPECIALLY THIS LAST YEAR.
...

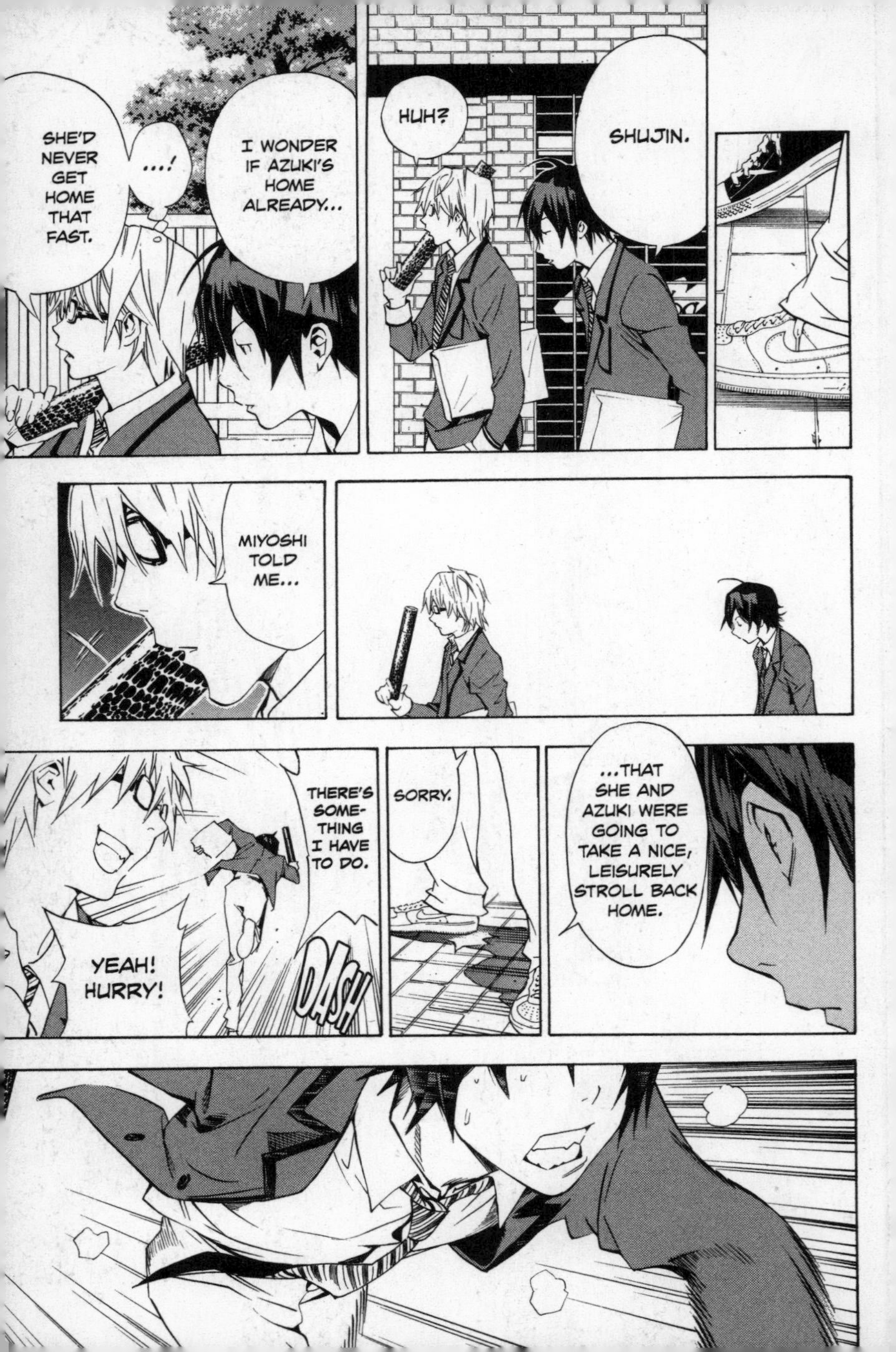
SHUJIN.
HUH?
I WONDER IF AZUKI'S HOME ALREADY...
...!
SHE'D NEVER GET HOME THAT FAST.
MIYOSHI TOLD ME...
...THAT SHE AND AZUKI WERE GOING TO TAKE A NICE, LEISURELY STROLL BACK HOME.
SORRY.
THERE'S SOME-THING I HAVE TO DO.
DASH
YEAH! HURRY!

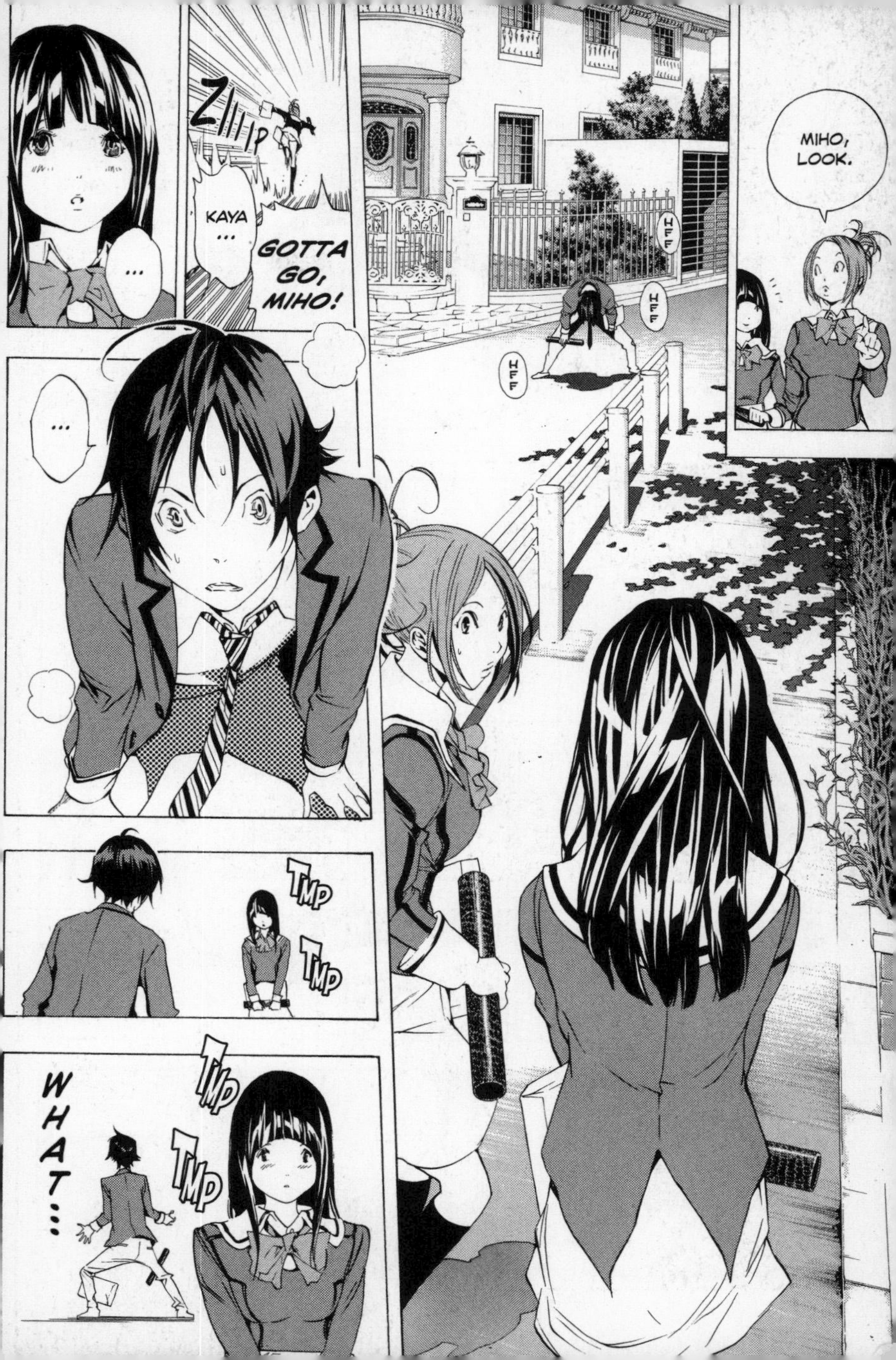

MIHO, LOOK.
HFF
HFF
HFF
ZIIIP
KAYA ...
GOTTA GO, MIHO!
...
...
TMP
TMP
TMP
TMP
WHAT...

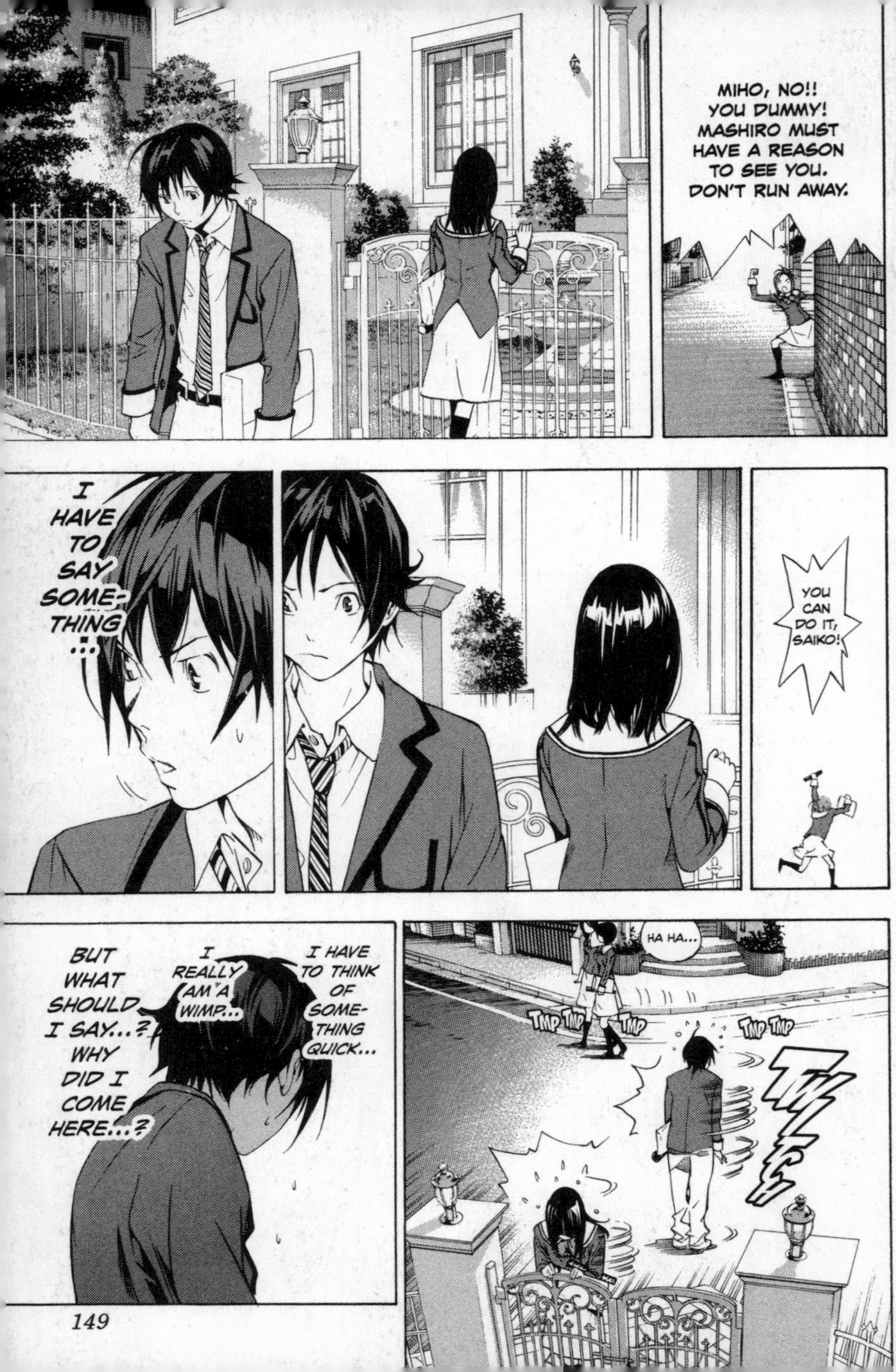
MIHO, NO!! YOU DUMMY! MASHIRO MUST HAVE A REASON TO SEE YOU. DON'T RUN AWAY.
YOU CAN DO IT, SAIKO!
I HAVE TO SAY SOME-THING...
HA HA...
TMP TMP
TMP TMP
TMP
I HAVE TO THINK OF SOME-THING QUICK...
I REALLY AM A WIMP...
BUT WHAT SHOULD I SAY...? WHY DID I COME HERE...?

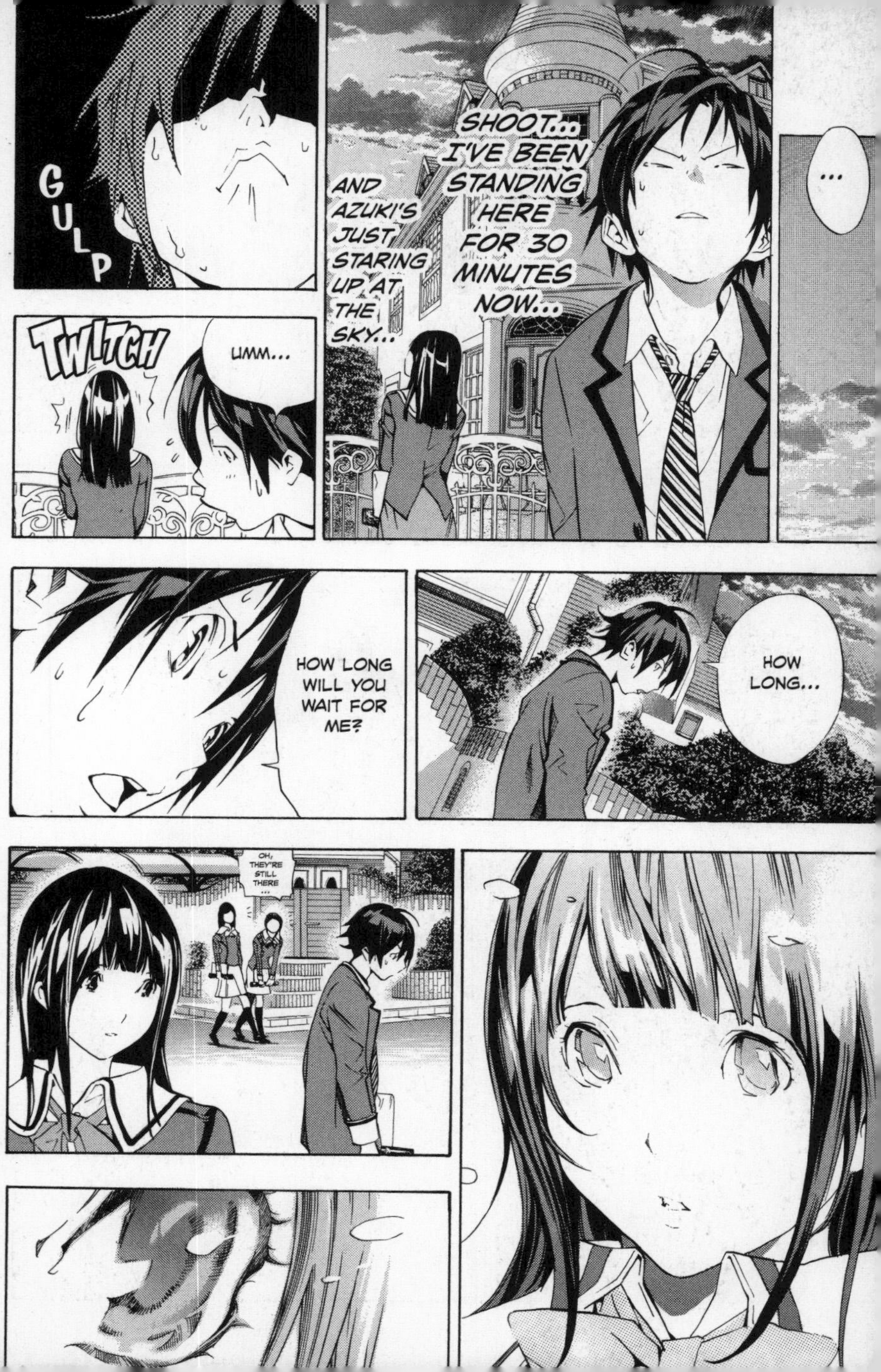
...
SHOOT... I'VE BEEN STANDING HERE FOR 30 MINUTES NOW...
AND AZUKI'S JUST STARING UP AT THE SKY...
GULP
TWITCH
UMM...
HOW LONG...
HOW LONG WILL YOU WAIT FOR ME?
OH, THEY'RE STILL THERE ...

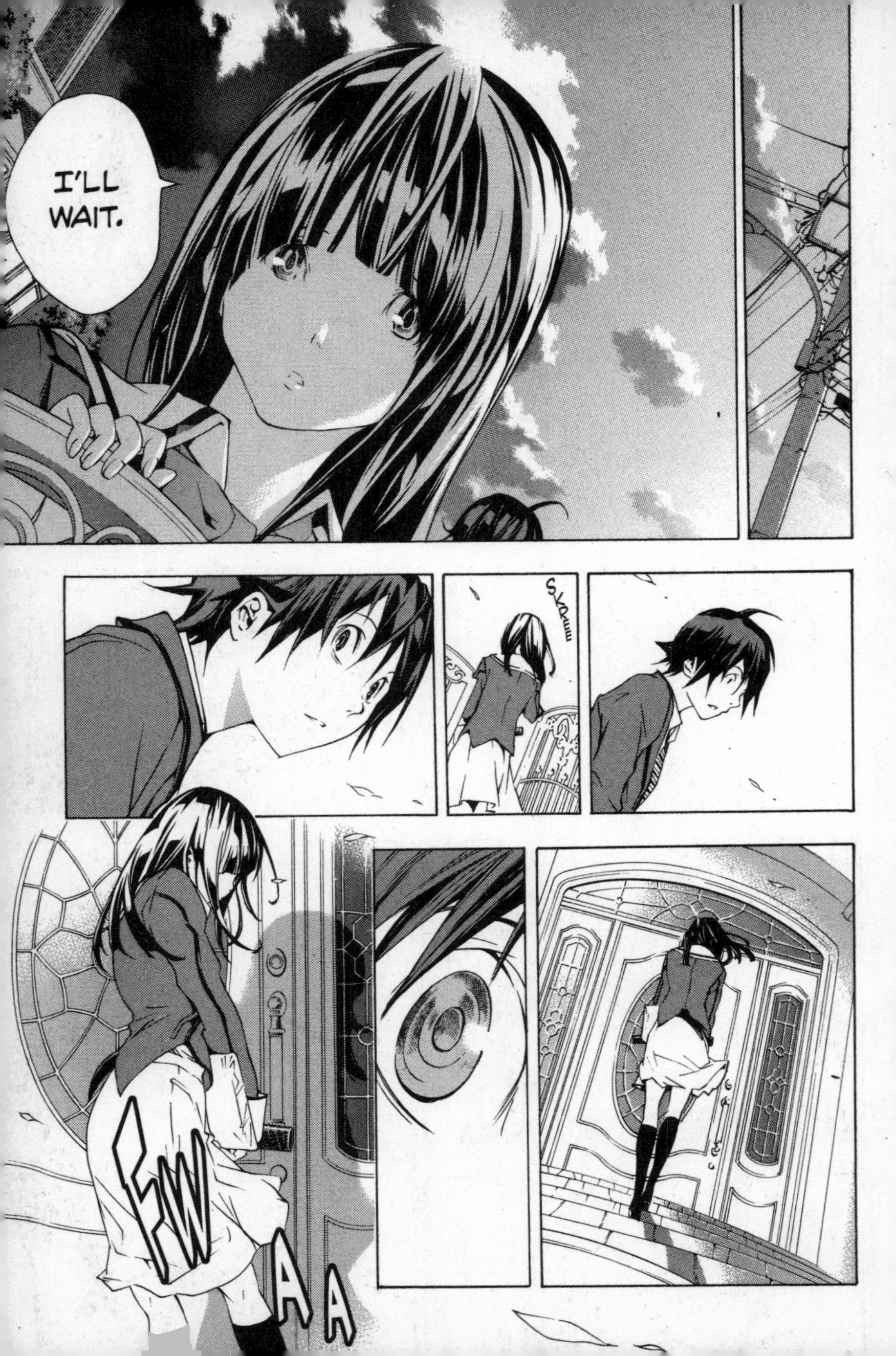
I'LL WAIT.
SKREEE
FWAA

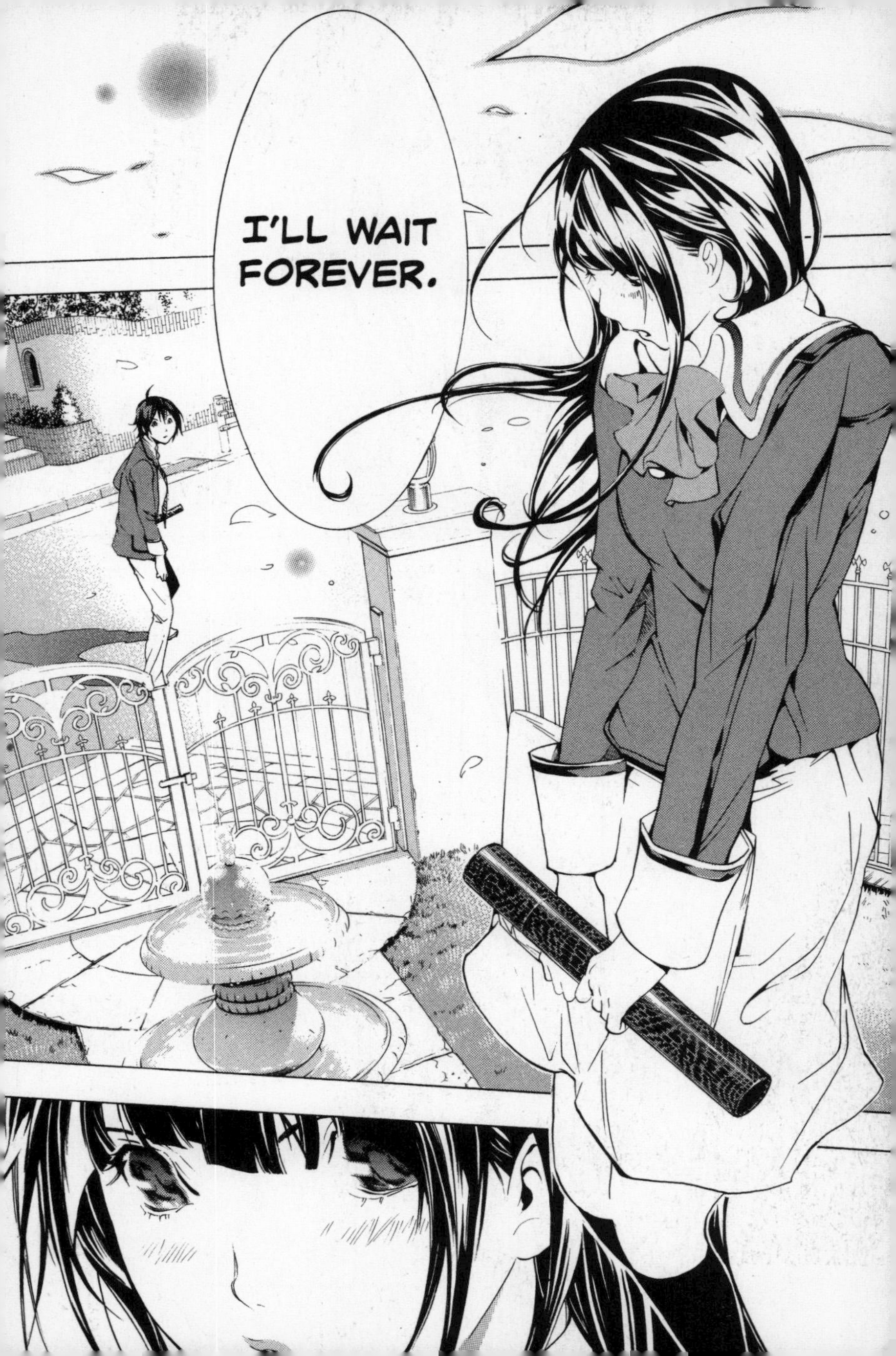
I'LL WAIT FOREVER.

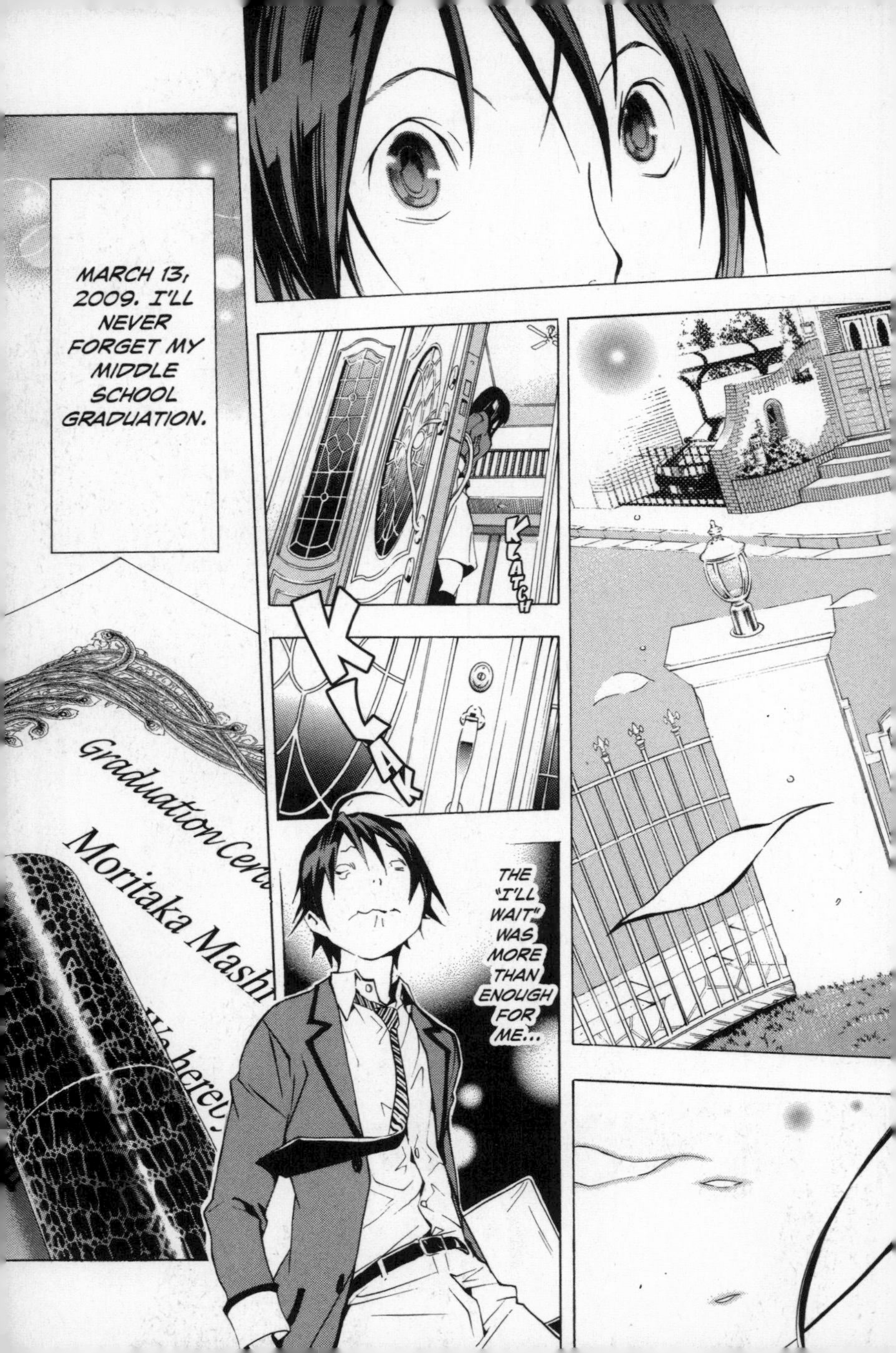
KLATCH
KLAK
THE "I'LL WAIT" WAS MORE THAN ENOUGH FOR ME...
MARCH 13, 2009. I'LL NEVER FORGET MY MIDDLE SCHOOL GRADUATION.
Graduation Cert
Moritaka Mashi

OHBA'S STORYBOARD

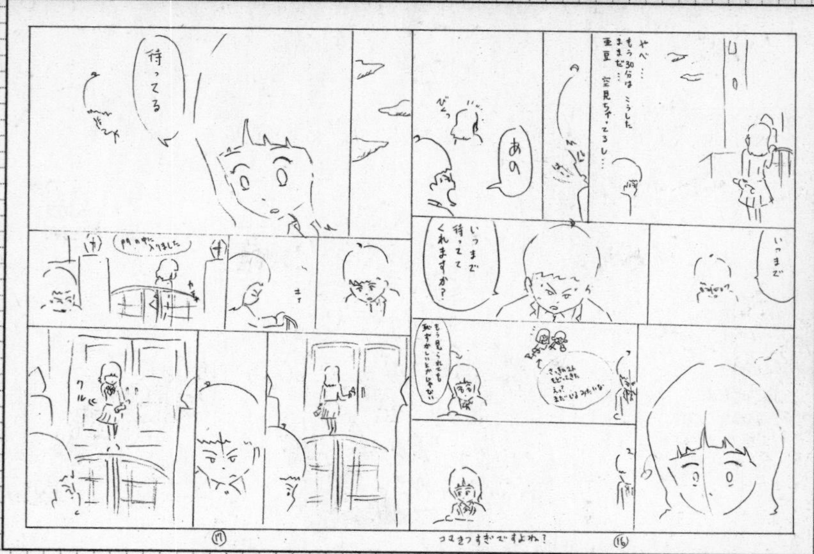
やべ…もう30分は こうしたままだ…亜豆 空見ちゃってるし…
びくっ
あの
いつまで
いつまで待っててくれますか?
待ってる
門の中に入りました
カチャ
キィ
クルッ
コマきつすぎですよね?

OBATA'S STORYBOARD

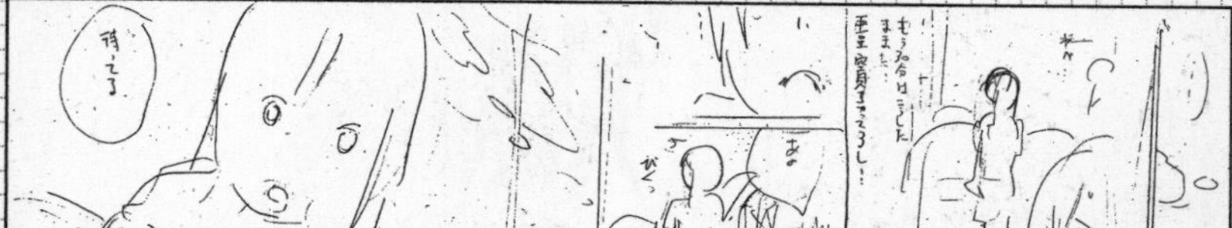
もう30分は こうしたままだ…亜豆 空見ちゃってるし…
びくっ
あの
いつまで待っててくれますか
いつまで
待ってる

COMPLETE!

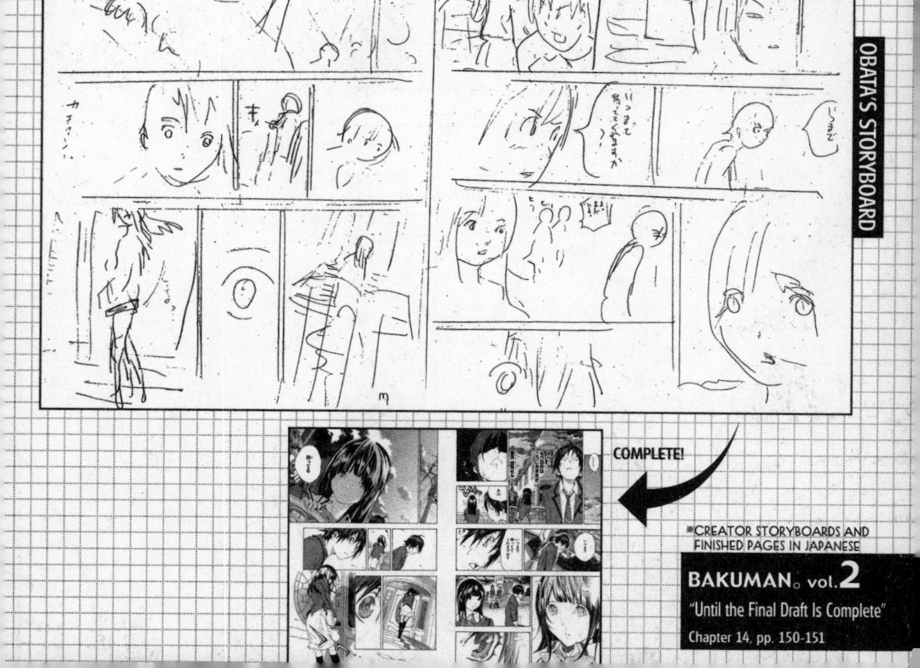

*CREATOR STORYBOARDS AND FINISHED PAGES IN JAPANESE

**BAKUMAN。 vol.2**

"Until the Final Draft Is Complete"

Chapter 14, pp. 150-151

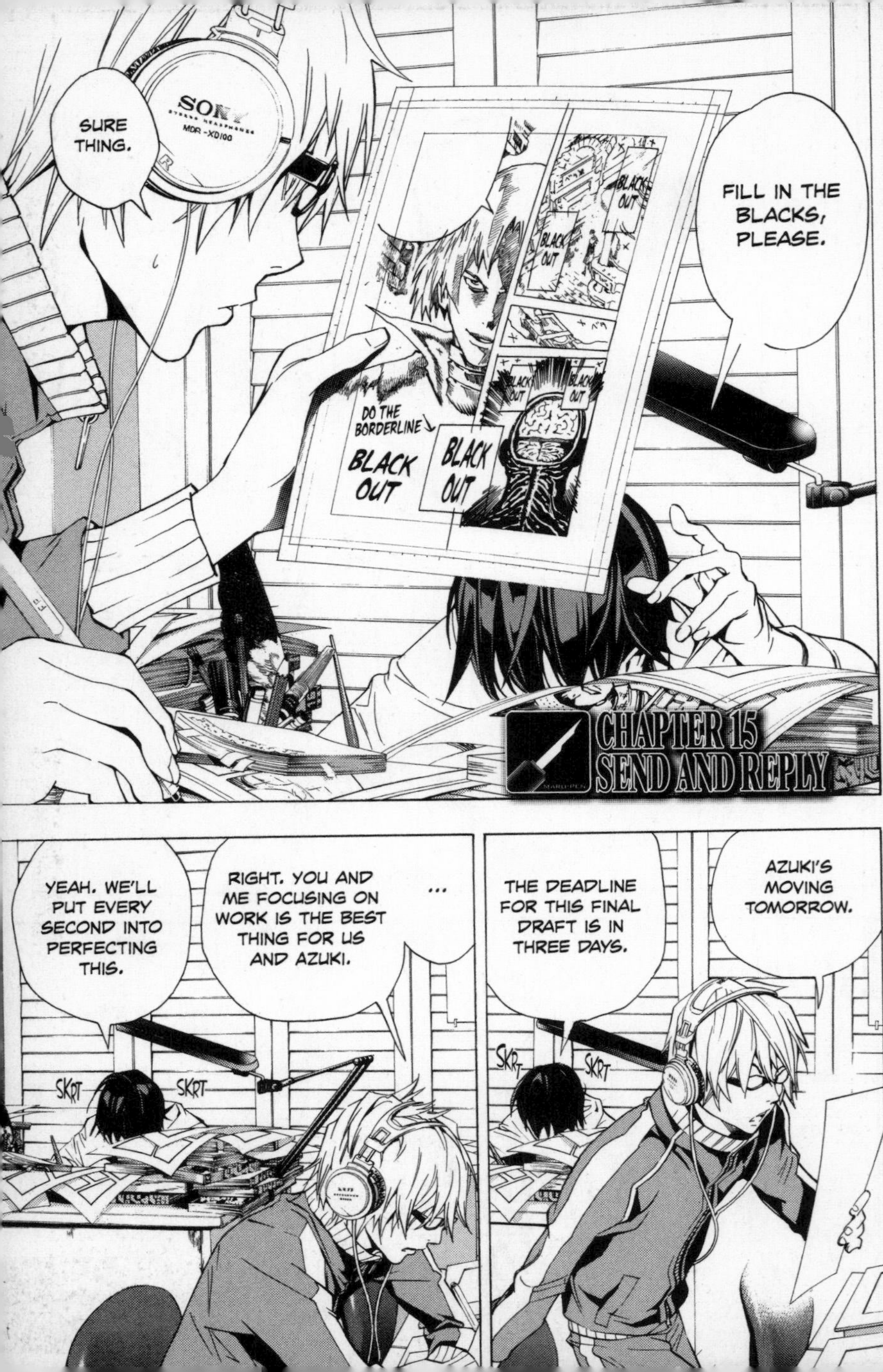
CHAPTER 15
SEND AND REPLY
FILL IN THE BLACKS, PLEASE.
BLACK OUT
BLACK OUT
BLACK OUT
BLACK OUT
BLACK OUT
DO THE BORDERLINE
BLACK OUT
SONY
MDR-XD100
SURE THING.
AZUKI'S MOVING TOMORROW.
THE DEADLINE FOR THIS FINAL DRAFT IS IN THREE DAYS.
SKRT
SKRT
...
RIGHT. YOU AND ME FOCUSING ON WORK IS THE BEST THING FOR US AND AZUKI.
YEAH. WE'LL PUT EVERY SECOND INTO PERFECTING THIS.
SKRT
SKRT

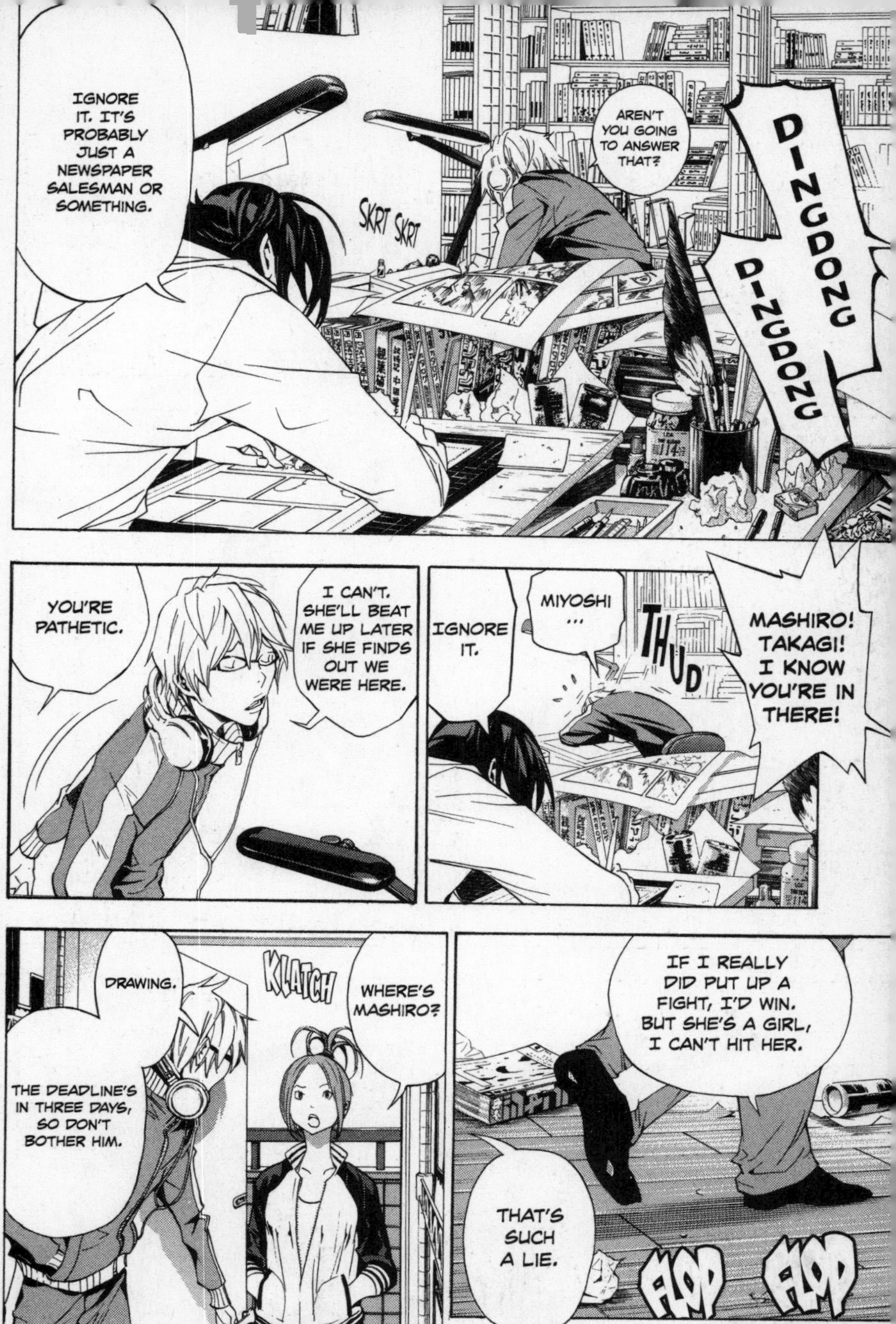
DINGDONG
DINGDONG
AREN'T YOU GOING TO ANSWER THAT?
SKRT SKRT
IGNORE IT. IT'S PROBABLY JUST A NEWSPAPER SALESMAN OR SOMETHING.
MASHIRO! TAKAGI! I KNOW YOU'RE IN THERE!
MIYOSHI ...
THUD
IGNORE IT.
I CAN'T. SHE'LL BEAT ME UP LATER IF SHE FINDS OUT WE WERE HERE.
YOU'RE PATHETIC.
IF I REALLY DID PUT UP A FIGHT, I'D WIN. BUT SHE'S A GIRL, I CAN'T HIT HER.
FLOP FLOP
THAT'S SUCH A LIE.
WHERE'S MASHIRO?
KLATCH
DRAWING.
THE DEADLINE'S IN THREE DAYS, SO DON'T BOTHER HIM.

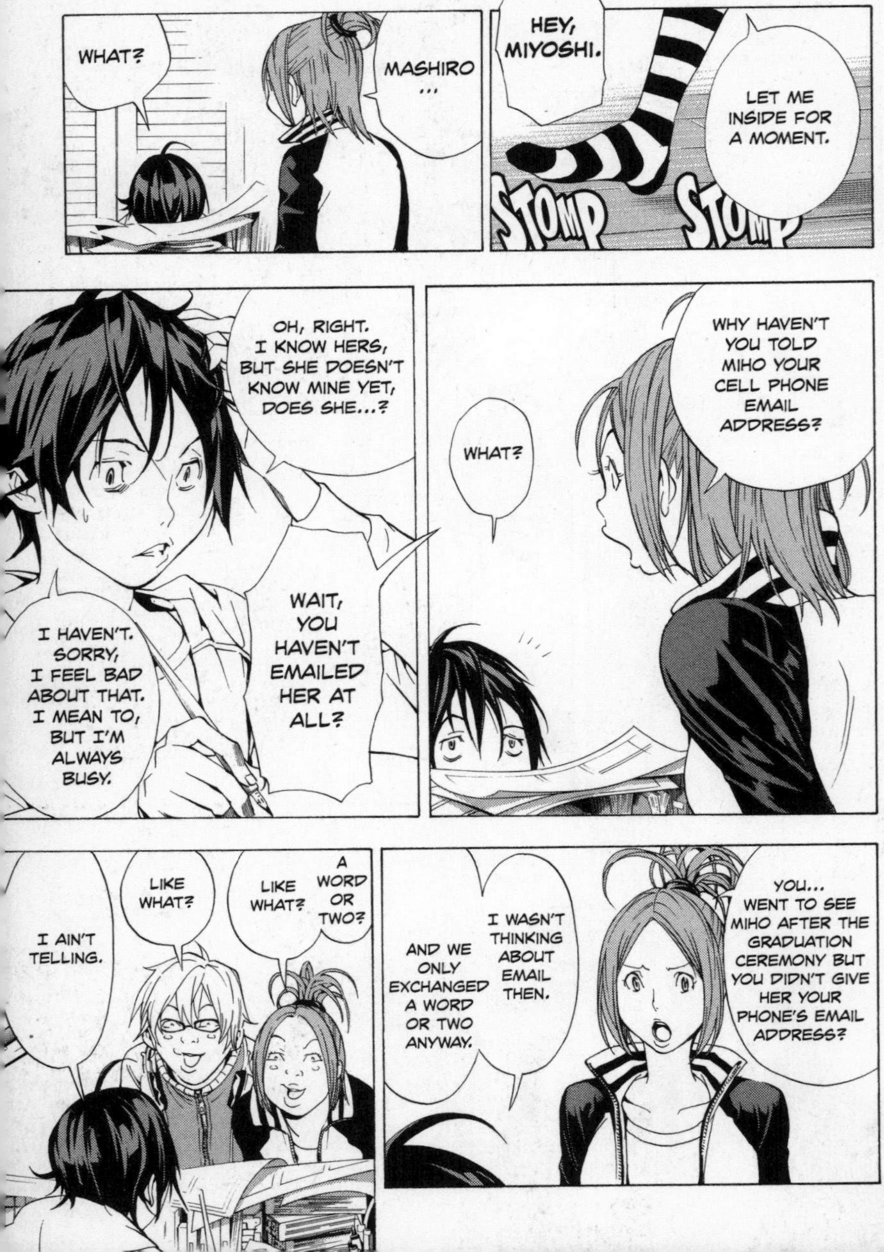
HEY, MIYOSHI.
LET ME INSIDE FOR A MOMENT.
STOMP
STOMP
MASHIRO ...
WHAT?
WHY HAVEN'T YOU TOLD MIHO YOUR CELL PHONE EMAIL ADDRESS?
WHAT?
OH, RIGHT. I KNOW HERS, BUT SHE DOESN'T KNOW MINE YET, DOES SHE...?
WAIT, YOU HAVEN'T EMAILED HER AT ALL?
I HAVEN'T. SORRY, I FEEL BAD ABOUT THAT. I MEAN TO, BUT I'M ALWAYS BUSY.
YOU... WENT TO SEE MIHO AFTER THE GRADUATION CEREMONY BUT YOU DIDN'T GIVE HER YOUR PHONE'S EMAIL ADDRESS?
I WASN'T THINKING ABOUT EMAIL THEN.
AND WE ONLY EXCHANGED A WORD OR TWO ANYWAY.
A WORD OR TWO?
LIKE WHAT?
LIKE WHAT?
I AIN'T TELLING.

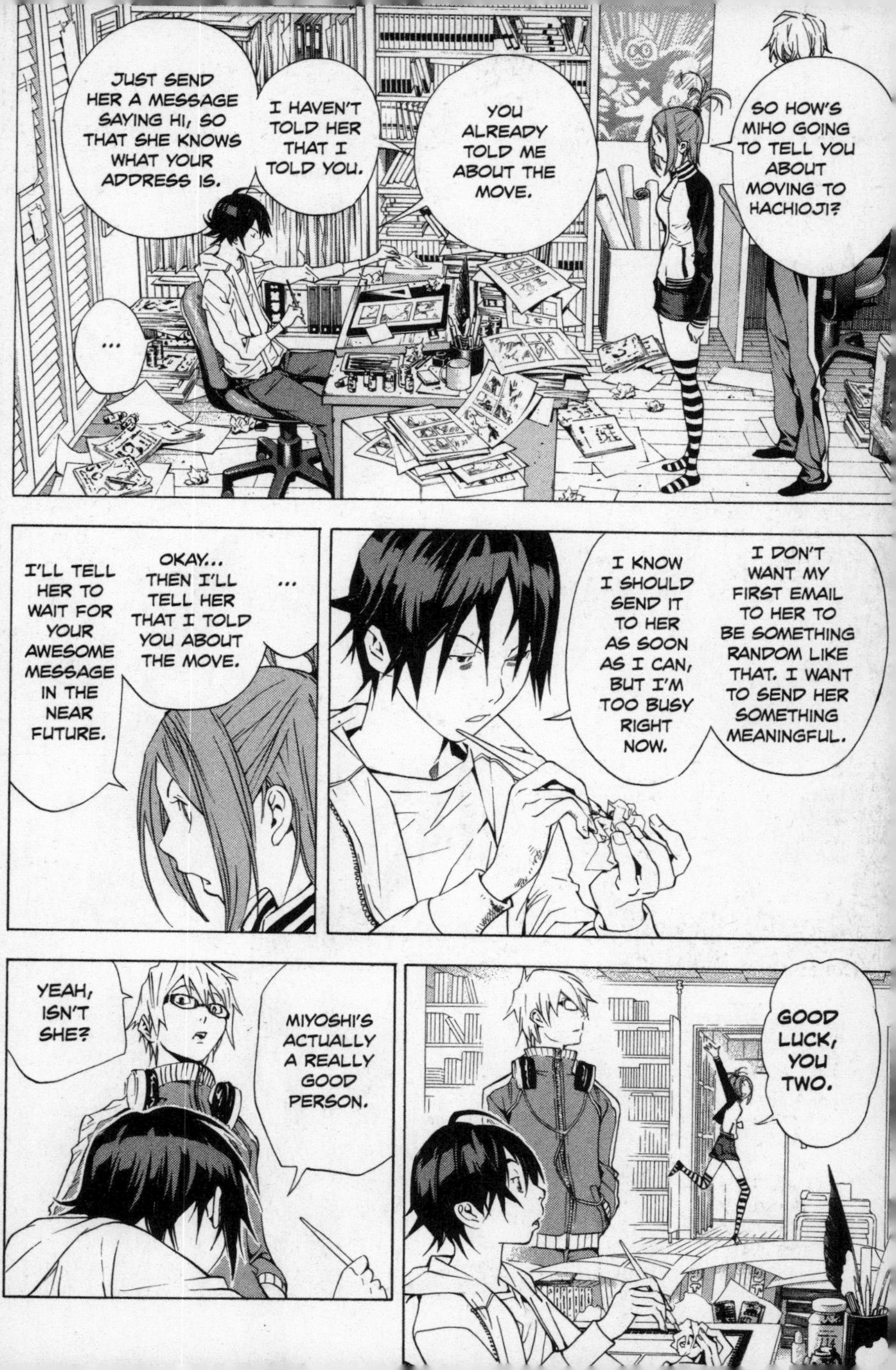
SO HOW'S MIHO GOING TO TELL YOU ABOUT MOVING TO HACHIOJI?
YOU ALREADY TOLD ME ABOUT THE MOVE.
I HAVEN'T TOLD HER THAT I TOLD YOU.
JUST SEND HER A MESSAGE SAYING HI, SO THAT SHE KNOWS WHAT YOUR ADDRESS IS.
...
I DON'T WANT MY FIRST EMAIL TO HER TO BE SOMETHING RANDOM LIKE THAT. I WANT TO SEND HER SOMETHING MEANINGFUL.
I KNOW I SHOULD SEND IT TO HER AS SOON AS I CAN, BUT I'M TOO BUSY RIGHT NOW.
...
OKAY... THEN I'LL TELL HER THAT I TOLD YOU ABOUT THE MOVE.
I'LL TELL HER TO WAIT FOR YOUR AWESOME MESSAGE IN THE NEAR FUTURE.
GOOD LUCK, YOU TWO.
MIYOSHI'S ACTUALLY A REALLY GOOD PERSON.
YEAH, ISN'T SHE?

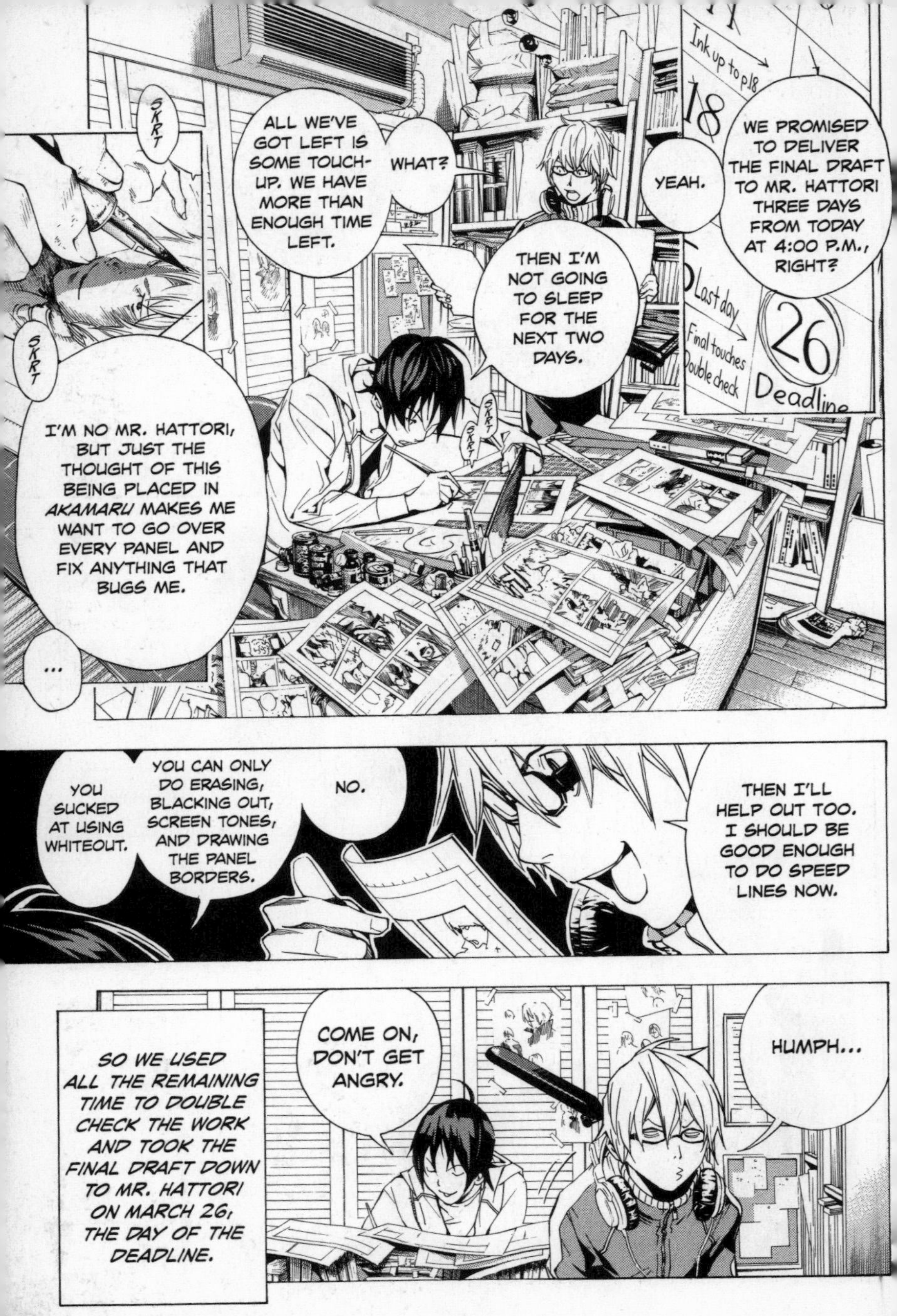
Ink up to p.18
18
Last day
Final touches
Double check
26
Deadline
WE PROMISED TO DELIVER THE FINAL DRAFT TO MR. HATTORI THREE DAYS FROM TODAY AT 4:00 P.M., RIGHT?
YEAH.
THEN I'M NOT GOING TO SLEEP FOR THE NEXT TWO DAYS.
SKRT
SKRT
WHAT?
ALL WE'VE GOT LEFT IS SOME TOUCH-UP. WE HAVE MORE THAN ENOUGH TIME LEFT.
SKRT
SKRT
I'M NO MR. HATTORI, BUT JUST THE THOUGHT OF THIS BEING PLACED IN *AKAMARU* MAKES ME WANT TO GO OVER EVERY PANEL AND FIX ANYTHING THAT BUGS ME.
...
THEN I'LL HELP OUT TOO. I SHOULD BE GOOD ENOUGH TO DO SPEED LINES NOW.
NO.
YOU CAN ONLY DO ERASING, BLACKING OUT, SCREEN TONES, AND DRAWING THE PANEL BORDERS.
YOU SUCKED AT USING WHITEOUT.
HUMPH...
COME ON, DON'T GET ANGRY.
SO WE USED ALL THE REMAINING TIME TO DOUBLE CHECK THE WORK AND TOOK THE FINAL DRAFT DOWN TO MR. HATTORI ON MARCH 26, THE DAY OF THE DEADLINE.

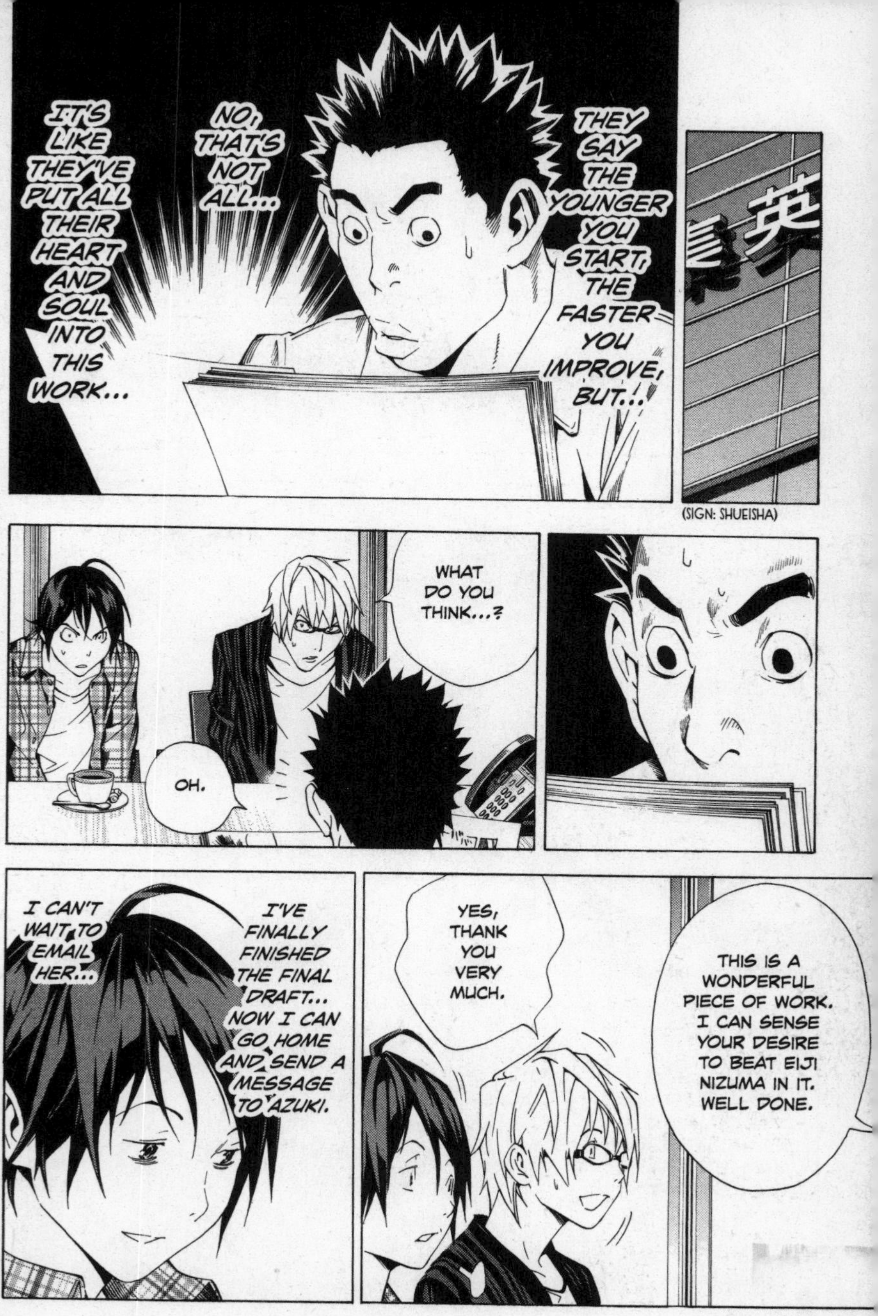
(SIGN: SHUEISHA)
THEY SAY THE YOUNGER YOU START, THE FASTER YOU IMPROVE, BUT...
NO, THAT'S NOT ALL...
IT'S LIKE THEY'VE PUT ALL THEIR HEART AND SOUL INTO THIS WORK...
WHAT DO YOU THINK...?
OH.
THIS IS A WONDERFUL PIECE OF WORK. I CAN SENSE YOUR DESIRE TO BEAT EIJI NIZUMA IN IT. WELL DONE.
YES, THANK YOU VERY MUCH.
I'VE FINALLY FINISHED THE FINAL DRAFT... NOW I CAN GO HOME AND SEND A MESSAGE TO AZUKI.
I CAN'T WAIT TO EMAIL HER...

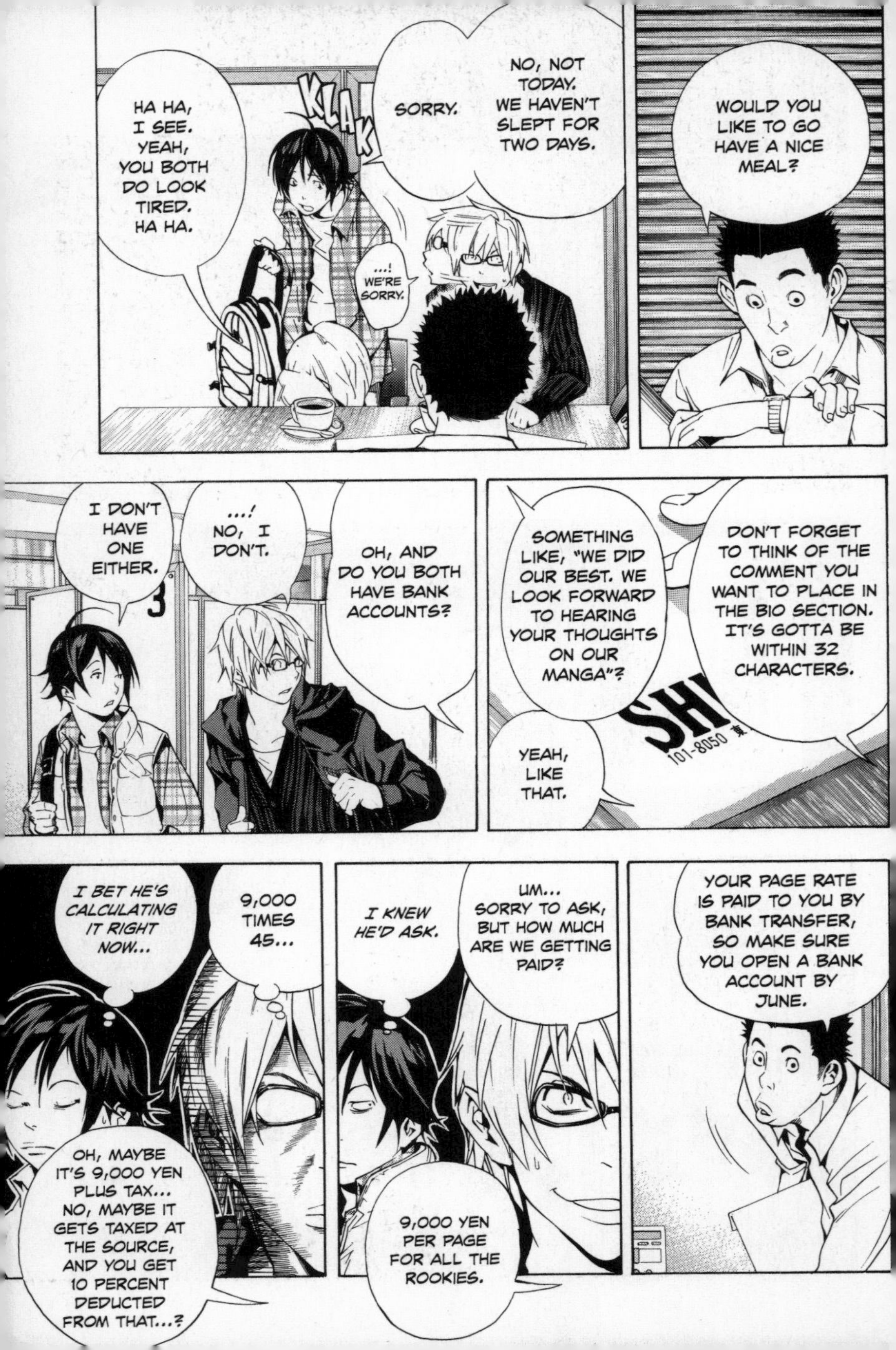
WOULD YOU LIKE TO GO HAVE A NICE MEAL?
NO, NOT TODAY. WE HAVEN'T SLEPT FOR TWO DAYS.
SORRY.
KLAK
HA HA, I SEE. YEAH, YOU BOTH DO LOOK TIRED. HA HA.
...! WE'RE SORRY.
DON'T FORGET TO THINK OF THE COMMENT YOU WANT TO PLACE IN THE BIO SECTION. IT'S GOTTA BE WITHIN 32 CHARACTERS.
SOMETHING LIKE, "WE DID OUR BEST. WE LOOK FORWARD TO HEARING YOUR THOUGHTS ON OUR MANGA"?
YEAH, LIKE THAT.
OH, AND DO YOU BOTH HAVE BANK ACCOUNTS?
...! NO, I DON'T.
I DON'T HAVE ONE EITHER.
YOUR PAGE RATE IS PAID TO YOU BY BANK TRANSFER, SO MAKE SURE YOU OPEN A BANK ACCOUNT BY JUNE.
UM... SORRY TO ASK, BUT HOW MUCH ARE WE GETTING PAID?
I KNEW HE'D ASK.
9,000 YEN PER PAGE FOR ALL THE ROOKIES.
9,000 TIMES 45...
I BET HE'S CALCULATING IT RIGHT NOW...
OH, MAYBE IT'S 9,000 YEN PLUS TAX... NO, MAYBE IT GETS TAXED AT THE SOURCE, AND YOU GET 10 PERCENT DEDUCTED FROM THAT...?

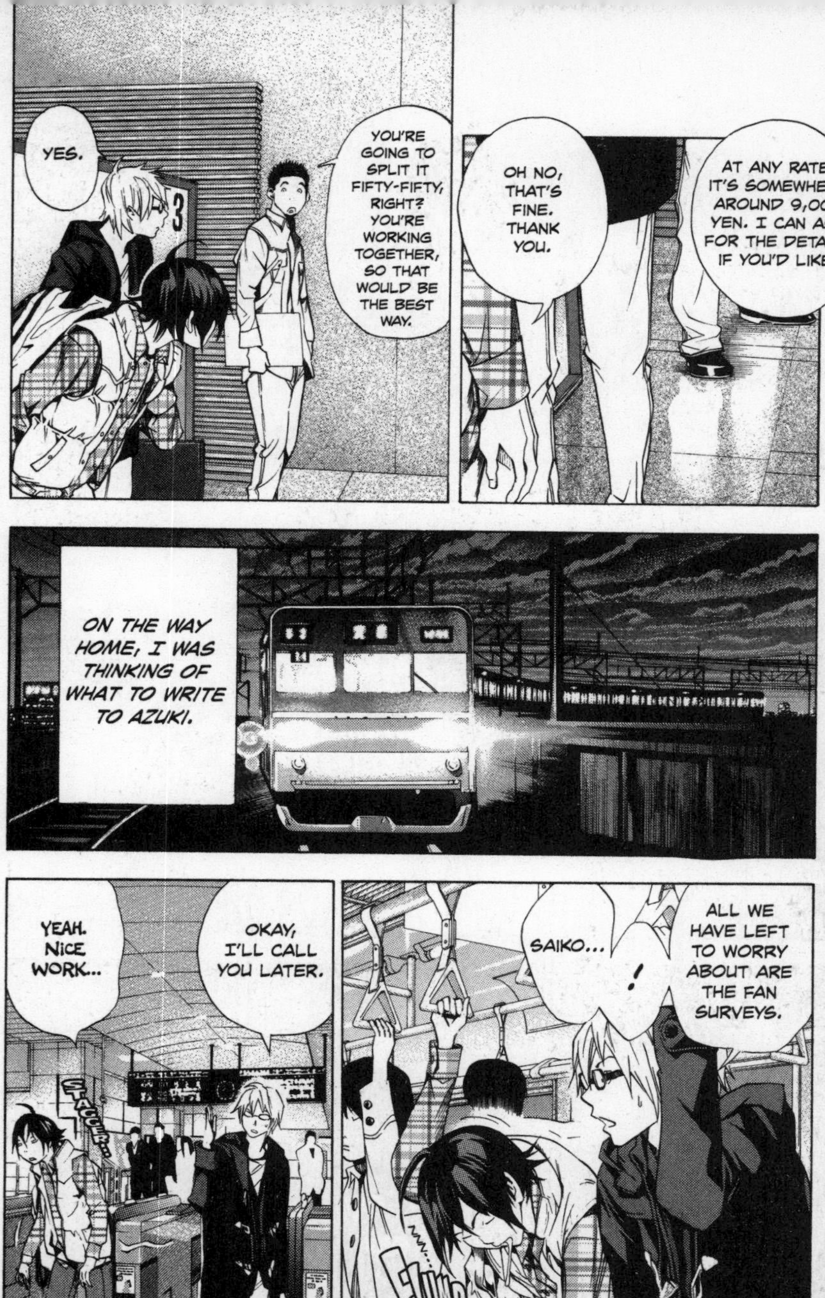
AT ANY RATE, IT'S SOMEWHERE AROUND 9,000 YEN. I CAN ASK FOR THE DETAILS IF YOU'D LIKE.
OH NO, THAT'S FINE. THANK YOU.
YOU'RE GOING TO SPLIT IT FIFTY-FIFTY, RIGHT? YOU'RE WORKING TOGETHER, SO THAT WOULD BE THE BEST WAY.
YES.
ON THE WAY HOME, I WAS THINKING OF WHAT TO WRITE TO AZUKI.
ALL WE HAVE LEFT TO WORRY ABOUT ARE THE FAN SURVEYS.
SAIKO...
!
FLUMP
OKAY, I'LL CALL YOU LATER.
YEAH. NICE WORK...

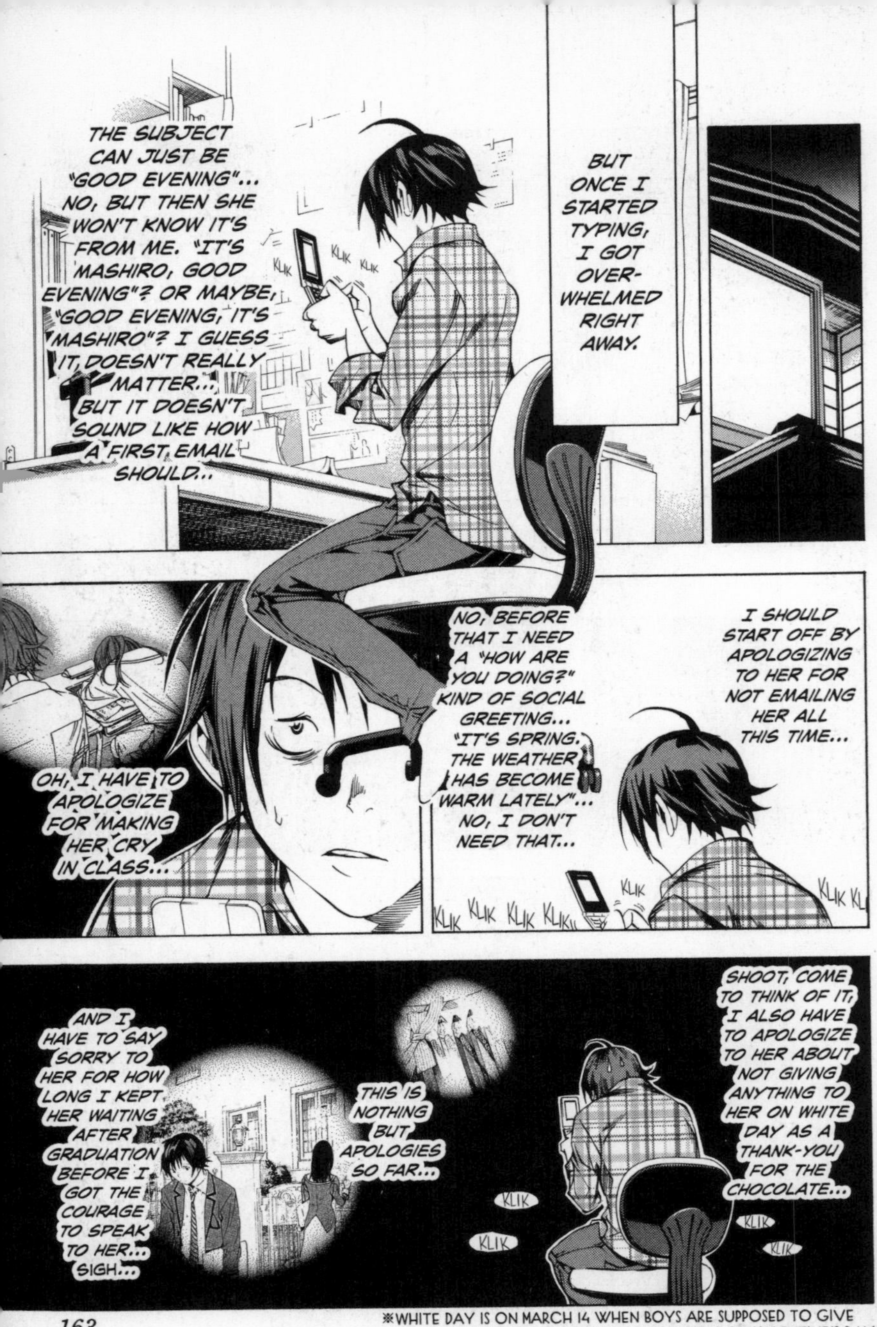
BUT ONCE I STARTED TYPING, I GOT OVER-WHELMED RIGHT AWAY.
THE SUBJECT CAN JUST BE "GOOD EVENING"... NO, BUT THEN SHE WON'T KNOW IT'S FROM ME. "IT'S MASHIRO, GOOD EVENING"? OR MAYBE, "GOOD EVENING, IT'S MASHIRO"? I GUESS IT DOESN'T REALLY MATTER... BUT IT DOESN'T SOUND LIKE HOW A FIRST EMAIL SHOULD...
KLIK KLIK
KLIK
I SHOULD START OFF BY APOLOGIZING TO HER FOR NOT EMAILING HER ALL THIS TIME...
NO, BEFORE THAT I NEED A "HOW ARE YOU DOING?" KIND OF SOCIAL GREETING... "IT'S SPRING. THE WEATHER HAS BECOME WARM LATELY"... NO, I DON'T NEED THAT...
KLIK KL
KLIK
KLIK KLIK KLIK KLIK
OH, I HAVE TO APOLOGIZE FOR MAKING HER CRY IN CLASS...
SHOOT, COME TO THINK OF IT, I ALSO HAVE TO APOLOGIZE TO HER ABOUT NOT GIVING ANYTHING TO HER ON WHITE DAY AS A THANK-YOU FOR THE CHOCOLATE...
KLIK
KLIK
KLIK
KLIK
THIS IS NOTHING BUT APOLOGIES SO FAR...
AND I HAVE TO SAY SORRY TO HER FOR HOW LONG I KEPT HER WAITING AFTER GRADUATION BEFORE I GOT THE COURAGE TO SPEAK TO HER... SIGH...

※WHITE DAY IS ON MARCH 14 WHEN BOYS ARE SUPPOSED TO GIVE GIFTS TO THE GIRLS WHO GAVE THEM GIFTS ON VALENTINE'S DAY.

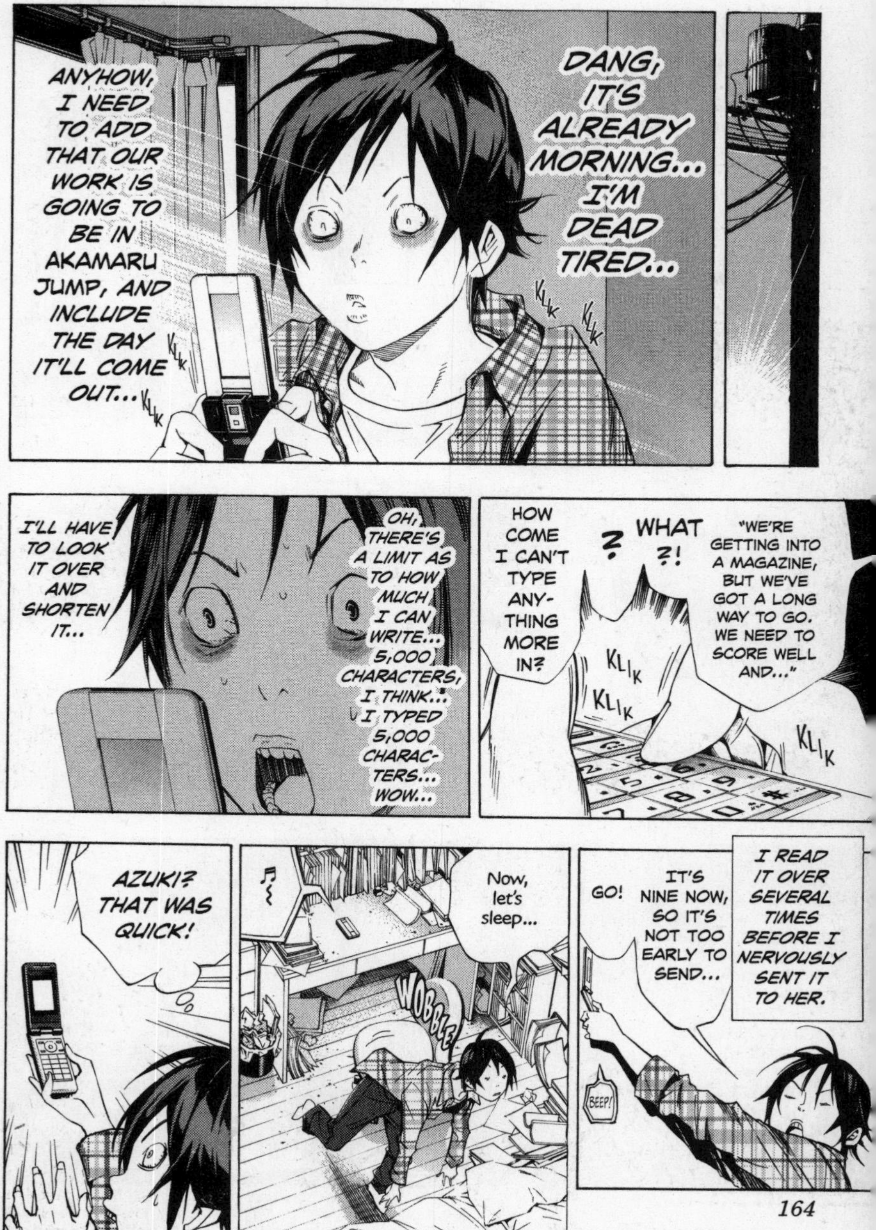
DANG, IT'S ALREADY MORNING... I'M DEAD TIRED...
KLIK
KLIK
ANYHOW, I NEED TO ADD THAT OUR WORK IS GOING TO BE IN AKAMARU JUMP, AND INCLUDE THE DAY IT'LL COME OUT...
KLIK
KLIK
"WE'RE GETTING INTO A MAGAZINE, BUT WE'VE GOT A LONG WAY TO GO. WE NEED TO SCORE WELL AND..."
WHAT ?!
HOW COME I CAN'T TYPE ANY-THING MORE IN?
KLIK
KLIK
KLIK
OH, THERE'S A LIMIT AS TO HOW MUCH I CAN WRITE... 5,000 CHARACTERS, I THINK... I TYPED 5,000 CHARAC-TERS... WOW...
I'LL HAVE TO LOOK IT OVER AND SHORTEN IT...
I READ IT OVER SEVERAL TIMES BEFORE I NERVOUSLY SENT IT TO HER.
IT'S NINE NOW, SO IT'S NOT TOO EARLY TO SEND...
GO!
BEEP!
Now, let's sleep...
WOBBLE
AZUKI? THAT WAS QUICK!

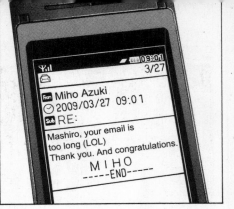

09:01
3/27
Miho Azuki
2009/03/27 09:01
RE:
Mashiro, your email is too long (LOL)
Thank you. And congratulations.
MIHO
-----END-----
IT'S SO SHORT!
I'M GLAD SHE SENT ME A REPLY, BUT IT'S SO SHORT! I FEEL SO EMBARRASSED FOR USING UP ALL 5,000 CHARACTERS...
OKAY, I'M GOING TO SOUND A LITTLE CHILDISH...
"AZUKI, WASN'T THAT EMAIL A LITTLE SHORT?" I'LL ADD A SMILEY FACE HERE... "NOW THAT WE CAN EMAIL, SHOULDN'T WE TALK TO EACH OTHER MORE?" ANOTHER SMILEY...
KLIK
KLIK
KLIK
KLIK
AND SEND...
BEEP
♬♪
AGAIN WITH THE SPEED!
09:16
3/27
Miho Azuki
2009/03/27 09:16
RE:
You should be drawing manga if you have so much free time! (LOL)
Bad boy!
MIHO
-----END-----
Menu
Reply
"BAD BOY!" THAT'S CUTE. I NEVER KNEW SHE COULD BE LIKE THIS... IT'S STILL SO SHORT...
BUT I GUESS SHE'S RIGHT... HMM...
BEEP
BEEP
HEY, SHUJIN, YOU SHOULD THINK UP THE STORYBOARDS IN CASE WE GET FIRST PLACE IN THE READER SURVEYS AND *MONEY AND INTELLIGENCE* BECOMES A SERIES.
GOT THAT? WE DON'T HAVE TIME TO BE PLAYING AROUND, SO HOP TO IT!
UNDERSTAND?!
HUH? WHY ARE YOU SO ANGRY? AND WHY ARE YOU ORDERING ME AROUND?

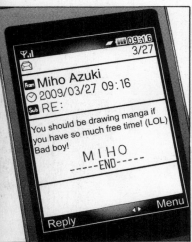

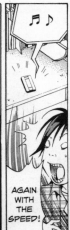

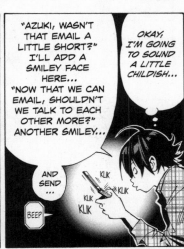

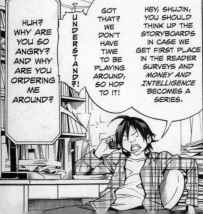

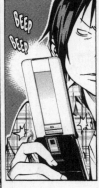

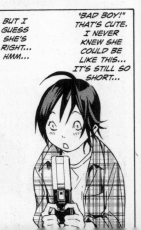

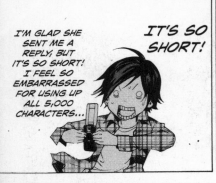

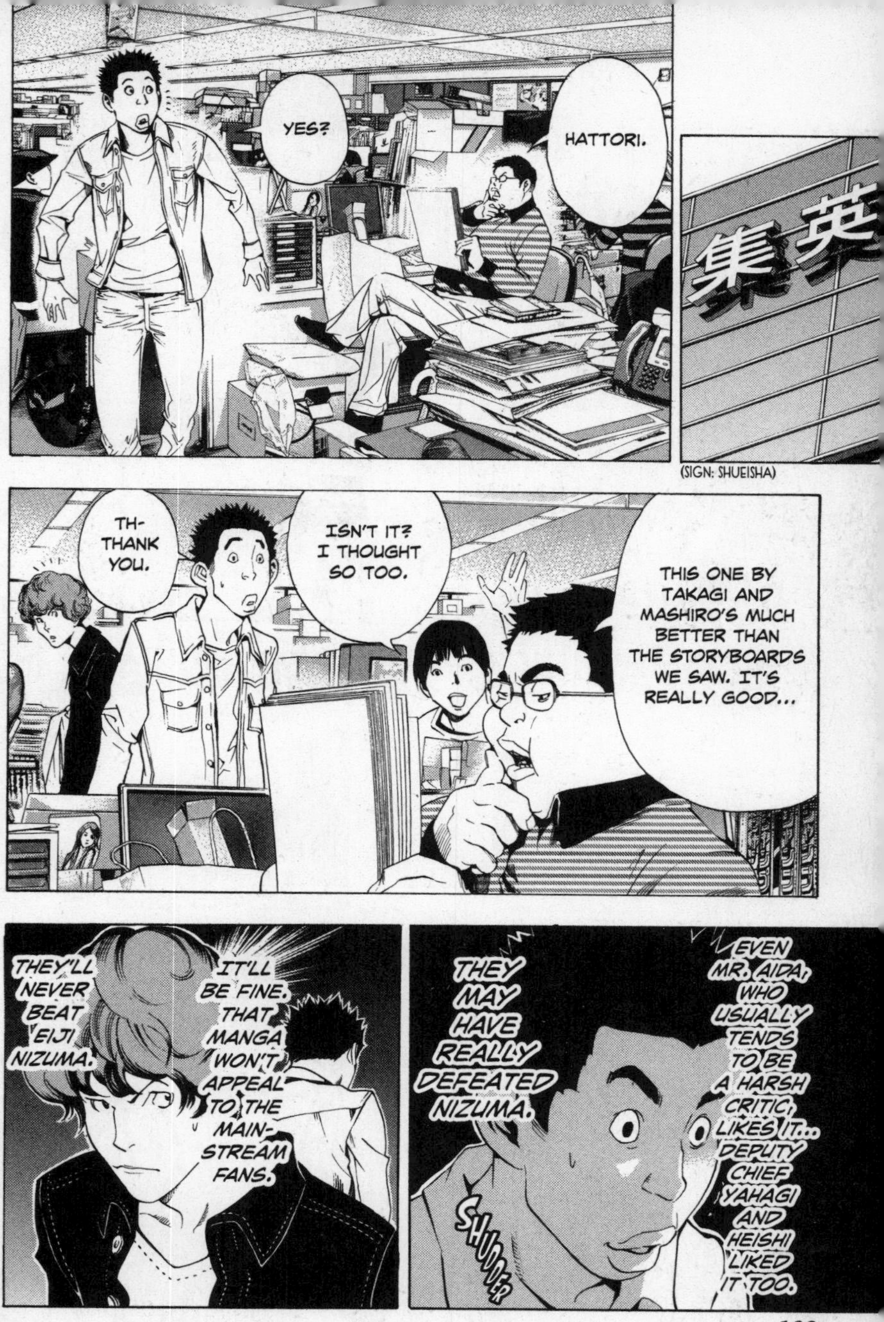
集英
(SIGN: SHUEISHA)
HATTORI.
YES?
THIS ONE BY TAKAGI AND MASHIRO'S MUCH BETTER THAN THE STORYBOARDS WE SAW. IT'S REALLY GOOD...
ISN'T IT? I THOUGHT SO TOO.
TH-THANK YOU.
EVEN MR. AIDA, WHO USUALLY TENDS TO BE A HARSH CRITIC, LIKES IT... DEPUTY CHIEF YAHAGI AND HEISHI LIKED IT TOO.
THEY MAY HAVE REALLY DEFEATED NIZUMA.
SHUDDER
IT'LL BE FINE. THAT MANGA WON'T APPEAL TO THE MAIN-STREAM FANS.
THEY'LL NEVER BEAT EIJI NIZUMA.

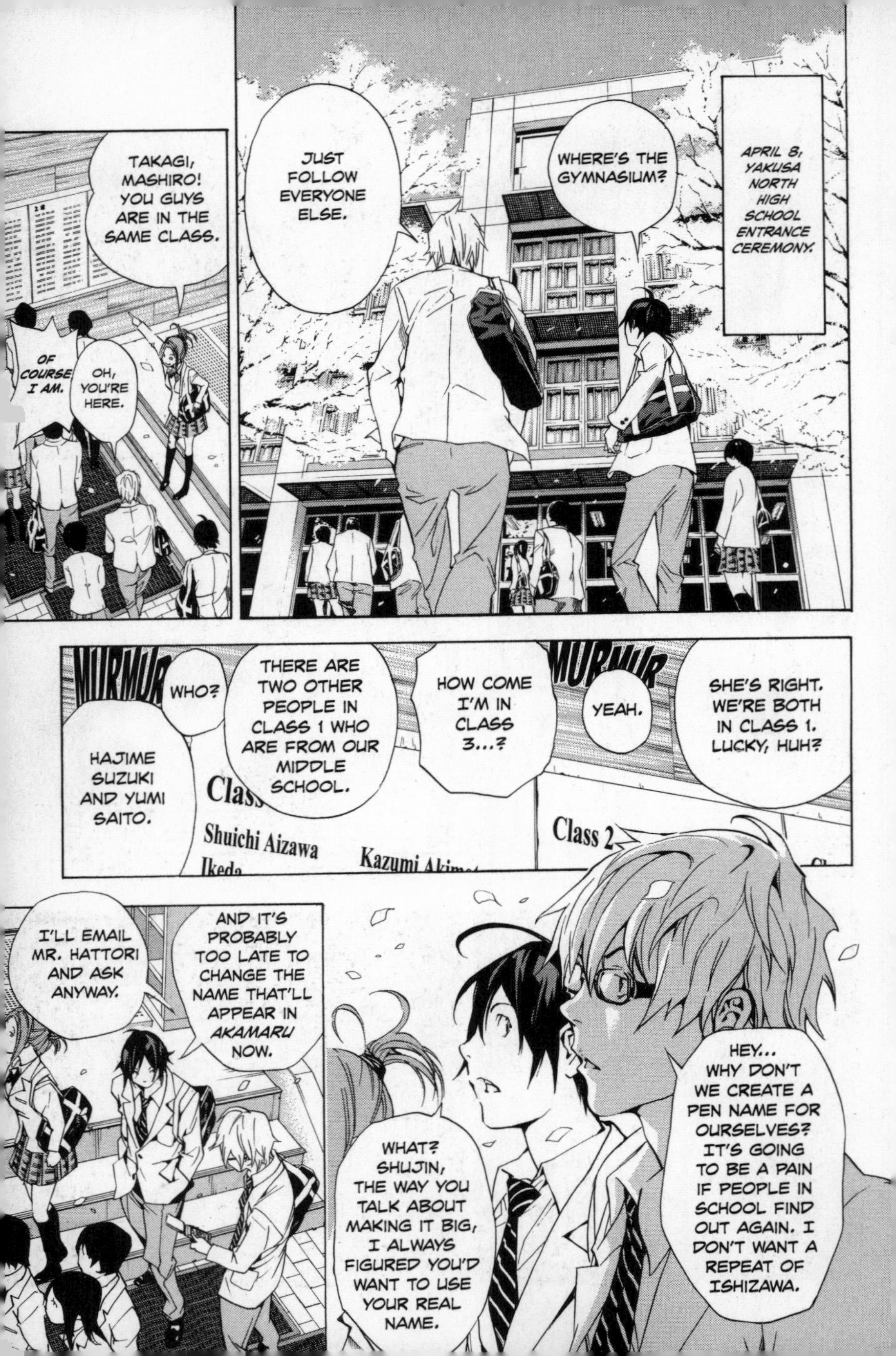
APRIL 8, YAKUSA NORTH HIGH SCHOOL ENTRANCE CEREMONY.
WHERE'S THE GYMNASIUM?
JUST FOLLOW EVERYONE ELSE.
TAKAGI, MASHIRO! YOU GUYS ARE IN THE SAME CLASS.
OH, YOU'RE HERE.
OF COURSE I AM.
SHE'S RIGHT. WE'RE BOTH IN CLASS 1. LUCKY, HUH?
YEAH.
MURMUR
Class 2
HOW COME I'M IN CLASS 3...?
THERE ARE TWO OTHER PEOPLE IN CLASS 1 WHO ARE FROM OUR MIDDLE SCHOOL.
WHO?
HAJIME SUZUKI AND YUMI SAITO.
MURMUR
Shuichi Aizawa
HEY... WHY DON'T WE CREATE A PEN NAME FOR OURSELVES? IT'S GOING TO BE A PAIN IF PEOPLE IN SCHOOL FIND OUT AGAIN. I DON'T WANT A REPEAT OF ISHIZAWA.
WHAT? SHUJIN, THE WAY YOU TALK ABOUT MAKING IT BIG, I ALWAYS FIGURED YOU'D WANT TO USE YOUR REAL NAME.
AND IT'S PROBABLY TOO LATE TO CHANGE THE NAME THAT'LL APPEAR IN *AKAMARU* NOW.
I'LL EMAIL MR. HATTORI AND ASK ANYWAY.

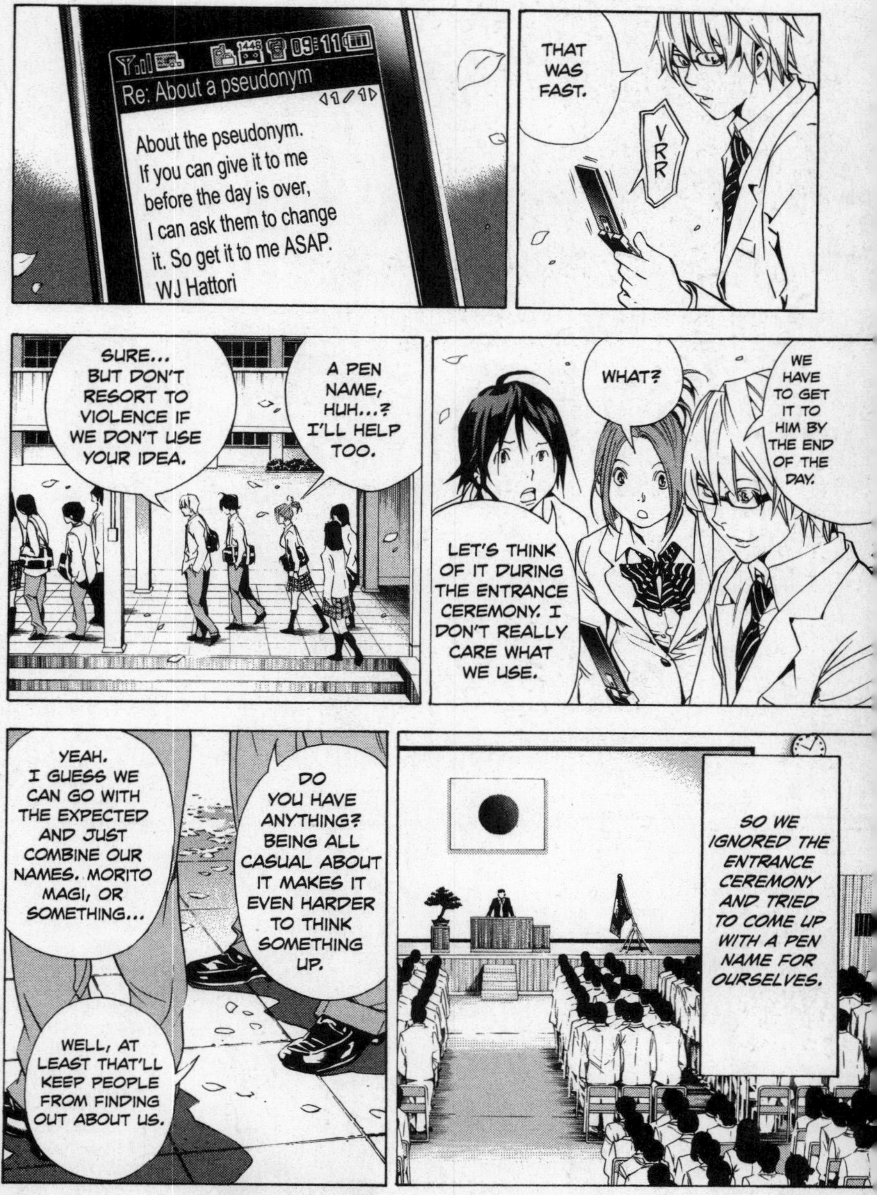
THAT WAS FAST.
VRR
Re: About a pseudonym
About the pseudonym. If you can give it to me before the day is over, I can ask them to change it. So get it to me ASAP. WJ Hattori
WE HAVE TO GET IT TO HIM BY THE END OF THE DAY.
WHAT?
LET'S THINK OF IT DURING THE ENTRANCE CEREMONY. I DON'T REALLY CARE WHAT WE USE.
A PEN NAME, HUH...? I'LL HELP TOO.
SURE... BUT DON'T RESORT TO VIOLENCE IF WE DON'T USE YOUR IDEA.
SO WE IGNORED THE ENTRANCE CEREMONY AND TRIED TO COME UP WITH A PEN NAME FOR OURSELVES.
DO YOU HAVE ANYTHING? BEING ALL CASUAL ABOUT IT MAKES IT EVEN HARDER TO THINK SOMETHING UP.
YEAH. I GUESS WE CAN GO WITH THE EXPECTED AND JUST COMBINE OUR NAMES. MORITO MAGI, OR SOMETHING...
WELL, AT LEAST THAT'LL KEEP PEOPLE FROM FINDING OUT ABOUT US.

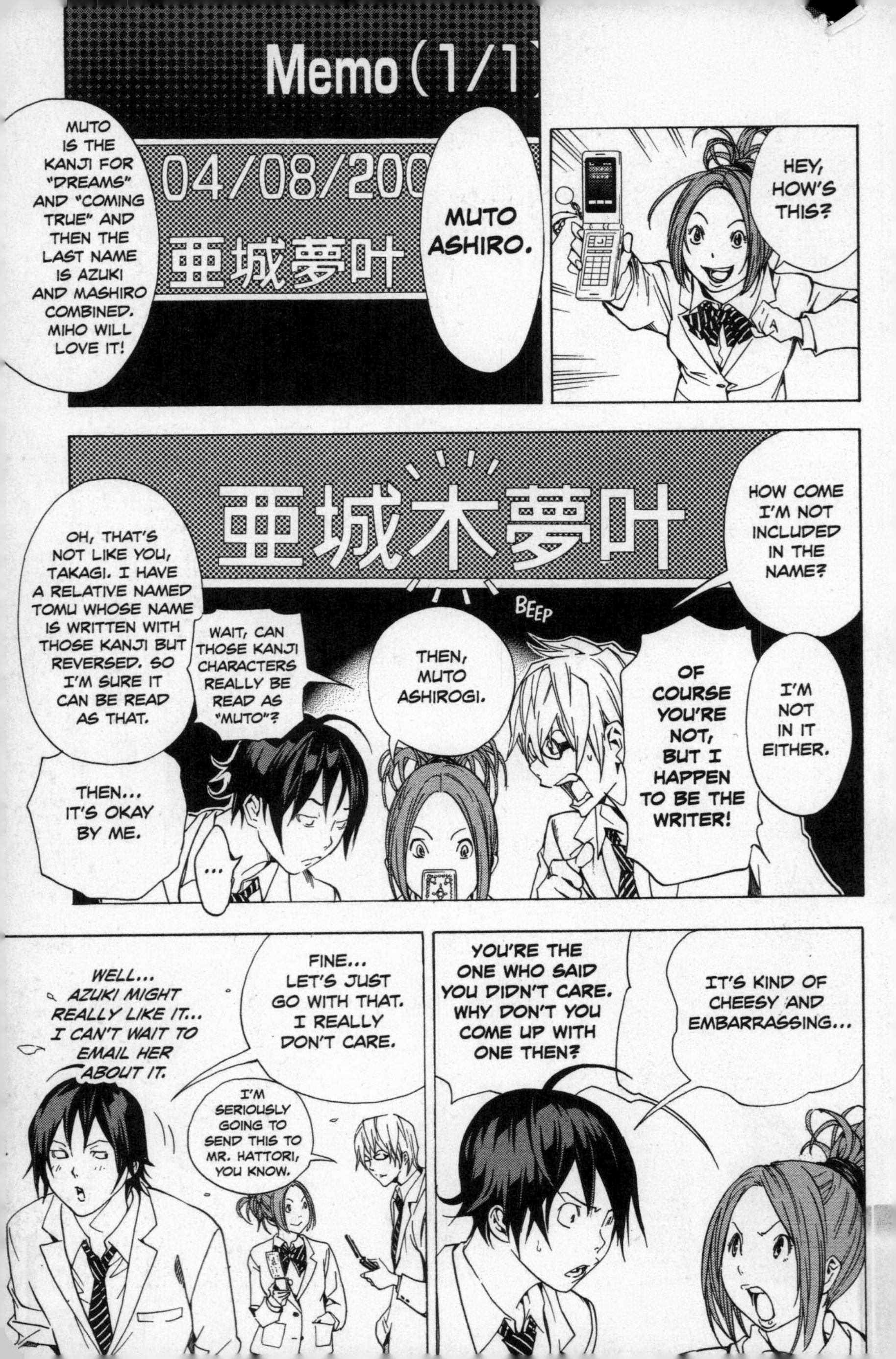

HEY, HOW'S THIS?
Memo (1/1)
04/08/200
亜城夢叶
MUTO ASHIRO.
MUTO IS THE KANJI FOR "DREAMS" AND "COMING TRUE" AND THEN THE LAST NAME IS AZUKI AND MASHIRO COMBINED. MIHO WILL LOVE IT!
亜城木夢叶
HOW COME I'M NOT INCLUDED IN THE NAME?
BEEP
I'M NOT IN IT EITHER.
OF COURSE YOU'RE NOT, BUT I HAPPEN TO BE THE WRITER!
THEN, MUTO ASHIROGI.
WAIT, CAN THOSE KANJI CHARACTERS REALLY BE READ AS "MUTO"?
OH, THAT'S NOT LIKE YOU, TAKAGI. I HAVE A RELATIVE NAMED TOMU WHOSE NAME IS WRITTEN WITH THOSE KANJI BUT REVERSED. SO I'M SURE IT CAN BE READ AS THAT.
THEN... IT'S OKAY BY ME.
...
IT'S KIND OF CHEESY AND EMBARRASSING...
YOU'RE THE ONE WHO SAID YOU DIDN'T CARE. WHY DON'T YOU COME UP WITH ONE THEN?
FINE... LET'S JUST GO WITH THAT. I REALLY DON'T CARE.
I'M SERIOUSLY GOING TO SEND THIS TO MR. HATTORI, YOU KNOW.
WELL... AZUKI MIGHT REALLY LIKE IT... I CAN'T WAIT TO EMAIL HER ABOUT IT.

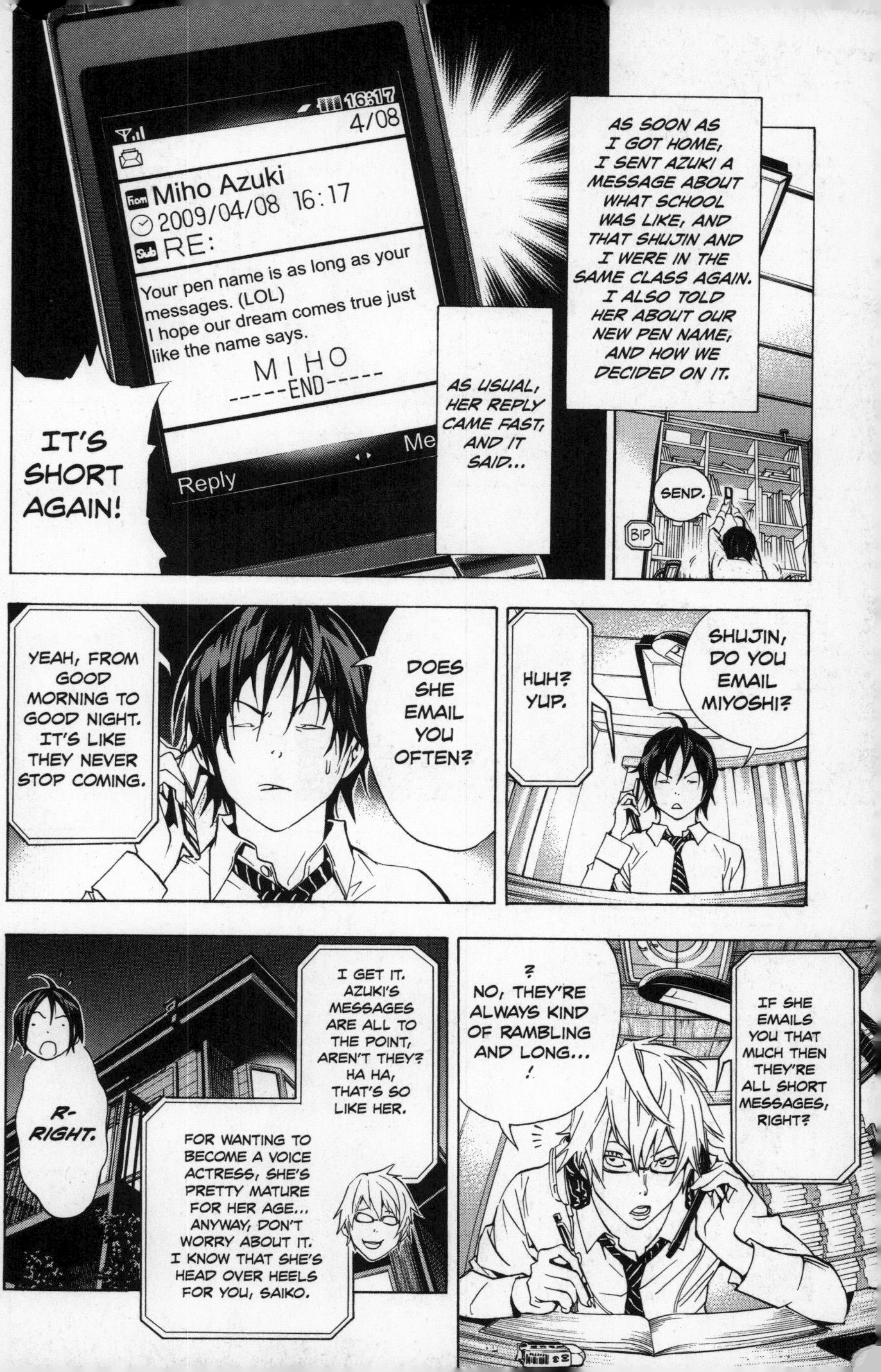
AS SOON AS I GOT HOME, I SENT AZUKI A MESSAGE ABOUT WHAT SCHOOL WAS LIKE, AND THAT SHUJIN AND I WERE IN THE SAME CLASS AGAIN. I ALSO TOLD HER ABOUT OUR NEW PEN NAME, AND HOW WE DECIDED ON IT.
SEND.
BIP
AS USUAL, HER REPLY CAME FAST, AND IT SAID...
16:17
4/08
Miho Azuki
2009/04/08 16:17
RE:
Your pen name is as long as your messages. (LOL)
I hope our dream comes true just like the name says.
MIHO
-----END-----
Reply
IT'S SHORT AGAIN!
SHUJIN, DO YOU EMAIL MIYOSHI?
HUH? YUP.
DOES SHE EMAIL YOU OFTEN?
YEAH, FROM GOOD MORNING TO GOOD NIGHT. IT'S LIKE THEY NEVER STOP COMING.
IF SHE EMAILS YOU THAT MUCH THEN THEY'RE ALL SHORT MESSAGES, RIGHT?
? NO, THEY'RE ALWAYS KIND OF RAMBLING AND LONG... !
I GET IT. AZUKI'S MESSAGES ARE ALL TO THE POINT, AREN'T THEY? HA HA, THAT'S SO LIKE HER.
FOR WANTING TO BECOME A VOICE ACTRESS, SHE'S PRETTY MATURE FOR HER AGE... ANYWAY, DON'T WORRY ABOUT IT. I KNOW THAT SHE'S HEAD OVER HEELS FOR YOU, SAIKO.
R-RIGHT.

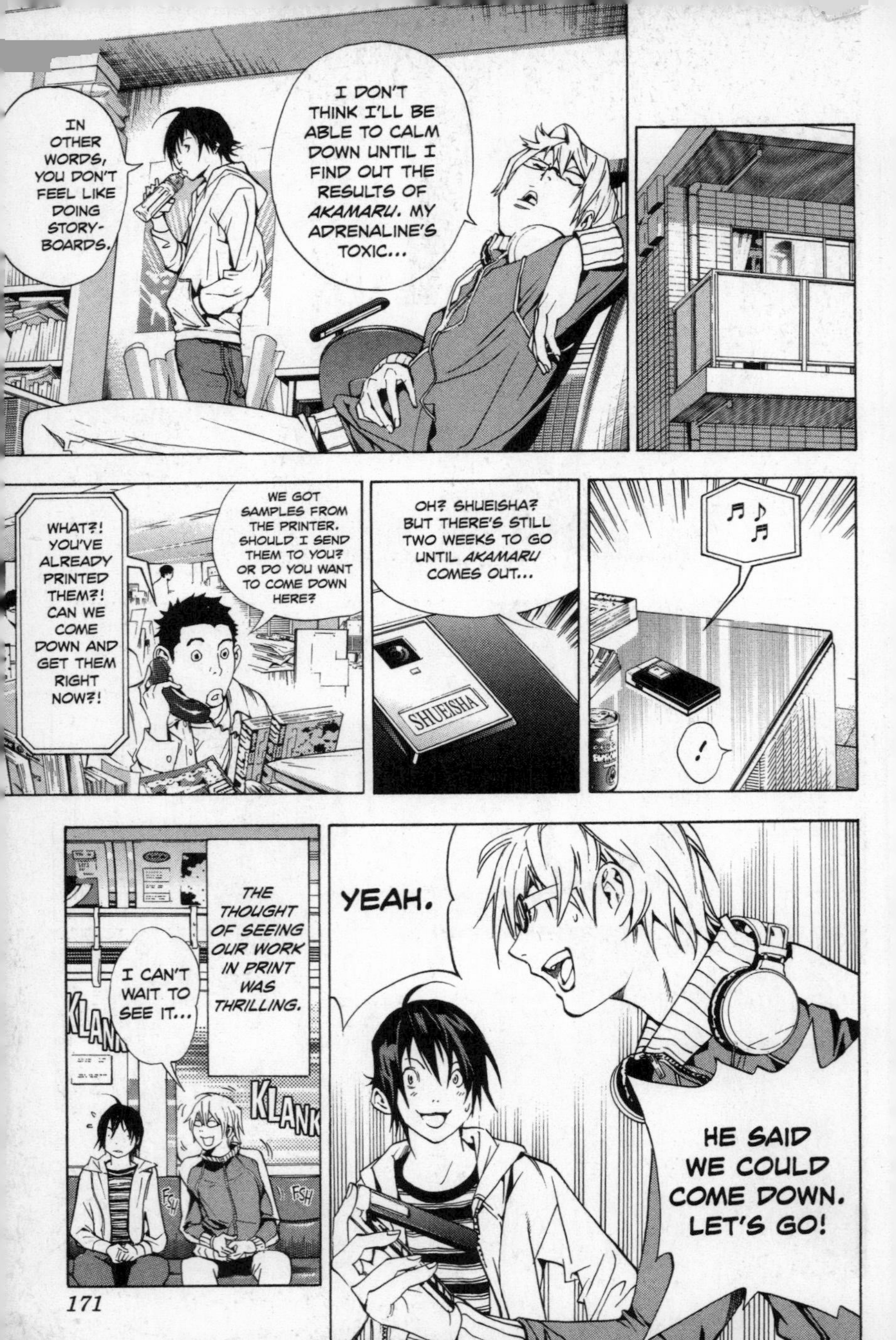
I DON'T THINK I'LL BE ABLE TO CALM DOWN UNTIL I FIND OUT THE RESULTS OF *AKAMARU*. MY ADRENALINE'S TOXIC...
IN OTHER WORDS, YOU DON'T FEEL LIKE DOING STORY-BOARDS.
♬ ♪ ♬
!
OH? SHUEISHA? BUT THERE'S STILL TWO WEEKS TO GO UNTIL *AKAMARU* COMES OUT...
SHUEISHA
WE GOT SAMPLES FROM THE PRINTER. SHOULD I SEND THEM TO YOU? OR DO YOU WANT TO COME DOWN HERE?
WHAT?! YOU'VE ALREADY PRINTED THEM?! CAN WE COME DOWN AND GET THEM RIGHT NOW?!
HE SAID WE COULD COME DOWN. LET'S GO!
YEAH.
*THE THOUGHT OF SEEING OUR WORK IN PRINT WAS THRILLING.*
I CAN'T WAIT TO SEE IT...
KLANK
KLANK
FSH
FSH

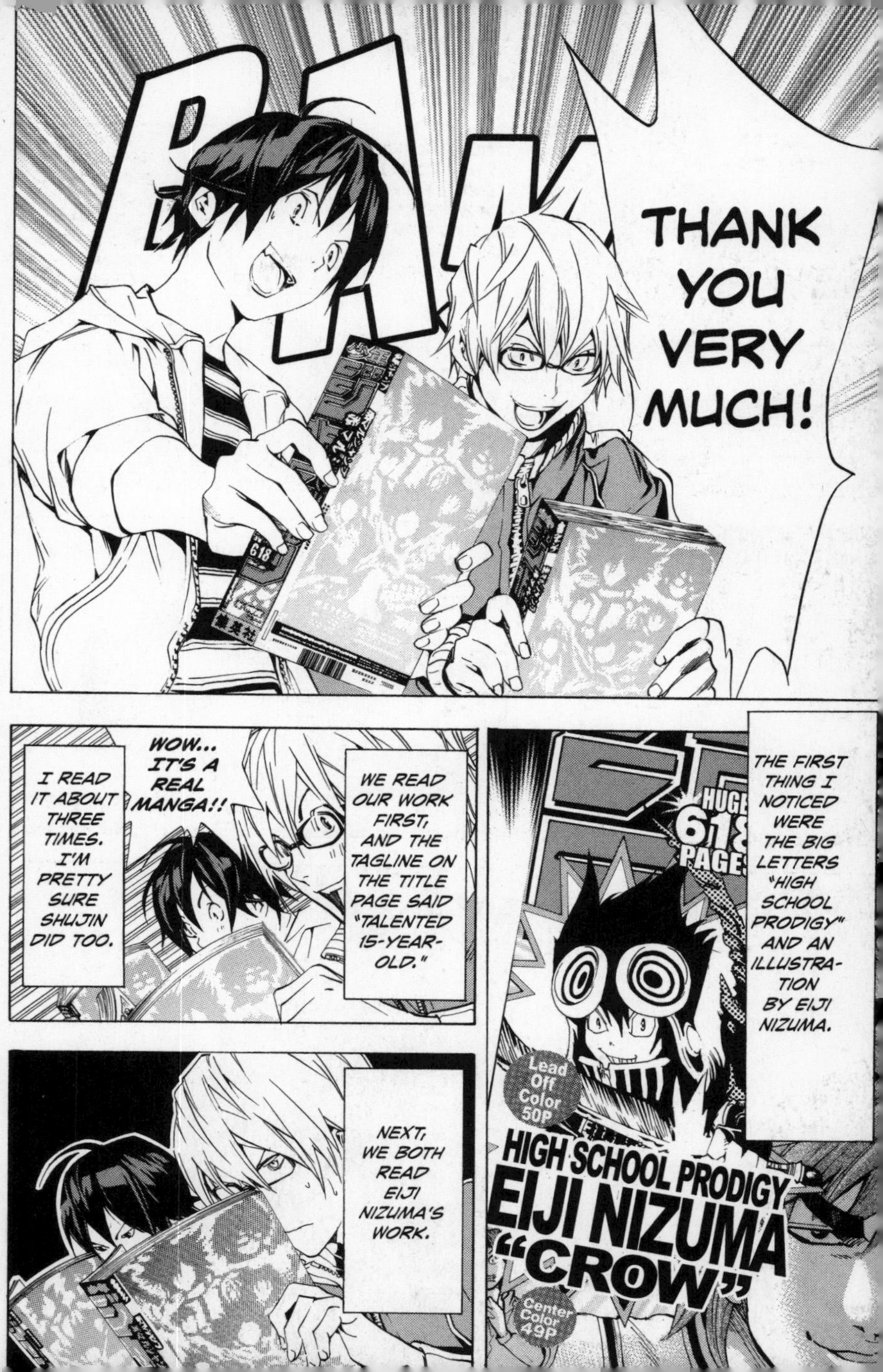
THANK YOU VERY MUCH!
THE FIRST THING I NOTICED WERE THE BIG LETTERS "HIGH SCHOOL PRODIGY" AND AN ILLUSTRATION BY EIJI NIZUMA.
Lead Off Color 50P
HIGH SCHOOL PRODIGY
EIJI NIZUMA
"CROW"
Center Color 49P
WE READ OUR WORK FIRST, AND THE TAGLINE ON THE TITLE PAGE SAID "TALENTED 15-YEAR-OLD."
WOW... IT'S A REAL MANGA!!
I READ IT ABOUT THREE TIMES. I'M PRETTY SURE SHUJIN DID TOO.
NEXT, WE BOTH READ EIJI NIZUMA'S WORK.

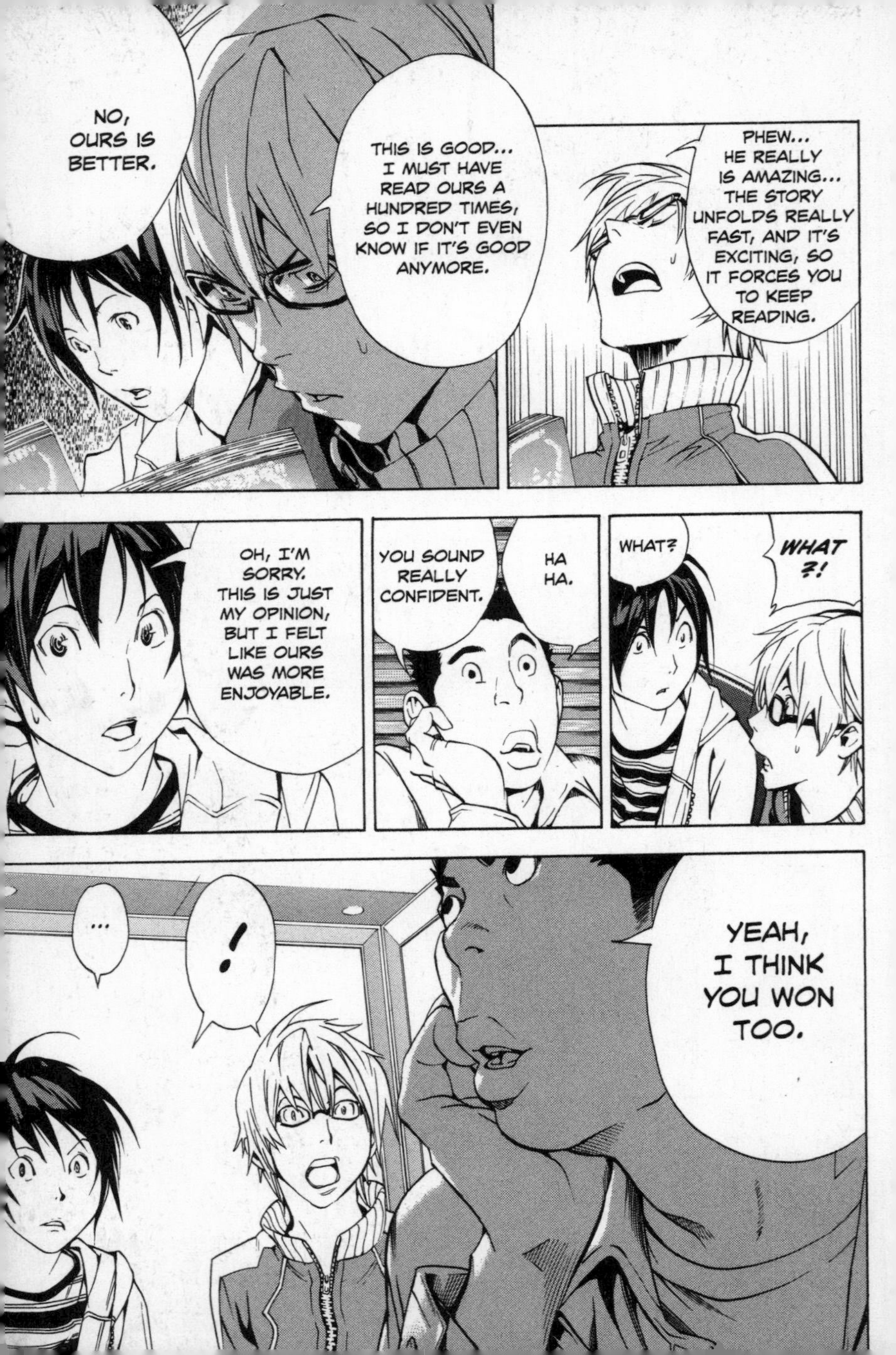
PHEW... HE REALLY IS AMAZING... THE STORY UNFOLDS REALLY FAST, AND IT'S EXCITING, SO IT FORCES YOU TO KEEP READING.
THIS IS GOOD... I MUST HAVE READ OURS A HUNDRED TIMES, SO I DON'T EVEN KNOW IF IT'S GOOD ANYMORE.
NO, OURS IS BETTER.
WHAT ?!
WHAT?
HA HA.
YOU SOUND REALLY CONFIDENT.
OH, I'M SORRY. THIS IS JUST MY OPINION, BUT I FELT LIKE OURS WAS MORE ENJOYABLE.
YEAH, I THINK YOU WON TOO.
!
...

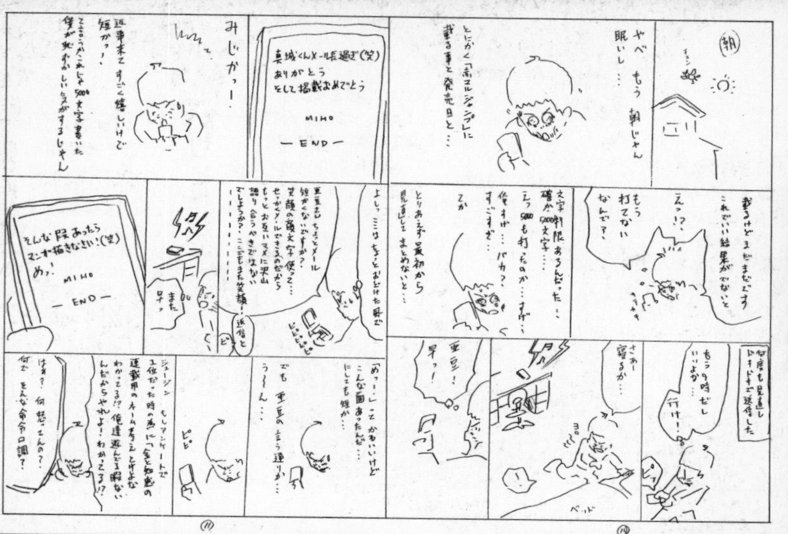
(朝)
ヤベ もう 朝じゃん 眠いし…
とにかく「赤マルジャンプ」に載る事と発売日と…
真城くんメール長過ぎ(笑)
ありがとう
そして掲載おめでとう
MIHO
—END—
みじかっ…
返事来てすごく嬉しいけど短かっ！
てゆうかこれじゃ5000文字書いた僕が恥ずかしい気がするじゃん
載るけどまだまだです
これでいい結果がでないと
えっ!?
もう打てない
なんで?
文字制限あるんだった…
確か5000文字…
てか
とりあえず最初から見直してまとめないと…
よしっ ここはちょっとおどけた風で
そんな暇あったらマンガ描きなさい!(笑)
めっ!
MIHO
—END—
何度も見直しドキドキで送信した
もう9時だし いいよな… 行け!
さぁー寝るか…
亜豆! 早っ!
はぁ? 何怒ってんの? 何でそんな命令口調?

OHBA'S STORYBOARD

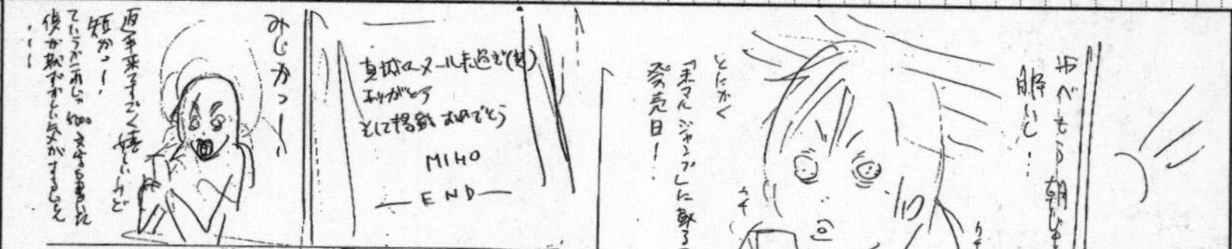

OBATA'S STORYBOARD

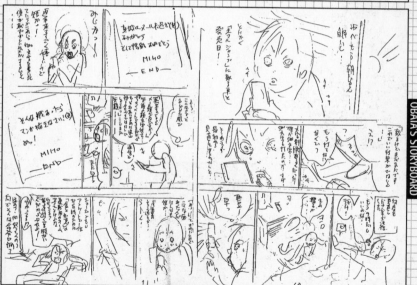

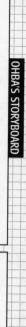

COMPLETE!

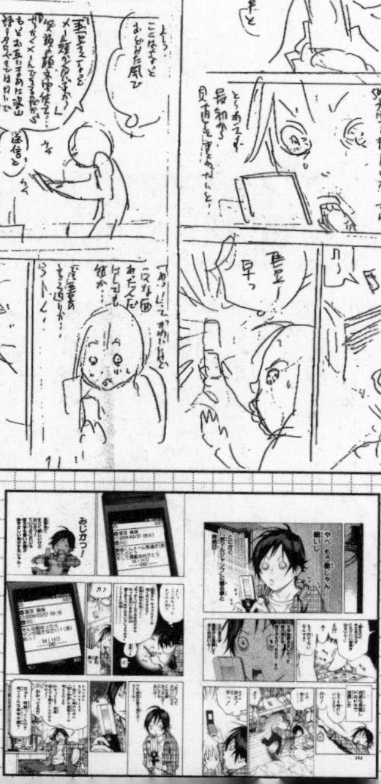

※CREATOR STORYBOARDS AND FINISHED PAGES IN JAPANESE

**BAKUMAN。vol.2**

"Until the Final Draft Is Complete"

Chapter 15, pp.164-165

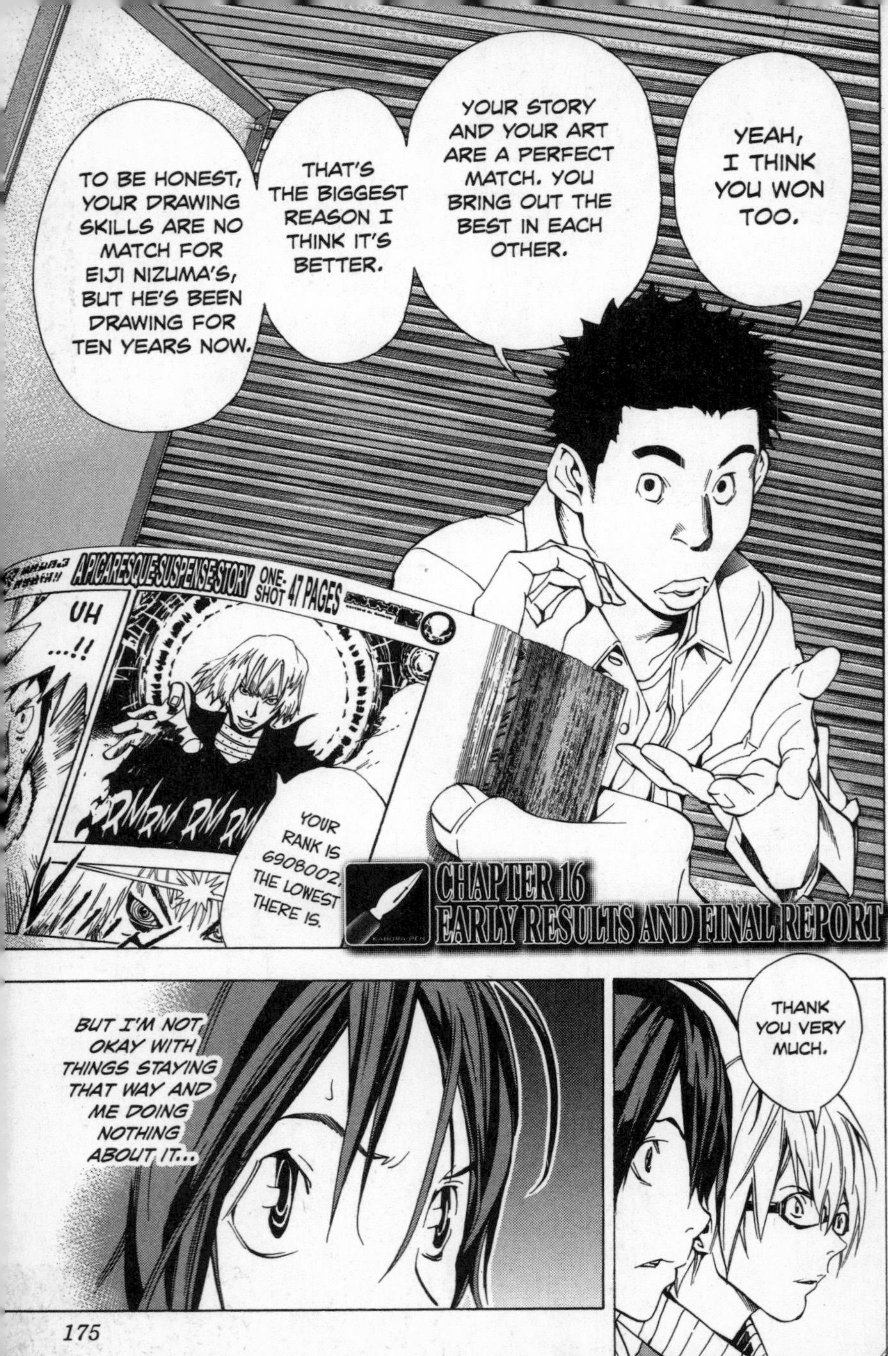
YEAH, I THINK YOU WON TOO.
YOUR STORY AND YOUR ART ARE A PERFECT MATCH. YOU BRING OUT THE BEST IN EACH OTHER.
THAT'S THE BIGGEST REASON I THINK IT'S BETTER.
TO BE HONEST, YOUR DRAWING SKILLS ARE NO MATCH FOR EIJI NIZUMA'S, BUT HE'S BEEN DRAWING FOR TEN YEARS NOW.
A PICARESQUE SUSPENSE STORY
ONE-SHOT 47 PAGES
UH ...!!
DRM DRM DRM DRM
YOUR RANK IS 6908002, THE LOWEST THERE IS.
CHAPTER 16
EARLY RESULTS AND FINAL REPORT
THANK YOU VERY MUCH.
BUT I'M NOT OKAY WITH THINGS STAYING THAT WAY AND ME DOING NOTHING ABOUT IT...

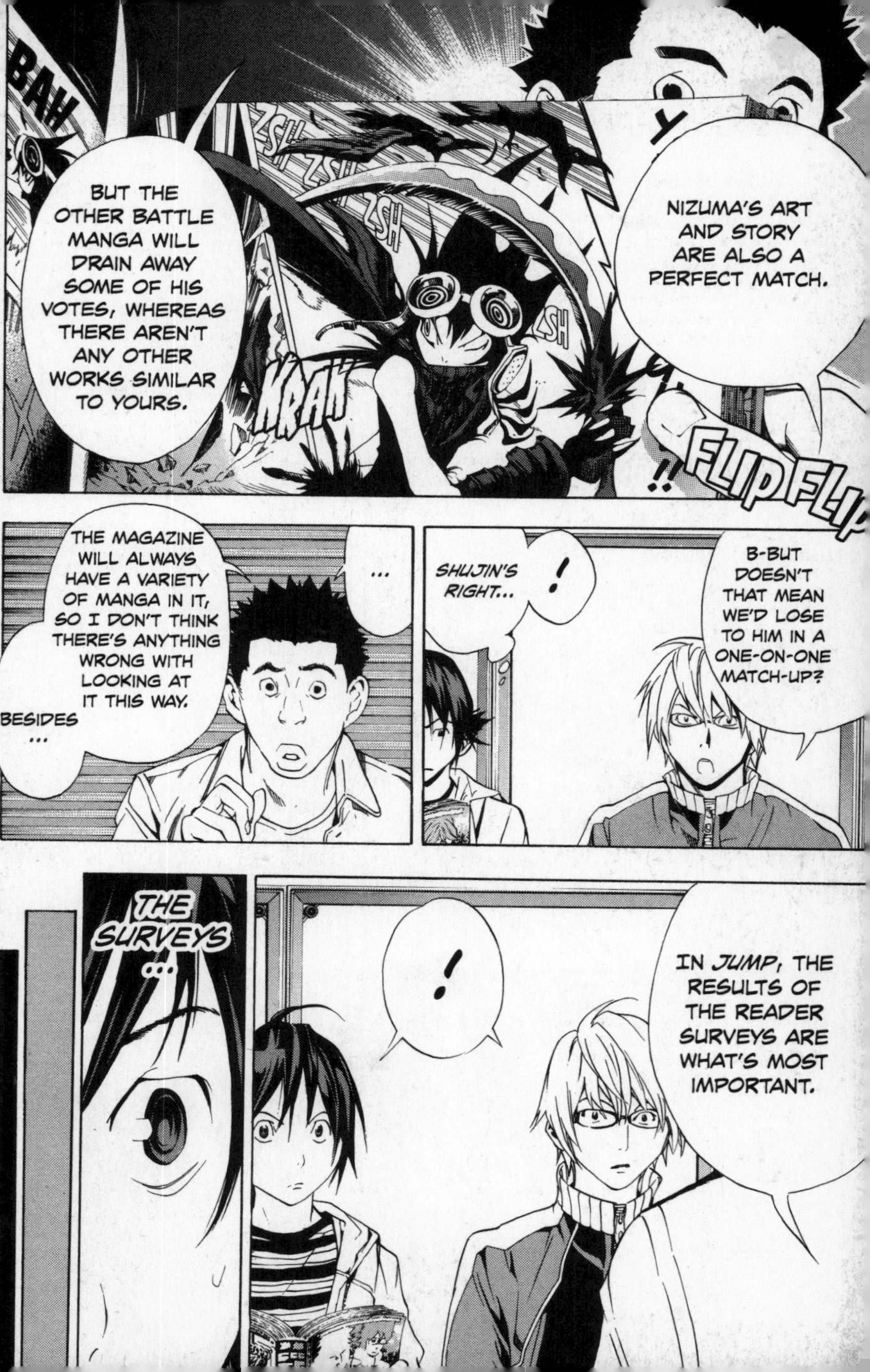
NIZUMA'S ART AND STORY ARE ALSO A PERFECT MATCH.
FLIP FLIP
!!
ZSH ZSH ZSH ZSH ZSH
KRAK
BUT THE OTHER BATTLE MANGA WILL DRAIN AWAY SOME OF HIS VOTES, WHEREAS THERE AREN'T ANY OTHER WORKS SIMILAR TO YOURS.
BAH
B-BUT DOESN'T THAT MEAN WE'D LOSE TO HIM IN A ONE-ON-ONE MATCH-UP?
!
SHUJIN'S RIGHT...
...
THE MAGAZINE WILL ALWAYS HAVE A VARIETY OF MANGA IN IT, SO I DON'T THINK THERE'S ANYTHING WRONG WITH LOOKING AT IT THIS WAY.
BESIDES ...
IN JUMP, THE RESULTS OF THE READER SURVEYS ARE WHAT'S MOST IMPORTANT.
!
THE SURVEYS ...

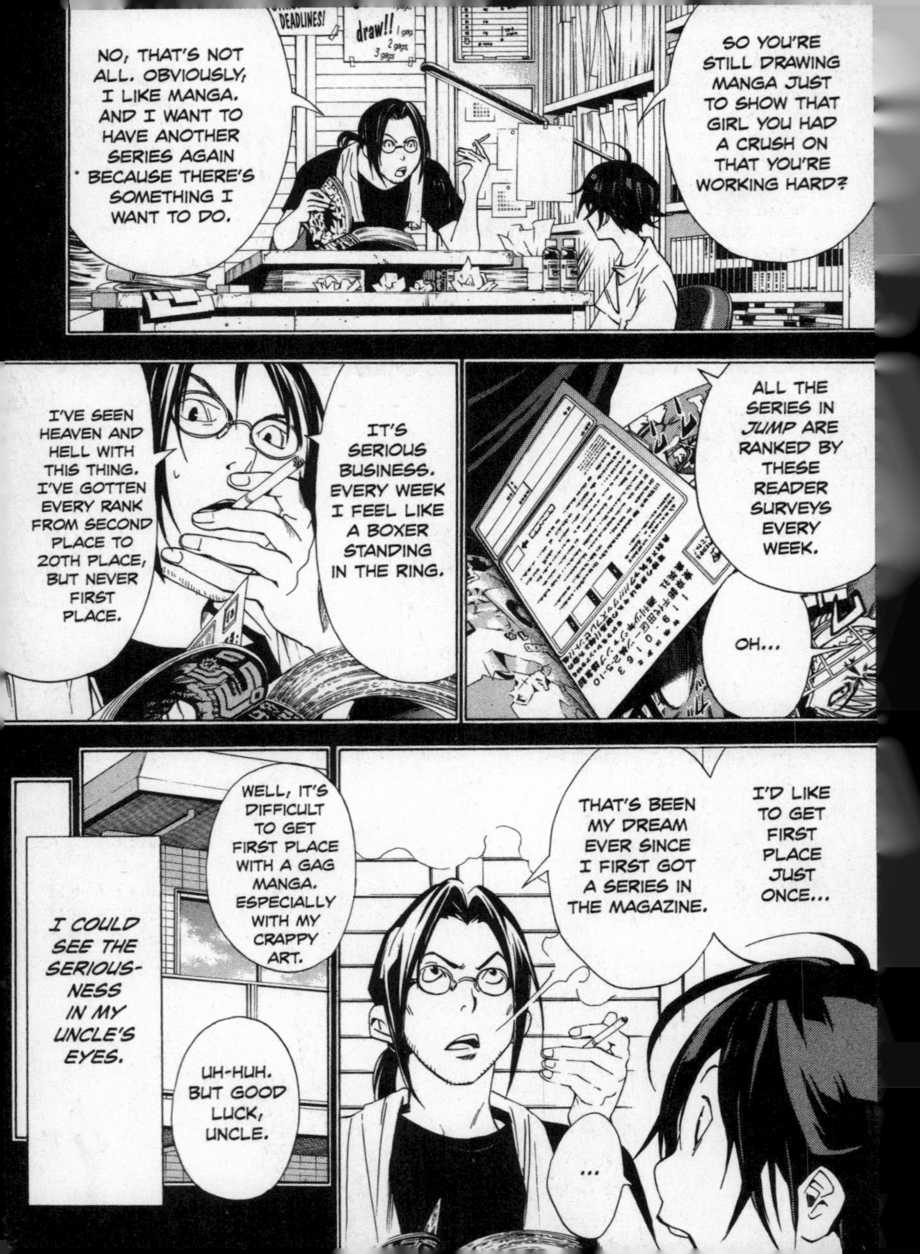
DEADLINES!
draw!! 1 gag 2 gags 3 gags
SO YOU'RE STILL DRAWING MANGA JUST TO SHOW THAT GIRL YOU HAD A CRUSH ON THAT YOU'RE WORKING HARD?
NO, THAT'S NOT ALL. OBVIOUSLY, I LIKE MANGA. AND I WANT TO HAVE ANOTHER SERIES AGAIN BECAUSE THERE'S SOMETHING I WANT TO DO.
ALL THE SERIES IN *JUMP* ARE RANKED BY THESE READER SURVEYS EVERY WEEK.
OH...
IT'S SERIOUS BUSINESS. EVERY WEEK I FEEL LIKE A BOXER STANDING IN THE RING.
I'VE SEEN HEAVEN AND HELL WITH THIS THING. I'VE GOTTEN EVERY RANK FROM SECOND PLACE TO 20TH PLACE, BUT NEVER FIRST PLACE.
I'D LIKE TO GET FIRST PLACE JUST ONCE...
THAT'S BEEN MY DREAM EVER SINCE I FIRST GOT A SERIES IN THE MAGAZINE.
WELL, IT'S DIFFICULT TO GET FIRST PLACE WITH A GAG MANGA. ESPECIALLY WITH MY CRAPPY ART.
UH-HUH. BUT GOOD LUCK, UNCLE.
...
I COULD SEE THE SERIOUSNESS IN MY UNCLE'S EYES.

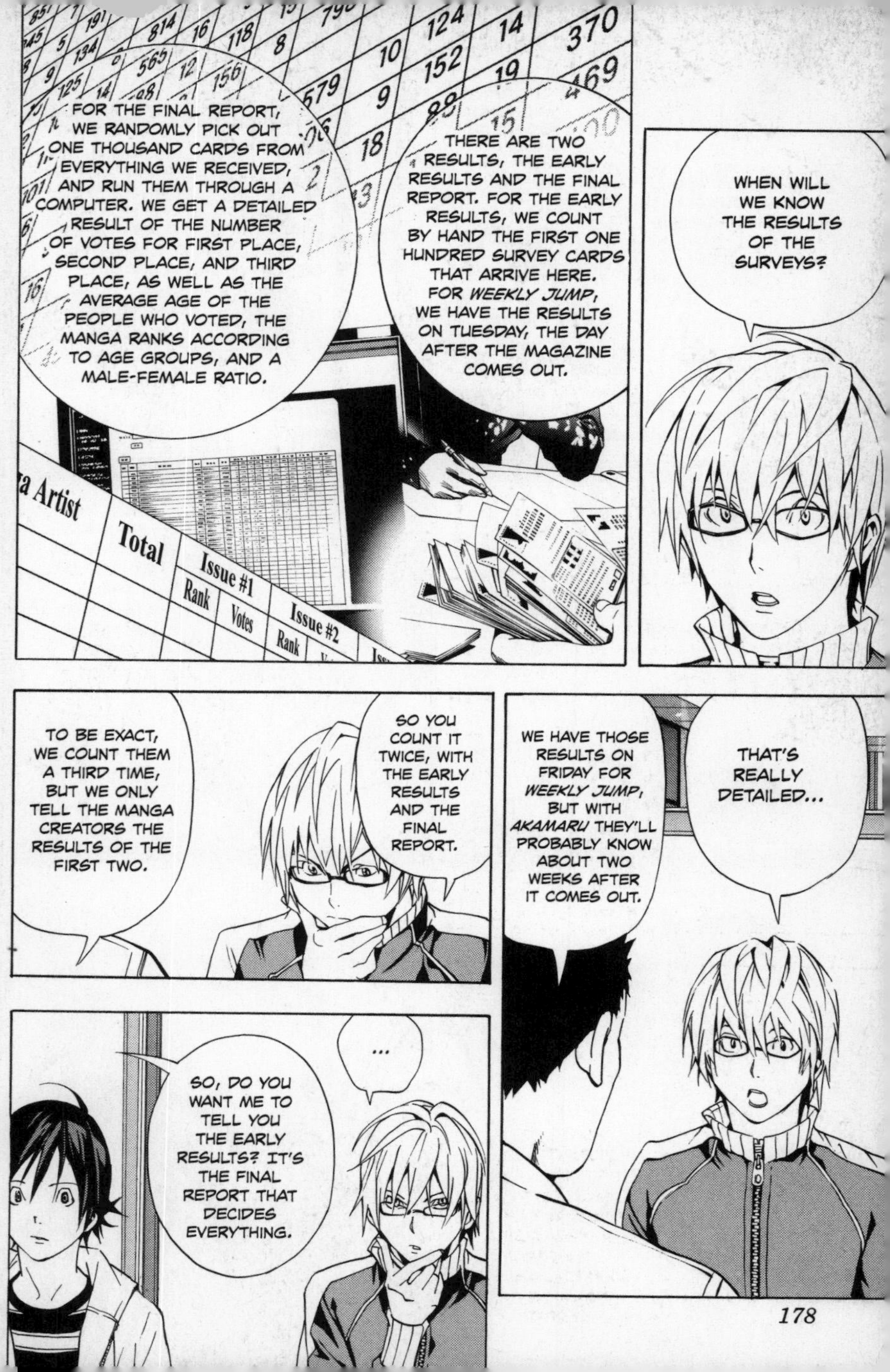
WHEN WILL WE KNOW THE RESULTS OF THE SURVEYS?
THERE ARE TWO RESULTS, THE EARLY RESULTS AND THE FINAL REPORT. FOR THE EARLY RESULTS, WE COUNT BY HAND THE FIRST ONE HUNDRED SURVEY CARDS THAT ARRIVE HERE. FOR *WEEKLY JUMP*, WE HAVE THE RESULTS ON TUESDAY, THE DAY AFTER THE MAGAZINE COMES OUT.
FOR THE FINAL REPORT, WE RANDOMLY PICK OUT ONE THOUSAND CARDS FROM EVERYTHING WE RECEIVED, AND RUN THEM THROUGH A COMPUTER. WE GET A DETAILED RESULT OF THE NUMBER OF VOTES FOR FIRST PLACE, SECOND PLACE, AND THIRD PLACE, AS WELL AS THE AVERAGE AGE OF THE PEOPLE WHO VOTED, THE MANGA RANKS ACCORDING TO AGE GROUPS, AND A MALE-FEMALE RATIO.
a Artist
Total
Issue #1
Rank
Votes
Issue #2
Rank
THAT'S REALLY DETAILED...
WE HAVE THOSE RESULTS ON FRIDAY FOR *WEEKLY JUMP*, BUT WITH *AKAMARU* THEY'LL PROBABLY KNOW ABOUT TWO WEEKS AFTER IT COMES OUT.
SO YOU COUNT IT TWICE, WITH THE EARLY RESULTS AND THE FINAL REPORT.
TO BE EXACT, WE COUNT THEM A THIRD TIME, BUT WE ONLY TELL THE MANGA CREATORS THE RESULTS OF THE FIRST TWO.
...
SO, DO YOU WANT ME TO TELL YOU THE EARLY RESULTS? IT'S THE FINAL REPORT THAT DECIDES EVERYTHING.

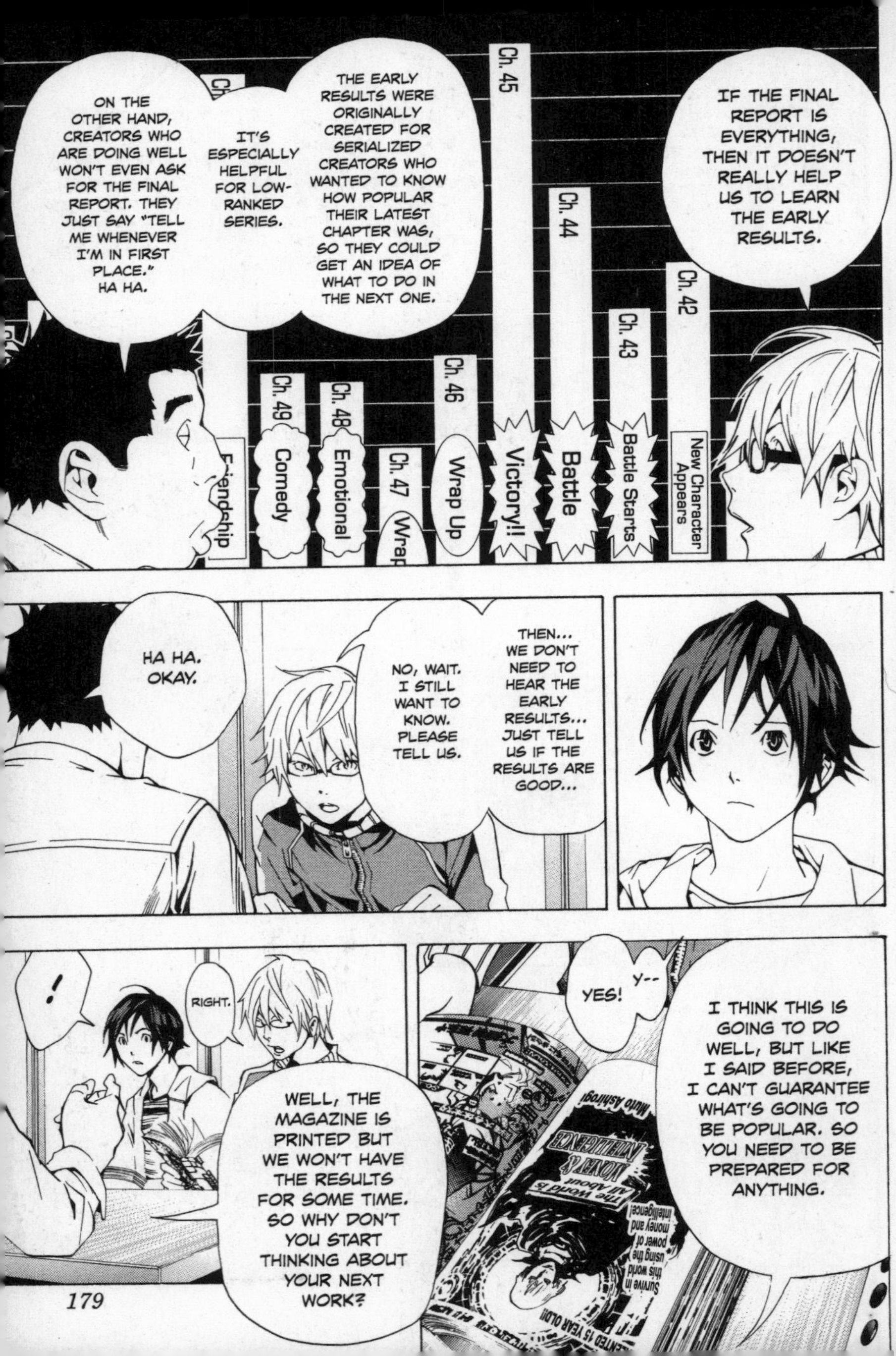
IF THE FINAL REPORT IS EVERYTHING, THEN IT DOESN'T REALLY HELP US TO LEARN THE EARLY RESULTS.
Ch. 42
New Character Appears
Ch. 43
Battle Starts
Ch. 44
Battle
Ch. 45
Victory!!
Ch. 46
Wrap Up
Ch. 47
Wrap
Ch. 48
Emotional
Ch. 49
Comedy
THE EARLY RESULTS WERE ORIGINALLY CREATED FOR SERIALIZED CREATORS WHO WANTED TO KNOW HOW POPULAR THEIR LATEST CHAPTER WAS, SO THEY COULD GET AN IDEA OF WHAT TO DO IN THE NEXT ONE.
IT'S ESPECIALLY HELPFUL FOR LOW-RANKED SERIES.
ON THE OTHER HAND, CREATORS WHO ARE DOING WELL WON'T EVEN ASK FOR THE FINAL REPORT. THEY JUST SAY "TELL ME WHENEVER I'M IN FIRST PLACE." HA HA.
THEN... WE DON'T NEED TO HEAR THE EARLY RESULTS... JUST TELL US IF THE RESULTS ARE GOOD...
NO, WAIT. I STILL WANT TO KNOW. PLEASE TELL US.
HA HA. OKAY.
Y--
YES!
I THINK THIS IS GOING TO DO WELL, BUT LIKE I SAID BEFORE, I CAN'T GUARANTEE WHAT'S GOING TO BE POPULAR. SO YOU NEED TO BE PREPARED FOR ANYTHING.
Muto Ashirogi
The World Is All About MONEY & INTELLIGENCE
Survive in this world using the power of money and intelligence!
RIGHT.
!
WELL, THE MAGAZINE IS PRINTED BUT WE WON'T HAVE THE RESULTS FOR SOME TIME. SO WHY DON'T YOU START THINKING ABOUT YOUR NEXT WORK?

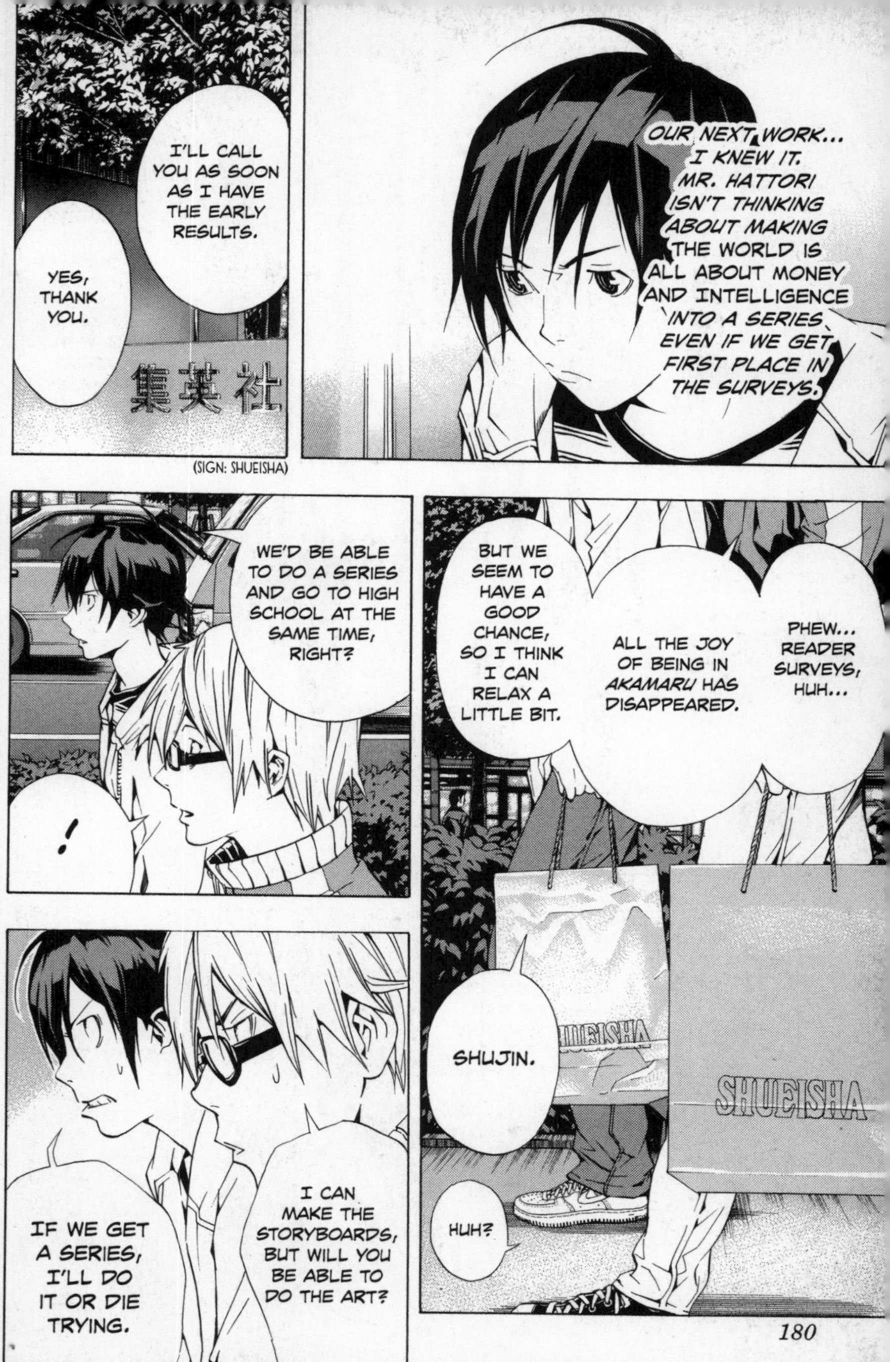
OUR NEXT WORK... I KNEW IT. MR. HATTORI ISN'T THINKING ABOUT MAKING THE WORLD IS ALL ABOUT MONEY AND INTELLIGENCE INTO A SERIES EVEN IF WE GET FIRST PLACE IN THE SURVEYS.
I'LL CALL YOU AS SOON AS I HAVE THE EARLY RESULTS.
YES, THANK YOU.
集英社
(SIGN: SHUEISHA)
PHEW... READER SURVEYS, HUH...
ALL THE JOY OF BEING IN *AKAMARU* HAS DISAPPEARED.
BUT WE SEEM TO HAVE A GOOD CHANCE, SO I THINK I CAN RELAX A LITTLE BIT.
SHUEISHA
SHUJIN.
SHUEISHA
HUH?
WE'D BE ABLE TO DO A SERIES AND GO TO HIGH SCHOOL AT THE SAME TIME, RIGHT?
!
I CAN MAKE THE STORYBOARDS, BUT WILL YOU BE ABLE TO DO THE ART?
IF WE GET A SERIES, I'LL DO IT OR DIE TRYING.

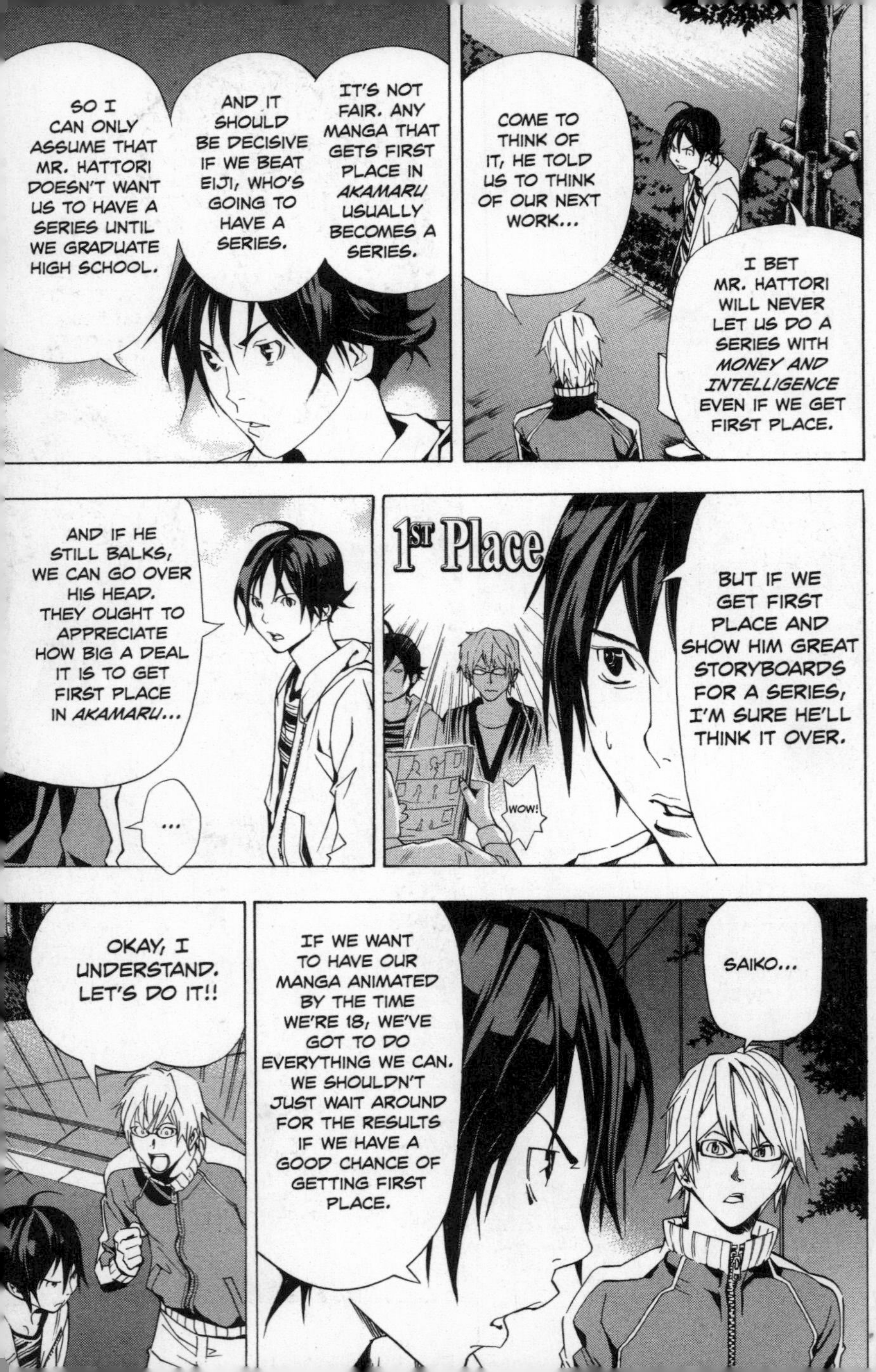
COME TO THINK OF IT, HE TOLD US TO THINK OF OUR NEXT WORK...
I BET MR. HATTORI WILL NEVER LET US DO A SERIES WITH *MONEY AND INTELLIGENCE* EVEN IF WE GET FIRST PLACE.
IT'S NOT FAIR. ANY MANGA THAT GETS FIRST PLACE IN *AKAMARU* USUALLY BECOMES A SERIES.
AND IT SHOULD BE DECISIVE IF WE BEAT EIJI, WHO'S GOING TO HAVE A SERIES.
SO I CAN ONLY ASSUME THAT MR. HATTORI DOESN'T WANT US TO HAVE A SERIES UNTIL WE GRADUATE HIGH SCHOOL.
1ST Place
BUT IF WE GET FIRST PLACE AND SHOW HIM GREAT STORYBOARDS FOR A SERIES, I'M SURE HE'LL THINK IT OVER.
WOW!
AND IF HE STILL BALKS, WE CAN GO OVER HIS HEAD. THEY OUGHT TO APPRECIATE HOW BIG A DEAL IT IS TO GET FIRST PLACE IN *AKAMARU*...
...
SAIKO...
IF WE WANT TO HAVE OUR MANGA ANIMATED BY THE TIME WE'RE 18, WE'VE GOT TO DO EVERYTHING WE CAN. WE SHOULDN'T JUST WAIT AROUND FOR THE RESULTS IF WE HAVE A GOOD CHANCE OF GETTING FIRST PLACE.
OKAY, I UNDERSTAND. LET'S DO IT!!

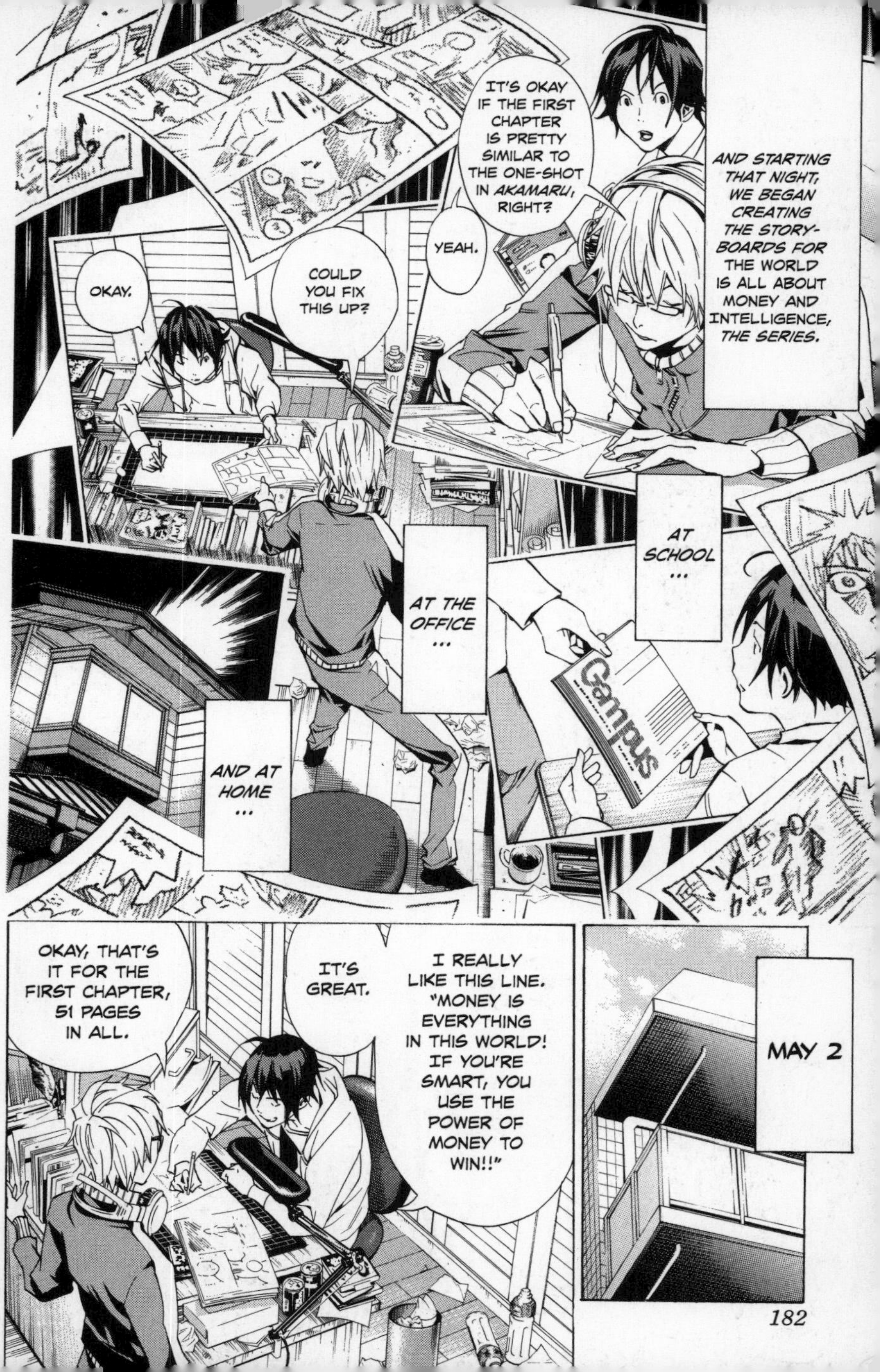
AND STARTING THAT NIGHT, WE BEGAN CREATING THE STORY-BOARDS FOR THE WORLD IS ALL ABOUT MONEY AND INTELLIGENCE, THE SERIES.
IT'S OKAY IF THE FIRST CHAPTER IS PRETTY SIMILAR TO THE ONE-SHOT IN AKAMARU, RIGHT?
YEAH.
COULD YOU FIX THIS UP?
OKAY.
AT SCHOOL ...
AT THE OFFICE ...
AND AT HOME ...
MAY 2
I REALLY LIKE THIS LINE. "MONEY IS EVERYTHING IN THIS WORLD! IF YOU'RE SMART, YOU USE THE POWER OF MONEY TO WIN!!"
IT'S GREAT.
OKAY, THAT'S IT FOR THE FIRST CHAPTER, 51 PAGES IN ALL.

READ THIS WAY

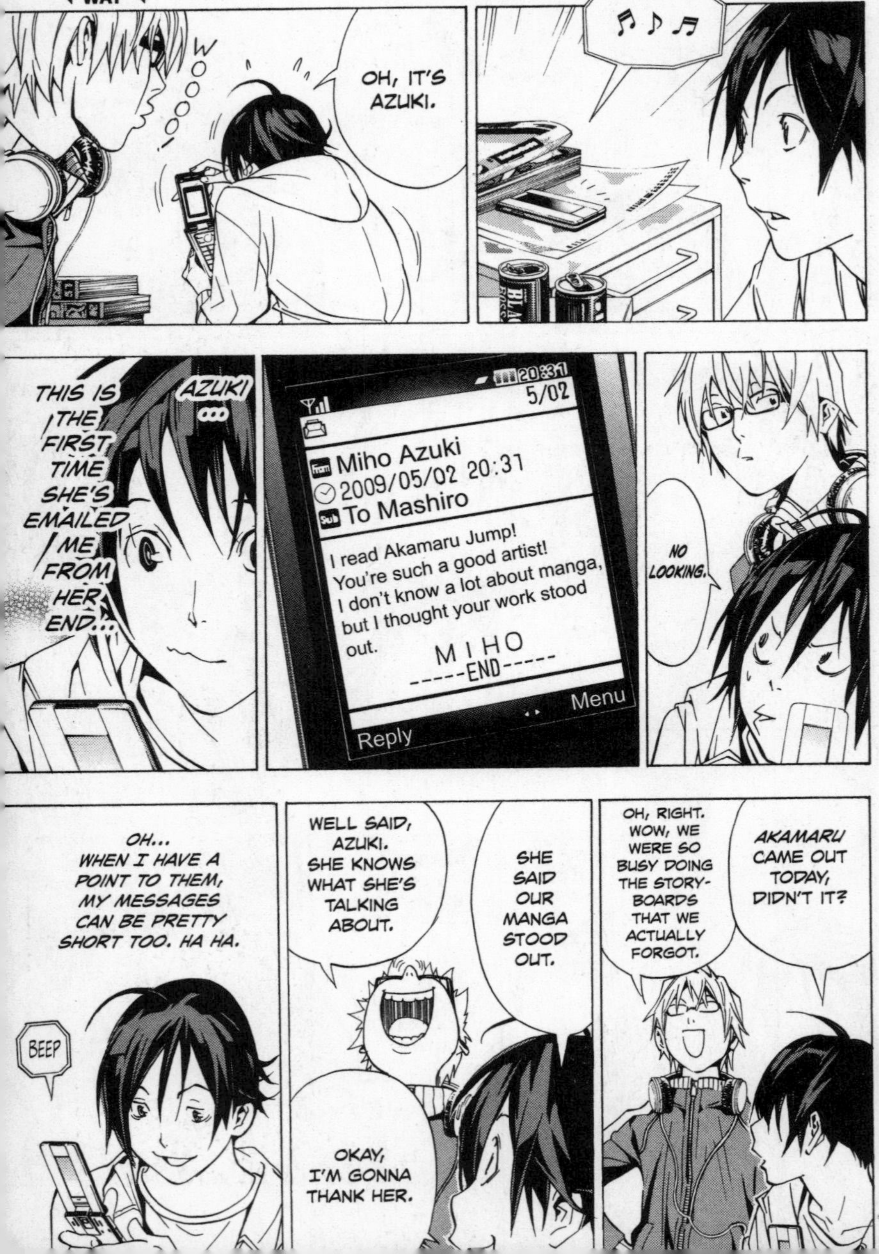
♬ ♪ ♬
WOOOOO
OH, IT'S AZUKI.
NO LOOKING.
20:31
5/02
Miho Azuki
2009/05/02 20:31
To Mashiro
I read Akamaru Jump! You're such a good artist! I don't know a lot about manga, but I thought your work stood out.
MIHO
-----END-----
Menu
Reply
AZUKI ...
THIS IS THE FIRST TIME SHE'S EMAILED ME FROM HER END...
AKAMARU CAME OUT TODAY, DIDN'T IT?
OH, RIGHT. WOW, WE WERE SO BUSY DOING THE STORY-BOARDS THAT WE ACTUALLY FORGOT.
SHE SAID OUR MANGA STOOD OUT.
WELL SAID, AZUKI. SHE KNOWS WHAT SHE'S TALKING ABOUT.
OKAY, I'M GONNA THANK HER.
OH... WHEN I HAVE A POINT TO THEM, MY MESSAGES CAN BE PRETTY SHORT TOO. HA HA.
BEEP

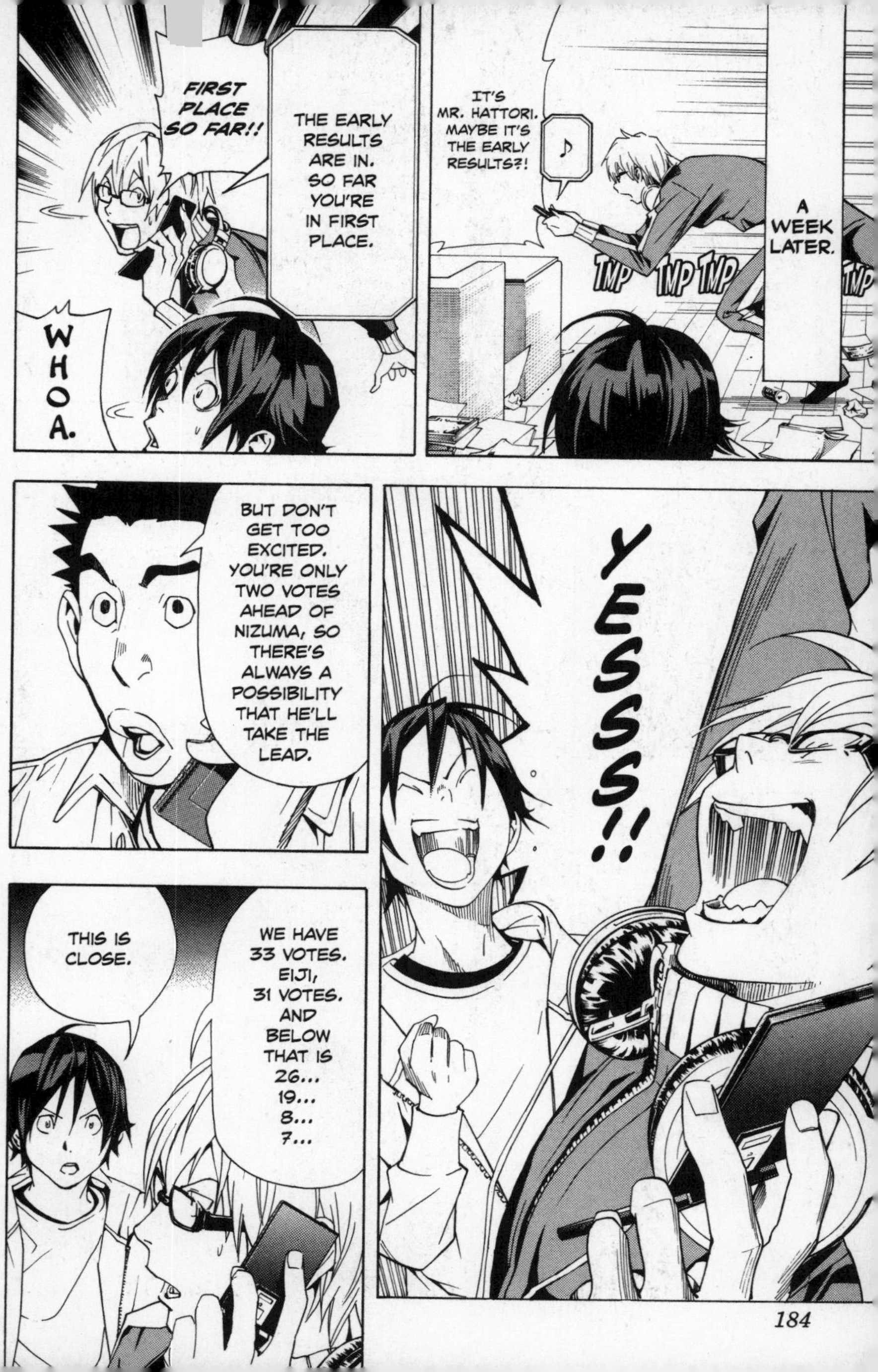
A WEEK LATER.
TMP TMP TMP
TMP
IT'S MR. HATTORI. MAYBE IT'S THE EARLY RESULTS?!
♪
THE EARLY RESULTS ARE IN. SO FAR YOU'RE IN FIRST PLACE.
FIRST PLACE SO FAR!!
WHOA.
YESSS!!
BUT DON'T GET TOO EXCITED. YOU'RE ONLY TWO VOTES AHEAD OF NIZUMA, SO THERE'S ALWAYS A POSSIBILITY THAT HE'LL TAKE THE LEAD.
WE HAVE 33 VOTES. EIJI, 31 VOTES. AND BELOW THAT IS 26... 19... 8... 7...
THIS IS CLOSE.

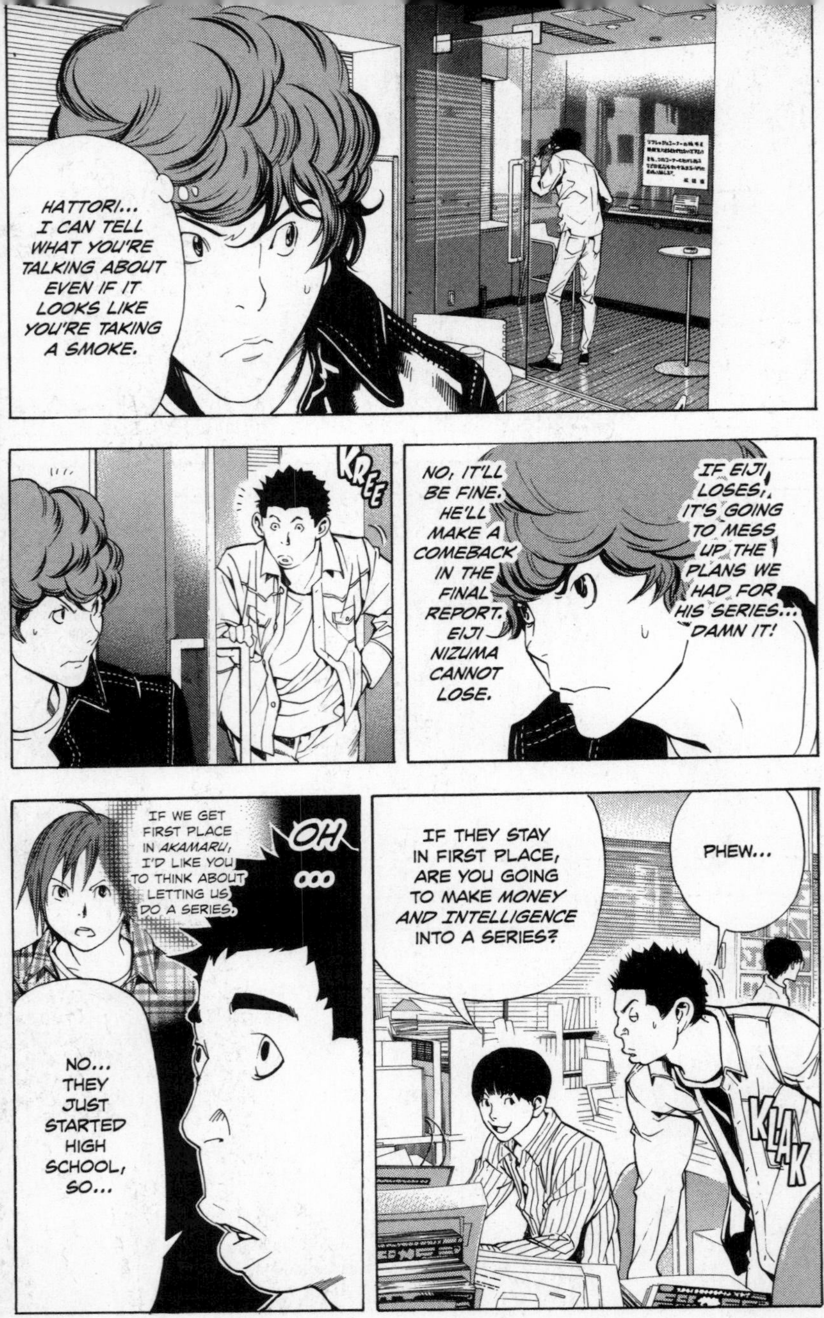
HATTORI... I CAN TELL WHAT YOU'RE TALKING ABOUT EVEN IF IT LOOKS LIKE YOU'RE TAKING A SMOKE.
IF EIJI LOSES, IT'S GOING TO MESS UP THE PLANS WE HAD FOR HIS SERIES... DAMN IT!
NO, IT'LL BE FINE. HE'LL MAKE A COMEBACK IN THE FINAL REPORT. EIJI NIZUMA CANNOT LOSE.
KREE
PHEW...
IF THEY STAY IN FIRST PLACE, ARE YOU GOING TO MAKE *MONEY AND INTELLIGENCE* INTO A SERIES?
KLAK
OH
OOO
IF WE GET FIRST PLACE IN *AKAMARU*, I'D LIKE YOU TO THINK ABOUT LETTING US DO A SERIES.
NO... THEY JUST STARTED HIGH SCHOOL, SO...

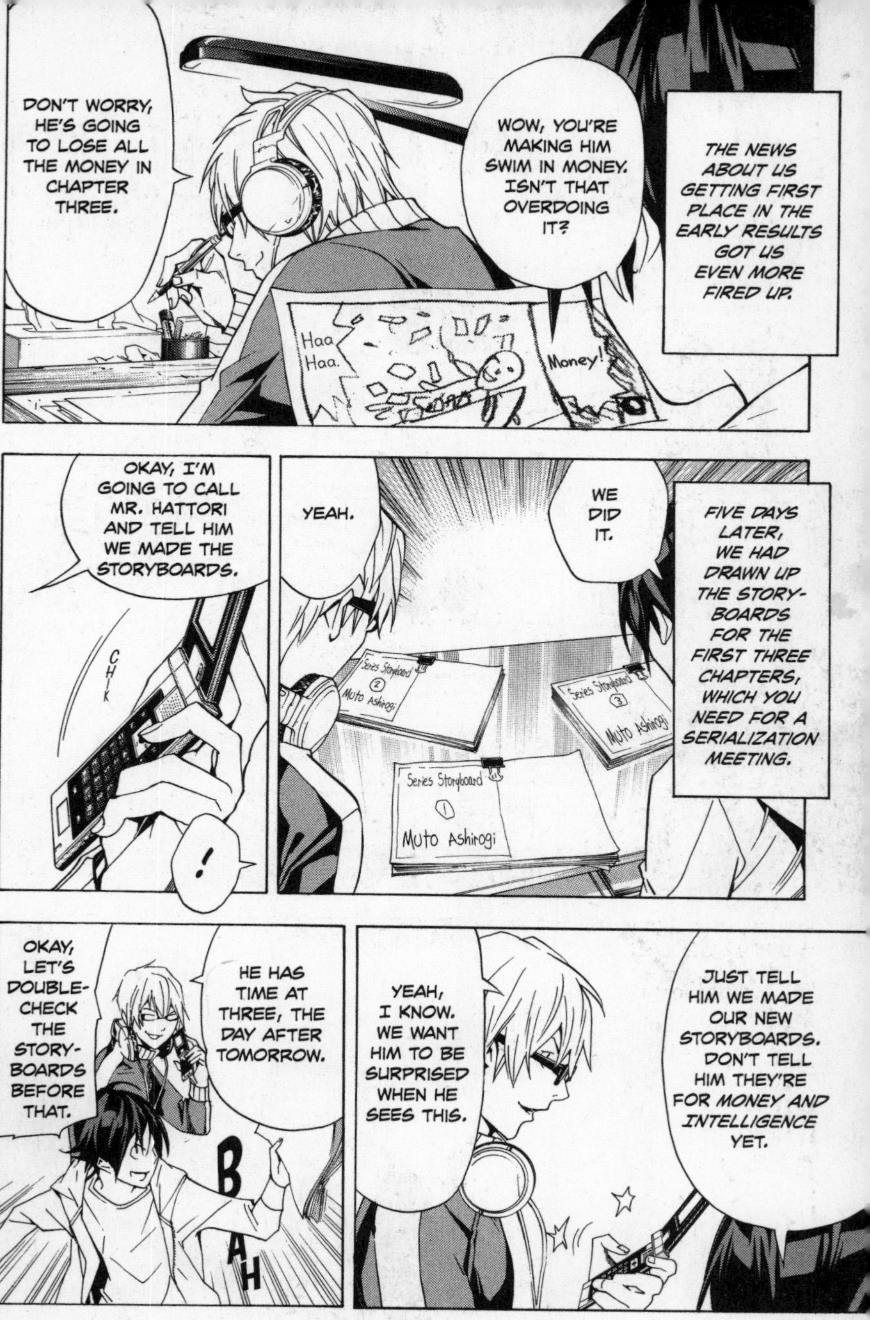
THE NEWS ABOUT US GETTING FIRST PLACE IN THE EARLY RESULTS GOT US EVEN MORE FIRED UP.
WOW, YOU'RE MAKING HIM SWIM IN MONEY. ISN'T THAT OVERDOING IT?
DON'T WORRY, HE'S GOING TO LOSE ALL THE MONEY IN CHAPTER THREE.
Money!
Haa Haa.
FIVE DAYS LATER, WE HAD DRAWN UP THE STORY-BOARDS FOR THE FIRST THREE CHAPTERS, WHICH YOU NEED FOR A SERIALIZATION MEETING.
WE DID IT.
YEAH.
Series Storyboard 3 Muto Ashirogi
Series Storyboard 2 Muto Ashirogi
Series Storyboard 1 Muto Ashirogi
OKAY, I'M GOING TO CALL MR. HATTORI AND TELL HIM WE MADE THE STORYBOARDS.
CHIK
!
JUST TELL HIM WE MADE OUR NEW STORYBOARDS. DON'T TELL HIM THEY'RE FOR *MONEY AND INTELLIGENCE* YET.
YEAH, I KNOW. WE WANT HIM TO BE SURPRISED WHEN HE SEES THIS.
HE HAS TIME AT THREE, THE DAY AFTER TOMORROW.
OKAY, LET'S DOUBLE-CHECK THE STORY-BOARDS BEFORE THAT.
BAH

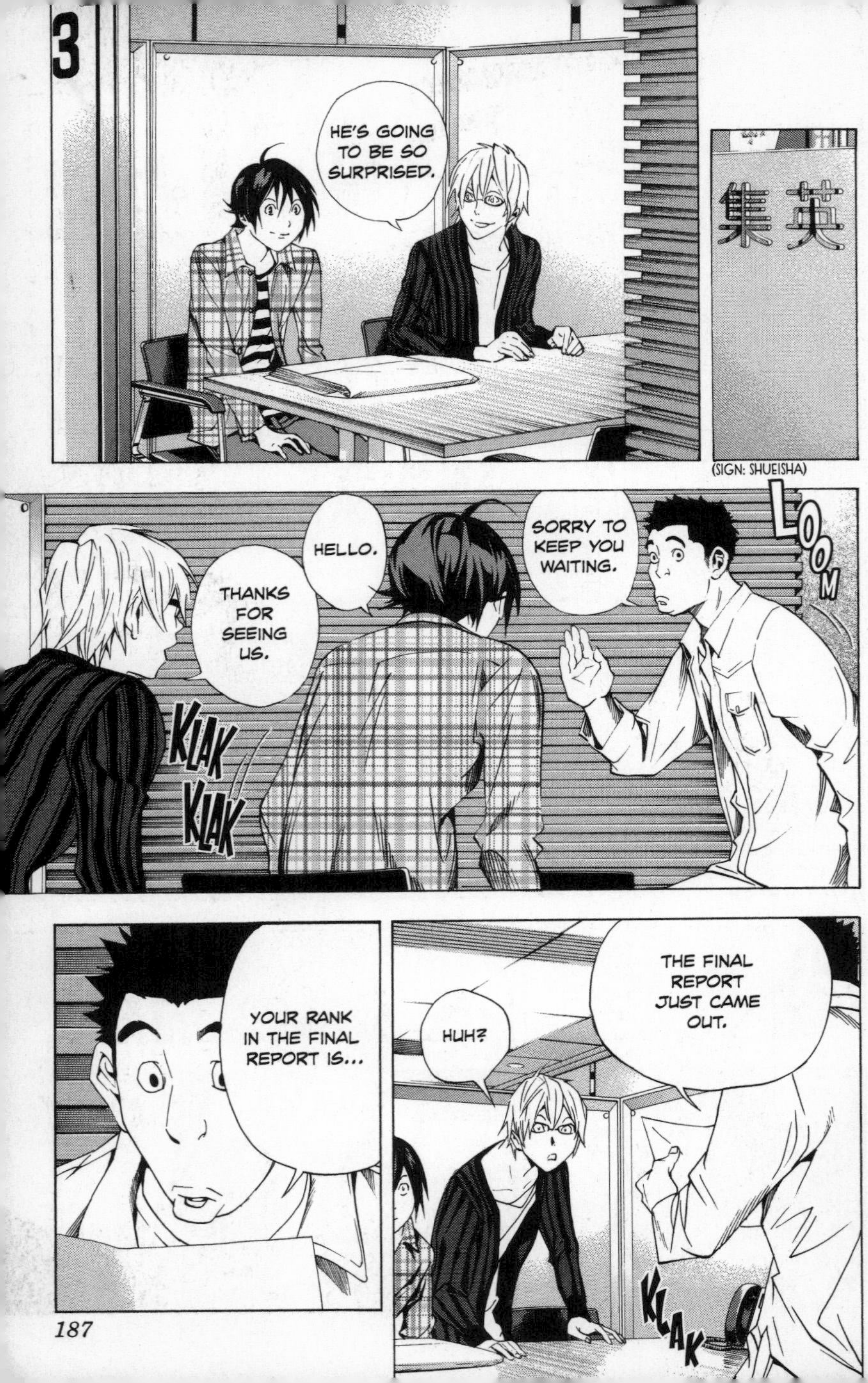
集英
(SIGN: SHUEISHA)
HE'S GOING TO BE SO SURPRISED.
LOOM
SORRY TO KEEP YOU WAITING.
HELLO.
THANKS FOR SEEING US.
KLAK KLAK
THE FINAL REPORT JUST CAME OUT.
HUH?
KLAK
YOUR RANK IN THE FINAL REPORT IS...

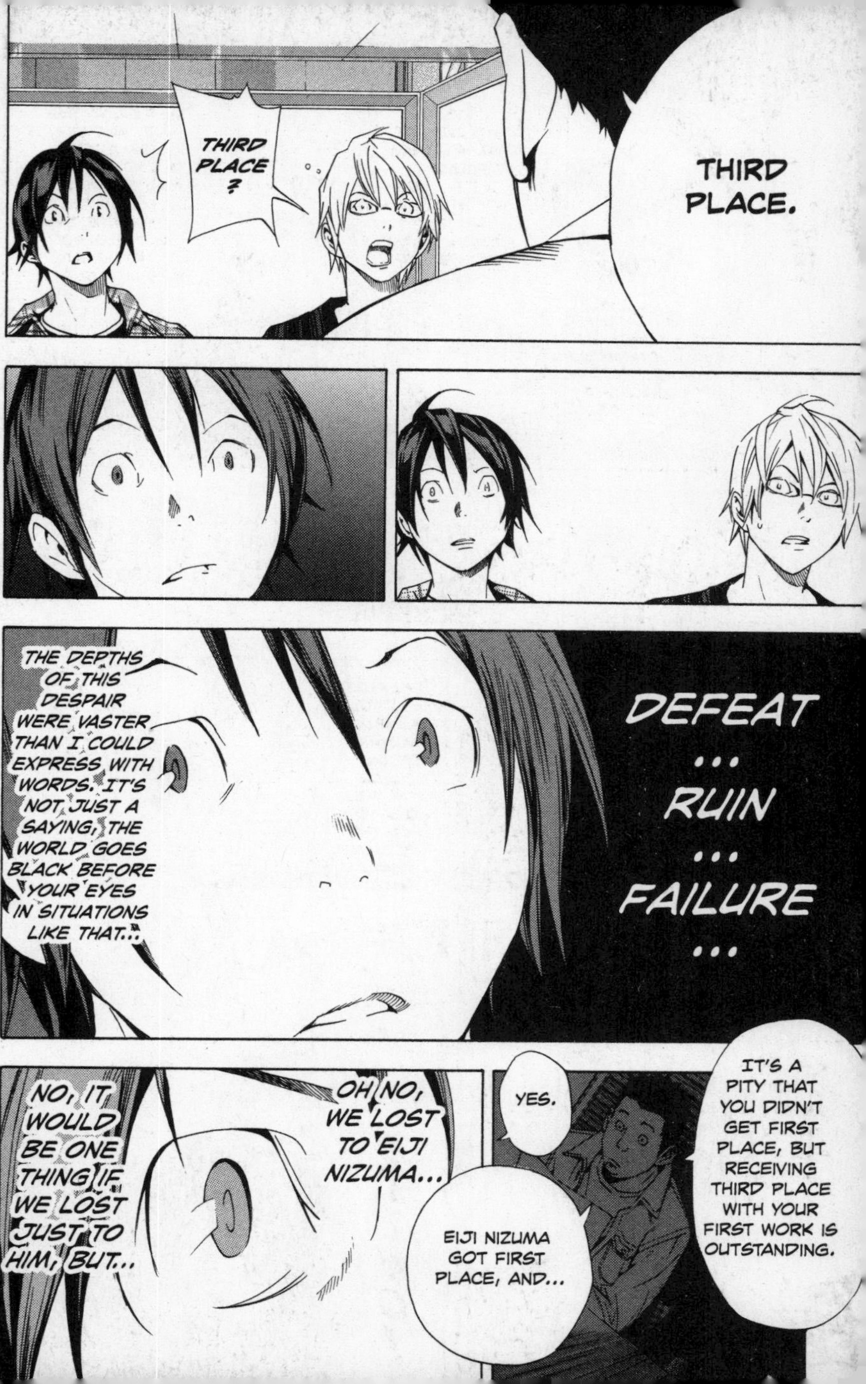
THIRD PLACE.
THIRD PLACE?
DEFEAT... RUIN... FAILURE...
THE DEPTHS OF THIS DESPAIR WERE VASTER THAN I COULD EXPRESS WITH WORDS. IT'S NOT JUST A SAYING, THE WORLD GOES BLACK BEFORE YOUR EYES IN SITUATIONS LIKE THAT...
IT'S A PITY THAT YOU DIDN'T GET FIRST PLACE, BUT RECEIVING THIRD PLACE WITH YOUR FIRST WORK IS OUTSTANDING.
YES.
EIJI NIZUMA GOT FIRST PLACE, AND...
OH NO, WE LOST TO EIJI NIZUMA...
NO, IT WOULD BE ONE THING IF WE LOST JUST TO HIM, BUT...

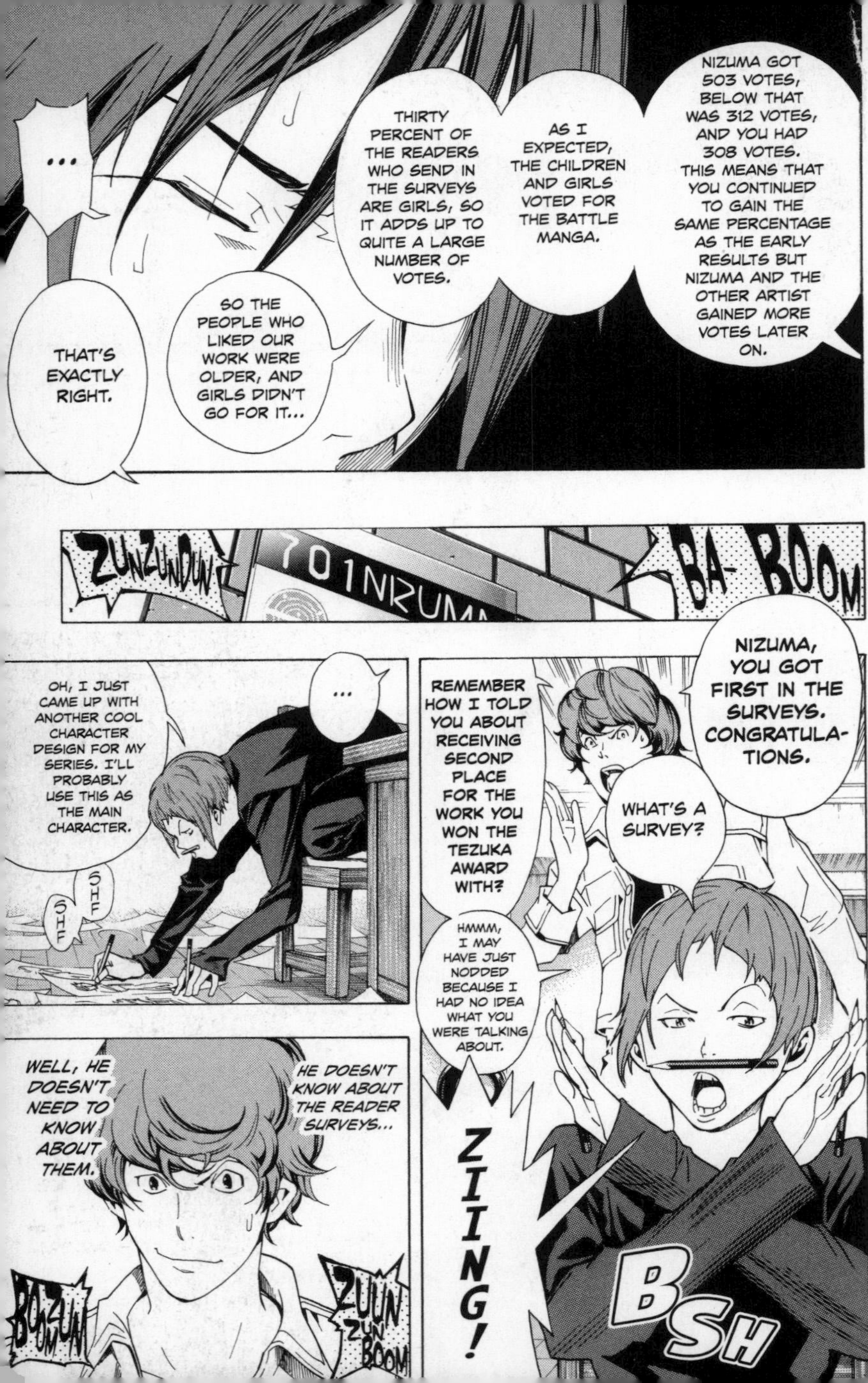
NIZUMA GOT 503 VOTES, BELOW THAT WAS 312 VOTES, AND YOU HAD 308 VOTES. THIS MEANS THAT YOU CONTINUED TO GAIN THE SAME PERCENTAGE AS THE EARLY RESULTS BUT NIZUMA AND THE OTHER ARTIST GAINED MORE VOTES LATER ON.
AS I EXPECTED, THE CHILDREN AND GIRLS VOTED FOR THE BATTLE MANGA.
THIRTY PERCENT OF THE READERS WHO SEND IN THE SURVEYS ARE GIRLS, SO IT ADDS UP TO QUITE A LARGE NUMBER OF VOTES.
...
SO THE PEOPLE WHO LIKED OUR WORK WERE OLDER, AND GIRLS DIDN'T GO FOR IT...
THAT'S EXACTLY RIGHT.
BA-BOOM
701 NIZUMA
ZUNZUNDUN
NIZUMA, YOU GOT FIRST IN THE SURVEYS. CONGRATULATIONS.
REMEMBER HOW I TOLD YOU ABOUT RECEIVING SECOND PLACE FOR THE WORK YOU WON THE TEZUKA AWARD WITH?
WHAT'S A SURVEY?
HMMM, I MAY HAVE JUST NODDED BECAUSE I HAD NO IDEA WHAT YOU WERE TALKING ABOUT.
ZIIING!
BSH
...
OH, I JUST CAME UP WITH ANOTHER COOL CHARACTER DESIGN FOR MY SERIES. I'LL PROBABLY USE THIS AS THE MAIN CHARACTER.
SHF
SHF
HE DOESN'T KNOW ABOUT THE READER SURVEYS...
WELL, HE DOESN'T NEED TO KNOW ABOUT THEM.
ZUUN ZUN BOOM

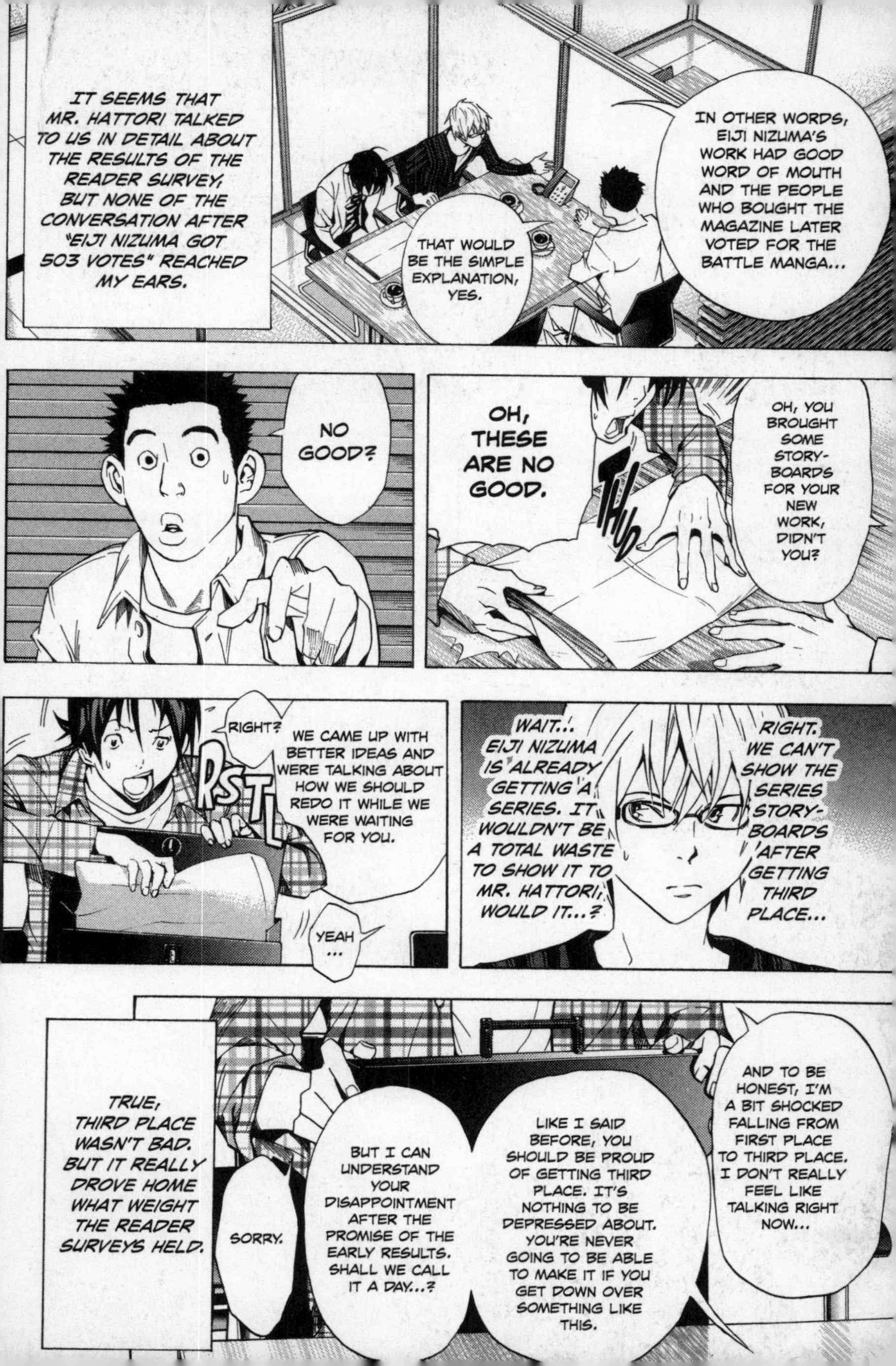
IN OTHER WORDS, EIJI NIZUMA'S WORK HAD GOOD WORD OF MOUTH AND THE PEOPLE WHO BOUGHT THE MAGAZINE LATER VOTED FOR THE BATTLE MANGA...
THAT WOULD BE THE SIMPLE EXPLANATION, YES.
IT SEEMS THAT MR. HATTORI TALKED TO US IN DETAIL ABOUT THE RESULTS OF THE READER SURVEY, BUT NONE OF THE CONVERSATION AFTER "EIJI NIZUMA GOT 503 VOTES" REACHED MY EARS.
OH, YOU BROUGHT SOME STORY-BOARDS FOR YOUR NEW WORK, DIDN'T YOU?
THUD
OH, THESE ARE NO GOOD.
NO GOOD?
RIGHT. WE CAN'T SHOW THE SERIES STORY-BOARDS AFTER GETTING THIRD PLACE...
WAIT... EIJI NIZUMA IS ALREADY GETTING A SERIES. IT WOULDN'T BE A TOTAL WASTE TO SHOW IT TO MR. HATTORI, WOULD IT...?
WE CAME UP WITH BETTER IDEAS AND WERE TALKING ABOUT HOW WE SHOULD REDO IT WHILE WE WERE WAITING FOR YOU.
RIGHT?
RSTL
YEAH...
AND TO BE HONEST, I'M A BIT SHOCKED FALLING FROM FIRST PLACE TO THIRD PLACE. I DON'T REALLY FEEL LIKE TALKING RIGHT NOW...
LIKE I SAID BEFORE, YOU SHOULD BE PROUD OF GETTING THIRD PLACE. IT'S NOTHING TO BE DEPRESSED ABOUT. YOU'RE NEVER GOING TO BE ABLE TO MAKE IT IF YOU GET DOWN OVER SOMETHING LIKE THIS.
BUT I CAN UNDERSTAND YOUR DISAPPOINTMENT AFTER THE PROMISE OF THE EARLY RESULTS. SHALL WE CALL IT A DAY...?
SORRY.
TRUE, THIRD PLACE WASN'T BAD. BUT IT REALLY DROVE HOME WHAT WEIGHT THE READER SURVEYS HELD.

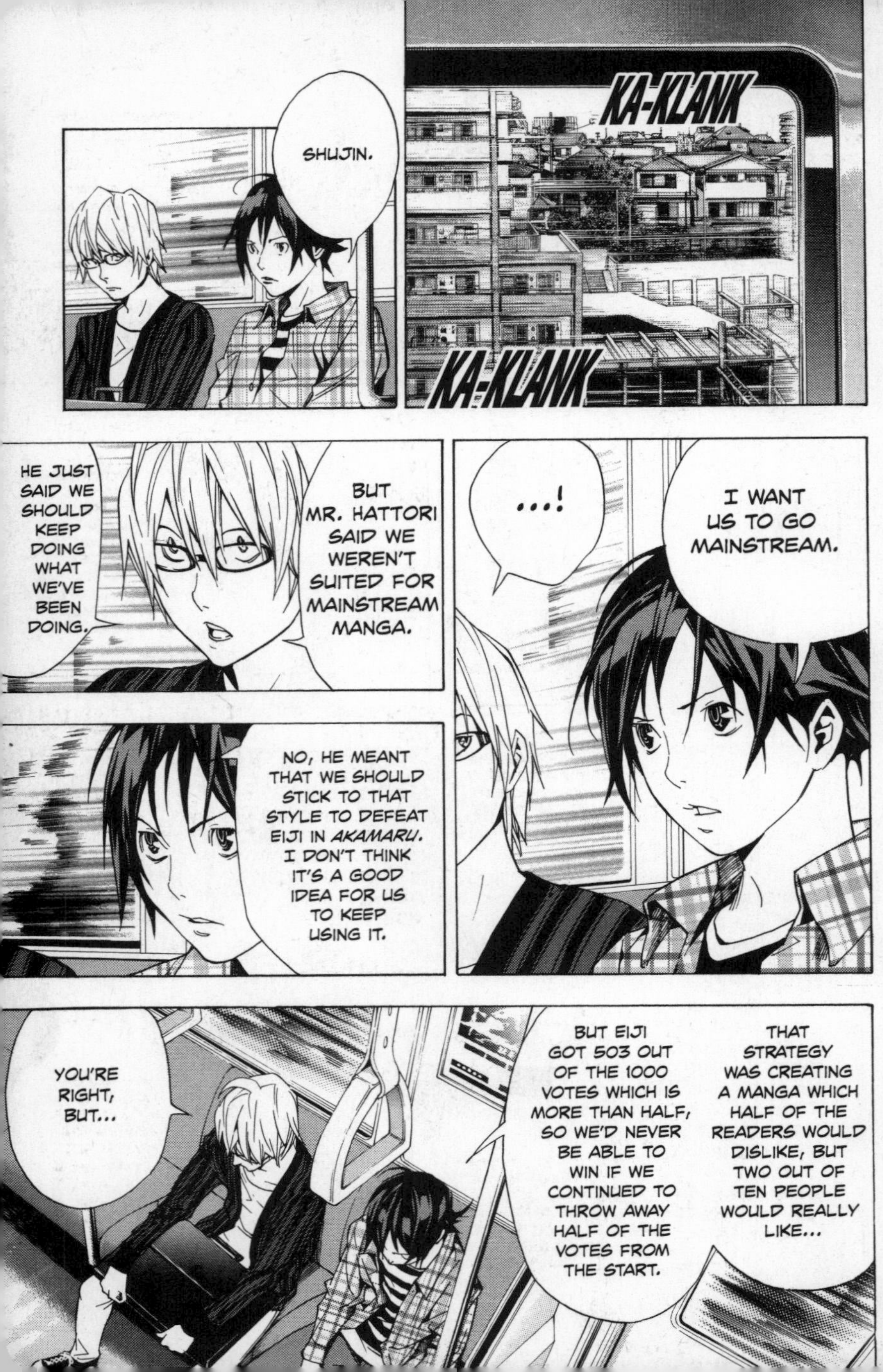
KA-KLANK
KA-KLANK
SHUJIN.
I WANT US TO GO MAINSTREAM.
...!
BUT MR. HATTORI SAID WE WEREN'T SUITED FOR MAINSTREAM MANGA.
HE JUST SAID WE SHOULD KEEP DOING WHAT WE'VE BEEN DOING.
NO, HE MEANT THAT WE SHOULD STICK TO THAT STYLE TO DEFEAT EIJI IN *AKAMARU*. I DON'T THINK IT'S A GOOD IDEA FOR US TO KEEP USING IT.
THAT STRATEGY WAS CREATING A MANGA WHICH HALF OF THE READERS WOULD DISLIKE, BUT TWO OUT OF TEN PEOPLE WOULD REALLY LIKE...
BUT EIJI GOT 503 OUT OF THE 1000 VOTES WHICH IS MORE THAN HALF, SO WE'D NEVER BE ABLE TO WIN IF WE CONTINUED TO THROW AWAY HALF OF THE VOTES FROM THE START.
YOU'RE RIGHT, BUT...

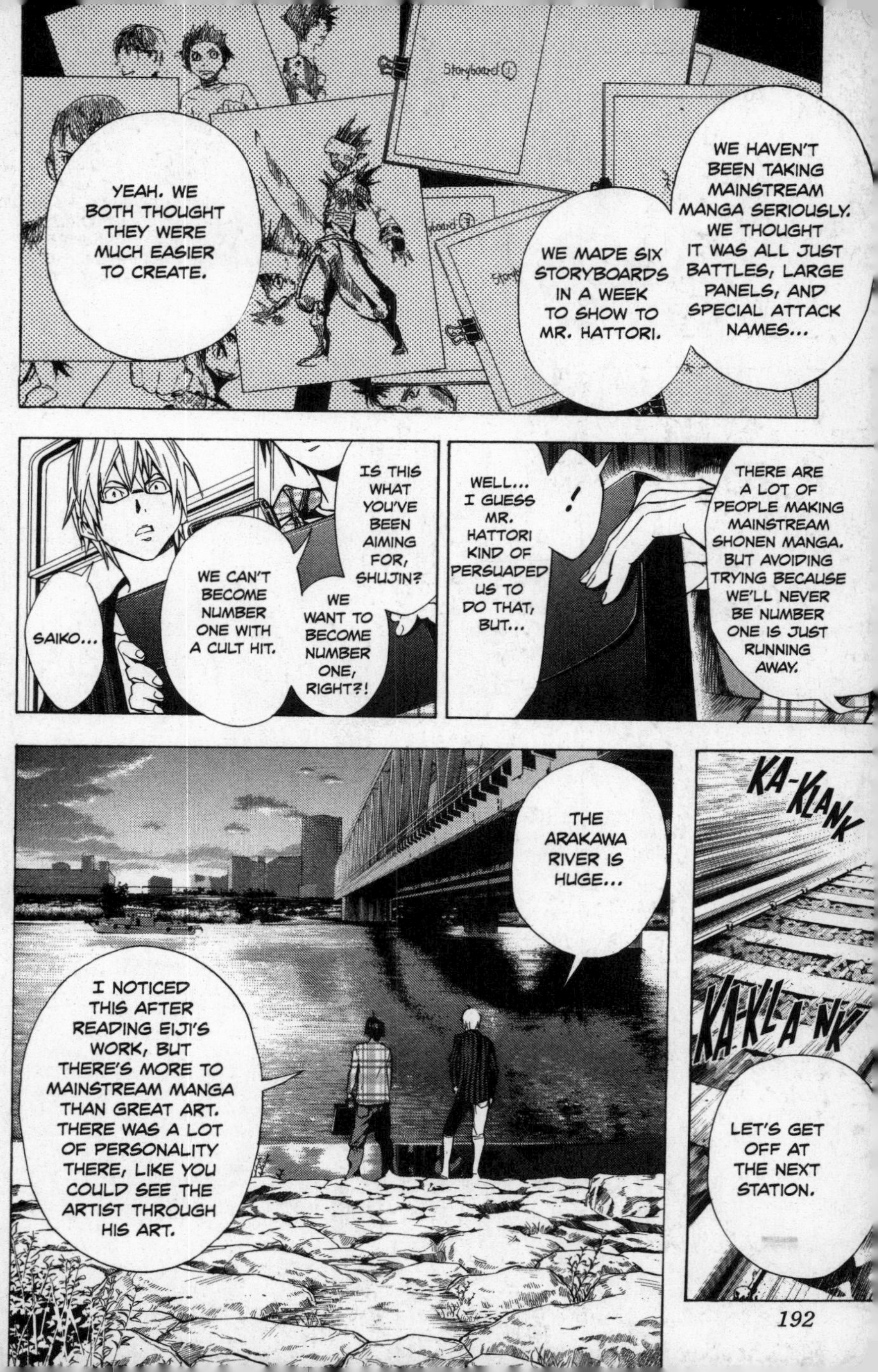

WE HAVEN'T BEEN TAKING MAINSTREAM MANGA SERIOUSLY. WE THOUGHT IT WAS ALL JUST BATTLES, LARGE PANELS, AND SPECIAL ATTACK NAMES...
WE MADE SIX STORYBOARDS IN A WEEK TO SHOW TO MR. HATTORI.
YEAH. WE BOTH THOUGHT THEY WERE MUCH EASIER TO CREATE.
THERE ARE A LOT OF PEOPLE MAKING MAINSTREAM SHONEN MANGA. BUT AVOIDING TRYING BECAUSE WE'LL NEVER BE NUMBER ONE IS JUST RUNNING AWAY.
!
WELL... I GUESS MR. HATTORI KIND OF PERSUADED US TO DO THAT, BUT...
IS THIS WHAT YOU'VE BEEN AIMING FOR, SHUJIN?
WE WANT TO BECOME NUMBER ONE, RIGHT?!
WE CAN'T BECOME NUMBER ONE WITH A CULT HIT.
SAIKO...
KA-KLANK
KA-KLANK
LET'S GET OFF AT THE NEXT STATION.
THE ARAKAWA RIVER IS HUGE...
I NOTICED THIS AFTER READING EIJI'S WORK, BUT THERE'S MORE TO MAINSTREAM MANGA THAN GREAT ART. THERE WAS A LOT OF PERSONALITY THERE, LIKE YOU COULD SEE THE ARTIST THROUGH HIS ART.

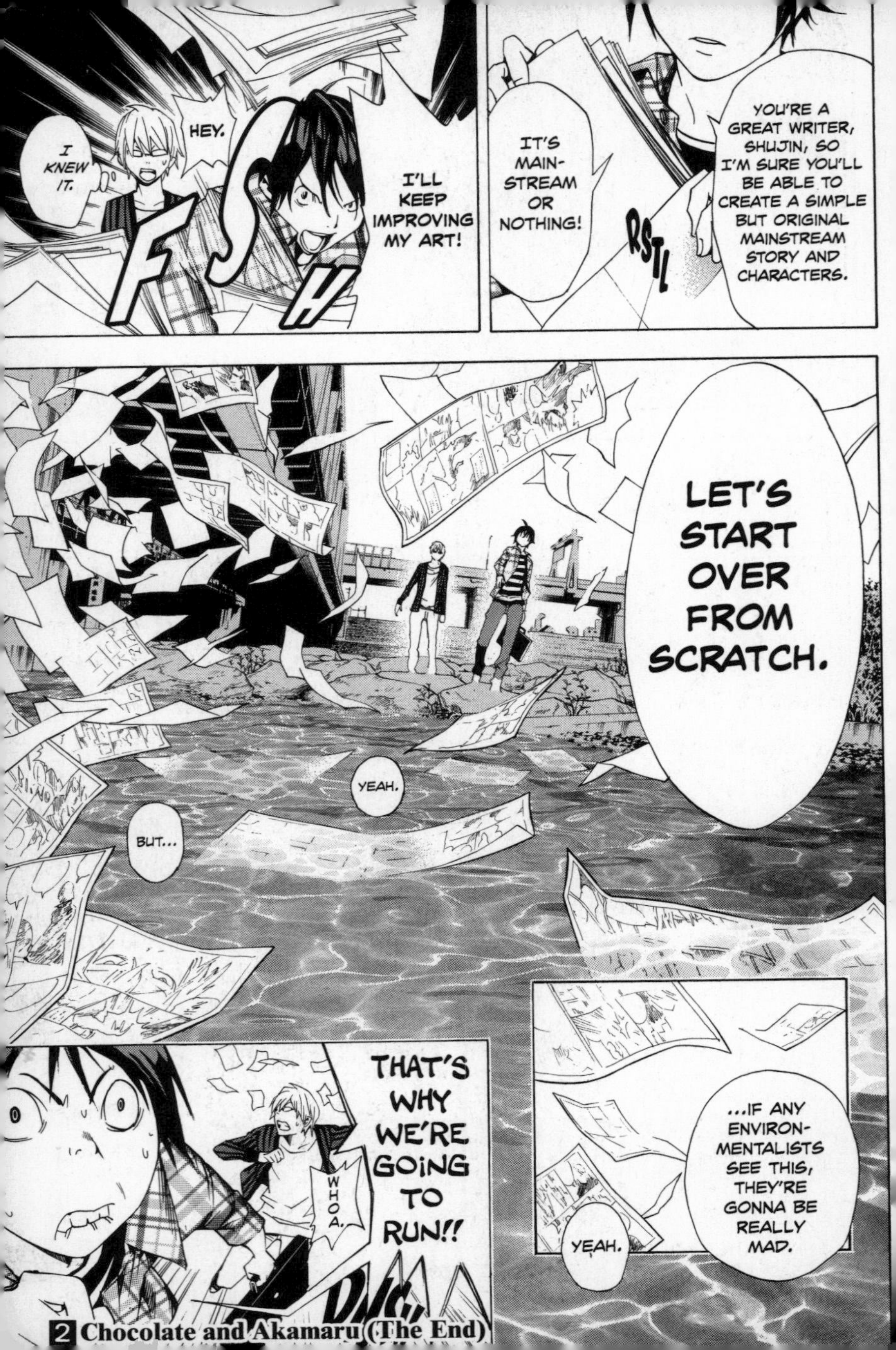
YOU'RE A GREAT WRITER, SHUJIN, SO I'M SURE YOU'LL BE ABLE TO CREATE A SIMPLE BUT ORIGINAL MAINSTREAM STORY AND CHARACTERS.
RSTL
IT'S MAIN-STREAM OR NOTHING!
I'LL KEEP IMPROVING MY ART!
HEY.
I KNEW IT.
F
H
LET'S START OVER FROM SCRATCH.
YEAH.
BUT...
...IF ANY ENVIRON-MENTALISTS SEE THIS, THEY'RE GONNA BE REALLY MAD.
YEAH.
THAT'S WHY WE'RE GOING TO RUN!!
WHOA.
2 Chocolate and Akamaru (The End)

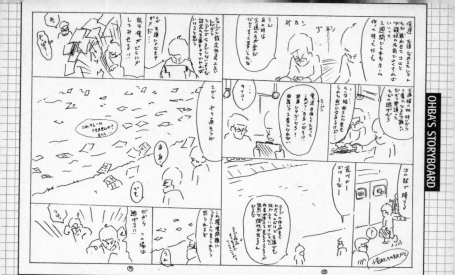

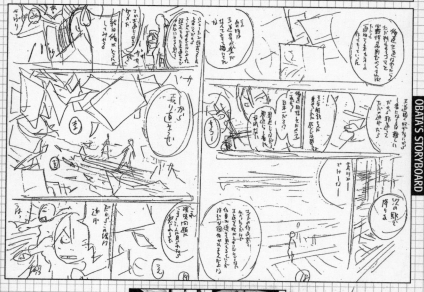

OHBA'S STORYBOARD

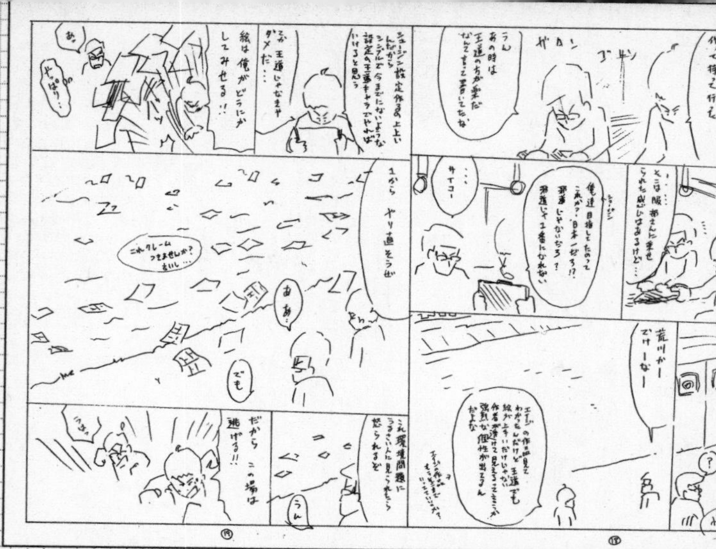

うん あの時は王道の方が楽だ なんて言って書いてたな
王道描く奴 多いから 1番になるのは難しい だから邪道って ただの逃げだろ
……そこは服部さんに乗せられた感じはあるけど……
俺達目指してたのって これか? 日本一だろ!? 邪道じゃないだろ? 邪道じゃ1番になれない
…サイコー
次の駅で降りる
荒川かー でけーなー
エイジの作品見てわかったんだけど 王道でも絵が上手いだけじゃない 作者が透けて見えるっていうか 強烈な個性が出てるんだよな
?
シュージン設定作るの上手いんだから シンプルで今までにないような設定の王道キャラでやれば いけると思う
でも王道じゃなきゃダメだ…
絵は俺がどうにかしてみせる!!
あっ
やっぱり…
1から やり直そうぜ
ああ
でも
これ環境問題に うるさい人に見られたら 怒られるぞ
うん
だから この場は 逃げる!!


OBATA'S STORYBOARD

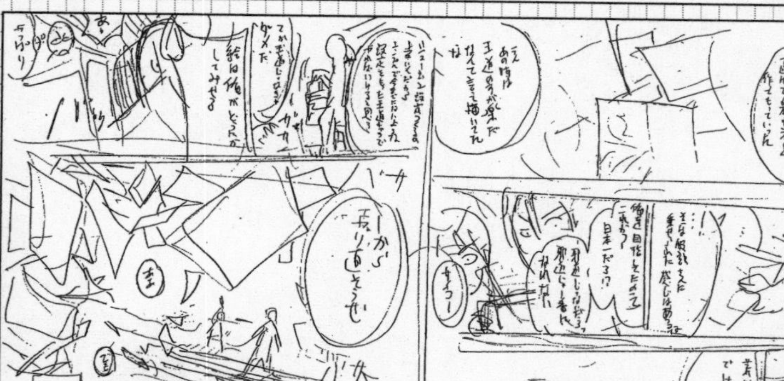

COMPLETE!

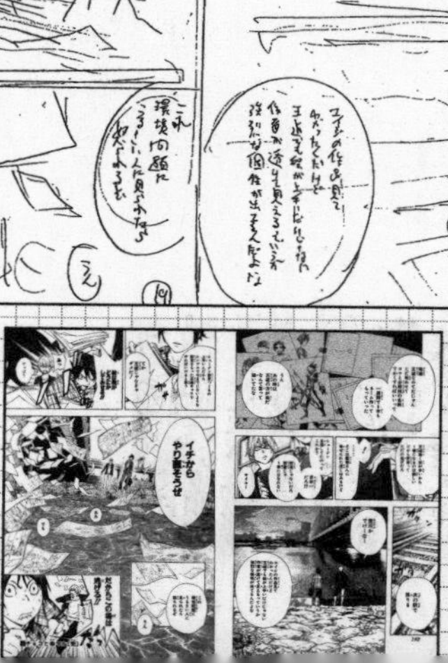

イチから やり直そうぜ


*CREATOR STORYBOARDS AND FINISHED PAGES IN JAPANESE

**BAKUMAN。 vol. 2**

"Until the Final Draft Is Complete"

Chapter 16, pp.192-193

**BAKUMAN.**

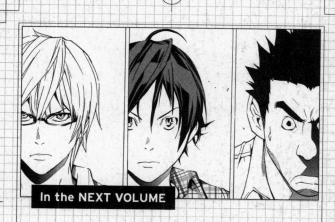

**In the NEXT VOLUME**

**In their quest to defeat Eiji Nizuma, Moritaka and Akito take a huge risk and defy their editor's wishes! Meanwhile, Eiji declares that he's a fan of the two boys?!**

**Available Now!**

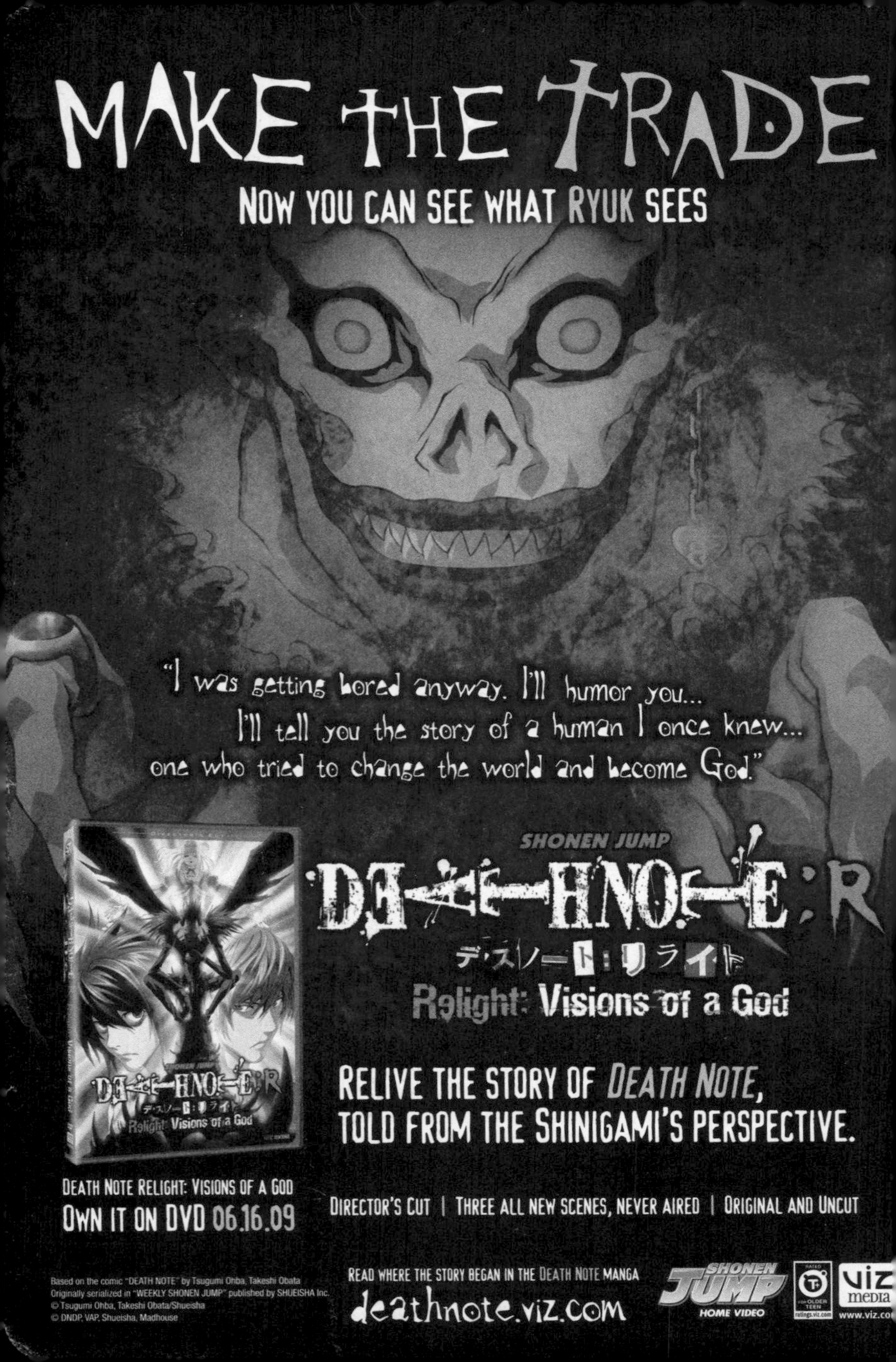
MAKE THE TRADE
NOW YOU CAN SEE WHAT RYUK SEES
"I was getting bored anyway. I'll humor you... I'll tell you the story of a human I once knew... one who tried to change the world and become God."
SHONEN JUMP
DEATH NOTE:R
デスノート：リライト
Relight: Visions of a God
RELIVE THE STORY OF DEATH NOTE, TOLD FROM THE SHINIGAMI'S PERSPECTIVE.
DEATH NOTE RELIGHT: VISIONS OF A GOD
OWN IT ON DVD 06.16.09
DIRECTOR'S CUT | THREE ALL NEW SCENES, NEVER AIRED | ORIGINAL AND UNCUT
Based on the comic "DEATH NOTE" by Tsugumi Ohba, Takeshi Obata
Originally serialized in "WEEKLY SHONEN JUMP" published by SHUEISHA Inc.
© Tsugumi Ohba, Takeshi Obata/Shueisha
© DNDP, VAP, Shueisha, Madhouse
READ WHERE THE STORY BEGAN IN THE DEATH NOTE MANGA
deathnote.viz.com
SHONEN JUMP HOME VIDEO
OLDER TEEN
ratings.viz.com
VIZ media
www.viz.com

# SHONEN JUMP

## THE WORLD'S MOST POPULAR MANGA

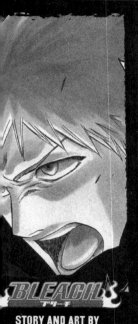

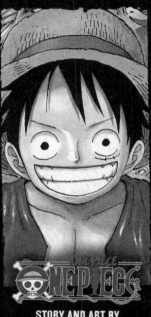

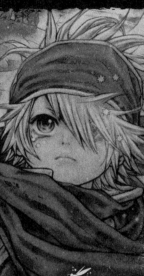

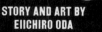

**BLEACH**

STORY AND ART BY
TITE KUBO

**ONE PIECE**

STORY AND ART BY
EIICHIRO ODA

**Tegami Bachi**
LETTER BEE

STORY AND ART BY
HIROYUKI ASADA

JUMP INTO THE ACTION BY TELLING US WHAT YOU LOVE (AND WHAT YOU DON'T)

# LET YOUR VOICE BE HEARD!

# SHONENJUMP.VIZ.COM/MANGASURVEY

## HELP US MAKE MORE OF THE WORLD'S MOST POPULAR MANGA!

RATED
T
FOR
TEEN
ratings.viz.com

VIZ
media

www.viz.com

# The World's Greatest Manga Now available on your iPad

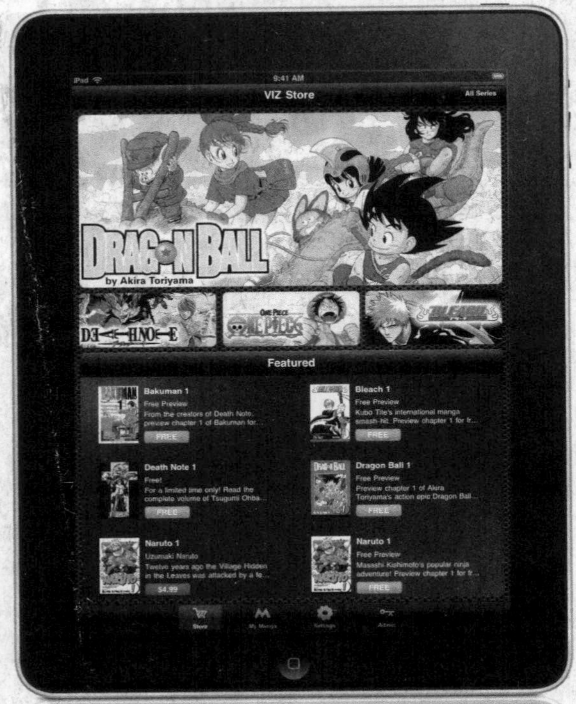
9:41 AM
VIZ Store
All Series
DRAGON BALL
by Akira Toriyama
Featured
Bakuman 1
Free Preview
From the creators of Death Note, preview chapter 1 of Bakuman for...
FREE
Bleach 1
Free Preview
Kubo Tite's international manga smash-hit. Preview chapter 1 for fr...
FREE
Death Note 1
Free!
For a limited time only! Read the complete volume of Tsugumi Ohba...
FREE
Dragon Ball 1
Free Preview
Preview chapter 1 of Akira Toriyama's action epic Dragon Ball...
FREE
Naruto 1
Uzumaki Naruto
Twelve years ago the Village Hidden in the Leaves was attacked by a fe...
$4.99
Naruto 1
Free Preview
Masashi Kishimoto's popular ninja adventure! Preview chapter 1 for fr...
FREE

**Full of FREE previews and tons of new manga for you to explore**

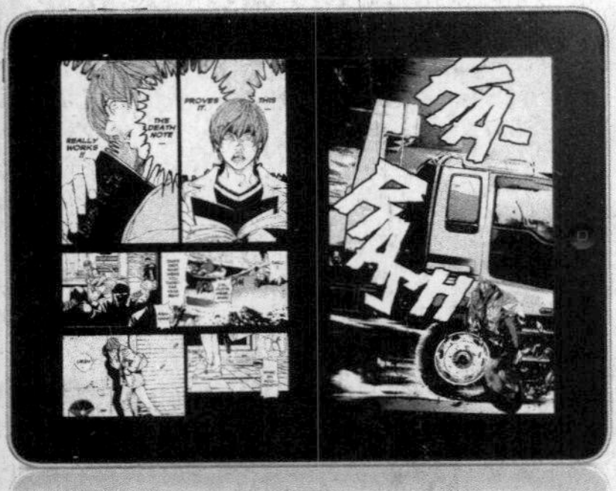

From legendary manga like *Dragon Ball* to *Bakuman。*, the newest series from the creators of *Death Note*, the best manga in the world is now available on the iPad through the official VIZ Manga app.

- Free App
- New content weekly
- Free chapter 1 previews

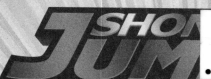

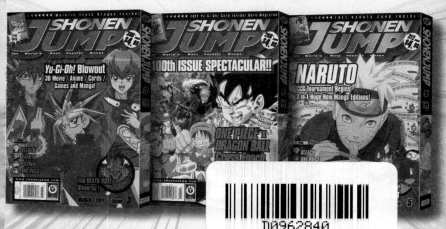
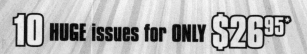

# BAKUMAN。

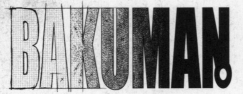

**Volume 2**

SHONEN JUMP Manga Edition

Story by **TSUGUMI OHBA**
Art by **TAKESHI OBATA**

Translation & Adaptation | **Tetsuichiro Miyaki**
Touch-up Art & Lettering | **James Gaubatz**
Design | **Fawn Lau**
Editor | **Alexis Kirsch**



Printed in the U.S.A.

Published by VIZ Media, LLC
P.O. Box 77010
San Francisco, CA 94107

10 9 8 7 6 5 4 3 2
First printing, November 2010
Second printing, April 2011

www.viz.com

RATED T FOR TEEN

**PARENTAL ADVISORY**
BAKUMAN。 is rated T for Teen and is recommended for ages 13 and up. This volume contains suggestive themes.
ratings.viz.com

www.shonenjump.com

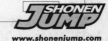

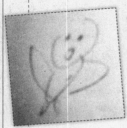

I know this is completely off topic,
but our editor likes Miyoshi. Kim,
another editor, likes Azuki, and
I like Iwase.

—Tsugumi Ohba

The title of this manga is *Bakuman*。
It means *bakuhatsu* (explosion),
*bakuchi* (gamble) and *baku* (an animal
that supposedly eats dreams)...
It has many meanings to it, and I
think it's a very fun title.

—Takeshi Obata

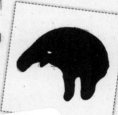

D0962839

## Tsugumi Ohba

Born in Tokyo, Tsugumi Ohba is the author of the hit series *Death Note*.
His current series *Bakuman*。 is serialized in *Weekly Shonen Jump*.

## Takeshi Obata

Takeshi Obata was born in 1969 in Niigata, Japan, and is the artist of
the wildly popular SHONEN JUMP title *Hikaru no Go*, which won the
2003 Tezuka Osamu Cultural Prize: Shinsei "New Hope" award and
the 2000 Shogakukan Manga award. Obata is also the artist of *Arabian
Majin Bokentan Lamp Lamp*, *Ayatsuri Sakon*, *Cyborg Jichan G.*, and the
smash hit manga *Death Note*. His current series *Bakuman*。 is serialized
in *Weekly Shonen Jump*.